A GUIDE TO
CONSUMER MARKETS
1976/1977

Helen Axel, Editor

CONTENTS

FOREWORD

Marketers and planners are called upon daily to make decisions that will affect their company's future position in the marketplace. The choice of an appropriate course of action depends on the scope of reliable and timely information that is available to these business executives. Their comprehensive understanding of the present economic scene, relevant past trends, and likely future growth are the necessary ingredients to intelligent decision making.

The *Guide to Consumer Markets* helps to meet this need. Culling its material from a large number of government and trade sources, the *Guide* offers an extensive collection of up-to-date statistics. Its focus is on the consumer, providing the user with basic data on the size and character of this special market sector and its economic significance. Information on the pace of population growth—shifts in geography, age structure, family composition, and income distribution; and the changing characteristics of family spending patterns—describes different dimensions of the consumer market. In addition, trends in employment, personal income, and expenditures —and the production, retail sales, and prices of consumer goods and services—provide historical perspective on this market's relative importance in the economy.

The 1976-1977 edition of *Guide to Consumer Markets* is the seventh annual issue of this statistical source book.

Although the figures in the *Guide* are the most current available at the time the book went to press, new material is issued throughout the year. In order to keep users abreast of new developments, the Board's Information Service maintains a reference file of updated tables. Those wishing to secure the most recent figures should contact the Board.

This publication was prepared and edited by Helen Axel, with the assistance of Joan Hom and Leslie Joseph of the Board's Consumer Research Department; Fabian Linden, Director.

Kenneth A. Randall
President

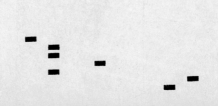

DO NOT REMOVE CARD
FROM THIS BOOK

A FINE OF $1.00 WILL BE CHARGED
FOR LOSS OR DAMAGE TO THIS CARD

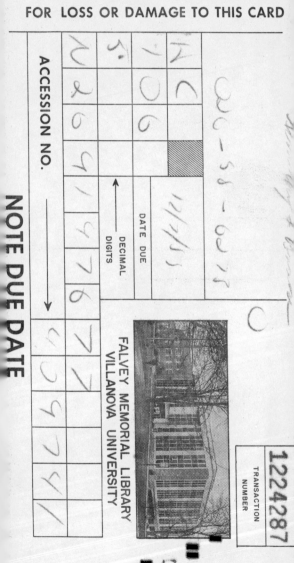

POPULATION

POPULATION

U.S. POPULATION AND GROWTH RATES

Year	Persons (Millions)	Annual Growth Rate[1] (Percent)
1930	123.1	1.47
1940	132.6	.72
1950	152.3	1.39
1951	154.9	1.71
1952	157.6	1.73
1953	160.2	1.67
1954	163.0	1.77
1955	165.9	1.78
1956	168.9	1.79
1957	172.0	1.82
1958	174.9	1.69
1959	177.8	1.69
1960	180.7	1.60
1961	183.7	1.67
1962	186.5	1.55
1963	189.2	1.45
1964	191.9	1.40
1965	194.3	1.26
1966	196.6	1.16
1967	198.7	1.09
1968	200.7	1.00
1969	202.7	.98
1970	204.9	1.09
1971	207.1	1.06
1972	208.8	.87
1973	210.4	.75
1974	211.9	.71
1975	213.6	.82
Projections:		
1980	222.8	.84
1985	234.1	.99
1990	245.1	.92

Note: Beginning 1940 data include Armed Forces overseas, Alaska and Hawaii. Estimates and projections (Series II) are as of July 1. For a brief description of the assumptions underlying these projections, see footnote to table on page 20

[1] From previous date shown (1920, for 1930). Growth rates computed from unrounded data

Source: Department of Commerce

U. S. POPULATION AND AREA

Year	Resident Population (Thousands)	Area (Thousand Sq. Miles)			Population per Sq. Mile Land Area
		Gross	Land	Water	
Conterminous U. S.[1]					
1900	75,995	3,022	2,970	53	25.6
1910	91,972	3,022	2,970	53	31.0
1920	105,711	3,022	2,969	53	35.6
1930	122,775	3,022	2,977	45	41.2
1940	131,669	3,022	2,977	45	44.2
1950	150,697	3,022	2,975	48	50.7
1960	178,464	3,022	2,968	54	60.1
1970	202,163	3,022	2,964	58	68.2
United States					
1950	151,326	3,615	3,552	63	42.6
1960	179,323	3,615	3,541	74	50.6
1970	203,235	3,615	3,537	78	57.5

Note: Data are census enumerations as of April 1

[1] Excludes Alaska and Hawaii

Source: Department of Commerce

POPULATION: UNITED STATES AND OUTLYING AREAS

Thousands of persons

Area	1940	1950	1960	1970
TOTAL	150,623a	154,233	183,285	207,976
United States:				
Total[1]	132,288	151,718	180,007	204,335
Resident Population	132,166	151,326	179,323	203,235
Conterminous U.S.........	131,669	150,697	178,464	202,163
Alaska	73	129	226	300
Hawaii	423	500	633	769
Civilian Population	131,859	150,219	177,472	201,064
Puerto Rico	1,869	2,211	2,350	2,712
Outlying Areas:				
American Samoa	13	19	20	27
Canal Zone	52	53	42	44
Guam	22	59	67	85
Pacific Trust Territory	[2]	55	71	91
Virgin Islands	25	27	32	62
Other	2	2	6	5
Persons Abroad, Total	119	482	1,374	1,738
Armed Forces	119	302	610	1,058
Other		180	765	680

Note: Data are census enumerations as of April 1

[1] Including Armed Forces overseas
[2] Not part of the United States in 1940
a—Also includes the population of the Philippines (16,356,000) not listed separately

Source: Department of Commerce

POPULATION BY BROAD DEMOGRAPHIC CHARACTERISTICS

Population in thousands

Year	Sex Male	Sex Female	Males per 100 Females	Race White	Race Negro	Negro as Percent Total	Median Age
1900	38,816	37,178	104.4	66,809	8,834	11.6	22.9
1910	47,332	44,640	106.0	81,732	9,828	10.7	24.1
1920	53,900	51,810	104.0	94,821	10,463	9.9	25.3
1930	62,137	60,638	102.5	110,287	11,891	9.7	26.4
1940	66,062	65,608	100.7	118,215	12,866	9.8	29.0
1950	75,187	76,139	98.7	135,150	15,045	9.9	30.2
1960	88,331	90,992	97.1	158,832	18,872	10.5	29.5
1970	100,020	104,315	95.9	179,065	22,699	11.1	27.9
1975	104,239	109,393	95.3	185,601	24,535	11.5	28.8
Projections:							
1980	108,474	114,295	94.9	192,162	26,371	11.8	29.9
1985	113,866	120,201	94.7	200,548	28,304	12.1	31.1
1990	119,154	125,921	94.6	208,686	30,148	12.3	32.3

Note: Data beginning 1950 include Alaska and Hawaii. Prior years refer to conterminous U. S. only. Figures for 1900-1970 are census enumerations; 1975 and projections (Series II) include Armed Forces overseas and are as of July 1

Source: Department of Commerce

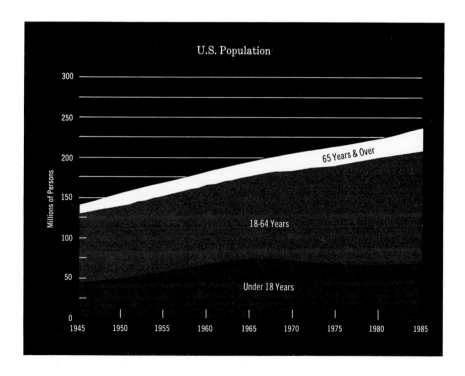

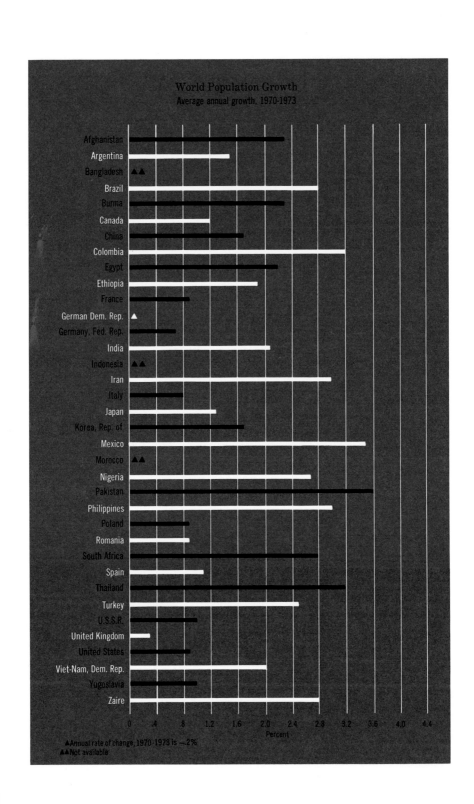

World Population Growth
Average annual growth, 1970-1973

Afghanistan	
Argentina	
Bangladesh ▲▲	
Brazil	
Burma	
Canada	
China	
Colombia	
Egypt	
Ethiopia	
France	
German Dem. Rep. ▲	
Germany, Fed. Rep.	
India	
Indonesia ▲▲	
Iran	
Italy	
Japan	
Korea, Rep. of	
Mexico	
Morocco ▲▲	
Nigeria	
Pakistan	
Philippines	
Poland	
Romania	
South Africa	
Spain	
Thailand	
Turkey	
U.S.S.R.	
United Kingdom	
United States	
Viet-Nam, Dem. Rep.	
Yugoslavia	
Zaire	

0   .4   .8   1.2   1.6   2.0   2.4   2.8   3.2   3.6   4.0   4.4
Percent

▲Annual rate of change, 1970-1973 is —.2%
▲▲Not available

12

POPULATION: UNITED STATES AND PRINCIPAL COUNTRIES

World Rank 1974	Country	1974 Population[1] (Millions)	1973 Population[1] Millions of Persons	1973 Population[1] Annual Percent Increase 1970-73	1973 Population[1] Per Square Mile	Area (Thousand Square Miles)
—	WORLD TOTAL	3,890.0	3,860.0	2.1	73	52,470
—	North America	235.0	236.0	1.3	29	8,307
—	South America	315.0	309.0	2.9	39	7,941
—	Europe[2]	470.0	472.0	.7	250	1,906
—	U.S.S.R.	252.1	250.0	1.0	29	8,650
—	Asia[2]	2,206.0	2,204.0	2.3	208	10,674
—	Africa................	391.0	374.0	2.8	31	11,706
—	Oceania	20.9	21.0	2.2	5	3,286
	PRINCIPAL COUNTRIES:					
34	Afghanistan[3]	18.8	18.3	2.3	73	250
26	Argentina	25.0	24.3	1.5	23	1,072
8	Bangladesh	75.0	[4]	[4]	[4]	56
7	Brazil	103.4	101.4	2.8	31	3,286
24	Burma[3]	30.3	29.6	2.3	114	262
31	Canada	22.5	22.1	1.2	5	3,852
1	China[3]	825.0	814.3	1.7	221	3,705
29	Colombia.............	24.0	23.2	3.2	52	440
19	Egypt[3]	36.4	35.6	2.2	94	387
25	Ethiopia	27.2	26.1	1.9	55	472
15	France	52.5	52.1	.9	247	211
35	German Dem. Rep. ...	16.9	17.0	−.2	408	42
10	Germany, Fed. Rep. ..	62.0	62.0	.7	647	96
2	India................	586.3	574.2	2.1	455	1,267
5	Indonesia	127.6	124.6	[4]	218	576
23	Iran	32.1	31.3	3.0	49	636
14	Italy	55.4	54.9	.8	473	116
6	Japan	109.7	108.3	1.3	757	144
22	Korea, Rep. of........	33.5	33.0	1.7	868	38
12	Mexico	58.1	54.3	3.5	13	762
36	Morocco	16.9	16.3	[4]	96	172
11	Nigeria[3]	61.3	59.6	2.7	169	357
9	Pakistan.............	68.2	66.7	3.6	216	310
16	Philippines	41.3	40.2	3.0	348	116
21	Poland	33.7	33.4	.9	278	121
33	Romania	21.0	20.8	.9	229	92
27	South Africa	24.9	23.7	2.8	49	471
20	Spain	35.2	34.9	1.1	179	195
17	Thailand[3]	41.0	39.8	3.2	200	198
18	Turkey	38.3	38.0	2.5	127	301
3	U.S.S.R.	252.1	249.7	1.0	29	8,650
13	United Kingdom	56.0	55.9	.3	595	94
4	United States	211.9	210.4	.9	57	3,615
30	Viet-Nam, Dem. Rep.[3]	23.2	22.5	2.0	369	61
32	Yugoslavia	21.2	21.0	1.0	213	99
28	Zaire	24.2	23.6	2.8	26	906

[1] Midyear estimates. 1974 world estimates not strictly comparable with 1973 data
[2] Excludes U.S.S.R., shown separately
[3] Population figures are United Nations estimates
[4] Comparable data for relevant years not available

Source: United Nations

PROJECTIONS OF THE POPULATION BY SINGLE YEARS TO 1990

Millions of persons

Year	Total Population	Age Group					
		Under 18	18-24	25-34	35-44	45-54	55 and Over
Estimates:							
1970	204.8	69.7	24.7	25.3	23.1	23.3	38.8
1975	213.6	66.3	27.6	30.9	22.8	23.8	42.2
Projections:							
1976	215.1	65.4	28.2	32.0	23.1	23.6	42.8
1977	216.8	64.6	28.6	33.1	23.5	23.4	43.5
1978	218.7	64.0	29.0	33.9	24.4	23.1	44.2
1979	220.7	63.5	29.3	35.0	25.1	22.9	44.9
1980	222.8	63.3	29.4	36.2	25.7	22.6	45.6
1981	225.0	63.2	29.5	37.4	26.2	22.5	46.1
1982	227.2	63.2	29.3	37.8	27.8	22.4	46.7
1983	229.5	63.4	29.0	38.5	29.0	22.3	47.2
1984	231.8	63.9	28.5	39.2	30.2	22.4	47.6
1985	234.1	64.6	27.8	39.8	31.3	22.4	48.1
1986	236.3	65.3	27.1	40.4	32.5	22.6	48.5
1987	238.6	65.9	26.4	40.8	33.5	23.1	48.8
1988	240.8	66.5	26.0	41.1	34.3	23.9	49.0
1989	243.0	67.0	25.6	41.2	35.4	24.6	49:2
1990	245.1	67.7	25.2	41.1	36.5	25.2	49.4

Note: Data include Armed Forces overseas and are as of July 1. Series II projections. For a brief description of the assumptions underlying these projections, see footnote to table on page 20

Source: Department of Commerce

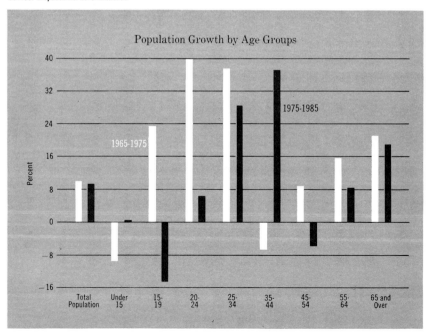

POPULATION BY BROAD AGE GROUPS

Millions of persons

	Total	Age Group				
Year	Population	Under 5	5-17	18-39	40-64	65 and Over
1920	106.5	11.6	28.0	38.3	23.7	4.9
1925	115.8	12.3	30.2	40.9	26.6	5.8
1930	123.1	11.4	31.6	43.7	29.6	6.7
1935	127.3	10.2	31.4	45.2	32.7	7.8
1940	132.1	10.6	29.8	47.7	35.1	9.0
1945	139.9	13.0	28.6	49.8	38.1	10.5
1950	152.3	16.4	30.9	51.5	41.1	12.4
1955	165.9	18.6	37.2	51.1	44.6	14.5
1960	180.7	20.3	44.2	51.6	47.9	16.7
1965	194.3	19.8	49.9	54.8	51.3	18.5
1970	204.9	17.1	52.5	61.1	54.0	20.1
1975	213.6	15.9	50.4	70.2	54.7	22.4
Projections:						
1980	222.8	17.3	46.0	79.6	55.4	24.5
1985	234.1	19.8	44.8	84.9	57.9	26.7
1990	245.1	20.1	47.6	85.5	63.0	28.9
1995	254.5	19.2	52.1	82.6	70.3	30.3

Note: Series II projections. Beginning 1940 data include Armed Forces overseas, Alaska and Hawaii. Estimates and projections are as of July 1. Beginning 1970 figures are based on the 1970 census. For brief description of the assumptions underlying the projections, see footnote to table on page 20   Source: Department of Commerce

POPULATION: SELECTED AGE GROUPS

As percent of total

Year	Under 6	Under 18	Under 25	Under 35	21 and Over	65 and Over
1920....................	13.1	37.2	49.4	65.8	57.5	4.6
1925....................	12.7	36.7	48.9	65.0	57.9	5.0
1930....................	11.3	34.9	47.5	63.0	59.5	5.4
1935....................	9.8	32.7	45.2	61.1	61.9	6.1
1940....................	9.6	30.5	43.1	59.4	63.9	6.8
1945....................	10.9	29.7	41.7	57.9	65.3	7.5
1950....................	12.6	31.0	41.6	57.4	64.6	8.1
1955....................	13.3	33.6	42.6	57.2	62.6	8.8
1960....................	13.4	35.7	44.6	57.3	60.2	9.2
1965....................	12.3	35.9	46.3	57.9	59.3	9.5
1970....................	10.2	34.0	46.1	58.4	60.5	9.8
1975....................	9.1	31.0	44.0	58.4	63.1	10.5
Projections:						
1980....................	9.1	28.4	41.6	57.8	65.8	11.0
1985....................	10.1	27.6	39.5	56.5	67.6	11.4
1990....................	9.9	27.6	37.9	54.6	67.9	11.8
1995....................	9.1	28.0	37.3	52.3	68.0	11.9

Note: Series II projections. Data include Armed Forces overseas beginning 1940, and Alaska and Hawaii beginning 1950. All figures are as of July 1. Beginning 1970 data are based on the 1970 census. For a brief description of the assumptions underlying the projections, see footnote to table on page 20   Source: Department of Commerce

POPULATION BY SINGLE YEARS OF AGE

Thousands of persons

Age	1960	1970	1971	1972	1973	1974	1975
TOTAL ...	180,671	204,878	207,053	208,846	210,410	211,894	213,631
Under 5 years	20,341	17,148	17,177	16,981	16,694	16,292	15,896
Under 1	4,094	3,503	3,579	3,261	3,081	3,009	3,081
1	4,104	3,400	3,485	3,560	3,254	3,067	2,999
2	4,080	3,292	3,337	3,419	3,493	3,193	3,014
3	4,078	3,403	3,323	3,368	3,450	3,524	3,225
4	3,985	3,551	3,454	3,372	3,417	3,499	3,577
5-9 years	18,810	19,898	19,319	18,720	18,104	17,584	17,334
5	3,959	3,753	3,543	3,446	3,364	3,407	3,493
6	3,852	3,943	3,776	3,565	3,466	3,383	3,430
7	3,798	4,014	3,956	3,789	3,576	3,476	3,397
8	3,636	4,029	3,965	3,908	3,742	3,531	3,436
9	3,566	4,159	4,079	4,013	3,955	3,786	3,577
10-14 years ...	16,925	20,835	21,032	20,992	20,879	20,717	20,418
10	3,473	4,261	4,325	4,241	4,173	4,113	3,942
11	3,490	4,134	4,118	4,179	4,098	4,033	3,977
12	3,492	4,172	4,163	4,147	4,208	4,127	4,065
13	3,700	4,171	4,179	4,170	4,154	4,215	4,138
14	2,770	4,098	4,247	4,254	4,245	4,230	4,296
15-19 years ...	13,442	19,315	19,724	20,184	20,554	20,826	21,028
15	2,759	4,041	4,089	4,237	4,244	4,236	4,225
16	2,751	3,928	4,004	4,050	4,196	4,205	4,201
17	2,939	3,844	3,941	4,015	4,062	4,210	4,222
18	2,613	3,780	3,875	3,970	4,045	4,093	4,246
19	2,381	3,723	3,815	3,911	4,007	4,082	4,135
20-24 years ...	11,134	17,184	18,089	18,033	18,345	18,740	19,242
20	2,296	3,651	3,788	3,882	3,978	4,076	4,157
21	2,266	3,553	3,541	3,675	3,766	3,858	3,957
22	2,239	3,491	3,494	3,485	3,615	3,704	3,799
23	2,174	3,710	3,438	3,444	3,434	3,561	3,652
24	2,160	2,779	3,827	3,548	3,553	3,541	3,677
25-29 years ...	10,936	13,718	13,968	15,097	15,574	16,232	16,941
25	2,166	2,798	2,741	3,774	3,498	3,502	3,495
26	2,111	2,800	2,756	2,701	3,717	3,445	3,453
27	2,164	2,997	2,832	2,789	2,733	3,757	3,488
28	2,225	2,641	3,003	2,839	2,795	2,739	3,769
29	2,270	2,482	2,635	2,995	2,831	2,788	2,737
30-34 years ...	11,983	11,576	11,873	12,306	13,035	13,544	13,994
30	2,311	2,486	2,627	2,789	3,167	2,995	2,953
31	2,356	2,318	2,356	2,489	2,641	3,001	2,839
32	2,404	2,303	2,333	2,371	2,504	2,656	3,020
33	2,441	2,217	2,285	2,315	2,352	2,483	2,637
34	2,471	2,252	2,272	2,342	2,372	2,409	2,545

POPULATION BY SINGLE YEARS OF AGE (continued)

Thousands of persons

Age	1960	1970	1971	1972	1973	1974	1975
35-39 years ...	12,542	11,151	11,115	11,154	11,265	11,444	11,630
35	2,497	2,224	2,248	2,267	2,335	2,365	2,404
36	2,524	2,184	2,223	2,247	2,265	2,333	2,365
37	2,534	2,221	2,185	2,223	2,246	2,265	2,335
38	2,515	2,230	2,225	2,188	2,226	2,250	2,270
39	2,473	2,291	2,235	2,230	2,192	2,231	2,256
40-44 years ...	11,679	11,991	11,855	11,699	11,538	11,374	11,195
40	2,425	2,420	2,295	2,239	2,233	2,196	2,236
41	2,370	2,363	2,424	2,299	2,243	2,237	2,201
42	2,322	2,397	2,363	2,424	2,298	2,242	2,238
43	2,290	2,392	2,391	2,356	2,418	2,292	2,237
44	2,271	2,418	2,382	2,380	2,346	2,407	2,283
45-49 years ...	10,914	12,147	12,140	12,034	11,963	11,852	11,790
45	2,251	2,465	2,407	2,370	2,369	2,335	2,397
46	2,228	2,433	2,451	2,392	2,356	2,355	2,322
47	2,195	2,415	2,422	2,441	2,382	2,346	2,346
48	2,148	2,448	2,411	2,419	2,437	2,379	2,344
49	2,092	2,386	2,449	2,411	2,419	2,438	2,380
50-54 years ...	9,664	11,163	11,376	11,656	11,850	11,966	11,981
50	2,036	2,428	2,383	2,446	2,409	2,417	2,437
51	1,977	2,299	2,425	2,379	2,443	2,406	2,415
52	1,926	2,199	2,288	2,414	2,368	2,432	2,396
53	1,883	2,130	2,178	2,267	2,392	2,347	2,413
54	1,841	2,107	2,102	2,150	2,239	2,364	2,320
55-59 years ...	8,471	9,998	10,062	10,108	10,162	10,298	10,537
55	1,796	2,105	2,080	2,075	2,122	2,211	2,337
56	1,752	2,049	2,077	2,052	2,047	2,095	2,185
57	1,700	2,009	2,019	2,048	2,023	2,018	2,067
58	1,642	1,941	1,977	1,988	2,016	1,991	1,988
59	1,582	1,894	1,909	1,945	1,955	1,983	1,960
60-64 years ...	7,154	8,666	8,835	8,990	9,102	9,201	9,243
65-69 years ...	6,280	7,023	7,160	7,391	7,616	7,838	8,099
70-74 years ...	4,773	5,465	5,512	5,514	5,605	5,701	5,775
75-79 years ...	3,080	3,859	3,929	3,948	3,917	3,930	4,001
80-84 years ...	1,601	2,309	2,390	2,479	2,571	2,607	2,649
85 yrs. & over .	940	1,432	1,497	1,562	1,637	1,748	1,877

Note: Data refer to total population including Armed Forces overseas and are as of July 1. Projections of births by single years and of the population by selected age groups are shown elsewhere in this chapter

Source: Department of Commerce

POPULATION BY AGE AND SEX: ESTIMATES AND PROJECTIONS

Millions of persons

Age and Sex	1960	1970	1975	1980	1985	1990
Both Sexes, Total	180.7	204.9	213.6	222.8	234.1	245.1
0-4	20.4	17.1	15.9	17.3	19.8	20.1
5-9	18.8	19.9	17.3	16.1	17.5	20.0
10-14	16.9	20.8	20.4	17.8	16.6	18.0
15-19	13.4	19.3	21.0	20.6	18.0	16.8
20-24	11.1	17.2	19.2	20.9	20.5	18.0
25-29	11.0	13.7	16.9	18.9	20.6	20.2
30-34	12.0	11.6	14.0	17.2	19.3	20.9
35-39	12.5	11.2	11.6	14.0	17.2	19.3
40-44	11.7	12.0	11.2	11.7	14.1	17.3
45-49	10.9	12.1	11.8	11.0	11.5	13.9
50-54	9.7	11.2	12.0	11.6	10.9	11.4
55-59	8.5	10.0	10.5	11.3	11.0	10.3
60-64	7.2	8.7	9.2	9.7	10.5	10.2
65-69	6.3	7.0	8.1	8.7	9.2	9.9
70-74	4.8	5.5	5.8	6.7	7.2	7.7
75-79	3.1	3.9	4.0	4.3	5.0	5.4
80 and over	2.5	3.7	4.5	4.8	5.2	6.0
Male, Total	89.3	100.3	104.2	108.5	113.9	119.2
0-4	10.3	8.7	8.1	8.8	10.1	10.3
5-9	9.6	10.1	8.8	8.2	9.0	10.3
10-14	8.6	10.6	10.4	9.1	8.5	9.2
15-19	6.8	9.8	10.7	10.5	9.1	8.6
20-24	5.6	8.6	9.7	10.5	10.3	9.0
25-29	5.4	6.8	8.4	9.4	10.2	10.0
30-34	5.9	5.7	6.9	8.5	9.6	10.4
35-39	6.1	5.5	5.7	6.9	8.5	9.5
40-44	5.7	5.8	5.5	5.7	6.9	8.5
45-49	5.4	5.9	5.7	5.4	5.6	6.8
50-54	4.8	5.4	5.8	5.6	5.3	5.5
55-59	4.1	4.8	5.0	5.4	5.3	4.9
60-64	3.4	4.0	4.3	4.5	4.9	4.8
65-69	2.9	3.1	3.6	3.8	4.0	4.3
70-74	2.2	2.3	2.4	2.8	3.0	3.2
75-79	1.4	1.6	1.6	1.7	1.9	2.1
80 and over	1.0	1.4	1.6	1.6	1.7	1.9
Female, Total	91.4	104.6	109.4	114.3	120.2	125.9
0-4	10.0	8.4	7.8	8.4	9.7	9.8
5-9	9.2	9.8	8.5	7.9	8.5	9.8
10-14	8.3	10.2	10.0	8.7	8.1	8.8
15-19	6.6	9.5	10.4	10.1	8.9	8.2
20-24	5.6	8.5	9.6	10.4	10.2	8.9
25-29	5.5	6.9	8.5	9.5	10.3	10.1
30-34	6.1	5.9	7.1	8.7	9.7	10.5
35-39	6.4	5.7	6.0	7.2	8.8	9.8
40-44	5.9	6.1	5.7	6.0	7.2	8.8
45-49	5.5	6.3	6.1	5.6	5.9	7.1
50-54	4.9	5.8	6.2	6.0	5.6	5.9
55-59	4.3	5.2	5.5	5.9	5.7	5.3
60-64	3.7	4.6	4.9	5.2	5.6	5.4
65-69	3.3	3.9	4.5	4.8	5.1	5.5
70-74	2.6	3.1	3.3	3.9	4.2	4.5
75-79	1.7	2.3	2.4	2.6	3.1	3.3
80 and over	1.5	2.4	3.0	3.2	3.5	4.1

Note: Series II projections for years 1980-1990. Figures include Armed Forces overseas and are as of July 1. For a brief description of the assumptions underlying these projections, see footnote for table on page 20

Source: Department of Commerce

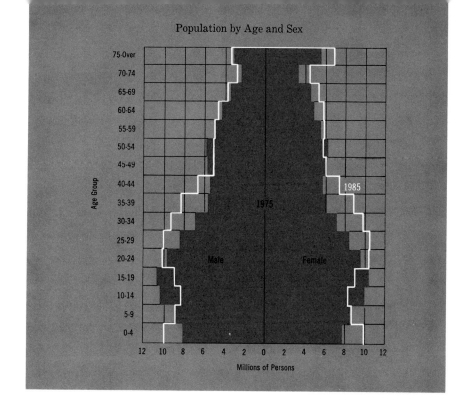

Population by Age and Sex

Age Group (vertical axis, top to bottom): 75-Over, 70-74, 65-69, 60-64, 55-59, 50-54, 45-49, 40-44, 35-39, 30-34, 25-29, 20-24, 15-19, 10-14, 5-9, 0-4

Male | Female

1975 | 1985

Horizontal axis: 12 10 8 6 4 2 0 2 4 6 8 10 12

Millions of Persons

SEX RATIO OF THE POPULATION BY AGE AND RACE

Males per 100 females

Age and Race	1950	1960	1970	1975	1980	1985
TOTAL, ALL RACES ...	99.2	97.8	95.9	95.3	94.9	94.7
Under 15	103.8	103.4	103.9	104.1	104.5	104.8
15-24	100.0	101.4	102.3	102.2	102.0	102.1
25-44	97.2	96.9	96.9	97.3	97.4	97.5
45-64	100.1	95.7	91.7	91.7	91.8	92.0
65 and over	89.5	82.6	72.1	69.3	67.9	66.9
WHITE	99.6	98.2	96.3	95.8	95.5	95.4
Under 15	104.2	103.9	104.5	104.7	105.0	105.3
15-24	101.0	102.2	103.1	103.1	102.9	103.0
25-44	97.8	97.9	98.5	99.2	99.6	99.8
45-64	99.9	95.7	92.2	92.3	92.6	93.0
65 and over	89.2	82.3	71.5	68.7	67.3	66.4
NEGRO	94.7	93.8	91.8	91.5	91.2	91.1
Under 15	100.4	99.7	100.4	101.2	101.9	102.8
15-24	90.7	94.5	96.5	96.9	97.4	97.7
25-44	89.0	88.0	85.0	85.0	85.2	85.8
45-64	99.9	92.3	85.9	85.8	86.1	86.1
65 and over	91.3	86.9	76.4	72.9	70.7	69.3

Note: Ratios for all races and all data for 1975 refer to total population including Armed Forces overseas and are as of July 1; those by race for 1950-1970 are census counts as of April 1. Projections for 1980 and 1985 are Series II (moderate series)

Source: Department of Commerce

PROJECTIONS OF THE POPULATION BY SEX AND RACE

Millions of persons

Year and Series	Total	Sex		Race	
		Male	Female	White	Negro, Other
Estimates:					
1960	180.7	89.3	91.4	160.0	20.6
1965	194.3	95.6	98.7	171.2	23.1
1966	196.6	96.6	99.9	173.0	23.6
1967	198.7	97.6	101.1	174.7	24.0
1968	200.7	98.4	102.3	176.2	24.5
1969	202.7	99.3	103.4	177.8	24.9
1970	204.9	100.3	104.6	179.5	25.4
1971	207.1	101.3	105.8	181.1	25.9
1972	208.8	102.1	106.8	182.4	26.4
1973	210.4	102.8	107.6	183.5	26.9
1974	211.9	103.4	108.4	184.5	27.4
1975	213.6	104.2	109.4	185.6	28.0
Projections:					
1980: Series I	225.7	110.0	115.7	194.7	31.0
Series II	222.8	108.5	114.3	192.2	30.6
Séries III	220.4	107.2	113.1	190.1	30.2
1985: Series I	241.3	117.6	123.7	206.9	34.4
Series II	234.1	113.9	120.2	200.5	33.5
Series III	228.4	110.9	117.4	195.7	32.6
1990: Series I	257.7	125.6	132.1	219.7	37.9
Series II	245.1	119.2	125.9	208.7	36.4
Series III	235.6	114.3	121.3	200.7	34.9
1995: Series I	272.7	133.0	139.7	231.2	41.5
Series II	254.5	123.7	130.8	215.4	39.1
Series'III	241.2	116.9	124.3	204.2	37.0
2000: Series I	287.0	140.1	146.9	241.9	45.1
Series II	262.5	127.5	135.0	220.8	41.7
Series III	245.1	118.6	126.5	206.2	38.9

Note: Data refer to total population including Armed Forces overseas and are as of July 1. The projection series are based primarily on differing assumptions of completed fertility rates of all women, that is, the average number of children per 1,000 women at the end of childbearing. Series I forecasts that women, on the average, will each bear 2.7 children in their lifetime. The corresponding ultimate completed fertility rates for Series II and Series III are 2.1 and 1.7 children respectively

Source: Department of Commerce

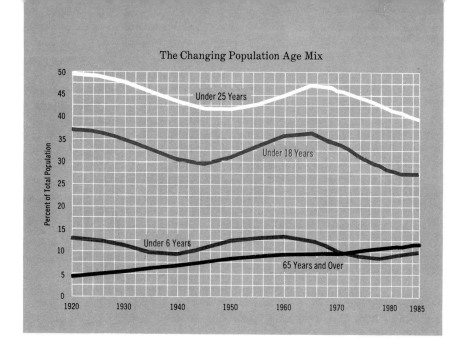

The Changing Population Age Mix

POPULATION BY RACE, NATIVITY AND SEX

Millions of persons

Race, Nativity, Sex	1930	1940	1950	1960	1970
TOTAL	122.8	131.7	150.2	179.3	203.2
Native	108.6	120.1	139.9	169.6	193.6
Foreign Born	14.2	11.6	10.3	9.7	9.6
White	110.3	118.2	134.9	158.8	178.1
Native	96.3	106.8	124.8	149.5	169.4
Foreign Born	14.0	11.4	10.2	9.3	8.7
Negro	11.9	12.9	15.0	18.8	22.5
Other Races	.6	.6	.7	1.6	2.6
MALE	62.1	66.1	74.2	88.3	98.9
Native	54.5	59.9	68.9	83.5	94.5
Foreign Born	7.6	6.1	5.3	4.8	4.4
White	55.9	59.4	67.1	78.3	86.7
Native	48.4	53.4	62.0	73.8	82.9
Foreign Born	7.5	6.0	5.2	4.5	4.0
Negro	5.9	6.3	7.3	9.1	10.7
Other Races	.4	.3	.4	.9	1.4
FEMALE	60.6	65.6	76.0	91.0	104.3
Native	54.1	60.1	70.9	86.0	99.1
Foreign Born	6.6	5.5	5.1	5.0	5.2
White	54.4	58.8	67.8	80.5	91.0
Native	47.9	53.4	62.8	75.7	86.5
Foreign Born	6.5	5.4	5.0	4.8	4.8
Negro	6.0	6.6	7.7	9.8	11.8
Other Races	.2	.2	.3	.8	1.4

Source: Department of Commerce

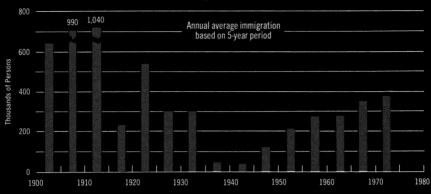

Immigrants Admitted

IMMIGRANTS BY COUNTRY OF ORIGIN

Totals for periods shown, in thousands

Country	1820-1975	1951-1960	1961-1970	1974	1975
ALL COUNTRIES	47,099	2,515	3,322	395	386
Europe	35,961	1,326	1,123	80	73
Austria[1]	4,312	67	21	1	1
France	742	51	45	2	2
Germany[1]	6,954	478	191	7	6
Great Britain[2]	4,852	195	210	12	12
Greece	629	48	86	11	10
Ireland[3]	4,720	57	37	1	1
Italy	5,270	185	214	15	11
Portugal	411	20	76	11	11
Sweden..............	1,270	22	17	1	1
U.S.S.R.[1]	3,354	1	2	1	5
Other Europe	3,446	202	224	19	14
Asia[5]	2,275	150	428	127	129
China[4]	488	10	35	10	9
India	107	2	27	12	14
Japan	391	46	40	5	5
Turkey	382	4	10	1	1
Other Asia...........	906	89	316	98	100
America	8,348	997	1,716	179	175
Canada	4,048	378	413	12	11
Mexico	1,912	300	454	72	63
West Indies	1,408	123	470	61	67
Central America.......	263	45	101	9	10
South America	607	92	258	24	24
Other America	109	60	20	[6]	[6]
Africa	104	14	29	5	6
Australia, New Zealand ..	111	12	20	2	2
All Other Countries	300	17	6	1	2

Note: Country of origin refers to country of last permanent residence
[1] Austria included with Germany, 1938-1945; 1899-1919 Poland included with Austria-Hungary, Germany and U.S.S.R.
[2] Beginning 1952, includes data for United Kingdom not specified, formerly with "Other Europe"
[3] Comprises Eire and Northern Ireland
[4] Beginning 1957, includes Taiwan   [6] Less than 500
[5] Beginning 1952, Philippines included with Asia
Source: Department of Justice

ALIENS ADMITTED, BY CLASSES

Thousands of persons

Year	Total Admitted	Immigrants	Nonimmigrants Total	Temp. Visitors for Pleasure	Other
1950	676	249	427	220	207
1955	859	238	621	332	289
1960	1,406	265	1,141	671	470
1961	1,492	271	1,220	742	478
1962	1,615	284	1,331	811	521
1963	1,813	306	1,507	945	562
1964	2,037	292	1,745	1,105	640
1965	2,373	297	2,076	1,323	752
1966	2,665	323	2,342	1,473	869
1967	2,970	362	2,608	1,629	980
1968	3,655	454	3,200	2,043	1,158
1969	4,004	359	3,645	2,382	1,263
1970	4,805	373	4,432	3,020	1,412
1971	4,774	370	4,404	3,128	1,276
1972	5,556	385	5,171	3,475	1,696
1973	6,377	400	5,977	4,087	1,890
1974	7,304	395	6,909	4,783	2,216
1975	7,470	386	7,084	5,060	2,024

Note: Data are for years ending June 30

Source: Department of Justice

POPULATION BY ETHNIC ORIGIN, 1973

Origin	Thousands of Persons	Males per 100 Females	Median Age (Years)	Percent Under 18 Years	Percent 65 Years and Over	Median School Years Completed[1]
TOTAL POPULATION	206,295	94.0	28.1	33.1	9.8	12.2
English	25,993	90.2	39.0	20.8	15.2	12.5
French	3,939	92.6	36.7	19.2	13.3	12.1
German	20,517	103.1	35.5	21.3	13.3	12.3
Irish	12,240	87.4	38.1	19.9	14.6	12.2
Italian	7,101	103.5	38.4	18.2	11.2	12.1
Polish	3,686	92.8	41.8	15.0	12.5	12.1
Russian	1,747	96.5	45.5	12.8	17.7	12.7
Spanish[2]	10,577	96.5	20.1	46.1	3.8	9.2
Other[3]	97,593	92.6	21.5	43.1	7.0	12.2
Not reported	22,902	96.9	30.0	27.5	10.3	12.0

[1] Persons 25 years and over
[2] Includes persons of Mexican, Puerto Rican, Cuban, Central or South American or other Spanish origin
[3] Includes all origin groups not shown separately, of whom more than 20 million were Negroes

Source: Department of Commerce

PERSONS OF FOREIGN WHITE STOCK

Thousands of persons, except percent

Country of Origin	1950	1960	1970 Total Number	1970 Total Percent	Foreign Born	Native Born[1]
ALL COUNTRIES	33,751	33,078	31,888	100.0	8,734	23,154
United Kingdom	2,736	2,623	2,451	7.7	681	1,770
Ireland (Eire)	2,396	1,771	1,445	4.5	250	1,195
Norway	855	774	613	1.9	97	516
Sweden...................	1,190	1,046	805	2.5	127	678
Denmark	427	399	324	1.0	61	263
Netherlands...............	375	398	382	1.2	110	272
France	362	349	339	1.1	104	235
Germany	4,727	4,313	3,606	11.3	830	2,776
Poland	2,786	2,778	2,371	7.4	547	1,824
Czechoslovakia	984	917	758	2.4	161	597
Austria	1,225	1,098	974	3.1	214	760
Hungary	705	701	603	1.9	183	420
Yugoslavia................	384	448	446	1.4	153	293
U.S.S.R.	2,542	2,287	1,938	6.1	461	1,477
Lithuania	398	402	331	1.0	76	255
Greece	364	378	432	1.4	176	256
Italy	4,571	4,540	4,232	13.3	1,006	3,226
Other Europe	1,455	1,683	1,421	4.5	451	970
Asia	420	483	709	2.2	274	435
Canada	2,982	3,154	2,997	9.4	799	2,198
Mexico..................	1,343	1,725	2,298	7.2	746	1,552
Other America............	222	389	1,163	3.6	815	348
All Other[2]	304	425	1,250	3.9	412	838

[1] Of foreign or mixed parentage
[2] Includes persons not reporting country of origin

Source: Department of Commerce

THE NONWHITE POPULATION

Thousands of persons

Color or Race	1920	1940	1950	1960	1970
TOTAL POPULATION	105,711	131,669	150,697	179,323	203,212
White......................	94,821	118,215	134,942	158,832	177,749
Nonwhite	10,890	13,454	15,755	20,491	25,463
Negro	10,463	12,866	15,042	18,872	22,580
Indian	244	334	343	524	793
Japanese	111	127	142	464	591
Chinese	62	78	118	237	435
Filipino .... } 9	46	62	176	343
Other[1] .... }	5	49	218	721

Note: Data are census enumerations as of April 1 and include Alaska and Hawaii beginning 1960

Asian Indians, Koreans, Hawaiians, Eskimos, and other races not shown separately

Source: Department of Commerce

THE NONWHITE POPULATION BY REGION, 1970

Thousands of persons

Region	All Races	Negro	American Indian	Japanese	Chinese	Filipino	All Other[1]
TOTAL U.S.	203,212	22,580	793	591	435	343	721
Northeast..................	49,041	4,344	49	39	116	31	150
New England	11,842	388	11	7	18	7	21
Middle Atlantic	37,199	3,956	39	31	98	24	129
North Central	56,572	4,572	151	42	39	28	98
E. North Central	40,252	3,873	58	33	31	22	75
W. North Central	16,319	699	94	9	8	5	23
South	62,795	11,970	201	31	34	32	107
South Atlantic	30,671	6,388	67	17	19	24	43
E. South Central........	12,803	2,571	10	4	4	2	9
W. South Central	19,321	3,010	124	10	11	6	56
West	34,804	1,695	391	479	246	252	365
Mountain	8,282	180	235	20	9	4	34
Pacific	26,523	1,514	155	459	236	247	332

[1] Koreans. Hawaiians. Aleuts. Eskimos. Malayans. Polynesians. and other races

Source: Department of Commerce

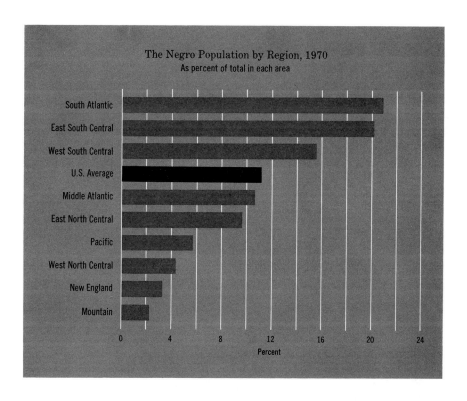

The Negro Population by Region, 1970
As percent of total in each area

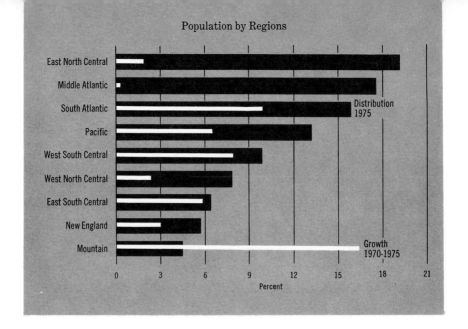

Population by Regions

POPULATION DENSITY OF STATES, 1975

State	Land Area (Thousand Sq. Miles)	Population per Sq. Mile	State	Land Area (Thousand Sq. Miles)	Population per Sq. Mile
Alabama.......	50.7	71.3	Missouri.......	69.0	69.0
Alaska	566.4	.6	Montana.......	145.6	5.1
Arizona	113.4	19.6	Nebraska	76.5	20.2
Arkansas	51.9	40.7	Nevada........	109.9	5.4
California......	156.4	135.5	New Hampshire	9.0	90.6
Colorado	103.8	24.4	New Jersey	7.5	972.7
Connecticut....	4.9	636.6	New Mexico ...	121.4	9.4
Delaware	2.0	292.1	New York	47.8	378.8
District of			North Carolina	48.8	111.7
Columbia	[1]	11,737.7	North Dakota ..	69.3	9.2
Florida	54.1	154.5	Ohio	41.0	262.6
Georgia	58.1	84.8	Oklahoma	68.8	39.4
Hawaii	6.4	134.6	Oregon	96.2	23.8
Idaho	82.7	9.9	Pennsylvania ...	45.0	263.0
Illinois	55.7	199.9	Rhode Island ..	1.0	883.7
Indiana	36.1	147.1	South Carolina .	30.2	93.2
Iowa	55.9	51.3	South Dakota ..	76.0	9.0
Kansas	81.8	27.7	Tennessee	41.3	101.3
Kentucky	39.6	85.6	Texas	262.1	46.7
Louisiana	44.9	84.4	Utah	82.1	14.7
Maine	30.9	34.2	Vermont.......	9.3	50.8
Maryland	9.9	414.3	Virginia	39.8	124.9
Massachusetts .	7.8	744.7	Washington	66.6	53.2
Michigan	56.8	161.2	West Virginia ..	24.1	74.9
Minnesota	79.3	49.5	Wisconsin	54.5	84.6
Mississippi.....	47.3	49.6	Wyoming	97.2	3.8

Note: Land area figures are as of April 1970; population data refer to total resident population as of July 1975

[1] 61 square miles

Source: Department of Commerce

POPULATION OF REGIONS

Millions of persons

Region	1960	1965	1970	1975	Percent Growth 1965-70	Percent Growth 1970-75
TOTAL U.S.	179.3	193.5	203.2	213.1	5.0	4.9
Northeast	44.7	47.5	49.1	49.5	3.4	.9
New England	10.5	11.3	11.8	12.2	4.5	3.0
Middle Atlantic	34.2	36.1	37.2	37.3	3.0	.2
North Central	51.6	54.2	56.6	57.7	4.3	1.9
East North Central	36.2	38.4	40.3	41.0	4.8	1.8
West North Central	15.4	15.8	16.3	16.7	3.2	2.3
South	55.0	59.6	62.8	68.1	5.4	8.5
South Atlantic	26.0	28.7	30.7	33.7	6.7	9.9
East South Central	12.0	12.6	12.8	13.5	1.4	5.8
West South Central	17.0	18.2	19.3	20.9	6.1	7.9
West	28.1	32.2	34.8	37.9	8.1	8.8
Mountain	6.9	7.7	8.3	9.6	7.0	16.4
Pacific	21.2	24.5	26.5	28.2	8.4	6.5

Note: Data refer to total resident population and are as of July 1, except 1960 and 1970 which are census enumerations as of April 1

Source: Department of Commerce

AGE COMPOSITION OF REGIONS, 1975

Region	Resident Population (Millions)	Percent Distribution by Age Group Total	Under 5	5-17	18-44	45-64	65 & Over
TOTAL U.S.	213.1	100.0	7.5	23.6	38.0	20.4	10.5
Northeast	49.5	100.0	6.7	23.0	36.9	22.2	11.2
New England	12.2	100.0	6.6	23.5	37.5	21.2	11.2
Middle Atlantic	37.3	100.0	6.7	22.9	36.7	22.5	11.2
North Central	57.7	100.0	7.5	24.2	37.7	20.1	10.6
East North Central .	41.0	100.0	7.6	24.4	37.9	20.2	9.9
West North Central .	16.7	100.0	7.2	23.9	37.0	19.8	12.2
South	68.1	100.0	7.9	23.7	38.1	19.7	10.5
South Atlantic	33.7	100.0	7.6	23.2	38.4	20.2	10.7
East South Central .	13.5	100.0	8.2	24.1	37.4	19.6	10.6
West South Central .	20.9	100.0	8.4	24.3	38.1	19.1	10.1
West	37.9	100.0	7.6	23.5	39.5	19.9	9.5
Mountain	9.6	100.0	8.7	24.9	38.8	18.8	8.8
Pacific	28.2	100.0	7.2	23.0	39.8	20.3	9.7

Note: Data based on estimates as of July 1

Source: Department of Commerce

POPULATION BY STATES

Thousands of persons, except percent

State	1970	1975	Annual Growth Rate (Percent)		
			1950-1960	1960-1970	1970-1975
TOTAL U.S.	203,235	213,121	1.7	1.3	1.0
Alabama	3,444	3,614	.7	.5	1.0
Alaska	302	352	5.8	2.9	3.1
Arizona	1,772	2,224	5.7	3.1	4.6
Arkansas.................	1,923	2,116	− .7	.7	1.9
California	19,953	21,185	4.0	2.4	1.2
Colorado	2,207	2,534	2.8	2.3	2.8
Connecticut	3,032	3,095	2.4	1.8	.4
Delaware	548	579	3.4	2.1	1.1
D.C.	757	716	− .5	− .1	−1.1
Florida	6,789	8,357	6.0	3.2	4.2
Georgia	4,590	4,926	1.4	1.5	1.4
Hawaii..................	770	865	2.4	2.0	2.4
Idaho	713	820	1.3	.7	2.8
Illinois	11,114	11,145	1.5	1.0	.1
Indiana	5,194	5,311	1.7	1.1	.4
Iowa	2,825	2,870	.5	.2	.3
Kansas	2,249	2,267	1.3	.3	.2
Kentucky	3,219	3,396	.3	.6	1.1
Louisiana	3,643	3,791	2.0	1.1	.8
Maine	994	1,059	.6	.2	1.3
Maryland	3,922	4,098	2.8	2.4	.9
Massachusetts	5,689	5,828	.9	1.0	.5
Michigan................	8,875	9,157	2.1	1.3	.6
Minnesota...............	3,805	3,926	1.4	1.1	.6
Mississippi	2,217	2,346	1	.3	1.1
Missouri	4,677	4,763	.9	.8	.4
Montana	694	748	1.3	.3	1.5
Nebraska	1,484	1,546	.6	.5	.8
Nevada	489	592	5.9	5.5	3.9
New Hampshire	738	818	1.3	2.0	2.1
New Jersey	7,168	7,316	2.3	1.7	.4
New Mexico	1,016	1,147	3.4	.7	2.5
New York	18,241	18,120	1.2	.8	− .1
North Carolina	5,082	5,451	1.2	1.1	1.4
North Dakota	618	635	.2	− .2	.5
Ohio....................	10,652	10,759	2.0	.9	.2
Oklahoma...............	2,559	2,712	.4	1.0	1.2
Oregon	2,091	2,288	1.5	1.7	1.8
Pennsylvania	11,794	11,827	.8	.4	.1
Rhode Island	950	927	.8	1.0	− .5
South Carolina	2,591	2,818	1.2	.8	1.7
South Dakota	666	683	.4	− .2	.5
Tennessee...............	3,924	4,188	.8	1.0	1.3
Texas...................	11,197	12,237	2.2	1.6	1.8
Utah	1,059	1,206	2.6	1.7	2.6
Vermont	445	471	.3	1.3	1.1
Virginia	4,648	4,967	1.8	1.6	1.3
Washington	3,409	3,544	1.8	1.8	.8
West Virginia............	1,744	1,803	− .7	− .6	.7
Wisconsin	4,418	4,607	1.4	1.1	.8
Wyoming	332	374	1.3	− .1	2.4

Note: Total resident population. 1970 figures are census enumerations as of April 1; 1975 data are estimates as of July 1

1 Less than .05 percent

Source: Department of Commerce

Population by States: 1975

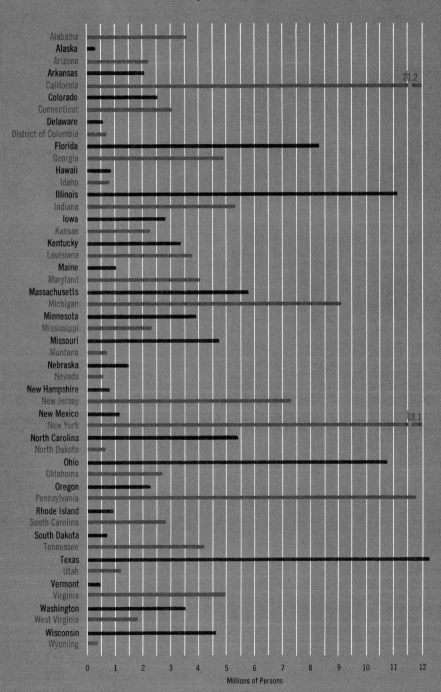

Alabama	
Alaska	
Arizona	
Arkansas	
California	21.2
Colorado	
Connecticut	
Delaware	
District of Columbia	
Florida	
Georgia	
Hawaii	
Idaho	
Illinois	
Indiana	
Iowa	
Kansas	
Kentucky	
Louisiana	
Maine	
Maryland	
Massachusetts	
Michigan	
Minnesota	
Mississippi	
Missouri	
Montana	
Nebraska	
Nevada	
New Hampshire	
New Jersey	
New Mexico	
New York	18.1
North Carolina	
North Dakota	
Ohio	
Oklahoma	
Oregon	
Pennsylvania	
Rhode Island	
South Carolina	
South Dakota	
Tennessee	
Texas	
Utah	
Vermont	
Virginia	
Washington	
West Virginia	
Wisconsin	
Wyoming	

0   1   2   3   4   5   6   7   8   9   10   11   12

Millions of Persons

POPULATION OF STATES BY RACE
Thousands of persons

State	1960			1970			
	Total	White	Negro, Other Races	Total	White	Negro, Other Races	Per- cent Negro
TOTAL U.S.	179,323	151,832	20,491	203,212	177,749	25,463	11.1
Alabama	3,267	2,284	983	3,444	2,534	910	26.2
Alaska	226	175	52	300	237	64	3.0
Arizona	1,302	1,170	133	1,771	1,605	166	3.0
Arkansas	1,786	1,396	391	1,923	1,566	357	18.3
California	15,717	14,455	1,262	19,953	17,761	2,192	7.0
Colorado	1,754	1,701	53	2,207	2,112	95	3.0
Connecticut	2,535	2,424	111	3,032	2,835	196	6.0
Delaware	446	384	62	548	466	82	14.3
D. C.	764	345	419	757	209	547	71.1
Florida	4,952	4,064	888	6,789	5,719	1,070	15.3
Georgia	3,943	2,817	1,126	4,590	3,391	1,198	25.9
Hawaii	633	202	431	769	298	470	1.0
Idaho	667	657	10	713	699	14	.3
Illinois	10,081	9,010	1,071	11,114	9,600	1,514	12.8
Indiana	4,662	4,389	274	5,194	4,820	373	6.9
Iowa	2,758	2,729	29	2,824	2,783	42	1.2
Kansas	2,179	2,079	100	2,247	2,122	125	4.8
Kentucky	3,038	2,820	218	3,219	2,982	237	7.2
Louisiana	3,257	2,212	1,045	3,641	2,541	1,100	29.8
Maine	969	963	6	992	985	7	.3
Maryland	3,101	2,574	527	3,922	3,195	728	17.8
Massachusetts ...	5,150	5,023	125	5,689	5,478	212	3.1
Michigan	7,823	7,086	738	8,875	7,833	1,042	11.2
Minnesota	3,414	3,372	42	3,805	3,736	69	.9
Mississippi	2,178	1,258	921	2,217	1,393	824	36.8
Missouri	4,320	3,923	397	4,677	4,177	499	10.3
Montana	675	651	24	694	663	31	.3
Nebraska	1,411	1,375	37	1,483	1,433	51	2.7
Nevada	285	263	22	489	448	41	5.7
New Hampshire .	607	604	3	738	733	5	.3
New Jersey	6,067	5,539	528	7,168	6,350	818	10.7
New Mexico	951	876	75	1,016	916	100	1.9
New York	16,782	15,287	1,495	18,237	15,834	2,403	11.9
North Carolina ..	4,556	3,399	1,157	5,082	3,902	1,180	22.2
North Dakota ...	632	620	13	618	599	18	.4
Ohio............	9,706	8,910	797	10,652	9,647	1,005	9.1
Oklahoma	2,327	2,108	220	2,559	2,280	279	6.7
Oregon	1,769	1,732	37	2,091	2,032	59	1.3
Pennsylvania	11,319	10,454	865	11,794	10,738	1,056	8.6
Rhode Island	859	839	21	947	915	32	2.7
South Carolina ..	2,383	1,551	832	2,591	1,794	796	30.5
South Dakota ...	681	653	27	666	630	35	.2
Tennessee	3,567	2,978	589	3,924	3,294	630	15.8
Texas...........	9,580	8,375	1,205	11,197	9,717	1,480	12.5
Utah	891	874	17	1,059	1,032	27	.6
Vermont	390	389	1	444	443	2	.2
Virginia	3,967	3,142	825	4,648	3,762	887	18.5
Washington	2,853	2,752	102	3,409	3,251	158	2.1
West Virginia ...	1,860	1,770	90	1,744	1,673	71	3.9
Wisconsin	3,953	3,859	93	4,418	4,259	159	2.9
Wyoming	330	323	7	332	323	9	.8

Note: Data are census enumerations as of April 1

Source: Department of Commerce

POPULATION BY STATES AND METROPOLITAN RESIDENCE, 1970

Thousands of persons, except percent

State	Metropolitan					Nonmetropolitan	
	Total			Inside Central Cities	Outside Central Cities	Number	Percent Change, 1960-1970
	Number	% of Pop.	% Chg. 1960-1970				
TOTAL U.S. ...	139,419	68.6	16.6	63,797	75,622	63,793	6.8
Alabama	1,801	52.3	6.5	882	919	1,643	4.2
Alaska	- -	- -	- -	- -	- -	300	32.8
Arizona	1,319	74.5	42.0	844	475	452	21.1
Arkansas	595	30.9	14.3	334	261	1,328	4.9
California	18,500	92.7	27.7	7,239	11,261	1,453	17.6
Colorado	1,582	71.7	32.7	747	835	626	11.3
Connecticut	2,505	82.6	17.4	1,067	1,438	527	31.2
Delaware	386	70.4	25.5	80	305	162	16.9
D.C.	757	100.0	−1.0	757	- -	- -	- -
Florida	4,657	68.6	37.2	1,946	2,711	2,132	37.0
Georgia	2,280	49.7	25.7	1,024	1,256	2,309	8.5
Hawaii	629	81.8	25.7	325	304	139	5.3
Idaho	112	15.7	20.1	75	37	600	4.6
Illinois	8,903	80.1	12.2	4,076	4,828	2,211	2.9
Indiana	3,214	61.9	12.7	1,790	1,424	1,980	9.3
Iowa	1,006	35.6	9.8	632	374	1,819	− 1.2
Kansas	949	42.2	11.4	402	548	1,297	− 2.2
Kentucky	1,288	40.0	14.1	549	739	1,931	1.1
Louisiana	1,996	54.8	14.0	1,143	851	1,645	9.2
Maine	214	21.6	2.2	129	85	778	2.4
Maryland	3,307	84.3	29.7	906	2,402	615	11.8
Massachusetts	4,818	84.7	8.5	1,726	3,092	871	23.4
Michigan	6,806	76.7	14.2	2,468	4,338	2,069	11.2
Minnesota	2,165	56.9	19.1	928	1,237	1,640	2.8
Mississippi	393	17.7	15.4	243	150	1,823	− .8
Missouri	2,997	64.1	13.0	1,376	1,621	1,679	.7
Montana	169	24.4	11.0	122	47	525	.6
Nebraska	634	42.8	17.0	497	137	849	− 2.3
Nevada	394	80.6	86.2	199	196	94	28.4
New Hampshire ..	202	27.2	25.0	144	58	536	20.3
New Jersey	5,511	76.9	12.6	1,167	4,344	1,657	41.3
New Mexico	316	31.1	20.4	244	72	700	1.7
New York	15,771	86.5	8.5	9,311	6,460	2,466	9.8
North Carolina ...	1,896	37.3	23.8	956	941	3,186	5.3
North Dakota	74	12.0	10.0	53	20	544	− 3.8
Ohio	8,273	77.7	11.0	3,429	4,844	2,380	5.5
Oklahoma	1,281	50.1	19.9	762	519	1,278	1.4
Oregon	1,281	61.3	23.3	527	753	811	11.0
Pennsylvania	9,366	79.4	4.9	3,372	5,993	2,428	1.4
Rhode Island	802	84.7	8.2	340	462	145	22.2
South Carolina	1,017	39.3	19.4	242	776	1,573	2.8
South Dakota	95	14.3	10.0	72	23	570	− 4.0
Tennessee	1,918	48.9	13.0	1,353	565	2,006	7.2
Texas	8,234	73.5	23.7	5,395	2,839	2,962	1.3
Utah	822	77.6	23.5	324	497	238	5.5
Vermont	- -	- -	- -	- -	- -	444	14.0
Virginia	2,846	61.2	27.6	1,125	1,721	1,802	3.7
Washington	2,249	66.0	24.9	910	1,339	1,160	10.3
West Virginia	545	31.3	− 5.2	221	324	1,199	− 6.7
Wisconsin	2,543	57.6	14.7	1,346	1,197	1,875	8.1
Wyoming	- -	- -	- -	- -	- -	332	.7

Note: Data are census enumerations as of April 1   Source: Department of Commerce

Projected Population Growth by States
Percent change, 1970 to 1980

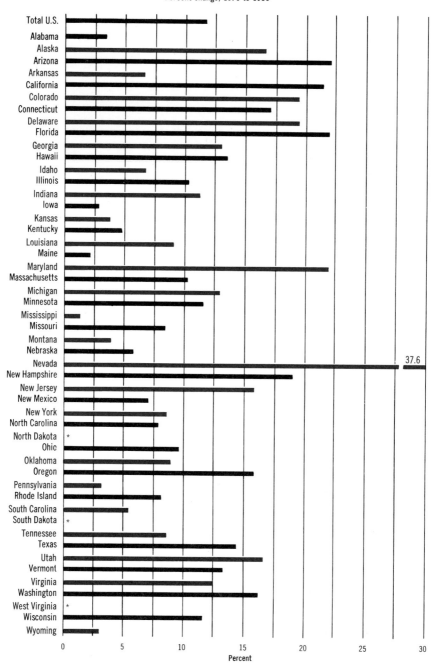

*Projected declines: North Dakota—2.9%, South Dakota—1.2%, and West Virginia—6.3%

PROJECTIONS OF THE POPULATION BY STATES
Thousands of persons

State	1970	1975	1980	1985	1990
TOTAL U.S.	203,235	214,883	226,934	239,329	250,630
Alabama.............	3,444	3,500	3,565	3,634	3,692
Alaska	302	328	352	374	392
Arizona	1,772	1,974	2,164	2,352	2,523
Arkansas	1,923	1,986	2,052	2,126	2,195
California	19,953	22,077	24,226	26,429	28,496
Colorado	2,207	2,423	2,636	2,848	3,042
Connecticut	3,032	3,288	3,551	3,825	4,082
Delaware	548	601	655	709	758
District of Columbia .	757	n.a.	n.a.	n.a.	n.a.
Florida	6,789	7,557	8,280	8,980	9,626
Georgia	4,590	4,887	5,191	5,494	5,761
Hawaii	770	828	874	908	933
Idaho	713	735	761	790	817
Illinois	11,114	11,666	12,256	12,885	13,464
Indiana	5,194	5,483	5,782	6,093	6,370
Iowa	2,825	2,861	2,908	2,962	3,009
Kansas	2,249	2,287	2,334	2,386	2,432
Kentucky	3,219	3,290	3,372	3,461	3,540
Louisiana	3,643	3,807	3,975	4,141	4,285
Maine	994	1,003	1,016	1,031	1,044
Maryland	3,922	4,348	4,782	5,225	5,637
Massachusetts	5,689	5,977	6,277	6,588	6,869
Michigan	8,875	9,445	10,031	10,639	11,193
Minnesota	3,805	4,021	4,245	4,483	4,703
Mississippi	2,217	2,227	2,245	2,268	2,288
Missouri	4,677	4,866	5,070	5,288	5,491
Montana.............	694	706	721	739	757
Nebraska	1,484	1,525	1,570	1,620	1,664
Nevada.............	489	584	673	759	836
New Hampshire	738	807	878	950	1,019
New Jersey..........	7,168	7,725	8,300	8,906	9,481
New Mexico	1,016	1,052	1,088	1,126	1,160
New York...........	18,241	18,964	19,789	20,660	21,461
North Carolina	5,082	5,277	5,482	5,682	5,852
North Dakota	618	607	600	597	594
Ohio	10,652	11,152	11,675	12,218	12,693
Oklahoma	2,559	2,669	2,787	2,912	3,029
Oregon	2,091	2,257	2,421	2,591	2,749
Pennsylvania	11,794	11,964	12,157	12,364	12,529
Rhode Island	950	985	1,027	1,068	1,104
South Carolina	2,591	2,658	2,731	2,800	2,855
South Dakota	666	660	658	660	662
Tennessee	3,924	4,089	4,259	4,430	4,581
Texas	11,197	12,002	12,812	13,625	14,358
Utah	1,059	1,146	1,234	1,322	1,400
Vermont.............	445	474	504	535	563
Virginia	4,648	4,936	5,229	5,512	5,755
Washington	3,409	3,682	3,958	4,236	4,489
West Virginia	1,744	1,681	1,634	1,598	1,565
Wisconsin	4,418	4,669	4,930	5,207	5,466
Wyoming	332	336	342	351	360

Note: Resident population. 1970 figures are census enumerations; projections are Series I-E which assume a low population growth and a continuation of 1960-1970 gross migration trends. These projections, developed in early 1972, are based on advance data from the 1970 Census and, in some cases, are not consistent with current area trends as shown in table on page 28

n.a.—Not available

Source: Department of Commerce

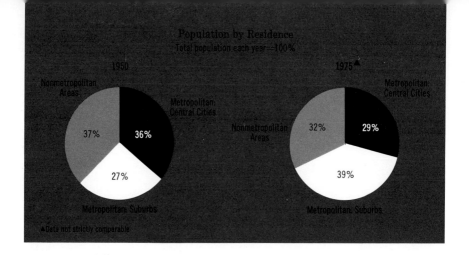

Population by Residence
Total population each year=100%

1950

Nonmetropolitan Areas

Metropolitan: Central Cities

37%   36%

27%

Metropolitan: Suburbs

▲Data not strictly comparable

1975 ▲

Metropolitan: Central Cities

Nonmetropolitan Areas   32%   29%

39%

Metropolitan: Suburbs

THE WHITE AND NEGRO POPULATION BY REGION AND RESIDENCE

Region and Residence	1970			1960		
	Total[1] (Thousands)	Percent of Total		Total[1] (Thousands)	Percent of Total	
		White	Negro		White	Negro
TOTAL U.S.	203,166	87.4	11.2	179,323	88.6	10.5
Metropolitan[2]	140,156	86.5	12.0	120,159	88.5	10.7
Inside Central Cities	63,824	77.5	20.6	60,630	82.6	16.3
Outside Central Cities[2] ...	76,331	94.1	4.8	59,529	94.6	4.8
Nonmetropolitan	63,010	89.4	9.3	59,164	88.7	10.3
Northeast..............	48,994	90.4	8.9	44,678	92.9	6.8
Metropolitan[2]	39,925	88.7	10.5	36,620	91.8	7.9
Inside Central Cities	17,233	79.0	19.5	17,576	86.3	13.2
Outside Central Cities[2] ...	22,692	96.0	3.6	19,045	96.9	3.0
Nonmetropolitan	9,069	97.8	1.8	8,058	98.2	1.6
North Central	56,572	91.3	8.1	51,619	93.0	6.7
Metropolitan	37,658	88.0	11.4	33,351	90.2	9.6
Inside Central Cities	17,077	77.4	21.7	17,121	83.3	16.3
Outside Central Cities	20,582	96.8	2.8	16,230	97.4	2.5
Nonmetropolitan	18,913	97.8	1.5	18,268	98.2	1.4
South	62,795	80.1	19.2	54,973	79.1	20.6
Metropolitan	35,199	80.2	19.1	28,860	80.2	19.6
Inside Central Cities	17,955	71.7	27.6	16,139	74.6	25.1
Outside Central Cities	17,244	89.0	10.3	12,721	87.2	12.6
Nonmetropolitan	27,596	80.1	19.3	26,113	77.9	21.7
West	34,804	90.2	4.9	28,053	92.1	3.9
Metropolitan	27,373	89.5	5.9	21,328	91.7	4.8
Inside Central Cities	11,560	84.3	9.7	9,794	87.6	7.6
Outside Central Cities	15,813	93.3	3.2	11,533	95.2	2.4
Nonmetropolitan	7,431	92.7	1.0	6,725	93.3	1.0

Note: Figures are based on census enumerations as of April 1. Metropolitan area data have been adjusted for comparability between the two years

[1] Totals include other nonwhite races not shown separately

[2] Includes Middlesex and Somerset counties in New Jersey, which are part of the New York-Northeastern New Jersey Standard Consolidated Area, but not part of any SMSA   Source: Department of Commerce

POPULATION BY RESIDENCE AND RACE

Residence and Race	Thousands of Persons		Annual Average Percent Change	
	1970	1975	1960-1970[1]	1970-1975
WHITE	175,276	181,636	1.1	.7
Metropolitan Areas[2]	118,938	121,277	1.3	.4
Inside Central Cities[3]	48,909	45,559	--	− 1.4
Outside Central Cities	70,029	75,718	2.3	1.6
Nonmetropolitan Areas	56,338	60,359	.8	1.4
NEGRO, OTHER RACES	24,543	27,047	2.2	1.9
Metropolitan Areas[2]	18,120	20,716	3.1	2.7
Inside Central Cities[3]	13,967	15,343	3.1	1.9
Outside Central Cities	4,153	5,373	3.2	5.2
Nonmetropolitan Areas	6,423	6,331	− .2	− .3

Note: Figures for 1970 have been adjusted for comparability with the Current Population Survey, and exclude inmates of institutions and members of the Armed Forces in barracks and similar quarters. Data for 1975 are April-centered averages

[1] Based on the total 1970 and 1960 censuses of population, including persons not covered in the Current Population Survey
[2] Population of 243 metropolitan areas as defined in the 1970 census
[3] 1975 data refer to Jan. 1, 1970 boundaries

Source: Department of Commerce

THE 50 LARGEST METROPOLITAN AREAS IN 1974

Rank	Standard Metropolitan Statistical Area	Population (Thousands)	Rank	Standard Metropolitan Statistical Area	Population (Thousands)
1	New York, N.Y.-N.J. ...	9,634	26	Tampa-St. Petersburg, Fla.	1,333
2	Chicago, Ill.	6,971	27	Buffalo, N.Y.	1,331
3	Los Angeles-Long Beach, Calif. ...	6,926	28	Kansas City, Mo.-Kans.	1,302
4	Philadelphia, Pa.-N.J. ...	4,810	29	Riverside-San Bernardino-etc., Calif.	1,214
5	Detroit, Mich.	4,434	30	San Jose, Calif.	1,182
6	Boston-Lowell-etc., Mass.-N.H.[1]	3,918	31	Phoenix, Ariz.	1,172
7	San Francisco-Oakland, Calif.	3,136	32	Indianapolis, Ind.	1,144
8	Washington, D.C.-Md.-Va.	3,015	33	New Orleans, La.......	1,090
9	Nassau-Suffolk, N.Y. ...	2,621	34	Portland, Oreg.-Wash. ..	1,080
10	Dallas-Fort Worth, Tex.	2,498	35	Columbus, Ohio	1,067
11	St. Louis, Mo.-Ill.	2,371	36	Hartford-etc., Conn[1] ...	1,059
12	Pittsburgh, Pa.	2,334	37	San Antonio, Tex.	980
13	Houston, Tex..........	2,223	38	Rochester, N.Y........	966
14	Baltimore, Md.	2,140	39	Louisville, Ky.-Ind.	892
15	Newark, N.J.	2,019	40	Sacramento, Calif.	883
16	Minneapolis-St. Paul, Minn.-Wis.	2,011	41	Providence-Warwick-Pawtucket-R.I.[1]	854
17	Cleveland, Ohio	1,984	42	Memphis, Tenn.-Ark.-Miss.	853
18	Atlanta, Ga............	1,776	43	Dayton, Ohio	845
19	Anaheim-Santa Ana-etc., Calif.	1,661	44	Fort Lauderdale-Hollywood, Fla.	807
20	San Diego, Calif.	1,518	45	Albany-Schenectady-Troy, N.Y.	799
21	Miami, Fla.	1,416	46	Bridgeport-etc., Conn.[1]	791
22	Milwaukee, Wis........	1,415	47	Birmingham, Ala.	785
23	Seattle-Everett, Wash. ..	1,396	48	Toledo, Ohio-Mich.	781
24	Denver-Boulder, Colo. .	1,391	49	Oklahoma City, Okla. ..	766
25	Cincinnati, Ohio-Ky.-Ind.	1,376	50	Norfolk-Virginia Beach-etc., Va.-N.C.	766

Note: Metropolitan areas as currently defined, and not comparable to all SMSA's on page 36
[1] Metropolitan state economic area

Source: Department of Commerce

POPULATION OF LEADING METROPOLITAN AREAS, 1970

Thousands of persons, except percent

Standard Metropolitan Statistical Area	Total SMSA	Inside Central Cities	Outside Central Cities		Percent Change, 1960-1970	
			Number	Percent of SMSA	Inside C. C.	Outside C. C.
TOTAL, 243 AREAS	139,419	63,797	75,622	54.2	6.4	26.8
New York, N. Y...........	11,572	7,895	3,667	31.7	1.5	26.2
Los Angeles-Long Beach, Calif.	7,032	3,175	3,857	54.8	12.5	20.0
Chicago, Ill.	6,979	3,367	3,612	51.8	− 5.2	35.3
Philadelphia, Pa.-N. J........	4,818	1,949	2,869	59.5	− 2.7	22.6
Detroit, Mich.	4,200	1,511	2,688	64.0	− 9.5	28.5
San Francisco-Oakland, Calif.	3,110	1,077	2,032	65.3	− 2.8	31.9
Washington, D.C.-Md.-Va. ...	2,861	757	2,105	73.6	− 1.0	60.3
Boston, Mass...............	2,754	641	2,113	76.7	− 8.1	11.3
Pittsburgh, Pa.	2,401	520	1,881	78.3	−13.9	4.4
St. Louis, Mo.-Ill...........	2,363	622	1,741	73.7	−17.0	28.5
Baltimore, Md...............	2,071	906	1,165	56.3	− 3.6	34.7
Cleveland, Ohio	2,064	751	1,313	63.6	−14.3	27.1
Houston, Tex.	1,985	1,231	754	38.0	31.2	57.0
Newark, N. J.	1,857	382	1,474	79.4	− 5.6	14.8
Minneapolis-St. Paul, Minn. ..	1,814	744	1,069	58.9	− 6.5	55.9
Dallas, Tex.	1,556	844	712	45.7	24.2	61.8
Seattle-Everett, Wash.	1,422	584	837	58.9	− 2.2	64.3
Anaheim-Santa Ana-etc., Calif.	1,420	446	975	68.7	54.4	134.7
Milwaukee, Wis.	1,404	717	687	48.9	− 3.3	27.7
Atlanta, Ga.	1,390	497	893	64.2	2.0	68.6
Cincinnati, Ohio-Ky.-Ind.	1,385	453	932	67.3	−10.0	21.7
Paterson-Clifton-Passaic, N.J.	1,359	282	1,076	79.2	1.0	18.7
San Diego, Calif.............	1,358	694	664	48.9	21.1	44.4
Buffalo, N. Y.	1,349	463	886	65.7	−13.1	14.5
Miami, Fla.	1,268	335	933	73.6	14.8	45.0
Kansas City, Mo.-Kans.	1,254	502	752	60.0	5.5	21.9
Denver, Colo...............	1,228	515	713	58.1	4.2	63.7
San Bernardino-etc., Calif. ...	1,143	308	835	73.1	38.4	42.2
Indianapolis, Ind.............	1,110	743	367	33.0	56.0	−21.7
San Jose, Calif.	1,065	444	621	58.3	117.4	41.7
New Orleans, La.	1,046	592	454	43.4	− 5.8	62.5
Tampa-St. Petersburg, Fla....	1,013	494	519	51.2	8.3	64.0
Portland, Ore.-Wash.	1,009	383	627	62.1	2.7	39.5
Phoenix, Ariz.	968	582	386	39.9	32.4	72.0
Columbus, Ohio	916	540	377	41.2	14.5	32.8
Providence-etc., R. I.-Mass. .	911	340	571	62.7	− 4.8	23.0
Rochester, N. Y.	883	296	586	66.4	− 7.0	41.7
San Antonio, Tex.	864	654	210	24.3	11.3	63.4
Dayton, Ohio	850	244	607	71.4	− 7.2	30.5
Louisville, Ky.-Ind...........	827	361	465	56.2	− 7.5	39.0
Sacramento, Calif............	801	254	546	68.2	32.7	25.9
Memphis, Tenn.-Ark.	770	623	147	19.1	25.3	−17.2
Fort Worth, Tex.	762	393	369	48.4	10.4	69.9
Birmingham, Ala.............	739	301	438	59.3	−11.7	15.3
Albany-Schenectady, etc. N.Y.	722	257	465	64.5	− 8.0	22.9
Toledo, Ohio-Mich...........	693	384	309	44.6	20.7	− 1.3
Norfolk-Portsmouth, Va.	681	419	262	38.5	− .2	64.7
Akron, Ohio	679	275	404	59.5	− 5.2	28.2
Hartford, Conn.	664	158	506	76.2	− 2.6	30.7
Oklahoma City, Okla.	641	366	274	42.7	13.0	46.3

Note: Figures are census enumerations as of April 1 and refer to SMSA's as defined at that time

Source: Department of Commerce

POPULATION MOBILITY BY SELECTED CHARACTERISTICS

March 1970 to March 1975

Characteristic	Total Population[1] (Millions)	Percent of Population Moving			
		Total	Same County	Different County in State	Different State
TOTAL U.S.	193.5	41.3	24.2	8.4	8.6
Race					
White	169.1	40.7	22.7	9.0	9.0
Negro, Other Races	24.4	44.9	34.5	4.3	6.1
Negro	21.4	45.7	35.7	4.1	5.9
Sex					
Male	93.4	41.5	24.0	8.5	8.9
Female	100.1	41.0	24.4	8.4	8.3
Household Status					
Head of Household	71.1	42.2	25.0	8.6	8.6
Husband-Wife	47.0	41.7	23.3	9.0	9.4
Other Primary Family Head .	8.6	44.7	31.5	6.7	6.5
Primary Individual	15.6	42.4	26.5	8.3	7.6
Relative of Household Head[2] .	118.6	40.1	23.5	8.1	8.5
All Others	3.8	60.6	32.4	16.1	12.1
Residence					
Metropolitan	131.8	41.0	25.1	7.7	8.3
Central Cities	56.5	40.9	28.3	5.3	7.2
Outside Central Cities	75.3	41.2	22.6	9.5	9.0
Nonmetropolitan	61.7	41.7	22.3	10.0	9.4
Age					
5-13	33.6	47.7	28.2	9.4	10.1
14-17	16.7	34.0	20.9	6.1	7.0
18-24	26.3	54.8	32.5	11.8	10.5
25-34	30.1	66.5	36.1	14.9	15.5
35-44	22.6	39.7	23.4	7.7	8.6
45-64	43.1	24.4	15.4	4.6	4.4
65 and over	21.1	20.1	12.2	4.1	3.9
Region					
Northeast	44.9	30.7	19.7	6.3	4.8
North Central	52.4	38.9	24.1	8.4	6.4
South	61.5	46.3	25.6	9.2	11.5
West	34.7	49.4	27.6	10.0	11.8
Education, Total 18 Yrs. & Over	143.2	40.6	23.7	8.5	8.4
Less than High School	26.6	29.2	20.3	5.1	3.9
Some High School	23.1	39.9	26.5	6.9	6.5
High School Graduate	54.3	41.2	25.1	8.2	7.9
Some College	21.1	46.1	24.0	10.8	11.3
College Graduate	18.2	49.8	20.2	13.7	15.8
Income, Male, 18 Yrs. & Over	67.9	40.7	23.4	8.6	8.8
Under $3,000	11.9	33.4	20.5	6.4	6.5
$ 3,000-5,000	7.9	38.3	21.6	8.7	8.1
5,000-7,000	7.6	43.8	24.9	8.9	9.9
7,000-10,000	11.0	47.0	27.3	9.8	10.0
10,000-15,000	15.8	43.1	25.5	9.3	8.2
15,000 and over	13.7	39.1	20.3	8.6	10.1

[1] Population five years of age and over
[2] Includes wife in husband-wife households

Source: Department of Commerce

POPULATION PROFILE OF MAJOR CITIES

Thousands of persons, except as indicated

City	1950	1960	1970 Number	Percent Change, 1960-1970	Percent Negro	Persons per Sq. Mile
Akron, Ohio	275	290	275	− 5.1	17.5	5,082
Albuquerque, N.M.	97	201	244	21.2	2.2	2,965
Atlanta, Ga.	331	487	497	2.0	51.3	3,779
Austin, Tex.	132	187	252	35.0	11.8	3,492
Baltimore, Md.	950	939	906	− 3.6	46.4	11,568
Birmingham, Ala.	326	341	301	−11.7	42.0	3,785
Boston, Mass.	801	697	641	− 8.1	16.3	13,936
Buffalo, N.Y.	580	533	463	−13.1	20.4	11,205
Charlotte, N.C.	134	202	241	19.7	30.3	3,173
Chicago, Ill.	3,621	3,550	3,367	− 5.2	32.7	15,126
Cincinnati, Ohio	504	503	453	−10.0	27.6	5,794
Cleveland, Ohio	915	876	751	−14.3	38.3	9,893
Columbus, Ohio	376	471	540	14.5	18.5	4,009
Corpus Christi, Tex.	108	168	205	22.0	5.1	2,033
Dallas, Tex.	434	680	844	24.2	24.9	3,179
Dayton, Ohio	244	262	244	− 7.1	30.5	6,360
Denver, Colo.	416	494	515	4.2	9.1	5,406
Des Moines, Iowa	178	209	201	− 4.0	5.7	3,174
Detroit, Mich.	1,850	1,670	1,511	− 9.5	43.7	10,953
El Paso, Tex.	130	277	322	16.5	2.3	2,724
Fort Worth, Tex.	279	356	393	10.4	19.9	1,919
Honolulu, Hawaii	248	294	325	10.4	.7	3,872
Houston, Tex.	596	938	1,233	31.4	25.7	2,841
Indianapolis, Ind.	427	476	745	56.3	18.0	1,963
Jacksonville, Fla	205	201	529	163.1	22.3	690
Jersey City, N.J.	299	276	261	− 5.6	21.0	17,255
Kansas City, Mo.	457	476	507	6.6	22.1	1,603
Long Beach, Calif.	251	344	359	4.2	5.3	7,364
Los Angeles, Calif.	1,970	2,479	2,816	13.6	17.9	6,073
Louisville, Ky.	369	391	361	− 7.5	23.8	6,025
Memphis, Tenn.	396	498	624	25.3	38.9	2,868
Miami, Fla.	249	292	335	14.8	22.7	9,763
Milwaukee, Wis.	637	741	717	− 3.3	14.7	7,548
Minneapolis, Minn.	522	483	434	− 10.0	4.4	8,135
Nashville, Tenn.[1]	174	171	448	162.2	19.6	882
New Orleans, La.	570	628	593	− 5.4	45.0	3,011
New York, N.Y.	7,892	7,782	7,895	1.5	21.2	26,343
Newark, N.J.	439	405	382	−5.6	54.2	16,273
Norfolk, Va.	214	306	308	1.0	28.3	5,855
Oakland, Calif.	385	368	362	−1.6	34.5	6,771
Oklahoma City, Okla.	244	324	366	13.0	13.7	576
Omaha, Neb.	251	302	347	15.2	9.9	4,534
Philadelphia, Pa.	2,071	2,003	1,949	−2.7	33.6	15,164
Phoenix, Ariz.	107	439	582	32.4	4.8	2,346
Pittsburgh, Pa.	677	604	520	−13.9	20.2	9,422
Portland, Ore.	374	373	383	2.7	5.6	4,294
Richmond, Va.	230	220	250	13.5	42.0	4,140
Rochester, N.Y.	332	319	296	− 7.0	16.8	8,072

POPULATION PROFILE OF MAJOR CITIES (Continued)

Thousands of persons, except as indicated

City	1950	1960	1970 Number	Percent Change, 1960-1970	Percent Negro	Persons per Sq. Mile
Sacramento, Calif.	138	192	254	32.7	10.7	2,712
St. Louis, Mo.	857	750	622	−17.0	40.9	10,167
St. Paul, Minn.	311	313	310	−1.1	3.5	5,938
St. Petersburg, Fla	97	181	216	19.3	14.8	3,903
San Antonio, Tex.	408	588	654	11.3	7.6	3,555
San Diego, Calif.	334	573	697	21.6	7.6	2,199
San Francisco, Calif.	775	740	716	−3.3	13.4	15,764
San Jose, Calif.	95	204	446	118.3	2.5	3,273
Seattle, Wash.	468	557	531	−4.7	7.1	6,350
Tampa, Fla.	125	275	278	1.0	19.7	3,287
Toledo, Ohio	304	318	384	20.7	13.8	4,727
Tucson, Ariz.	45	213	263	23.5	3.5	3,287
Tulsa, Okla.	183	262	332	26.7	10.6	1,929
Washington, D.C.	802	764	757	−1.0	71.1	12,321
Wichita, Kans.	168	255	277	8.6	9.7	3,197
Yonkers, N.Y.	153	191	204	7.2	6.4	11,542

[1] Nashville-Davidson, Tenn. Nashville and Davidson counties were consolidated between 1960 and 1970

Source: Department of Commerce

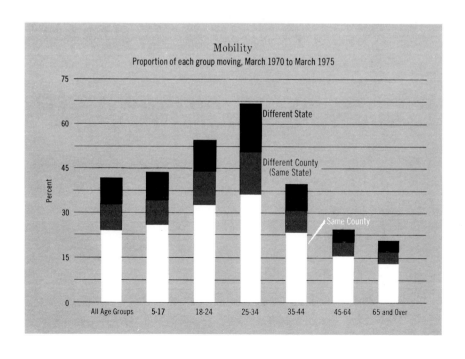

Mobility
Proportion of each group moving, March 1970 to March 1975

CHARACTERISTICS OF THE FARM POPULATION

Characteristic	Thousands			Percent Distribution		
	1960	1970	1974	1960	1970	1974
TOTAL	15,669	9,712	9,264	100.0	100.0	100.0
Sex						
Male	8,184	5,004	4,785	52.2	51.5	51.7
Female	7,485	4,708	4,478	47.8	48.5	48.3
Race						
White	13,092	8,775	8,608	83.6	90.4	92.9
Negro, Other Races	2,577	938	655	16.4	9.7	7.1
Age						
Under 14	4,995	2,490	1,999	31.9	25.6	21.6
14 and over	10,674	7,222	7,265	68.1	74.4	78.4
14-19	1,868	1,316	1,297	11.9	13.6	14.0
20-24	763	502	584	4.9	5.2	6.3
25-34	1,461	770	790	9.3	7.9	8.5
35-44	1,803	1,061	1,037	11.5	10.9	11.2
45-54	1,963	1,250	1,237	12.5	12.9	13.4
55-64	1,490	1,202	1,160	9.5	12.4	12.5
65 and over	1,326	1,122	1,159	8.5	11.6	12.5
Labor Force Status[1]	10,674	7,222	7,265	100.0	100.0	100.0
In Labor Force	6,266	4,293	4,419	58.7	59.4	60.8
Employed	6,089	4,211	4,321	57.0	58.3	97.8
Agriculture	4,025	2,333	2,242	37.7	32.3	50.7
Nonagriculture	2,064	1,878	2,078	19.3	26.0	47.0
Unemployed	177	82	98	1.7	1.1	2.2
Not in Labor Force	4,408	2,929	2,846	41.3	40.6	39.2

Note: Data for 1970 and 1974 are April-centered averages; figures for 1960 are for the month of April
[1] 14 years and over

Source: Department of Commerce

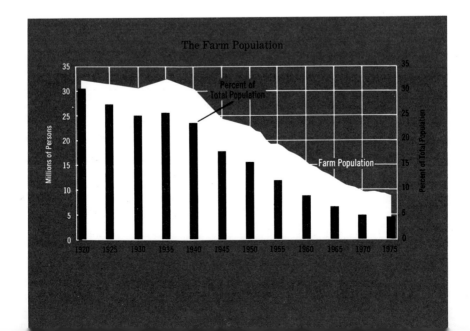

The Farm Population

FARM AND NONFARM POPULATION

Millions of Persons

Year	Total	Farm	Nonfarm	Farm as Percent of Total
1920	106.5	31.9	74.5	30.0
1930	123.2	30.5	92.7	24.8
1940	132.1	30.5	101.6	23.1
1950	151.7	23.0	128.6	15.2
1960	180.7	15.6	165.0	8.7
1961	183.7	14.8	168.9	8.1
1962	186.5	14.3	172.2	7.7
1963	189.2	13.4	175.9	7.1
1964	191.9	13.0	178.9	6.8
1965	194.3	12.4	181.9	6.4
1966	196.6	11.6	185.0	5.9
1967	198.7	10.9	187.8	5.5
1968	200.7	10.5	190.3	5.2
1969	202.7	10.3	192.3	5.1
1970	204.9	9.7	195.2	4.7
1971	207.0	9.4	197.6	4.6
1972	208.8	9.6	199.2	4.6
1973	210.4	9.5	200.9	4.5
1974	211.9	9.3	202.6	4.4
1975p	213.1	8.9	204.7	4.2

Note: Farm population figures are as of April 1; total population (including Armed Forces overseas) as of July 1

p—Preliminary   Sources: Departments of Agriculture and Commerce

METROPOLITAN AREA MOBILITY BY RACE

March 1970 to March 1975

Item	All Races	White	Negro	Percent Negro
TOTAL POPULATION[1]	193,512	169,147	21,377	11.0
Same House (Nonmovers)	99,651	88,248	10,217	10.3
Different House (Movers)	79,838	68,910	9,778	12.2
Within or Between SMSA's	48,962	41,098	6,994	14.3
Same SMSA	36,710	29,911	6,125	16.7
Between SMSA's	12,252	11,187	869	7.1
Within or to Central Cities	20,941	15,071	5,481	26.2
Within or to Suburbs	28,020	26,028	1,512	5.4
Outside SMSA to SMSA	5,127	4,615	463	9.0
Inside SMSA to Outside SMSA	6,721	6,349	325	4.8
Remaining Outside SMSA's	19,029	16,848	1,994	10.5

[1] Population 5 years of age and older. Total includes movers from abroad, as well as those not reporting mobility status
Source: Department of Commerce

CHARACTERISTICS OF VOTERS IN NATIONAL ELECTIONS

	Congressional Elections			Presidential Elections		
	1974		1970	1972		1968
Characteristic	Voters (Thousands)	Percent of Population	Percent of Population	Voters (Thousands)	Percent of Population	Percent of Population
TOTAL	63,164	44.7	54.6	85,766	63.0	67.8
Sex						
Male	30,675	46.2	56.8	40,908	64.1	69.8
Female	32,489	43.4	52.7	44,858	62.0	66.0
Race						
White	57,918	46.3	56.0	78,166	64.5	69.1
Negro, Other ..	5,246	32.4	43.0	7,600	50.8	56.2
Negro	4,786	33.8	43.5	7,032	52.7	57.6
Age						
18-20	2,412	20.8	n.a.	5,318	48.2	n.a.
21-24	3,718	26.4	30.4	6,896	50.7	51.1
25-34	10,834	37.0	46.2	16,072	59.7	62.5
35-44	10,971	49.1	58.1	14,747	66.3	70.8
45-64	24,466	56.9	64.2	29,991	70.8	74.9
65 and over ...	10,764	51.4	57.0	12,741	63.5	65.8
Family Income[1]				75,988	63.9	68.8
Under $5,000 ..	5,387	32.3	43.7	10,921	49.5	56.0
$5,000-10,000 ..	11,704	39.3	51.7	20,207	57.9	69.0
10,000-15,000 ..	15,081	46.9	63.3	21,344	70.5	78.5
15,000 and over	19,603	57.7	71.2	18,328	79.3	84.1
Not reported ..	4,255	43.1	53.9	5,189	61.0	66.5
Region						
North and West	47,058	48.8	59.0	62,193	66.4	71.0
South	16,105	36.0	44.7	23,573	55.4	60.1
Residence						
Metropolitan ..	45,262	44.7	55.3	63,799	64.3	68.0
Central Cities	18,700	42.6	53.8	26,357	62.2	65.6
Outside C.C.	26,562	46.3	56.6	37,442	65.9	70.1
Nonmetropolitan	17,901	44.7	53.2	21,967	59.4	67.3

Note: Data based on post-election surveys of persons reporting voter participation. Figures for 1968 and 1970 include persons 18-20 years old for states where voting age was under 21, but these figures are not shown by age

[1] Refers to persons in primary families only   Source: Department of Commerce

n.a.—Not available

CHURCH MEMBERSHIP
Thousands of persons, except as indicated

				1974	
Item	1950	1960	1965	Members	Churches (Number)
TOTAL	86,830	114,449	124,682	132,287	332,485
Eastern Churches	1,650	2,699	3,172	3,696	1,598
Jewish Congregations	5,000	5,367	5,600	6,115	5,000a
The Roman Catholic Church	28,635	42,105	46,246	48,702	23,793
Protestants[1]	51,080 }	64,279	69,664	{ 72,485	300,159
All other[2]	465 }			1,290	1,935

[1] Includes nonprotestant bodies such as "Latter Day Saints" and "Jehovah's Witnesses"

[2] Includes Old Catholic, Polish National Catholic and Armenian churches, as well as nonchristian bodies such as "Spiritualists", "Ethical Culture Movement" and "Buddhists"

a—1973 data   Source: National Council of Churches of Christ in America

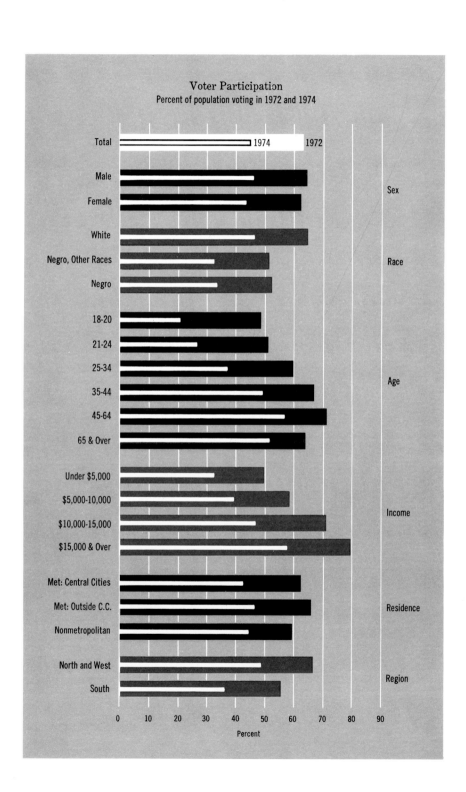

Voter Participation
Percent of population voting in 1972 and 1974

MEDIAN AGE AT MARRIAGE

Year	Age at First Marriage: Years	
	Male	Female
1920	24.6	21.2
1930	24.3	21.3
1940	24.3	21.5
1950	22.8	20.3
1960	22.8	20.3
1965	22.8	20.6
1966	22.8	20.5
1967	23.1	20.6
1968	23.1	20.8
1969	23.2	20.8
1970	23.2	20.8
1971	23.1	20.9
1972	23.3	20.9
1973	23.2	21.0
1974	23.1	21.1
1975	23.5	21.1

Source: Department of Commerce

MARITAL STATUS BY AGE, SEX AND RACE, 1975

Thousands of persons, 18 years and over

Age and Sex	Total	Single	Married, Spouse Present	Married, Spouse Absent	Widowed	Divorced
ALL RACES						
Male, Total	67,869	14,098	47,523	1,886	1,817	2,545
18-24	12,833	8,970	3,539	187	9	128
25-34	14,776	2,539	11,030	510	20	677
35-44	10,992	870	9,119	408	42	553
45-54	11,366	716	9,584	316	188	561
55-64	9,181	596	7,509	292	371	413
65 and over	8,722	407	6,742	171	1,187	214
Female, Total	75,345	11,007	47,366	2,891	10,104	3,978
18-24	13,484	6,961	5,591	549	31	351
25-34	15,316	1,672	11,666	841	103	1,036
35-44	11,615	568	9,254	595	323	877
45-54	12,220	563	9,318	450	1,045	845
55-64	10,305	529	6,873	269	2,087	546
65 and over	12,405	715	4,664	187	6,517	323
WHITE						
Male	60,442	12,061	43,436	1,259	1,480	2,205
Female	66,332	9,091	43,326	1,766	8,811	3,338
NEGRO, OTHER RACES						
Male	7,426	2,036	4,087	626	337	340
Female	9,013	1,916	4,039	1,125	1,293	639

Source: Department of Commerce

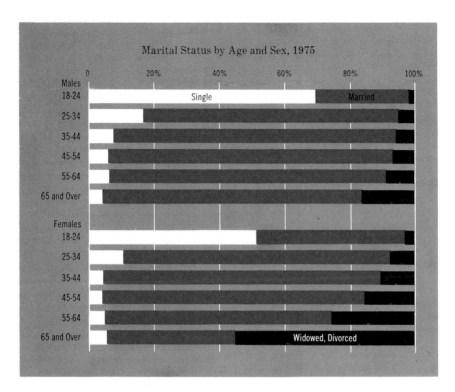

Marital Status by Age and Sex, 1975

MARITAL STATUS OF PERSONS BY HOUSEHOLD HEADSHIP, 1975

Numbers in thousands, except percent

| | | Head of Household | | | | |
Age and Sex	Total Persons	Total	Single	Married, Spouse Present	Other Marital Status	Not Head of Household
TOTAL, 14 YRS. & OVER	159,948	71,120	6,244	46,951	17,925	88,827
Male, Total	76,349	54,348	3,189	46,951	4,209	22,000
14-24	21,313	4,443	963	3,362	118	16,870
25-44	25,768	22,539	1,321	19,939	1,279	3,228
45-64	20,546	19,098	606	16,995	1,497	1,448
65 and over	8,722	8,268	298	6,655	1,315	454
Female, Total	83,599	16,772	3,056	- -	13,716	66,827
14-24	21,738	1,392	875	- -	517	20,346
25-44	26,931	4,269	1,088	- -	3,181	22,662
45-64	22,525	5,120	614	- -	4,505	17,405
65 and over	12,405	5,991	478	- -	5,513	6,414
PERCENT DISTRIBUTION						
Male	100.0	71.2	4.2	61.5	5.5	28.8
Female	100.0	20.1	3.7	- -	16.4	79.9

Source: Department of Commerce

MARITAL STATUS BY SEX

Year and Sex	Population 18 Years and Over (Millions)	Percent of Population		
		Single	Married	Widowed or Divorced
Male				
1940	45.7	27.8	66.1	6.1
1950	50.0	19.9	74.0	6.1
1955	51.4	17.4	76.1	6.5
1960	55.0	17.8	76.0	6.2
1965	58.0	17.7	76.2	6.1
1970	62.3	19.1	75.0	5.9
1971	63.7	19.9	74.1	6.0
1972	64.2	19.6	74.8	5.6
1973	65.2	19.5	74.5	6.0
1974	66.6	20.1	73.7	6.3
1975	67.9	20.8	72.8	6.4
Female				
1940	45.7	20.3	65.4	14.3
1950	52.5	13.8	70.9	15.3
1955	55.8	12.0	71.9	16.1
1960	59.4	11.8	71.3	16.8
1965	63.8	12.4	70.5	17.1
1970	69.5	13.7	68.5	17.8
1971	70.7	14.1	68.1	17.8
1972	71.6	13.8	68.5	17.7
1973	72.8	13.9	68.1	18.0
1974	74.0	14.3	67.6	18.2
1975	75.3	14.6	66.7	18.7

Source: Department of Commerce

MARRIAGES BY AGE, 1974

Thousands

Age	All Marriages[1]		First Marriages		Remarriages	
	Bride	Groom	Bride	Groom	Bride	Groom
TOTAL	1,791	1,791	1,271	1,253	494	514
Under 20	564	254	541	249	14	2
20-24	646	728	546	665	87	49
25-29	237	343	123	232	111	106
30-34	108	149	31	57	76	90
35-44	116	147	19	33	96	113
45 and over	122	172	11	17	110	154
Median Age	22.0	24.2	20.6	22.5	32.1	35.7

Note: Data based on marriage registration states only. These include 80 percent of all marriages registered in the U.S.

[1] Includes marriages where previous marital status was not reported

Source: Department of Health, Education and Welfare

MARRIAGES AND MARRIAGE RATES

Year	Marriages (Thousands)	Marriage Rate[1]	Year	Marriages (Thousands)	Marriage Rate[1]
1920	1,274	92.0	1959	1,494	73.6
1930	1,127	67.6			
1940	1,596	82.8	1960	1,523	73.5
			1961	1,548	72.2
1945	1,613	83.6	1962	1,577	71.2
1946	2,291	118.1	1963	1,654	73.4
1947	1,992	106.2	1964	1,725	74.6
1948	1,811	98.5			
1949	1,580	86.7	1965	1,800	75.0
			1966	1,857	75.6
1950	1,667	90.2	1967	1,927	76.4
1951	1,595	86.6	1968	2,069	79.1
1952	1,539	83.2	1969	2,145	80.0
1953	1,546	83.7			
1954	1,490	79.8	1970	2,159	76.5
			1971	2,190	76.2
1955	1,531	80.9	1972	2,282	77.9
1956	1,585	82.4	1973	2,284	76.0
1957	1,518	78.0	1974	2,230	72.0
1958	1,451	72.0	1975p	2,126	n.a.

[1] Rate per 1,000 unmarried females aged 15 years and over
n.a.—Not available
p—Preliminary

Source: Department of Health, Education and Welfare

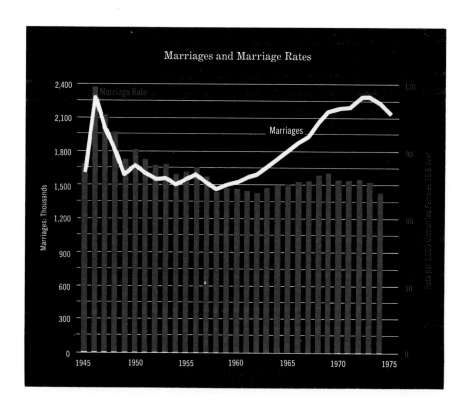

47

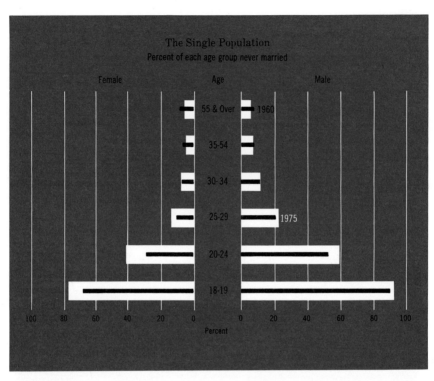

The Single Population
Percent of each age group never married

Female   Age   Male

55 & Over   1960

35-54

30-34

25-29   1975

20-24

18-19

100 80 60 40 20   0   0   20 40 60 80 100

Percent

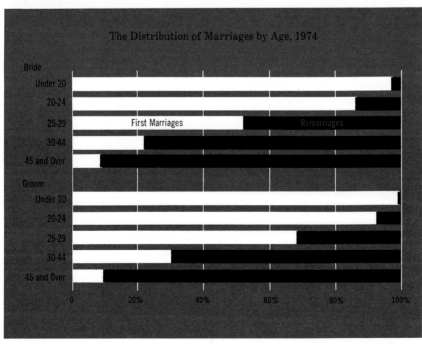

The Distribution of Marriages by Age, 1974

Bride
Under 20
20-24
25-29   First Marriages   Remarriages
30-44
45 and Over

Groom
Under 20
20-24
25-29
30-44
45 and Over

0   20%   40%   60%   80%   100%

THE SINGLE POPULATION BY AGE AND SEX
Persons 14 years and over

	Male			Female		
	1975		1960	1975		1960
Age	Thou-sands	Percent of Popu-lation	Percent of Popu-lation	Thou-sands	Percent of Popu-lation	Percent of Popu-lation
TOTAL SINGLE	22,519	29.5	25.0	19,023	22.8	19.0
14-17	8,421	99.3	99.0	8,016	97.1	94.6
18-19	3,609	93.1	91.1	3,169	77.7	68.0
20-24	5,361	59.9	53.1	3,792	40.3	28.4
25-29	1,793	22.3	20.8	1,150	13.8	10.5
30-34	746	11.1	11.9	522	7.5	6.9
35-39	480	8.6	8.8	296	5.0	6.1
40-44	390	7.2	7.3	272	4.8	6.1
45-54	716	6.3	7.4	563	4.6	7.0
55-64	596	6.5	8.0	529	5.1	8.0
65 and over	407	4.7	7.7	715	5.8	8.5

Note: Single population refers to persons never married. Data for 1960 are taken from the Census of Population while figures for 1975 are from the Current Population Survey

Source: Department of Commerce

DIVORCED PERSONS BY AGE AND SEX
Persons 18 years and over

	Males			Females		
Year and Age	Number (Thou-sands)	Percent Distribu-tion	Percent of Age Group	Number (Thou-sands)	Percent Distribu-tion	Percent of Age Group
1960-TOTAL......	1,297	100.0	2.3	1,849	100.0	3.1
Under 25	57	4.4	.7	117	6.3	1.5
25-29	95	7.3	1.8	146	7.9	2.6
30-34	127	9.8	2.2	191	10.3	3.1
35-44	304	23.4	2.6	472	25.5	3.8
45-54	311	24.0	3.1	446	24.1	4.3
55 and over	403	31.1	2.7	477	25.8	2.8
1970-TOTAL......	1,577	100.0	2.5	2,693	100.0	3.9
Under 25	81	5.1	.8	204	7.6	1.7
25-29	154	9.8	2.3	296	11.0	4.3
30-34	160	10.1	2.9	268	10.0	4.6
35-44	325	20.6	2.9	633	23.5	5.4
45-54	403	25.5	3.6	591	22.0	4.9
55 and over	456	28.9	2.7	699	26.0	3.3
1975-TOTAL......	2,545	100.0	3.7	3,978	100.0	5.4
Under 25	128	5.0	1.0	351	8.8	2.6
25-29	338	13.3	4.2	540	13.6	6.5
30-34	339	13.3	5.0	496	12.5	7.1
35-44	553	21.7	5.0	877	22.0	7.6
45-54	561	22.0	4.9	845	21.2	6.9
55 and over	627	24.6	3.5	869	21.8	3.8

Note: Data from 1960 are from Census of Population while figures for 1970 and 1975 are from the Current Population Survey
Source: Department of Commerce

DIVORCES AND DIVORCE RATES

Item	1950	1955	1960	1965	1970	1975p
DIVORCES (Thousands)	385	377	393	479	708	1,026
Divorce Rate						
Per 1,000 Population	2.6	2.3	2.2	2.5	3.5	4.8
Per 1,000 Married Women[1] . . .	10.3	9.3	9.2	10.6	14.9	21.6
Per Cent Divorced[2]						
Male	1.8	1.9	2.0	2.5	2.5	3.7
Female	2.3	2.4	2.9	3.3	3.9	5.4
Median Duration Marriage, Yrs..	5.3	6.2	7.1	7.2	6.7	n.a.
Percent Spouses Separated,						
All Families	1.3	1.5	1.5	2.0	2.0	2.7

Note: Data include annulments   n.a.—Not available
[1] 14 years and over, husband present   p—Preliminary
[2] Of population 18 years and over   Sources: Departments of Commerce and Health, Education and Welfare

BIRTH EXPECTATIONS

Total births expected per 1,000 wives

			1975	
Race and Age of Wives	1967	1971	Total Expected	Percent Already Born
All Races, 18-39 Years . . .	3,118	2,779	2,499	76.9
18-24	2,852	2,375	2,172	37.7
18-19	2,719	2,256	2,187	27.5
20-21	2,916	2,373	2,183	30.8
22-24	2,856	2,404	2,162	43.9
25-29	3,037	2,619	2,260	70.9
30-34	3,288	2,989	2,610	93.0
35-39	3,300	3,257	3,058	99.0
White, 18-39 Years	3,068	2,735	2,458	76.3
18-24	2,859	2,353	2,147	36.1
18-19	2,707	2,264	2,180	24.9
20-21	2,964	2,368	2,144	29.4
22-24	2,849	2,367	2,140	42.3
25-29	3,001	2,577	2,233	70.5
30-34	3,200	2,936	2,564	93.2
35-39	3,215	3,189	2,989	99.0
Negro, 18-39 Years	3,657	3,312	3,021	83.1
18-24	2,787	2,623	2,481	55.1
18-19	[1]	[1]	[1]	[1]
20-21	2,522	2,444	2,566	43.2
22-24	2,969	2,787	2,497	60.9
25-29	3,407	3,112	2,583	78.2
30-34	4,257	3,714	3,213	91.9
35-39	4,226	4,223	3,957	98.8

[1] Insufficient sample
Source: Department of Commerce

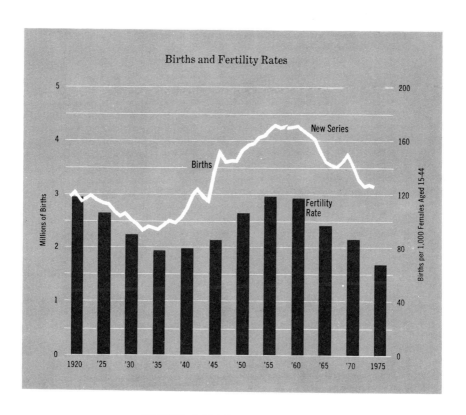

Births and Fertility Rates

BIRTHS AND FERTILITY RATES

Year	Births (Thousands)	Fertility Rate[1]	Year	Births (Thousands)	Fertility Rate[1]
1930	2,618	89.2	(New Series)		
1940	2,559	79.9	1959	4,245	118.8
			1960	4,258	118.0
1945	2,858	85.9	1961	4,268	117.2
1946	3,411	101.9	1962	4,167	112.2
1947	3,817	113.3	1963	4,098	108.5
1948	3,637	107.3	1964	4,027	105.0
1949	3,649	107.1			
			1965	3,760	96.6
1950	3,632	106.2	1966	3,606	91.3
1951	3,823	111.5	1967	3,521	87.6
1952	3,913	113.9	1968	3,502	85.7
1953	3,965	115.2	1969	3,600	86.5
1954	4,078	118.1			
			1970	3,731	87.9
1955	4,104	118.5	1971	3,556	81.8
1956	4,218	121.2	1972	3,258	73.4
1957	4,308	122.9	1973	3,137	69.2
1958	4,255	120.2	1974	3,160	68.4
1959	4,295	120.2	1975p	3,149	66.7

Note: Births through 1959 are adjusted for underregistration; beginning 1959 (new series) figures are for registered births only. Beginning 1970, data exclude births to nonresidents of U.S.

[1] Rate per 1,000 females aged 15-44 years

p—Preliminary

Source: Department of Health, Education and Welfare

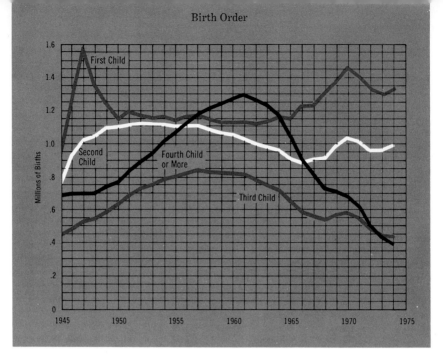

Birth Order

BIRTHS AND LIVE BIRTH ORDER
Thousands

Year	Total Births	First Child	Second Child	Third Child	Fourth Child and Over
1945	2,858	961	763	446	688
1946	3,411	1,291	935	487	699
1947	3,817	1,574	1,019	524	700
1948	3,637	1,343	1,047	545	701
1949	3,649	1,235	1,093	584	737
1950	3,632	1,140	1,097	630	764
1951	3,823	1,195	1,116	686	826
1952	3,913	1,169	1,122	733	889
1953	3,965	1,150	1,120	753	942
1954	4,078	1,160	1,119	785	1,014
1955	4,104	1,138	1,104	800	1,063
1956	4,218	1,166	1,109	821	1,122
1957	4,308	1,180	1,111	838	1,179
1958	4,255	1,140	1,085	826	1,203
1959	4,245	1,124	1,066	821	1,232
1960	4,258	1,122	1,053	820	1,263
1961	4,268	1,132	1,032	813	1,292
1962	4,167	1,118	1,002	782	1,265
1963	4,098	1,131	987	752	1,228
1964	4,027	1,167	965	721	1,175
1965	3,760	1,159	911	647	1,043
1966	3,606	1,226	888	585	908
1967	3,521	1,238	908	560	815
1968	3,502	1,312	919	539	731
1969	3,600	1,365	973	560	703
1970	3,731	1,450	1,025	579	677
1971	3,556	1,396	1,007	544	610
1972	3,258	1,329	956	473	500
1973	3,137	1,307	956	445	430
1974	3,160	1,336	995	442	387

Note: Births not stated by birth order are distributed. Beginning 1959 data are for registered births only; prior years are adjusted for underregistration

Source: Department of Health, Education and Welfare

BIRTHS AND BIRTH RATES BY SELECTED CHARACTERISTICS

Births in thousands

Item	1950	1955	1960	1965	1970	1974
LIVE BIRTHS	3,632	4,104	4,258	3,760	3,731	3,160
Percent Urban	60.6	61.0	62.3	54.5	n.a.	n.a.
White	3,108	3,488	3,601	3,124	3,091	2,576
Nonwhite	524	617	657	636	640	584
Male	1,863	2,103	2,180	1,927	1,915	1,622
Female	1,768	2,001	2,078	1,833	1,816	1,538
Males per 100 Females	105.4	105.1	104.9	105.1	105.5	105.5
BIRTH RATES[1]	24.1	25.0	23.7	19.4	18.4	14.9
White	23.0	23.8	22.7	18.3	17.4	14.0
Nonwhite	33.3	34.7	32.1	27.6	25.1	21.4
Male	24.9	25.8	24.7	20.3	19.1	15.8
Female	23.3	23.9	22.8	18.6	17.4	14.2
Plural Births, per 1,000 Live Births	20.9	21.1	20.4	20.1	n.a.	18.6

Note: Births for 1950 and 1955 are adjusted for underregistration; later years are registered births only

[1] Per 1,000 population in specified group
n.a.—Not available

Source: Department of Health, Education and Welfare

BIRTHS BY AGE OF MOTHER, 1974

Age of Mother	Total Births	First Child	Second Child	Third Child	Fourth Child and Over
			Thousands		
TOTAL	3,160	1,336	995	442	387
Under 20	608	484	106	15	2
20-24	1,108	526	411	126	46
25-29	923	261	357	184	121
30-34	373	54	101	92	126
35-39	118	11	18	21	69
40 and over	30	2	3	3	22
			Percent		
TOTAL	100.0	42.3	31.5	14.0	12.2
Under 20	19.2	15.3	3.4	.5	.1
20-24	35.1	16.6	13.0	4.0	1.5
25-29	29.2	8.3	11.3	5.8	3.8
30-34	11.8	1.7	3.2	2.9	4.0
35-39	3.7	.3	.6	.7	2.2
40 and over	.9	.1	.1	.1	.7

Note: Births not stated by birth order are distributed

Source: Department of Health, Education and Welfare

BIRTHS: ESTIMATES AND PROJECTIONS

Thousands

Year	Births	Year	Births Series I	Series II	Series III
1960	4,279	Projections:			
1961	4,350	1976	3,679	3,285	2,946
1962	4,259	1977	3,932	3,425	2,958
1963	4,185	1978	4,156	3,575	3,092
1964	4,119	1979	4,356	3,720	3,223
1965	3,940	1980	4,539	3,865	3,323
1966	3,716	1981	4,703	3,978	3,375
1967	3,608	1982	4,853	4,049	3,406
1968	3,520	1983	4,982	4,104	3,428
1969	3,583	1984	5,087	4,144	3,437
		1985	5,166	4,167	3,435
1970	3,676	1986	5,220	4,176	3,424
1971	3,713	1987	5,253	4,172	3,407
1972	3,393	1988	5,263	4,157	3,382
1973	3,195	1989	5,253	4,132	3,351
1974	3,115				
		1990	5,225	4,095	3,314
1975	3,187	2000	5,196	3,780	2,880

Note: All data are for years ending June 30 and include Alaska and Hawaii and Armed Forces overseas. Projections are based primarily on differing completed fertility levels for women. For a brief description of the assumptions underlying these projections, see footnote to table on page 20

Sources: Departments of Commerce and Health, Education and Welfare

CHILDREN EVER BORN BY AGE OF WOMAN

Number of children born per 1,000 women

Age Group	1940	1950	1960	1970	1975 Total	White	Negro
15-44 Years ...	1,238	1,395	1,746	1,616	1,440	1,421	1,593
15-19	68	105	127	75	66	63	79
20-24	522	738	1,032	678	514	500	622
25-29	1,132	1,436	2,006	1,738	1,360	1,349	1,494
30-34	1,678	1,871	2,445	2,596	2,209	2,174	2,538
35-39	2,145	2,061	2,523	2,980	2,856	2,777	3,487
40-44	2,490	2,170	2,409	2,927	3,144	3,090	3,591
45-49 Years ...	2,740	2,292	2,245	2,688	3,027	2,972	3,514

Note: Data for 1975 as of June; other years as of April

Source: Department of Commerce

CHILDREN EVER BORN TO WHITE AND NEGRO WOMEN, 1974

Children born per 1,000 women, 15-44 years

Characteristic of Woman	Race of Woman		Characteristic of Woman	Race of Woman	
	White	Negro		White	Negro
TOTAL	1,452	1,610	Residence:		
			Farm..............	1,728	n.a.
Age:			Nonfarm	1,441	1,613
15-19	63	86			
20-24	556	663	Northeast..........	1,350⎫	
25-29	1,428	1,610	North Central	1,494⎬	1,539
30-34	2,265	2,542	West	1,462⎭	
35-39	2,754	3,466	South	1,489	1,677
40-44	3,029	3,526			
			Metropolitan	1,383	1,551
Education:			Central Cities	1,283	1,550
Some Elem. or Less .	2,434⎫	2,122	Outside C.C.	1,444	1,551
Elementary, 8 yrs. ..	1,690⎭		Nonmetropolitan ...	1,606	1,818
Some High School ..	1,229	1,654			
High School Graduate	1,658	1,662	Labor Force Status:		
Some College	1,149⎫	1,073	In Labor Force	1,142	1,569
College Graduate ...	1,135⎭		Not in Labor Force .	1,817	1,663

Note: Data as of June

n.a. — Not available

Source: Department of Commerce

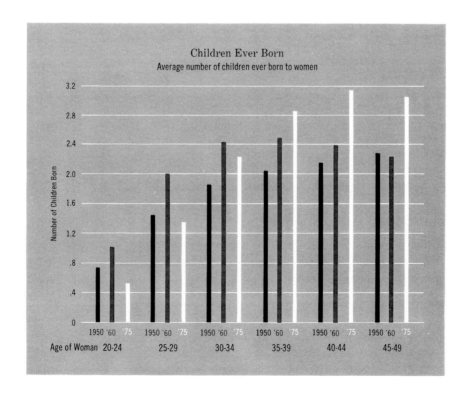

55

LIFE EXPECTATION AT BIRTH, BY SEX AND RACE

Years

Year	Total	Sex		Race	
		Male	Female	White	Negro, Other
1920	54.1	53.6	54.6	54.9	45.3
1930	59.7	58.1	61.6	61.4	48.1
1940	62.9	60.8	65.2	64.2	53.1
1950	68.2	65.6	71.1	69.1	60.8
1955	69.5	66.6	72.7	70.2	63.2
1960	69.7	66.6	73.1	70.6	63.6
1965	70.2	66.8	73.7	71.0	64.1
1970	70.9	67.1	74.8	71.7	65.3
1971	71.0	67.4	74.8	71.9	65.2
1972	71.1	67.4	75.1	72.0	65.6
1973	71.3	67.6	75.3	72.2	65.9
1974	71.9	68.2	75.9	72.7	67.0
1975p	72.4	68.5	76.4	73.1	68.0

p—Preliminary

Source: Department of Health, Education and Welfare

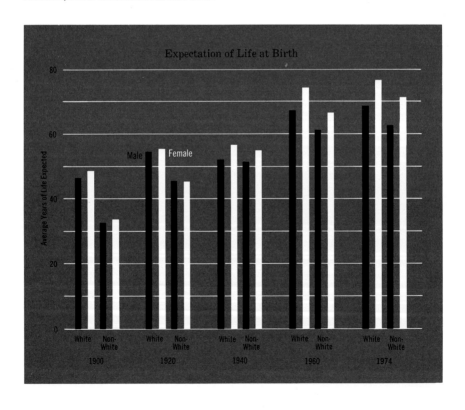

EXPECTATION OF LIFE AT SELECTED AGES, 1974

In years

Age	Total	White		Negro, Other Races	
		Male	Female	Male	Female
Under 1	71.9	68.9	76.6	62.9	71.2
5....................	68.4	65.3	72.7	60.0	68.1
10...................	63.5	60.5	67.8	55.1	63.2
15...................	58.6	55.6	62.9	50.3	58.3
20...................	53.9	51.0	58.1	45.7	53.5
25...................	49.3	46.5	53.3	41.5	48.8
30...................	44.6	41.8	48.4	37.4	44.2
35...................	39.9	37.2	43.6	33.2	39.7
40...................	35.3	32.6	38.9	29.3	35.3
45...................	30.9	28.1	34.3	25.5	31.1
50...................	26.7	24.0	29.8	22.0	27.1
55...................	22.7	20.1	25.5	18.7	23.4
60...................	19.0	16.5	21.4	16.0	19.9
65...................	15.6	13.4	17.6	13.4	16.7
70...................	12.5	10.6	14.0	11.1	13.7
75...................	9.8	8.3	10.7	9.6	11.8

Source: Department of Health, Education and Welfare

DEATHS AND DEATH RATES

Deaths in thousands

Item	1950	1955	1960	1965	1970	1975p
DEATHS, TOTAL	1,452	1,529	1,712	1,828	1,921	1,910
White................	1,276	1,351	1,505	1,605	1,682	1,676
Negro, Other Races	176	178	207	223	239	234
Male	828	873	976	1,035	1,078	1,061
Female	625	656	736	793	843	849
DEATH RATE[1]	9.6	9.3	9.5	9.4	9.5	9.0
White................	9.5	9.2	9.5	9.4	9.5	9.1
Negro, Other Races	11.2	10.0	10.1	9.6	9.4	8.4
Male	11.1	10.8	11.0	10.9	10.9	10.2
Female	8.2	7.9	8.1	8.0	8.1	7.8
INFANT MORTALITY RATE[2] ...	29.2	26.4	26.0	24.7	20.0	16.1

[1] Rate per 1,000 population in specified group

[2] Deaths per 1,000 live births of infants under 1 year, exclusive of fetal deaths

p—Preliminary

Source: Department of Health, Education and Welfare

HOUSEHOLDS AND FAMILIES

Thousands

Year	Households	Families	Net Annual Household Formation[1]
1955	47,874	41,951	912
1956	48,902	42,889	1,028
1957	49,673	43,497	771
1958	50,473	43,696	800
1959	51,435	44,232	962
1960	52,799	45,111	1,364
1961	53,557	45,539	758
1962	54,764	46,418	1,207
1963	55,270	47,059	506
1964	56,149	47,540	879
1965	57,436	47,956	1,287
1966	58,406	48,509	970
1967	59,236	49,214	830
1968	60,813	50,111	1,577
1969	62,214	50,823	1,401
1970	63,401	51,586	1,187
1971	64,778	52,227	1,904
1972	66,676	53,296	1,898
1973	68,251	54,373	1,575
1974	69,859	55,053	1,608
1975	71,120	55,712	1,261
Projections:			
1980	79,356	61,234	1,647
1985	87,188	66,255	1,566
1990	94,270	70,606	1,416

Note: Series B (moderate growth) projections.

[1] Net change from preceding year. For projections, total change is expressed as an annual average

Source: Department of Commerce

HOUSEHOLDS AND FAMILIES BY TYPE

Thousands

Item	1950	1960	1970	1975	1980
HOUSEHOLDS	43,554	52,799	62,874	71,120	79,356
Primary Families	38,838	44,905	51,110	55,563	61,144
Primary Individuals	4,716	7,895	11,765	15,557	18,211
FAMILIES	39,303	45,111	51,237	55,712	61,234
Husband-Wife	34,440	39,329	44,436	46,971	51,837e
Other Male Head	1,184	1,275	1,221	1,499	1,569e
Female Head	3,679	4,507	5,580	7,242	7,827e
UNRELATED INDIVIDUALS	9,136	11,092	14,827	19,100	21,477
Male	4,209	4,462	5,637	8,000	9,086
Female	4,927	6,630	9,190	11,101	12,391

Note: Series B (moderate growth) projections
e—Estimated, based on the distribution of secondary families in 1975
Source: Department of Commerce

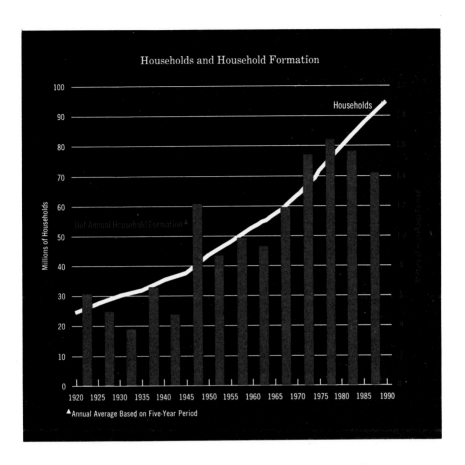

Households and Household Formation

Net Annual Household Formation ▲

Households

Millions of Households

100
90
80
70
60
50
40
30
20
10
0

1920 1925 1930 1935 1940 1945 1950 1955 1960 1965 1970 1975 1980 1985 1990

▲ Annual Average Based on Five-Year Period

FAMILIES AND CHILDREN

Thousands

Item	1960	1968	1970	1973	1974	1975
TOTAL FAMILIES	45,149	49,834	51,237	54,373	55,053	55,712
With Children:						
Under 18 Years .	25,690	27,809	28,665	29,571	29,750	30,057
Under 12	20,413	22,585	22,139	22,423	22,492	22,486
Under 6	13,924	13,720	13,865	13,802	13,752	13,812
Under 3	n.a.	8,189	8,122	8,403	7,886	7,623
TOTAL CHILDREN:						
Under 18 Years .	59,877	66,672	66,714	64,310	63,556	62,732
Under 12	43,128	45,187	44,278	41,168	40,077	39,199
Under 6	22,579	21,254	20,266	19,147	18,510	18,150
Under 3	n.a.	9,820	9,637	9,483	8,709	8,400

Note: Data refer to own children living in families. 1960 figures are based on a sample from the census of population. The number of total families for 1968 and 1970 do not reflect adjustments made according to the 1970 census

n.a. — Not available

Source: Department of Commerce

UNRELATED INDIVIDUALS BY AGE AND SEX
Persons 14 years and over

Age Group	1960		1975	
	Male	Female	Male	Female
Total (Thousands)	4,342	6,538	7,890	10,981
14-24	367	605	1,652	1,313
25-34	648	405	1,994	1,081
35-44	591	468	946	444
45-54	761	972	874	1,097
55-64	840	1,445	970	1,999
65 and over	1,136	2,644	1,455	5,047
Percent Distribution	100.0	100.0	100.0	100.0
14-24	8.5	9.3	20.9	12.0
25-34	14.9	6.2	25.3	9.8
35-44	13.6	7.2	12.0	4.0
45-54	17.5	14.9	11.1	10.0
55-64	19.3	22.1	12.3	18.2
65 and over	26.2	40.4	18.4	46.0

Source: Department of Commerce

SELECTED CHARACTERISTICS OF HOUSEHOLDS BY SIZE, 1975

Characteristic of Household Head	Total Households	Household Size (Persons)				
		One	Two	Three	Four	Five or More
TOTAL (Millions)	71.1	13.9	21.8	12.4	11.1	11.9
Percent Distribution	100.0	100.0	100.0	100.0	100.0	100.0
Sex						
Male	76.4	35.3	83.5	84.5	90.6	89.9
Female	23.6	64.7	16.5	15.5	9.4	10.1
Age						
Under 25	8.2	8.0	11.4	12.2	5.1	1.4
25-34	21.0	13.2	14.4	26.8	35.2	23.1
35-44	16.7	6.5	5.7	14.2	26.5	42.0
45-54	18.2	11.1	14.6	21.4	22.3	25.6
55-64	15.9	18.1	23.7	16.3	8.2	5.9
65 and over	20.1	43.1	30.2	9.1	2.8	2.1
Education						
Elementary or Less	22.4	30.6	26.8	17.4	12.7	18.8
Some High School	15.3	14.7	15.0	16.2	14.1	16.9
High School Graduate	33.0	27.1	29.9	37.1	39.0	35.6
College	29.3	27.5	28.2	29.2	34.1	28.7
Race						
White	88.5	87.7	91.3	87.9	89.4	84.2
Negro, Other Races	11.5	12.3	8.7	12.1	10.6	15.8
Negro	10.2	11.4	7.8	10.5	8.8	14.2
Employment Status						
Employed	67.3	46.0	59.9	76.0	82.8	82.0
Unemployed	4.8	3.8	4.2	5.7	5.3	5.7
Not in Civilian Labor Force ...	27.9	50.2	35.8	18.3	11.8	12.3

Source: Department of Commerce

HOUSEHOLDS AND FAMILIES BY AGE OF HEAD

Millions

Year and Unit	Total	Age Group					
		Under 25	25-34	35-44	45-54	55-64	65 and Over
HOUSEHOLDS							
1960..............	52.6	2.6	9.7	11.6	10.8	8.6	9.4
1965..............	57.3	3.4	9.9	12.0	11.5	9.6	10.9
1970..............	62.9	4.3	11.7	11.7	12.2	10.7	12.3
1975..............	71.1	5.8	14.9	11.9	12.9	11.3	14.3
Projections:							
1980..............	79.4	7.0	18.3	13.4	12.4	12.3	16.0
1985..............	87.2	7.1	20.7	16.6	12.4	12.7	17.7
FAMILIES							
1960..............	45.1	2.3	9.2	11.0	9.6	6.8	6.2
1965..............	47.8	2.9	9.3	11.2	10.3	7.5	6.7
1970..............	51.2	3.5	10.6	10.9	10.8	8.3	7.1
1975..............	55.7	4.2	12.7	10.9	11.2	8.7	8.0
Projections:							
1980..............	61.2	4.7	15.4	12.1	10.8	9.5	8.7
1985..............	66.3	4.6	17.1	14.9	10.7	9.7	9.2

Note: Series B (moderate growth) projections

Sources: Department of Commerce; The Conference Board

Households: Growth by Age of Head

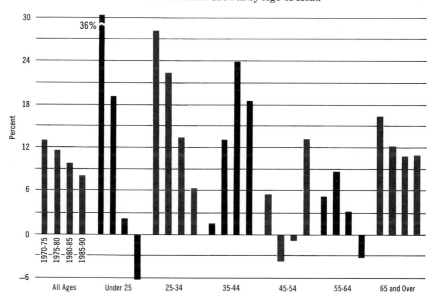

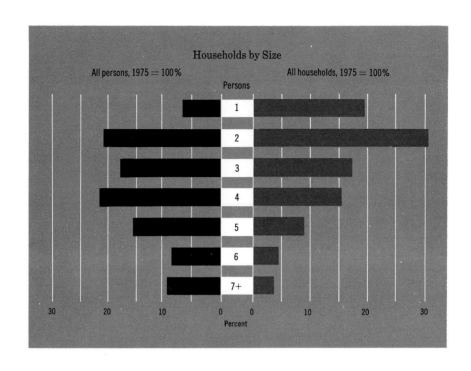

Households by Size

All persons, 1975 = 100%

All households, 1975 = 100%

Persons

Percent

HOUSEHOLDS BY SIZE

Household Size	1950	1960	1970	1975 Total	1975 Male Head	1975 Female Head
				Thousands		
TOTAL	43,468	52,610	62,874	71,120	54,343	16,777
One Person	4,737	6,871	10,692	13,939	4,918	9,021
Two	12,529	14,616	18,129	21,753	18,162	3,591
Three	9,808	9,941	10,903	12,384	10,470	1,915
Four	7,729	9,277	9,935	11,103	10,059	1,043
Five	4,357	6,064	6,532	6,399	5,818	581
Six	2,196	2,976	3,505	3,059	2,741	318
Seven or more	2,113	2,865	3,178	2,484	2,175	308
				Percent Distribution		
TOTAL	100.0	100.0	100.0	100.0	100.0	100.0
One Person	10.9	13.1	17.0	19.6	9.0	53.8
Two	28.8	27.8	28.8	30.6	33.4	21.4
Three	22.6	18.9	17.3	17.4	19.3	11.4
Four	17.8	17.6	15.8	15.6	18.5	6.2
Five	10.0	11.5	10.4	9.0	10.7	3.5
Six	5.1	5.7	5.6	4.3	5.0	1.9
Seven or more	4.9	5.4	5.1	3.5	4.0	1.8

Source: Department of Commerce

HOUSEHOLDS BY RESIDENCE AND SIZE, 1973

Household Size	Total U.S.	Metropolitan Total	Inside Central Cities	Outside Central Cities	Non-Metro-politan
TOTAL (Millions)	69.3	47.7	22.5	25.2	21.6
Percent Distribution, Total	100.0	100.0	100.0	100.0	100.0
One Person	20.1	20.7	26.3	15.7	18.7
Two Persons	30.3	29.6	29.8	29.4	32.0
Three and Four Persons	32.2	32.5	29.2	35.5	31.5
Five Persons or more	17.4	17.2	14.7	19.5	17.8
Percent Change, 1970-73, Total	9.3	8.8	5.1	12.3	10.3
One Person	24.7	24.4	20.2	31.1	25.7
Two Persons	12.0	11.0	5.1	16.8	14.2
Three and Four Persons	7.8	7.4	2.1	11.5	9.0
Five Persons or more	−5.8	−6.0	−9.8	−3.2	−5.5

Source: Department of Commerce

AVERAGE POPULATION PER HOUSEHOLD

Year	Persons Per Household All Ages	Under 18 Years	18 and Over
1940	3.67	1.14	2.53
1950	3.37	1.06	2.31
1960	3.33	1.21	2.12
1965	3.29	1.21	2.09
1966	3.27	1.19	2.08
1967	3.26	1.17	2.08
1968	3.20	1.14	2.06
1969	3.16	1.11	2.05
1970	3.14	1.09	2.05
1971	3.11	1.07	2.04
1972	3.06	1.03	2.03
1973	3.01	1.00	2.02
1974	2.97	.96	2.00
1975	2.94	.93	2.01
Projections:			
1980	2.75	.79	1.96
1985	2.64	.74	1.90
1990	2.55	.71	1.84

Note: Projections are based on Series B (moderate growth) households and Series II population data

Source: Department of Commerce

HOUSEHOLDS BY STATES

State	Households (Thousands)			Average Annual Percent Change	
	1960	1970	1975	1960-1970	1970-1975
TOTAL U.S.	53,021	63,450	71,537	1.8	2.3
Alabama............	884	1,034	1,162	1.6	2.2
Alaska	57	79	97	3.2	3.9
Arizona	367	539	730	3.9	5.8
Arkansas	524	615	717	1.6	2.9
California...........	4,981	6,574	7,639	2.8	2.9
Colorado	529	691	859	2.7	4.2
Connecticut	753	933	1,024	2.2	1.8
Delaware	129	165	187	2.5	2.4
District of Columbia ..	252	263	280	.4	1.2
Florida	1,550	2,285	3,039	3.9	5.4
Georgia	1,070	1,369	1,572	2.5	2.6
Hawaii	153	203	246	2.8	3.7
Idaho	194	219	266	1.2	3.7
Illinois	3,085	3,502	3,745	1.3	1.3
Indiana.............	1,388	1,609	1,755	1.5	1.7
Iowa	841	896	978	.6	1.7
Kansas	673	727	790	.8	1.6
Kentucky	852	984	1,102	1.4	2.2
Louisiana	892	1,052	1,183	1.6	2.2
Maine	280	303	345	.8	2.5
Maryland	863	1,175	1,324	3.1	2.3
Massachusetts	1,535	1,760	1,936	1.4	1.8
Michigan	2,239	2,653	2,947	1.7	2.0
Minnesota	992	1,154	1,292	1.5	2.2
Mississippi..........	568	637	719	1.1	2.3
Missouri............	1,360	1,521	1,649	1.1	1.5
Montana	202	217	253	.7	2.9
Nebraska	433	474	528	.9	2.1
Nevada.............	92	160	209	5.6	5.1
New Hampshire	180	225	266	2.2	3.1
New Jersey	1,806	2,218	2,408	2.1	1.6
New Mexico	251	289	358	1.4	4.0
New York	5,248	5,914	6,313	1.2	1.2
North Carolina	1,205	1,510	1,743	2.3	2.7
North Dakota	173	182	202	.5	2.0
Ohio	2,852	3,289	3,554	1.4	1.5
Oklahoma	735	851	959	1.5	2.3
Oregon	558	692	819	2.1	3.2
Pennsylvania	3,351	3,705	3,980	1.0	1.4
Rhode Island	257	292	307	1.3	.9
South Carolina	604	734	863	2.0	3.1
South Dakota	195	201	222	.3	1.9
Tennessee	1,003	1,213	1,383	1.9	2.5
Texas	2,778	3,434	4,011	2.1	3.0
Utah	242	298	358	2.1	3.5
Vermont............	111	132	152	1.8	2.6
Virginia	1,074	1,391	1,592	2.6	2.6
Washington	894	1,106	1,248	2.1	2.3
West Virginia	521	547	604	.5	1.9
Wisconsin	1,146	1,329	1,497	1.5	2.3
Wyoming	99	105	126	.5	3.5

Note: Data based on samples from census enumerations, except for 1975 which are estimates as of July 1

Source: Department of Commerce

Households: Growth Rates by States
Average annual growth rate, 1970-1975

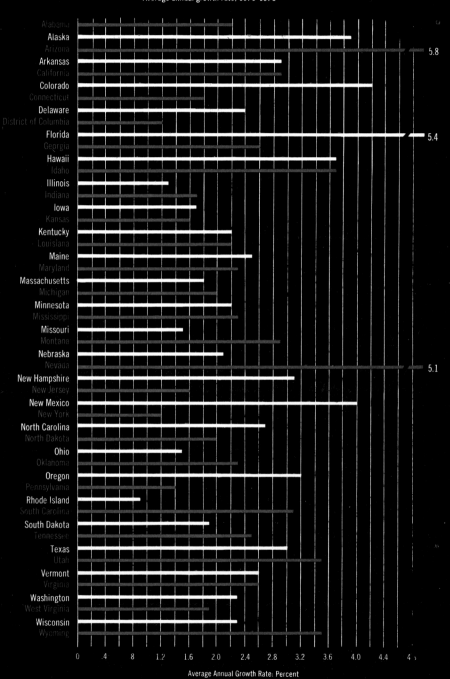

Average Annual Growth Rate: Percent

FAMILIES BY AGE OF HEAD AND PRESENCE OF CHILDREN, 1975

Numbers in thousands, except averages

Number of Children[1]	Total Families	Age of Head					
		Under 25	25-34	35-44	45-54	55-64	65 and Over
TOTAL	55,712	4,225	12,708	10,853	11,234	8,658	8,033
No Children	25,655	1,828	2,514	1,318	5,035	7,156	7,804
One Child	10,964	1,621	3,221	2,029	2,934	1,007	152
Two	10,036	622	4,158	3,101	1,778	320	55
Three	5,190	114	1,853	2,292	824	96	13
Four	2,304	32	643	1,186	402	36	5
Five	899	8	186	519	157	26	3
Six or more	663	- -	133	409	104	18	- -
TOTAL CHILDREN ..	62,732	3,280	20,731	24,329	11,788	2,278	325
Average per Family	1.13	.78	1.63	2.24	1.05	.26	.04
Average per Family with Children ...	2.09	1.37	2.03	2.55	1.90	1.52	1.42

[1] Own children under 18 years

Source: Department of Commerce

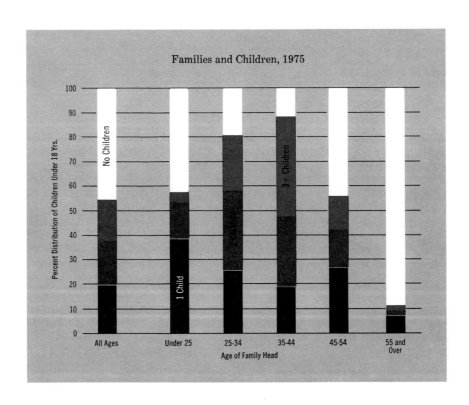

Families and Children, 1975

FAMILY LIFE CYCLE

Stage of Family Life Cycle	Period of Birth of Mother							
	1880's	1890's	1900's	1910's	1920's	1930's	1940's	1950's
Age of Mother, 1975	86-95	76-85	66-75	56-65	46-55	36-45	26-35	16-25
Median Age of Mother at:								
First Marriage.................	21.4	21.2	21.0	21.4	20.7	20.0	20.5	21.2
Birth of First Child	23.0	22.9	22.8	23.5	22.7	21.4	21.8	22.7
Birth of Last Child	32.9	32.0	31.0	32.0	31.5	31.2	30.1	29.6
Marriage of Last Child	55.4	54.8	53.0	53.2	53.2	53.6	52.7	52.3
Death of One Spouse	57.0	59.6	62.3	63.7	64.4	65.1	65.1	65.2
Median Years Between First Marriage and:								
Birth of First Child	1.6	1.7	1.8	2.1	2.0	1.4	1.3	1.5
Birth of Last Child	11.5	10.8	10.0	10.6	10.8	11.2	9.6	8.4
Marriage of Last Child	34.0	33.6	32.0	31.8	32.5	33.6	32.2	31.1
Death of One Spouse	35.6	38.4	41.3	42.3	43.7	45.1	44.6	44.0
Median Years Between:								
Birth of First and Last Child ...	9.9	9.1	8.2	8.5	8.8	9.8	8.3	6.9
Last Child's Marriage and Death of One Spouse	1.6	4.8	9.3	10.5	11.2	11.5	12.4	12.9

Source: Department of Commerce (from unpublished data developed by Paul C. Glick, Bureau of the Census)

CHILDREN BY AGE, RACE AND FAMILY STATUS, 1975

Thousands of persons under 18 years[1]

Item	Total, All Races	Race	
		White	Negro
TOTAL CHILDREN[1]	66,087	55,500	9,472
Under 3 Years.......................	9,180	7,636	1,371
3-5	10,342	8,610	1,546
6-8	10,288	8,608	1,491
9-11	11,606	9,739	1,683
12-13	8,209	6,940	1,138
14-17	16,463	13,966	2,242
Living with Both Parents	53,072	47,415	4,682
Living with One Parent	11,245	7,096	4,042
Other[2]............................	1,770	989	748

Note: Population figures for children, shown here, are based on household survey data and differ from those on page 59 which are derived from total population estimates by age
[1] Excludes persons under 18 years who are heads and wives of families and subfamilies
[2] Includes children not living in families

Source: Department of Commerce

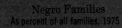

Negro Families
As percent of all families, 1975

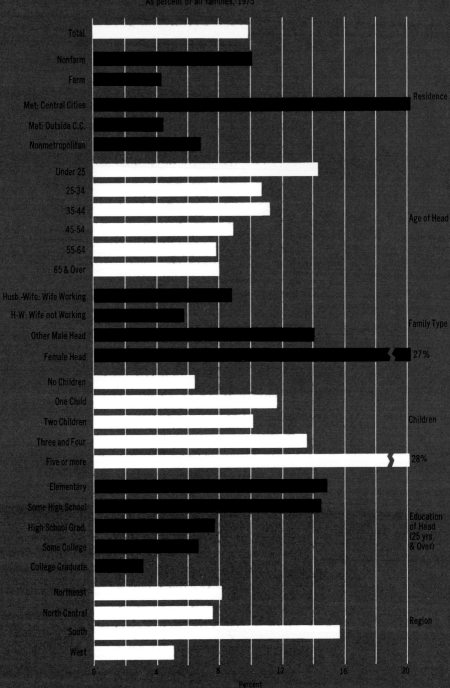

Total	
Nonfarm	
Farm	
Met: Central Cities	Residence
Met: Outside C.C.	
Nonmetropolitan	
Under 25	
25-34	
35-44	
45-54	Age of Head
55-64	
65 & Over	
Husb.-Wife: Wife Working	
H-W: Wife not Working	
Other Male Head	Family Type
Female Head	27%
No Children	
One Child	
Two Children	Children
Three and Four	
Five or more	28%
Elementary	
Some High School	
High School Grad.	Education of Head (25 yrs. & Over)
Some College	
College Graduate	
Northeast	
North Central	
South	Region
West	

0   4   8   12   16   20

Percent

WHITE AND NEGRO FAMILIES BY SELECTED CHARACTERISTICS, 1975

Characteristic	Total Families (Thousands)	White Families Number (Thousands)	White Families Percent Distribution	Negro Families Number (Thousands)	Negro Families Percent Distribution	As Percent of Total Families
TOTAL	55,712	49,451	100.0	5,498	100.0	9.9
Residence						
Nonfarm	53,314	47,166	95.4	5,396	98.1	10.1
Farm	2,398	2,284	4.6	102	1.9	4.3
Metropolitan	37,741	32,850	66.4	4,240	77.1	11.2
In Central Cities	16,012	12,388	25.1	3,271	59.5	20.4
Outside Central Cities	21,729	20,462	41.4	970	17.6	4.5
Nonmetropolitan	17,971	16,601	33.6	1,258	22.9	7.0
Age of Head						
Under 25	4,225	3,574	7.2	609	11.1	14.4
25-34	12,708	11,166	22.6	1,352	24.6	10.6
35-44	10,853	9,429	19.1	1,213	22.1	11.2
45-54	11,234	10,084	20.4	997	18.1	8.9
55-64	8,658	7,878	15.9	687	12.5	7.9
65 and over	8,034	7,319	14.8	641	11.7	8.0
Family Type						
Married, Wife Present	46,971	42,969	86.9	3,346	60.9	7.1
Wife Working	20,273	18,176	36.8	1,791	32.6	8.8
Wife not Working	26,698	24,793	50.1	1,555	28.3	5.8
Other Male Head	1,499	1,270	2.6	212	3.9	14.1
Female Head	7,242	5,212	10.5	1,940	35.3	26.8
Number of Children						
None	24,392	22,556	45.6	1,585	28.8	6.5
One	11,463	9,957	20.1	1,325	24.1	11.6
Two	10,282	9,048	18.3	1,037	18.9	10.1
Three and Four	7,846	6,669	13.5	1,069	19.4	13.6
Five or more	1,728	1,221	2.5	482	8.8	27.9
Earners						
None	6,181	5,217	10.5	914	16.6	14.8
One	19,584	17,369	35.1	1,935	35.2	9.9
Two	21,968	19,702	39.8	1,968	35.8	9.0
Three or more	7,979	7,162	14.5	682	12.4	8.5
Education of Head[1]						
Elementary, Total	11,219	9,420	20.5	1,686	34.5	15.0
Some High School	7,940	6,698	14.6	1,163	23.8	14.6
High School Graduate	17,214	15,678	34.2	1,336	27.3	7.8
Some College	6,700	6,157	13.4	446	9.1	6.7
College Graduate	8,415	7,924	17.3	258	5.3	3.1
Region						
Northeast	12,588	11,447	23.1	1,021	18.6	8.1
North Central	15,019	13,827	28.0	1,135	20.6	7.6
South	18,099	15,147	30.6	2,829	51.5	15.6
West	10,006	9,029	18.3	513	9.3	5.1

[1] Head 25 years and over

Source: Department of Commerce

SCHOOL ENROLLMENT BY SELECTED CHARACTERISTICS, 1974

Thousands of persons, except percent, as of fall opening

Characteristic	Population 3-34 Years	Number Enrolled	Percent of Population		
			Enrolled in School[1]	Enrolled in College	Not Enrolled; H.S. Grad.
TOTAL	112,390	60,259	53.6	7.9	32.1
Age					
3-4	6,966	2,006	28.8	- -	- -
5-6	6,817	6,421	94.2	- -	- -
7-9	10,677	10,585	99.1	- -	- -
10-13	16,334	16,248	99.5	- -	- -
14-15	8,413	8,238	97.9	.1	.1
16-17	8,298	7,291	87.9	3.7	2.8
18-19	7,822	3,375	43.1	33.2	40.2
20-21	7,471	2,254	30.2	29.3	54.0
22-24	10,377	1,562	15.1	14.7	69.7
25-29	15,900	1,525	9.6	9.3	74.3
30-34	13,315	753	5.7	5.4	72.7
Sex					
Male	55,711	31,177	56.0	8.8	30.1
Female	56,679	29,082	51.3	6.9	34.1
Race					
White	96,184	50,992	53.0	8.1	33.4
Negro	14,326	8,215	57.3	5.7	23.9
Spanish Origin	6,669	3,620	54.3	5.3	18.4
Residence					
Metropolitan	77,702	43,027	54.1	8.9	33.0
Central Cities	32,962	17,647	53.5	9.2	31.4
Outside Central Cities	44,739	24,380	54.5	8.7	34.2
Nonmetropolitan ...	34,688	18,231	52.6	5.5	30.2

[1] All levels, including college

Source: Department of Commerce

ENROLLMENT BY AGE

Percent of population enrolled in school or college, as of fall opening

Age Group	1947	1950	1955	1960	1965	1970	1975
Total, 5-34 Years	42.3	44.2	50.8	56.4	59.7	59.0	55.1
5	53.4	51.8	58.1	63.7	70.1	80.1 }	94.7
6	96.2	97.0	98.2	98.0	98.7	98.5 }	
7-9	98.4	98.9	99.2	99.6	99.3	99.3	99.3
10-13	98.6	98.6	99.2	99.5	99.4	99.2	99.3
14-15	91.6	94.7	95.9	97.8	98.9	98.1	98.2
16-17	67.6	71.3	77.4	82.6	87.4	90.0	89.0
18-19	24.3	29.4	31.5	38.4	46.3	47.7	46.9
20-24	10.2	9.0	11.1	13.1	19.0	21.5	22.4
25-29	3.0	3.0	4.2	4.9	6.1	7.5	10.1
30-34	1.0	.9	1.6	2.4	3.2	4.2	6.6

Source: Department of Commerce

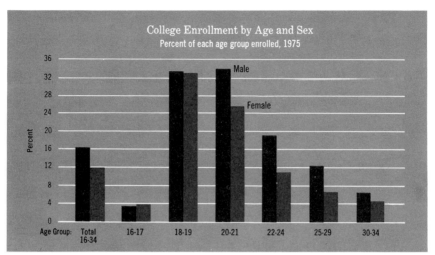

ENROLLMENT BY EDUCATIONAL LEVEL AND SEX
Millions of persons, 5-34 years

Year and Sex	Total Enrolled	Elementary School	High School	College
TOTAL PERSONS				
1950	30.3	21.4	6.7	2.2
1960	46.3	32.4	10.2	3.6
1965	53.8	35.1	13.0	5.7
1970	58.8	36.7	14.7	7.4
1974	58.3	34.0	15.4	8.8
1975	58.9	33.5	15.7	9.7
Projections:				
1980	59.4	32.8	15.1	11.4
1985	62.3	36.1	14.4	11.9
MALE				
1950	15.9	11.0	3.3	1.5
1960	24.2	16.7	5.2	2.3
1965	28.1	18.0	6.5	3.5
1970	30.6	18.8	7.4	4.4
1974	30.2	17.4	7.8	4.9
1975	30.5	——25.2——		5.3
Projections:				
1980	31.4	16.8	7.7	6.9
1985	32.9	18.5	7.2	7.1
FEMALE				
1950	14.4	10.4	3.3	.7
1960	22.0	15.7	5.1	1.2
1965	25.7	17.1	6.5	2.2
1970	28.2	17.9	7.3	3.0
1974	28.1	16.6	7.6	3.9
1975	28.4	——24.0——		4.4
Projections:				
1980	28.0	16.0	7.5	4.6
1985	29.4	17.6	7.1	4.7

Note: Series E-1 projections (moderate population series; relatively rapid increase in age-specific enrollment rates)

Source: Department of Commerce

COLLEGE PLANS OF HIGH SCHOOL SENIORS, 1974

Thousands of persons, except percent, as of October

Characteristic	All High School Seniors	With Plans to Continue Education in: College Number	College Percent	Vocational School
TOTAL	3,518	1,486	42.2	162
Sex				
Male	1,707	675	39.5	86
Female	1,811	810	44.7	76
Race				
White.........................	3,006	1,304	43.4	134
Negro	454	152	33.5	28
Residence				
Metropolitan	2,376	1,064	44.8	86
In Central Cities	935	381	40.7	24
Outside Central Cities	1,441	683	47.4	61
Nonmetropolitan	1,142	421	36.9	76
Family Income[1]				
Under $5,000	340	88	25.8	31
$5,000- 7,500	345	116	33:6	23
7,500-10,000	326	99	30.3	20
10,000-15,000	909	375	41.3	33
15,000-25,000	849	438	51.7	29
25,000 and over	282	191	67.6	9
Not reported	325	132	40.7	14

[1] Data for primary families only

Source: Department of Commerce

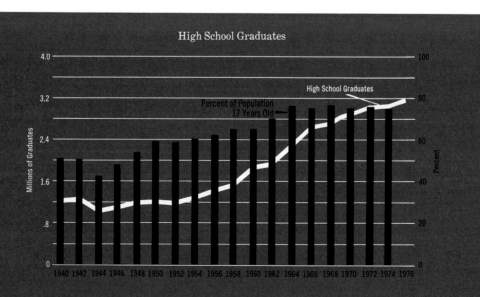

High School Graduates

HIGH SCHOOL GRADUATES

Thousands of persons, except percent

Year of High School Graduation	High School Graduates			Graduates as Percent of Population 17 Years Old
	Total	Male	Female	
1930	667	300	367	29.0
1940	1,221	579	643	50.8
1950	1,200	571	629	59.0
1952	1,197	569	627	58.6
1954	1,276	613	664	60.0
1956	1,415	680	735	62.3
1958	1,506	726	780	64.8
1960	1,864	898	966	65.1
1962	1,925	941	984	69.5
1964	2,290	1,121	1,169	76.3
1966	2,632	1,308	1,324	74.9
1968	2,702	1,341	1,361	76.7
1970	2,896	1,433	1,463	75.7
1972	3,006	1,490	1,516	76.0
1974	3,069	1,512	1,557	74.9
1975p	3,139	1,554	1,585	n.a.
Projections:				
1976	3,137	1,552	1,585	n.a.
1980	3,083	1,527	1,556	n.a.
1985	2,680	1,327	1,353	n.a.

n.a.—Not available
p—Preliminary

Source: Department of Health, Education and Welfare

ENROLLMENT IN HIGHER EDUCATION

Thousands of degree-credit students, as of fall opening

Year	Total Enrolled	Sex		Level	
		Male	Female	Under-graduate[1]	Graduate[2]
1960	3,583	2,257	1,326	3,227	356
1962	4,175	2,587	1,588	3,753	422
1964	4,950	3,033	1.917	4,342	608
1966	5,928	3,577	2,351	5,160	768
1968	6,928	4,119	2,809	6,043	885
1970	7,920	4,637	3,284	6,889	1,031
1972	8,265	4,701	3,564	7,199	1,066
1974	9,023	4,969	4,054	7,833	1,190
1975p	9,328	5,132	4,196	8,096	1,232
Projections:					
1978	9,978	5,471	4,507	8,646	1,332
1980	10,173	5,572	4,601	8,806	1,367
1982	10,188	5,581	4,607	8,808	1,380
1984	9,811	5,376	4,435	8,475	1,336

[1] Including first professional
[2] Includes both resident and extension graduate students beginning 1964

p-Preliminary

Source: Department of Health, Education and Welfare

SCHOOL RETENTION RATES

Estimated retention rates per 1,000 pupils entering 5th grade

Year of Entrance into 5th Grade	Pupils Entering			High School Graduates	Year of High School Graduation	First Time College Students
	5th Grade	9th Grade	12th Grade			
1930	1,000	770	463	417	1938	148
1940	1,000	781	507	481	1948	[1]
1942	1,000	807	539	505	1950	205
1944	1,000	848	549	522	1952	234
1946	1,000	872	583	553	1954	283
1948	1,000	863	619	581	1956	301
1950	1,000	886	632	582	1958	308
1952	1,000	904	667	621	1960	328
1954	1,000	915	684	642	1962	343
1956	1,000	930	728	676	1964	362
1958	1,000	946	761	732	1966	384
1960	1,000	952	787	749	1968	452
1962	1,000	959	790	750	1970	461
1964	1,000	975	791	748	1972	433
1966	1,000	985	783	744	1974	449

[1] Not calculated because of influx of veterans in institutions of higher education
Source: Department of Health, Education and Welfare

COLLEGE ENROLLMENT BY FIELD OF STUDY, SEX AND LEVEL, 1974

Persons 14 years and over, as of October, in thousands

Field of Study	Total, Both Sexes	Males			Females		
		All Levels		Percent Enrolled 5th Year or Higher	All Levels		Percent Enrolled 5th Year or Higher
		Number	Percent Distri- bution		Number	Percent Distri- bution	
TOTAL, ALL FIELDS[1] . . .	9,856	5,404	100.0	20.8	4,449	100.0	18.4
Agriculture, Forestry	110	93	1.7	17.2	17	.4	17.6
Biological Sciences	339	199	3.7	15.6	140	3.1	15.0
Business, Commerce	1,546	1,052	19.5	16.5	494	11.1	8.9
Education	1,371	379	7.0	37.5	993	22.3	31.8
Engineering	430	402	7.4	19.7	28	.6	10.7
English, Journalism	281	116	2.1	20.7	166	3.7	16.9
Other Humanities	477	239	4.4	26.4	237	5.3	12.2
Health, Medical Professions	870	302	5.6	32.8	567	12.7	12.9
Law	290	219	4.1	50.2	71	1.6	54.9
Mathematics, Statistics . . .	184	105	1.9	12.4	78	1.8	23.1
Physical, Earth Sciences . .	140	100	1.9	23.0	39	.9	15.4
Social Sciences	885	468	8.7	23.7	417	9.4	19.9
Vocational Technical Studies	270	202	3.7	7.4	68	1.5	7.4
Computer Sciences	95	74	1.4	25.7	21	.5	23.8
Other Fields	1,531	892	16.5	20.1	640	14.4	19.1

[1] Includes those not reporting field of study

Source: Department of Commerce

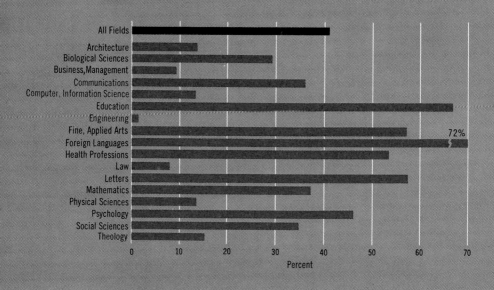

Women Earning Degrees, by Selected Fields of Study

Percent of total degrees conferred at all levels, 1973

DEGREES CONFERRED BY FIELD OF STUDY AND LEVEL, 1973

Field of Study	Level of Degree			Percent of Total	
	Bachelor's[1]	Master's	Doctorates	Advanced Degrees	Female Recipients, All Levels
ALL FIELDS	972,380	263,371	34,777	23.5	41.1
Agriculture, Natural Resources.	14,756	2,807	1,059	20.8	7.2
Architecture	6,962	2,307	58	25.4	13.8
Biological Sciences	42,233	6,263	3,636	19.0	29.2
Business, Management	126,830	31,166	932	20.2	9.4
Communications	14,317	2,406	139	15.1	36.3
Computer and Information Sci. ...	4,304	2,113	196	34.9	13.3
Education	194,210	105,242	7,314	36.7	67.1
Engineering	51,265	16,619	3,492	28.2	1.3
Fine, Applied Arts	36,017	7,254	616	17.9	57.3
Foreign Languages	18,964	4,289	991	21.8	72.2
Health Professions	50,789	8,362	646	15.1	53.4
Home Economics	13,533	1,679	165	12.0	95.5
Law	27,679	1,048	37	3.8	7.9
Letters	70,960	12,349	2,754	17.5	57.6
Library Sciences	1,159	7,696	102	87.1	79.6
Mathematics	23,067	5,028	1,068	20.9	37.3
Military Science[2]	253	--	--	--	--
Physical Sciences	20,696	6,257	4,006	33.2	13.5
Psychology	47,695	5,831	2,089	14.2	46.1
Public Affairs, Services	17,843	10,990	219	38.6	46.4
Social Sciences	156,361	17,318	4,230	12.1	34.8
Theology	8,817	2,778	666	28.1	15.2
Interdisciplinary and Area Studies	23,365	3,569	362	14.4	36.6

[1] Includes first professional degrees (principally in health professions, law and religion) requiring at least six years of study
[2] Includes naval and air force science

Source: Department of Health, Educaiton and Welfare

EARNED DEGREES CONFERRED IN HIGHER EDUCATION

Thousands

Year	Total Degrees Conferred	Level of Degree			Advanced Degrees as Percent of Total
		Bachelor's[1]	Master's	Doctor's	
1950	497	432	58	6	13.0
1952	401	330	64	8	17.8
1954	357	291	57	9	18.4
1956	377	309	59	9	18.1
1958	437	363	65	9	17.0
1960	477	389	78	10	18.4
1962	514	414	88	12	19.5
1964	614	494	106	15	19.5
1966	710	551	141	18	22.4
1968	867	667	177	23	23.1
1970	1,065	827	208	30	22.4
1972	1,216	931	252	33	23.4
1974p	1,310	1,000	277	34	23.7
1975p	1,326	999	292	36	24.7
Projections:					
1978	1,435	1,072	324	40	25.3
1980	1,492	1,115	338	39	25.3
1982	1,533	1,147	345	41	25.2
1984	1,538	1,150	345	43	25.2
1985	1,526	1,143	340	43	25.1

[1] Including first professional

p—Preliminary

Source: Department of Health, Education and Welfare

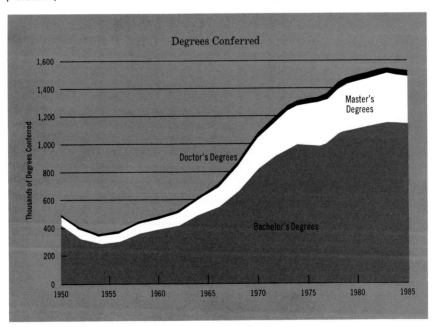

EDUCATIONAL ATTAINMENT: SELECTED METROPOLITAN AREAS, 1970

Persons 25 years and over

SMSA[1]	Total SMSA[1] (Millions)	Percent Distribution by Educational Level				
		Ele-mentary or Less	Some High School	High School Grad-uate	Some College	College Grad-uate
TOTAL, 30 AREAS	40.7	22.1	17.1	35.2	12.1	13.6
White	35.5	20.8	16.0	36.2	12.5	14.5
Negro, Other Races	5.2	30.8	24.4	28.5	9.0	7.3
In Central Cities	18.6	27.8	18.5	31.6	10.7	11.3
White	14.3	26.7	16.5	32.6	11.3	12.8
Negro, Other Races	4.2	31.6	25.3	28.1	8.6	6.3
Outside Central Cities	22.2	17.3	15.9	38.2	13.3	15.4
White	21.2	16.8	15.6	38.6	13.4	15.6
Negro, Other Races	1.0	27.4	20.7	30.2	10.4	11.6
INDIVIDUAL AREAS:						
Atlanta, Ga.	.8	24.1	17.6	29.9	12.8	15.6
Baltimore, Md.	1.0	32.5	22.4	28.3	7.9	9.0
Boston, Mass.	1.5	15.5	16.0	41.3	11.0	16.4
Buffalo, N. Y.	.7	23.5	18.9	35.1	10.7	11.6
Chicago, Ill.	3.7	23.7	17.4	33.7	12.6	12.5
Cincinnati, Ohio-Ky	.6	26.3	18.5	30.3	10.0	14.8
Cleveland, Ohio	1.0	19.0	21.8	36.8	10.2	12.3
Columbus, Ohio	.4	14.7	17.9	37.5	12.0	18.2
Dallas, Tex.	.8	16.2	17.5	33.9	16.0	16.5
Denver, Colo	.6	13.4	14.3	39.8	15.8	16.3
Detroit, Mich.	2.2	23.2	22.2	36.8	8.6	9.1
Houston, Tex.	.9	22.9	21.5	33.1	12.0	10.3
Indianapolis, Ind.	.4	19.0	22.9	35.2	13.3	10.1
Kansas City, Mo.-Kans.	.7	20.2	17.1	37.3	13.7	11.9
Los Angeles-Long Beach, Calif.	4.6	16.8	16.0	34.8	17.7	14.6
Memphis, Tenn.	.3	26.3	18.5	35.4	9.7	10.4
Milwaukee, Wis.	.7	23.7	14.6	38.9	10.5	12.4
Minneapolis-St. Paul, Minn.	.9	16.8	12.6	41.9	12.8	15.8
New Orleans, La.	.5	31.9	16.8	28.2	10.7	12.6
New York, N. Y.	6.7	26.7	15.6	34.4	10.0	13.1
Newark, N. J.	1.0	25.7	16.3	36.7	8.4	13.0
Philadelphia, Pa.-N. J.	2.6	23.8	19.8	36.0	7.9	12.5
Phoenix, Ariz.	.5	19.9	16.6	35.3	16.0	12.0
Pittsburgh, Pa.	1.3	26.6	17.4	40.8	6.5	8.7
St. Louis, Mo.-Ill.	1.3	30.3	18.6	30.7	9.9	10.5
San Antonio, Tex.	.4	34.1	15.5	27.8	11.5	10.5
San Diego, Calif.	.7	16.5	15.9	34.3	17.5	15.6
San Francisco-Oakland, Calif.	1.8	15.4	12.6	36.8	17.2	18.2
Seattle, Wash.	.7	14.6	15.1	37.6	17.3	15.3
Washington, D. C.-Md.-Va.	1.4	12.5	12.4	34.6	15.4	25.2

[1] Standard metropolitan statistical area

Source: Department of Commerce

EDUCATIONAL ATTAINMENT BY SELECTED CHARACTERISTICS, 1975

| Characteristic | Popu-lation, 25 Years and Over (Millions) | Percent Distribution by Years Completed | | | | | Median School Years Com-pleted |
		Total	Less Than H. S. Grad.	High School Grad.	Some College	College Grad.	
TOTAL	116.9	100.0	37.3	36.2	12.4	13.9	12.3
Sex							
Male	55.0	100.0	36.9	32.3	13.2	17.6	12.4
Female	61.9	100.0	38.1	39.7	11.7	10.6	12.3
Race							
White	104.1	100.0	35.6	37.3	12.8	14.5	12.4
Negro, Other Races	12.8	100.0	53.6	27.6	9.6	9.2	11.4
Negro	11.1	100.0	57.6	27.1	9.1	6.5	10.9
Age							
Male							
25-34	14.8	100.0	17.6	37.3	19.7	25.4	12.9
35-44	11.0	100.0	28.0	36.8	13.8	21.1	12.6
45-54	11.4	100.0	37.6	34.3	11.9	16.1	12.4
55-64	9.2	100.0	49.4	31.0	9.3	10.3	12.0
65 and over	8.7	100.0	66.6	16.8	7.2	9.4	9.1e
Female							
25-34	15.3	100.0	20.3	45.9	16.3	17.5	12.7
35-44	11.6	100.0	28.8	47.2	12.6	11.3	12.4
45-54	12.2	100.0	35.0	45.6	10.9	8.4	12.3
55-64	10.3	100.0	47.2	36.7	9.0	7.3	12.1
65 and over	12.4	100.0	63.6	21.8	8.4	6.3	9.6e
Residence							
Metropolitan Areas	79.8	100.0	33.7	36.7	13.7	15.8	12.4
In Central Cities	34.7	100.0	39.0	33.6	13.1	14.3	12.3
Outside Central Cities ..	45.2	100.0	29.8	39.1	14.2	16.8	12.5
Nonmetropolitan Areas ...	37.1	100.0	45.3	35.2	9.6	9.9	12.1
Nonfarm	32.9	100.0	44.6	35.1	9.8	10.4	12.2
Farm	4.2	100.0	49.6	35.8	8.0	6.6	12.0
Income[1]							
Under $3,000	5.8	100.0	68.1	17.6	7.2	7.1	9.1e
$3,000- 5,000	5.7	100.0	61.5	21.7	8.4	8.5	9.9e
5,000- 7,000	5.7	100.0	51.2	28.7	10.2	9.9	11.6e
7,000-10,000	9.2	100.0	40.7	36.7	11.3	11.3	12.2e
10,000-15,000	14.7	100.0	27.1	41.2	16.1	15.6	12.6
15,000-25,000	10.3	100.0	16.4	35.5	17.6	30.5	12.9
25,000 and over	3.2	100.0	8.7	21.2	16.6	53.5	16.1
Region							
Northeast	27.8	100.0	37.2	37.9	10.1	14.7	12.3
North Central	31.3	100.0	36.1	39.5	11.5	12.9	12.3
South	36.7	100.0	44.0	31.9	11.6	12.6	12.2
West	21.0	100.0	28.4	36.7	18.4	16.5	12.6

[1] Male income recipients by income of preceding year

e-Estimate
Source: Department of Commerce

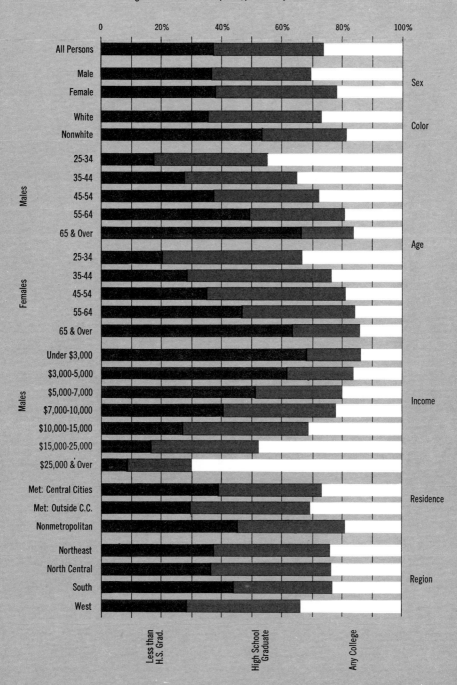

Educational Profile, 1975
Highest level of school completed, persons 25 years and over

	0	20%	40%	60%	80%	100%

All Persons

Sex
Male
Female

Color
White
Nonwhite

Age

Males
25-34
35-44
45-54
55-64
65 & Over

Females
25-34
35-44
45-54
55-64
65 & Over

Income

Males
Under $3,000
$3,000-5,000
$5,000-7,000
$7,000-10,000
$10,000-15,000
$15,000-25,000
$25,000 & Over

Residence
Met: Central Cities
Met: Outside C.C.
Nonmetropolitan

Region
Northeast
North Central
South
West

Less than H.S. Grad.   High School Graduate   Any College

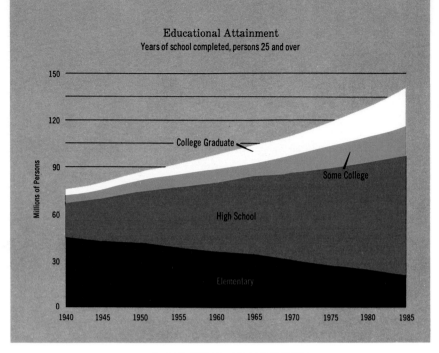

Educational Attainment
Years of school completed, persons 25 and over

EDUCATIONAL ATTAINMENT

Persons 25 years and over

Year	Total	Years of School Completed				
		Elementary or Less	Some High school	High School Graduate	Some College	College Graduate
		Millions of Persons				
1940........	74.8	45.2	11.4	10.7	4.1	3.4
1950........	86.0	41.8	14.9	17.7	6.3	5.3
1955........	91.3	38.0	16.3	23.3	6.9	6.8
1960........	97.3	36.3	17.6	27.0	8.3	8.2
1965........	103.2	34.0	18.6	31.7	9.1	9.7
1970........	109.3	30.3	18.7	37.1	11.2	12.1
1975........	116.9	25.5	18.2	42.4	14.5	16.2
Projections:						
1980........	128.5	23.5	20.9	48.7	16.1	19.3
1985........	139.9	20.1	21.6	54.4	19.2	24.5
		Percent Distribution				
1940........	100.0	60.4	15.2	14.3	5.5	4.6
1950........	100.0	48.6	17.3	20.6	7.3	6.2
1960........	100.0	37.3	18.1	27.7	8.5	8.4
1970........	100.0	27.8	17.0	34.0	10.3	11.1
1975........	100.0	21.9	15.6	36.2	12.4	13.9
Projections:						
1980........	100.0	18.3	16.3	37.9	12.5	15.0
1985........	100.0	14.4	15.4	38.9	13.7	17.5

Note: Series I (high series) projections

Source: Department of Commerce

EDUCATIONAL ATTAINMENT BY RACE, SEX AND AGE, 1975

Years of School Completed	Population 25 Years and Over	Age Group				
		25-34	35-44	45-54	55-64	65 & Over
TOTAL[1] (Millions)	116.9	30.1	22.6	23.6	19.5	21.1
WHITE, TOTAL (Millions) .	104.1	26.4	19.8	21.0	17.6	19.2
Percent Distribution	100.0	100.0	100.0	100.0	100.0	100.0
Some Elementary	10.0	3.4	5.9	7.9	11.8	23.6
Elementary, 8 Years	10.6	3.0	5.2	9.0	15.4	23.7
Some High School	15.0	11.4	15.0	16.4	18.1	15.4
High School Graduate	37.3	41.8	43.5	42.1	35.8	20.8
Some College	12.8	18.3	13.5	11.7	9.6	8.4
College Graduate	14.5	22.2	16.8	12.9	9.2	8.1
MALE (Millions)	49.3	13.1	9.7	10.2	8.3	7.9
Percent Distribution	100.0	100.0	100.0	100.0	100.0	100.0
Some Elementary	10.4	3.3	6.7	9.0	12.8	26.1
Elementary, 8 Years	10.5	3.2	5.7	9.7	16.0	23.9
Some High School	14.1	10.0	13.6	16.0	17.9	14.7
High School Graduate	33.1	37.1	37.8	35.7	32.6	17.6
Some College	13.6	20.1	14.2	12.3	9.6	7.6
College Graduate	18.4	26.4	22.0	17.1	11.1	10.1
FEMALE (Millions)	54.8	13.3	10.1	10.9	9.3	11.3
Percent Distribution	100.0	100.0	100.0	100.0	100.0	100.0
Some Elementary	9.4	3.4	5.0	6.8	10.9	21.8
Elementary, 8 Years	10.6	2.7	4.7	8.4	14.9	23.6
Some High School	15.9	12.8	16.4	16.7	18.4	15.9
High School Graduate	41.1	46.5	49.0	48.0	38.7	22.9
Some College	12.1	16.5	13.0	11.1	9.5	9.0
College Graduate	10.9	18.1	11.7	8.9	7.5	6.7
NEGRO, TOTAL (Millions) .	11.1	3.1	2.4	2.2	1.7	1.7
Percent Distribution	100.0	100.0	100.0	100.0	100.0	100.0
Some Elementary	26.7	5.1	14.8	26.7	43.6	64.6
Elementary, 8 Years	8.5	3.1	7.6	10.7	12.9	12.5
Some High School	22.4	22.5	28.1	26.5	21.0	10.0
High School Graduate	27.1	43.3	32.3	23.1	14.4	8.1
Some College	9.1	15.2	9.6	8.0	4.8	2.4
College Graduate	6.5	10.7	7.4	4.8	3.3	2.4
MALE (Millions)	4.9	1.4	1.0	1.0	.8	.7
Percent Distribution	100.0	100.0	100.0	100.0	100.0	100.0
Some Elementary	30.0	5.6	18.3	32.9	49.3	68.6
Elementary, 8 Years	8.1	3.2	6.6	11.4	12.2	10.6
Some High School	20.2	20.8	27.1	22.4	19.1	7.4
High School Graduate	25.2	41.9	29.5	20.8	11.8	7.6
Some College	9.8	16.6	10.5	7.6	5.5	2.6
College Graduate	6.7	12.0	8.0	4.7	2.1	2.8
FEMALE (Millions)	6.2	1.7	1.3	1.2	.9	1.0
Percent Distribution	100.0	100.0	100.0	100.0	100.0	100.0
Some Elementary . . . . . . , ...	23.8	4.7	12.1	21.6	38.8	61.5
Elementary, 8 Years	8.9	3.0	8.4	10.2	13.5	13.9
Some High School	24.0	24.0	28.9	29.9	22.7	12.0
High School Graduate	28.6	44.5	34.5	25.1	16.5	8.3
Some College	8.5	14.2	9.0	8.4	4.2	2.2
College Graduate	6.2	9.7	7.1	4.8	4.3	2.2

[1] Includes other races, not shown separately

Source: Department of Commerce

PUBLIC ELEMENTARY AND SECONDARY SCHOOLS, 1974-1975

State	Total Enrollment (Thousands)	Total Expenditures[1]		Current Expenditures per Pupil[2] (Dollars)
		Millions of Dollars	Percent of Pers. Income	
TOTAL U.S.	45,056	61,629	5.35	1,255
Alabama................	764	674	4.47	871
Alaska	87	184	7.75	1,624
Arizona	487	714	6.47	1,176
Arkansas	454	456	5.26	896
California	4,427	6,935	5.50	1,210
Colorado	568	759	5.51	1,188
Connecticut............	660	979	4.91	1,507
Delaware	131	205	5.68	1,485
District of Columbia	132	241	4.74	1,814
Florida	1,557	1,963	4.48	1,147
Georgia	1,081	1,082	4.67	1,000
Hawaii	177	263	5.14	1,384
Idaho	188	214	4.36	910
Illinois	2,296	3,425	4.94	1,376
Indiana	1,187	1,405	5.09	1,074
Iowa	617	805	5.34	1,240
Kansas	450	675	5.41	1,444
Kentucky	701	625	4.19	864
Louisiana	841	882	5.34	1,376
Maine	251	265	5.50	1,007
Maryland	894	1,410	5.79	1,369
Massachusetts	1,210	1,630	4.88	1,356
Michigan	2,138	3,450	6.45	1,547
Minnesota	890	1,482	6.98	1,423
Mississippi.............	513	477	5.40	834
Missouri...............	1,002	1,102	4.58	1,078
Montana...............	172	222	6.08	1,269
Nebraska	319	413	5.07	1,211
Nevada................	137	167	4.85	1,101
New Hampshire	172	187	4.68	1,095
New Jersey	1,470	2,420	5.29	1,565
New Mexico	282	356	7.67	1,052
New York	3,436	7,006	6.28	2,005
North Carolina	1,178	1,443	5.77	1,052
North Dakota	133	157	4.41	1,032
Ohio	2,330	2,749	4.64	1,144
Oklahoma	596	634	5.11	1,009
Oregon	477	717	5.99	1,425
Pennsylvania...........	2,277	3,548	5.50	1,446
Rhode Island	179	281	5.61	1,493
South Carolina	627	648	5.40	984
South Dakota	154	157	4.92	973
Tennessee	873	835	4.44	903
Texas	2,785	2,698	4.52	894
Utah	306	370	7.05	942
Vermont...............	105	127	5.96	1,095
Virginia	1,093	1,271	4.85	1,054
Washington	785	1,085	5.47	1,199
West Virginia	404	384	4.90	910
Wisconsin	974	1,334	5.57	1,323
Wyoming	87	116	5.97	1,322

[1] Current expenditures, capital outlays and interest
[2] In average daily attendance (excludes adult education, summer schools, community colleges, community services)

Sources: Departments of Commerce and Health Education and Welfare

EMPLOYMENT

EMPLOYMENT

POPULATION AND LABOR FORCE

Millions of persons 16 years and over, except percent

Year	Total Noninsti- tutional Population	Total Labor Force[1]		Not in Labor Force
		Number	Percent of Population	
1950	106.6	63.9	59.9	42.8
1951	107.7	65.1	60.4	42.6
1952	108.8	65.7	60.4	43.1
1953	110.6	66.6	60.2	44.0
1954	111.7	67.0	60.0	44.7
1955	112.7	68.1	60.4	44.7
1956	113.8	69.4	61.0	44.4
1957	115.1	69.7	60.6	45.3
1958	116.4	70.3	60.4	46.1
1959	117.9	70.9	60.2	47.0
1960	119.8	72.1	60.2	47.6
1961	121.3	73.0	60.2	48.3
1962	123.0	73.4	59.7	49.5
1963	125.2	74.6	59.6	50.6
1964	127.2	75.8	59.6	51.4
1965	129.2	77.2	59.7	52.1
1966	131.2	78.9	60.1	52.3
1967	133.3	80.8	60.6	52.5
1968	135.6	82.3	60.7	53.3
1969	137.8	84.2	61.1	53.6
1970	140.2	85.9	61.3	54.3
1971	142.6	86.9	61.0	55.7
1972	145.8	89.0	61.0	56.8
1973	148.3	91.0	61.4	57.2
1974	150.8	93.2	61.8	57.6
1975	153.4	94.8	61.8	58.7

Note: Population adjustments in 1953, 1960, 1962, 1972 and 1973 make subsequent data not strictly comparable with earlier years

[1] Includes Armed Forces

Source: Department of Labor

EMPLOYMENT STATUS OF THE LABOR FORCE BY SEX

Millions of persons 16 years and over, except percent

Sex and Year	Total Labor Force[1]	Civilian Labor Force				
		Employed			Unemployed	
		Total	Agri-cultural	Nonagri-cultural	Total	Percent of Labor Force
Total						
1960	72.1	65.8	5.5	60.3	3.9	5.5
1965	77.2	71.1	4.4	66.7	3.4	4.5
1966	78.9	72.9	4.0	68.9	2.9	3.8
1967	80.8	74.4	3.8	70.5	3.0	3.8
1968	82.3	75.9	3.8	72.1	2.8	3.6
1969	84.2	77.9	3.6	74.3	2.8	3.5
1970	85.9	78.6	3.5	75.2	4.1	4.9
1971	86.9	79.1	3.4	75.7	5.0	5.9
1972	89.0	81.7	3.5	78.2	4.8	5.6
1973	91.0	84.4	3.5	81.0	4.3	4.9
1974	93.2	85.9	3.5	82.4	5.1	5.6
1975	94.8	84.8	3.4	81.4	7.8	8.5
Male						
1960	48.9	43.9	4.5	39.4	2.5	5.4
1965	50.9	46.3	3.5	42.8	1.9	4.0
1966	51.6	46.9	3.2	43.7	1.6	3.2
1967	52.4	47.5	3.2	44.3	1.5	3.1
1968	53.0	48.1	3.2	45.0	1.4	2.9
1969	53.7	48.8	3.0	45.9	1.4	2.8
1970	54.3	49.0	2.9	46.1	2.2	4.4
1971	54.8	49.2	2.8	46.5	2.8	5.3
1972	55.7	50.6	2.8	47.8	2.6	4.9
1973	56.5	52.0	2.8	49.1	2.2	4.1
1974	57.3	52.5	2.9	49.6	2.7	4.8
1975	57.7	51.2	2.8	48.4	4.4	7.9
Female						
1960	23.3	21.9	1.0	20.9	1.4	5.9
1965	26.2	24.7	.8	23.9	1.5	5.5
1966	27.3	26.0	.7	25.2	1.3	4.8
1967	28.4	26.9	.7	26.2	1.5	5.2
1968	29.2	27.8	.7	27.1	1.4	4.8
1969	30.6	29.1	.6	28.4	1.4	4.7
1970	31.6	29.7	.6	29.1	1.9	5.9
1971	32.1	29.9	.6	29.3	2.2	6.9
1972	33.3	31.1	.6	30.4	2.2	6.6
1973	34.6	32.4	.6	31.8	2.1	6.0
1974	35.9	33.4	.6	32.8	2.4	6.7
1975	37.1	33.6	.6	33.0	3.4	9.3

Note: See note to table page 85

[1] Includes Armed Forces

Source: Department of Labor

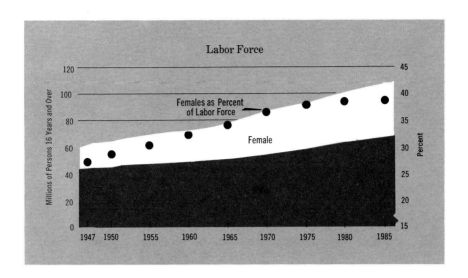

Labor Force

AGE COMPOSITION OF THE LABOR FORCE

Millions of persons 16 years and over

| Year | Total Labor Force[1] | Age Group | | | | | | |
		16-19	20-24	25-34	35-44	45-54	55-64	65 and Over
1950	63.9	4.5	7.9	15.1	14.1	11.5	7.6	3.0
1955	68.1	4.5	7.3	15.7	15.6	13.0	8.5	3.3
1960	72.1	5.2	7.5	15.1	16.8	14.7	9.4	3.4
1961	73.0	5.4	7.9	15.0	16.8	15.1	9.6	3.1
1962	73.4	5.4	8.1	14.8	17.0	15.2	9.8	3.2
1963	74.6	5.6	8.4	14.8	17.2	15.4	10.0	3.0
1964	75.8	5.9	8.9	14.8	17.2	15.7	10.2	3.1
1965	77.2	6.4	9.3	15.0	17.2	15.8	10.4	3.1
1966	78.9	7.0	9.7	15.3	17.2	16.1	10.6	3.1
1967	80.8	7.1	10.5	15.9	17.1	16.3	10.8	3.1
1968	82.3	7.1	11.0	16.5	17.0	16.5	11.0	3.2
1969	84.2	7.4	11.7	17.1	16.9	16.8	11.1	3.2
1970	85.9	7.6	12.3	17.7	16.8	17.0	11.3	3.2
1971	86.9	7.8	12.7	18.2	16.6	17.1	11.4	3.1
1972	89.0	8.4	13.1	19.3	16.7	17.0	11.4	3.1
1973	91.0	8.8	13.6	20.6	16.7	17.0	11.2	3.0
1974	93.2	9.2	14.0	21.8	17.0	17.2	11.2	2.9
1975	94.8	9.2	14.3	23.1	17.1	17.1	11.2	2.9
Projections:								
1980	101.8	8.3	15.4	26.8	18.7	16.4	12.8	3.3
1985	107.7	7.2	15.0	29.7	23.2	16.3	12.9	3.4
1990	112.6	7.1	13.2	30.5	27.6	18.3	12.3	3.5

Note: Projections are based on Series E (low series) population projections and do not reflect revision in population projections that are shown elsewhere in this volume. New labor force projections were in preparation at press time and are scheduled for publication in late 1976

[1] Includes Armed Forces

Source: Department of Labor

DISTRIBUTION OF THE LABOR FORCE BY AGE AND SEX

Age and Sex	1950	1960	1970	1975	1980	1985	1990
	Millions of Persons						
Male, Total	45.4	48.9	54.3	57.7	62.6	66.0	68.9
16-17	1.1	1.3	1.8	2.1	1.9	1.6	1.5
18-19	1.7	1.8	2.6	3.0	2.8	2.4	2.4
20-24	5.2	5.1	7.4	8.2	8.9	8.5	7.4
25-34	11.0	10.9	12.0	14.7	17.5	19.4	19.9
35-44	10.0	11.3	10.8	10.6	11.9	14.6	17.4
45-54	8.2	9.6	10.5	10.5	9.9	9.7	10.9
55-64	5.8	6.4	7.1	7.0	7.7	7.7	7.3
65 and over	2.5	2.3	2.2	1.9	2.1	2.1	2.1
Female, Total	18.4	23.3	31.6	37.1	39.2	41.7	43.7
16-17	.6	.8	1.3	1.7	1.4	1.2	1.2
18-19	1.1	1.3	1.9	2.4	2.2	2.0	2.0
20-24	2.7	2.6	4.9	6.1	6.6	6.5	5.8
25-34	4.1	4.1	5.7	8.5	9.3	10.3	10.7
35-44	4.2	5.3	6.0	6.5	6.9	8.6	10.2
45-54	3.3	5.3	6.5	6.7	6.5	6.5	7.4
55-64	1.8	3.0	4.2	4.2	5.1	5.2	5.0
65 and over	.6	.9	1.1	1.0	1.2	1.3	1.4
	Percent Distribution						
Male, Total	100.0	100.0	100.0	100.0	100.0	100.0	100.0
16-17	2.4	2.7	3.4	3.6	3.0	2.4	2.2
18-19	3.8	3.8	4.7	5.3	4.4	3.6	3.4
20-24	11.5	10.4	13.6	14.2	14.1	12.9	10.7
25-34	24.3	22.4	22.0	25.4	28.0	29.4	28.8
35-44	21.9	23.2	19.9	18.3	18.9	22.1	25.2
45-54	17.9	19.7	19.3	18.1	15.8	14.8	15.8
55-64	12.8	13.1	13.1	12.1	12.4	11.7	10.6
65 and over	5.4	4.7	4.0	3.3	3.3	3.2	3.1
Female, Total	100.0	100.0	100.0	100.0	100.0	100.0	100.0
16-17	3.3	3.5	4.2	4.5	3.6	3.0	2.8
18-19	6.0	5.4	6.1	6.5	5.7	4.7	4.5
20-24	14.6	11.1	15.5	16.5	16.8	15.6	13.3
25-34	22.3	17.8	18.1	22.8	23.6	24.8	24.5
35-44	22.6	22.8	18.9	17.5	17.5	20.5	23.4
45-54	18.1	22.7	20.7	18.0	16.7	15.7	16.9
55-64	10.0	12.8	13.2	11.4	12.9	12.5	11.5
65 and over	3.2	3.9	3.3	2.8	3.2	3.2	3.2

Note: Data include Armed Forces. Projections are based on Series E (low series) population projections and do not reflect revisions in population projections shown elsewhere in this volume. New labor force projections were in preparation at press time and are scheduled for publication in late 1976

Source: Department of Labor

THE LABOR FORCE BY AGE AND SEX: ESTIMATES AND PROJECTIONS

Thousands of persons 16 years and over, except percent

Age and Sex	1960	1970	1980	1990	Percent Change		
					1960-1970	1970-1980	1980-1990
Both Sexes	72,142	85,903	101,809	112,576	19.1	18.5	10.6
16-19	5,246	7,645	8,337	7,089	45.7	9.1	−15.0
20-24	7,679	12,271	15,444	13,230	59.8	25.9	−14.3
25-34	15,070	17,678	26,779	30,531	17.3	51.5	14.0
35-44	16,648	16,789	18,720	27,617	.8	11.5	47.5
45-54	14,914	17,020	16,445	18,273	14.1	−3.4	11.1
55-64	9,391	11,280	12,787	12,310	20.1	13.4	−3.7
65 and over	3,194	3,220	3,297	3,526	.8	2.4	6.9
Male, Total	48,870	54,343	62,590	68,907	11.2	15.2	10.1
16-19	3,184	4,395	4,668	3,901	38.0	6.2	−16.4
20-24	5,089	7,378	8,852	7,404	45.0	20.0	−16.4
25-34	10,930	11,974	17,523	19,853	9.6	46.3	13.3
35-44	11,340	10,818	11,851	17,398	−4.6	9.5	46.8
45-54	9,634	10,487	9,908	10,909	8.9	−5.5	10.1
55-64	6,405	7,127	7,730	7,307	11.3	8.5	−5.5
65 and over	2,287	2,164	2,058	2,135	−5.4	−4.9	3.7
Female, Total	23,272	31,560	39,219	43,669	35.6	24.3	11.3
16-19	2,062	3,250	3,669	3,188	57.6	12.9	−13.1
20-24	2,590	4,893	6,592	5,826	88.9	34.7	−11.6
25-34	4,140	5,704	9,256	10,678	37.8	62.3	15.4
35-44	5,308	5,971	6,869	10,219	12.5	15.0	48.8
45-54	5,280	6,533	6,537	7,364	23.7	.1	12.7
55-64	2,986	4,153	5,057	5,003	39.1	21.8	−1.1
65 and over	907	1,056	1,239	1,391	16.4	17.3	12.3

Note: Data include Armed Forces. Projections are based on Series E (low series) population projections and do not reflect revisions in population projections that are shown elsewhere in this volume. New labor force projections were in preparation at press time and are scheduled for release in late 1976   Source: Department of Labor

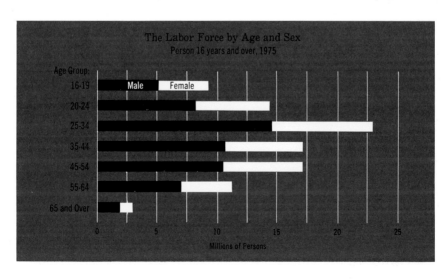

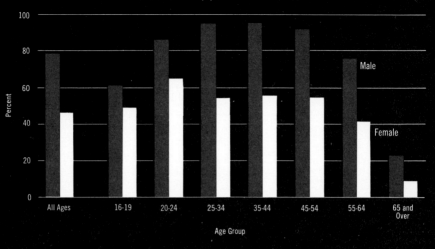

Labor Force Participation Rates
Percent of noninstitutional population in the labor force, 1975

LABOR FORCE PARTICIPATION RATES BY AGE, SEX AND RACE

Percent of total population 16 years and over in the labor force

Age, Sex, Race	1950	1960	1965	1970	1975	1980	1985
TOTAL	58.5	59.2	58.8	60.3	60.9	60.8	61.3
White	n.a.	58.8	58.5	60.2	61.1	n.a.	n.a.
Negro, Other	n.a.	63.0	62.1	61.1	58.7	n.a.	n.a.
MALE	84.3	82.4	80.1	79.2	77.2	78.0	78.3
White	n.a.	82.6	80.4	79.7	78.1	n.a.	n.a.
Negro, Other	n.a.	80.1	77.4	74.7	70.3	n.a.	n.a.
16-17	51.6	45.9	44.1	46.7	48.5	45.9	45.6
18-19	78.6	73.1	68.3	68.8	72.0	65.8	65.1
20-24	90.2	88.9	86.2	85.1	84.5	83.0	82.4
25-34	93.6	96.4	96.0	95.0	94.1	94.6	94.4
35-44	93.0	96.4	96.2	95.7	94.9	95.1	94.9
45-54	93.5	94.3	94.3	92.9	91.1	91.9	91.7
55-64	86.4	85.2	83.2	81.5	74.7	79.1	78.1
65 and over	41.9	32.2	26.9	25.8	20.8	21.2	20.0
FEMALE	33.3	37.1	38.8	42.8	45.8	45.0	45.6
White	n.a.	36.0	37.7	42.0	45.4	n.a.	n.a.
Negro, Other	n.a.	47.2	48.1	48.9	48.7	n.a.	n.a.
16-17	29.7	28.6	27.5	34.6	39.9	36.0	36.7
18-19	50.6	51.0	48.6	53.4	58.0	54.8	55.7
20-24	45.5	46.1	49.7	57.5	64.0	63.4	64.9
25-34	33.5	35.8	38.5	44.8	54.4	50.2	50.9
35-44	38.1	43.1	45.9	50.9	55.7	53.2	54.4
45-54	38.1	49.3	50.5	54.0	54.3	56.2	57.4
55-64	27.5	36.7	40.6	42.5	40.7	44.7	45.4
65 and over	8.9	10.5	9.5	9.2	7.8	8.6	8.5

Note: Projections are based on Series E (low series) population projections and do not reflect revisions in population projections that are shown elsewhere in this volume. New labor force projections were in preparation at press time and are scheduled for release in late 1976

n.a.—Not available

Source: Department of Labor

PARTICIPATION IN THE LABOR FORCE BY SEX AND AGE

Percent of noninstitutional population, 16 years and over

Age Group	Male			Female		
	1960	1970	1975	1960	1970	1975
TOTAL	84.0	80.6	78.5	37.8	43.4	46.4
16-17	46.8	47.5	49.0	29.1	34.9	40.2
18-19	73.6	69.9	73.0	51.1	53.7	58.3
20-24	90.2	86.6	85.9	46.2	57.8	64.3
25-34	97.7	96.6	95.5	36.0	45.0	54.6
35-44	97.7	97.0	95.8	43.5	51.1	55.8
45-54	95.8	94.3	92.1	49.8	54.4	54.6
55-64	86.8	83.0	75.8	37.2	43.0	41.0
65 and over	33.1	26.8	21.7	10.8	9.7	8.3

Note: The difference between these figures and the labor force participation rates found in table on page 90 is in the population base used. These data are based on the noninstitutional population, rather than the total population from which the others are derived

Source: Department of Labor

CIVILIAN LABOR FORCE BY SEX AND RACE

Thousands of persons 16 years and over

Year	Total	White		Negro, Other Races	
		Male	Female	Male	Female
1955	65,023	40,196	17,886	4,279	2,663
1956	66,552	40,734	18,693	4,359	2,768
1957	66,929	40,821	18,920	4,376	2,812
1958	67,639	41,080	19,213	4,442	2,905
1959	68,369	41,397	19,556	4,490	2,928
1960	69,628	41,742	20,171	4,645	3,069
1961	70,459	41,986	20,668	4,666	3,136
1962	70,614	41,931	20,819	4,668	3,195
1963	71,833	42,404	21,426	4,725	3,279
1964	73,091	42,893	22,028	4,785	3,384
1965	74,455	43,400	22,736	4,855	3,464
1966	75,770	43,572	23,702	4,899	3,597
1967	77,347	44,042	24,657	4,945	3,704
1968	78,737	44,554	25,424	4,979	3,780
1969	80,733	45,185	26,594	5,036	3,918
1970	82,715	46,013	27,505	5,182	4,015
1971	84,113	46,801	27,989	5,220	4,102
1972	86,542	47,930	29,028	5,335	4,249
1973	88,714	48,648	30,041	5,555	4,470
1974	91,011	49,486	31,192	5,700	4,633
1975	92,613	49,881	32,203	5,734	4,795

Source: Department of Labor

PROJECTIONS OF EMPLOYMENT BY REGIONS

Thousands of persons, except percent

Region	1970	Projections		Percent Change	
		1980	1990	1970-1980	1980-1990
TOTAL U.S.	79,307	96,114	106,388	21.2	10.7
Northeast.................	19,624	23,508	25,690	19.8	9.3
New England	4,889	5,897	6,464	20.6	9.6
Middle Atlantic	14,735	17,611	19,226	19.5	9.2
North Central	22,120	26,586	28,840	20.2	8.5
East North Central	15,730	19,200	20,955	22.1	9.1
West North Central.......	6,390	7,386	7,885	15.6	6.8
South	23,974	29,422	33,354	22.7	13.4
South Atlantic	12,170	15,273	17,577	25.5	15.1
East South Central	4,614	5,658	6,355	22.6	12.3
West South Central.......	4,190	8,491	9,422	18.1	11.0
West :....................	13,587	16,597	18,503	22.2	11.5
Mountain	3,124	3,895	4,377	24.7	12.4
Pacific	10,463	12,702	14,126	21.4	11.2

Note: Projections were prepared by the Bureau of Economic Analysis in conjunction with their projections of state and personal income (see pp. 122-123) and are based primarily on economic rather than demographic assumptions. Nationally, these projections assume an annual 2.9 percent growth in private output per man-hour and a 4 percent unemployment rate.

Source: Department of Commerce

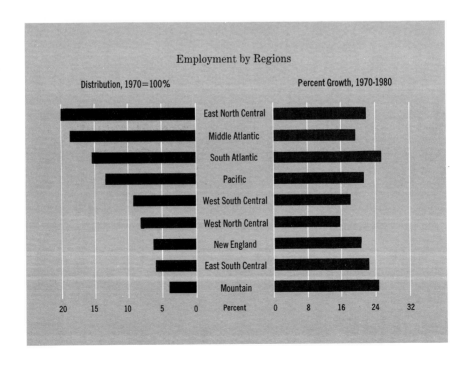

PROJECTIONS OF EMPLOYMENT BY STATES
Thousands of persons

State	1970	1980	1990
TOTAL U. S.	79,307	96,114	106,388
Alabama	1,235	1,474	1,633
Alaska	122	152	178
Arizona	648	883	1,057
Arkansas	664	796	884
California	7,900	9,658	10,785
Colorado	885	1,144	1,276
Connecticut	1,279	1,555	1,720
Delaware	219	274	311
District of Columbia	345	457	606
Florida	2,550	3,498	4,189
Georgia	1,843	2,298	2,632
Hawaii	338	404	460
Idaho	267	297	312
Illinois	4,519	5,449	5,919
Indiana	2,094	2,550	2,827
Iowa	1,108	1,262	1,308
Kansas	900	972	1,004
Kentucky	1,137	1,418	1,603
Louisiana	1,204	1,380	1,478
Maine	381	411	425
Maryland	1,618	1,972	2,259
Massachusetts	2,351	2,858	3,143
Michigan	3,308	4,108	4,530
Minnesota	1,494	1,824	2,032
Mississippi	748	876	941
Missouri	1,821	2,175	2,361
Montana	254	270	271
Nebraska	598	659	690
Nevada	209	284	344
New Hampshire	302	380	418
New Jersey	2,931	3,659	4,071
New Mexico	342	398	430
New York	7,209	8,550	9,356
North Carolina	2,104	2,580	2,901
North Dakota	219	225	222
Ohio	4,124	5,025	5,485
Oklahoma	974	1,136	1,249
Oregon	793	972	1,064
Pennsylvania	4,594	5,402	5,799
Rhode Island	406	486	526
South Carolina	1,033	1,235	1,369
South Dakota	250	269	268
Tennessee	1,495	1,891	2,178
Texas	4,348	5,180	5,812
Utah	389	479	544
Vermont	170	206	230
Virginia	1,903	2,320	2,646
Washington	1,311	1,516	1,638
West Virginia	554	638	663
Wisconsin	1,730	2,067	2,195
Wyoming	129	140	142

Note: See note to table on page 92 for a description of these projections
Source: Department of Commerce

EMPLOYED PERSONS BY OCCUPATION, SEX AND RACE, 1975

Thousands of persons 16 years and over

Occupation	Total	Sex		Race	
		Male	Female	White	Negro, Other
TOTAL EMPLOYED	84,783	51,230	33,553	75,713	9,070
White-Collar Workers	42,227	21,134	21,092	39,126	3,101
Professional, Technical	12,748	7,481	5,267	11,711	1,037
Managers, Administrators	8,891	7,162	1,729	8,493	398
Clerical Workers	15,128	3,355	11,772	13,705	1,423
Sales Workers..................	5,460	3,137	2,324	5,218	242
Blue-Collar Workers	27,962	23,220	4,742	24,568	3,394
Craft Workers.................	10,972	10,472	500	10,177	795
Operatives	12,856	8,971	3,885	11,042	1,814
Nonfarm Laborers	4,134	3,777	357	3,349	785
Service Workers.................	11,657	4,400	7,258	9,319	2,339
Private Household	1,171	29	1,141	728	443
Other Services	10,486	4,370	6,117	8,590	1,896
Farm Workers	2,936	2,476	460	2,700	237

Note: Civilian employment only

Source: Department of Labor

EMPLOYMENT BY OCCUPATION

Millions of persons

Occupation	1950	1960	1970	1975	1980	1985
TOTAL EMPLOYED	59.6	66.7	78.6	84.8	95.8	101.5
White-Collar Workers	22.4	28.7	38.0	42.2	49.4	53.7
Professional, Technical ...	4.5	7.5	11.1	12.7	15.0	17.0
Mgrs., Administrators	6.4	7.1	8.3	8.9	10.1	10.5
Clerical Workers	7.6	9.8	13.7	15.1	17.9	19.7
Sales Workers	3.8	4.4	4.9	5.5	6.3	6.5
Blue-Collar Workers	23.3	24.2	27.8	28.0	31.7	32.8
Craft Workers	7.7	8.6	10.2	11.0	12.2	13.0
Operatives	12.1	12.0	13.9	12.9	15.0	15.3
Nonfarm Laborers	3.5	3.7	3.7	4.1	4.5	4.5
Service Workers	6.5	8.3	9.7	11.7	12.7	13.4
Private Household	1.9	2.2	1.6	1.2	1.3	1.1
Other Services	4.7	6.1	8.2	10.5	11.4	12.3
Farm Workers............	7.4	5.4	3.1	2.9	2.0	1.6

Note: Data for 1950 and 1960 are for persons 14 years and over; later years refer to population 16 years and over. All years refer to civilian employment only. Projections are based on Series E (low) population projections and assume an annual 3 percent unemployment rate and an annual increase in real GNP of 4 percent to 1980 and 3.2 percent 1980-85. New labor force projections were in preparation at press time and are scheduled for publication in late 1976

Source: Department of Labor

DISTRIBUTION OF EMPLOYMENT BY OCCUPATION

Percent distribution

Occupation	1950	1960	1970	1975	1980	1985
TOTAL EMPLOYED	100.0	100.0	100.0	100.0	100.0	100.0
White-Collar Workers	37.5	43.1	48.3	49.8	51.5	52.9
Professional, Technical	7.5	11.2	14.2	15.0	15.7	16.8
Managers, Administrators	10.8	10.6	10.5	10.5	10.5	10.3
Clerical Workers	12.8	14.7	17.4	17.8	18.7	19.4
Sales Workers	6.4	6.6	6.2	6.4	6.6	6.4
Blue-Collar Workers	39.1	36.3	35.3	33.0	33.1	32.3
Craft Workers	12.9	12.8	12.9	12.9	12.8	12.8
Operatives	20.4	18.0	17.7	15.2	15.6	15.1
Nonfarm Laborers	5.9	5.5	4.7	4.9	4.7	4.4
Service Workers	11.0	12.5	12.4	13.7	13.3	13.2
Private Household	3.2	3.3	2.0	1.4	1.3	1.1
Other Services..................	7.8	9.2	10.4	12.4	12.0	12.9
Farm Workers	12.4	8.1	4.0	3.5	2.1	1.6

Note: Data for 1950 and 1960 are for persons 14 years and over; later years refer to population 16 years and over. All years refer to civilian employment only. See also footnote to table on preceding page

Source: Department of Labor

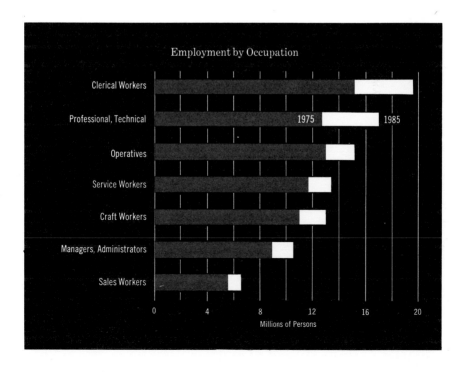

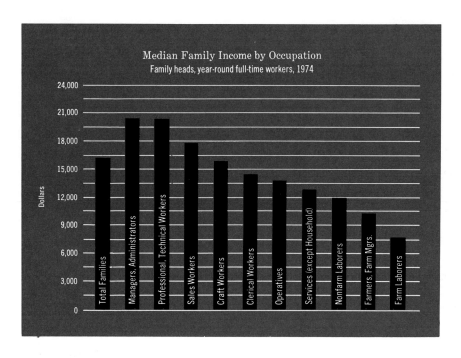

Median Family Income by Occupation
Family heads, year-round full-time workers, 1974

MEDIAN FAMILY INCOME BY OCCUPATION OF HEAD, 1974

| | Total Families | | Head, Full-Time Worker[1] | |
Occupation of Family Head	Number (Thousands)	Median Income (Dollars)	Percent of all Families	Median Income (Dollars)
TOTAL[2]	55,712	12,836	62.4	16,072
Professional, Technical Workers ...	6,312	19,441	86.2	20,361
Self-Employed	681	23,553	75.0	27,963
Salaried	5,632	19,202	87.6	20,035
Managers, Administrators	6,364	19,707	90.2	20,396
Self-Employed	1,218	15,278	83.7	16,521
Salaried	5,146	20,506	91.7	21,057
Clerical Workers	3,361	13,325	79.5	14,407
Sales Workers...................	2,481	16,593	81.8	17,761
Craft Workers...................	8,336	14,838	80.6	15,798
Operatives.....................	6,691	12,894	76.5	13,775
Nonfarm Laborers...............	1,831	10,979	68.6	11,952
Private Household Workers	166	4,166	24.5	[3]
Other Service Workers...........	3,224	11,098	71.9	12,842
Farmers, Farm Managers	1,254	9,498	80.6	10,234
Farm Labor.....................	398	7,164	70.0	7,717

[1] Year-round; excludes Armed Forces
[2] Total also includes families with head unemployed, in Armed Forces, and not in the labor force
[3] Not calculated because of insufficient numbers   Source: Department of Commerce

EDUCATIONAL ATTAINMENT OF EMPLOYEES, 1975

Employed civilian labor force 16 years and over

Occupation	Males: Percent With			Females: Percent With		
	No High School Diploma	4 Years High School Only	4 Years College or More	No High School Diploma	4 Years High School Only	4 Years College or More
ALL OCCUPATIONS	29.3	36.3	18.5	25.2	45.0	14.1
Professional, Technical	3.1	13.5	66.1	3.3	17.7	60.5
Managers, Administrators	12.3	34.7	31.0	16.4	44.1	18.9
Sales Workers	13.9	34.5	25.1	26.7	51.0	6.6
Clerical Workers	17.0	43.8	12.3	11.7	61.0	6.2
Craft Workers	34.6	49.4	3.2	34.4	50.7	4.1
Operatives (exc. Transport) ...	46.0	42.2	1.7	55.8	38.3	1.2
Transport Equip. Operatives ..	46.6	42.0	2.2	34.2	57.2	.8
Nonfarm Laborers	54.0	33.8	2.2	41.2	47.8	2.2
Private Household Workers ...	} 44.0	36.0	4.6	{ 70.1	24.7	.9
Other Service Workers				43.3	43.7	2.0
Farm Workers	53.7	32.4	5.1	40.5	41.7	4.7

Source: Department of Labor

USUAL WEEKLY EARNINGS BY OCCUPATION

Full-time wage and salary workers, May 1975

Occupation	Workers (Thousands)	Median Earnings (Dollars)	Occupation	Workers (Thousands)	Median Earnings (Dollars)
ALL OCCUPATIONS .	61,765	185	Operatives (exc. trans.)..	8,169	157
			Motor Vehicles, etc. ..	414	222
White-Collar Workers	31,660	204	Other Durable Ind.....	3,457	165
Professional, Tech. ...	10,272	246	Nondurable Industry ···	2,654	129
Engineers	1,175	350	Mine Workers	229	245
Medical Personnel ..	1,125	223	Other Industry	1,415	145
Teachers (exc. coll.)	2,582	217			
Other Professions ..	5,090	252e	Transport Operatives ...	2,518	198
			Drivers	2,108	197
Mgrs, Administrators	6,897	274	Others	411	201
Clerical Workers	11,286	150	Nonfarm Laborers	2,955	154
Steno, Secretaries ..	3,428	143	Construction..........	684	164
Other Clerical	7,858	155	Manufacturing	815	157
			Other Industries	1,456	147
Sales Workers	3,205	189			
Retail Sales	1,430	119	Service Workers	6,299	120
Other Sales	1,776	257	Private Household	326	54
Blue-Collar Workers ..	23,045	186	Other Services	5,973	123
Craft Workers.......	9,403	223	Protective	1,060	228
Carpenters	709	213	Cleaning	1,408	128
Construction	1,772	236	Food	1,633	96
Foremen	1,388	250	Health	1,307	118
Machinists	511	215	Personal	566	118
Mechanics, auto	919	196			
Mechanics, other ...	1,571	216			
Metal Craftsmen ...	509	237	Farm Workers	761	111
Other Craftsmen ...	2,024	218	Farm Laborers	723	109

Note: Data refer to earnings usually received each week by full-time wage and salary workers at their principal job, and not to earnings for a specific calendar week. Median earnings are calculated on the basis of those reporting and not total workers
e—Estimate   Source: Department of Labor

EMPLOYMENT STATUS: HIGH SCHOOL GRADUATES AND DROPOUTS

Persons 16-21 years not enrolled in college, in thousands except percent

Characteristic	Graduates			Dropouts		
	1965	1970	1974	1965	1970	1974
TOTAL	4,898	5,823	7,406	2,986	2,757	3,266
Percent of Population[1]	62.1	67.9	69.4	37.9	32.1	30.6
Not in Labor Force..................	1,129	1,257	1,225	1,123	1,146	1,134
In Labor Force	3,769	4,566	6,181	1,863	1,611	2,132
Percent of Total	76.9	78.4	83.5	62.4	58.4	65.3
Percent Distribution	100.0	100.0	100.0	100.0	100.0	100.0
Male	42.9	43.1	48.8	67.9	63.6	65.5
Female	57.1	56.9	51.2	32.1	36.4	34.5
White	89.5	89.0	89.4	78.9	77.2	82.5
Negro, Other Races	10.5	11.0	10.6	21.1	22.8	17.5
Employed	91.6	88.4	89.0	85.1	78.5	78.0
Unemployed	8.4	11.6	11.0	14.9	21.5	22.0

Note: Data refer to the civilian noninstitutional population and are as of October

[1] Total population 16-21 years not enrolled

Source: Department of Labor

FULL-TIME AND PART-TIME EMPLOYMENT, 1975

Thousands of nonagricultural workers 16 years and over

Race, Age and Marital Status	Male Workers		Female Workers	
	Full-Time	Part-Time	Full-Time	Part-Time
TOTAL	40,663	3,310	21,663	7,270
Race				
White	36,814	2,986	18,876	6,605
Negro, Other Races	3,849	324	2,787	665
Age Group				
16-17	294	919	186	916
18-24	6,151	1,092	4,836	1,439
25-44	19,773	371	9,326	2,587
45-64	13,713	368	6,935	1,884
65 and over	729	560	378	445
Marital Status				
Single	6,243	2,062	4,709	2,090
Married[1]......................	31,865	1,070	12,505	4,281
Other	1,705	140	3,492	745

Note: Full-time workers are those who worked 35 hours or more during the survey week, as well as those usually working full time but who worked part time in survey week for temporary noneconomic reasons. *Part-time workers* are those voluntarily working less than 35 hours per week. Not included in table are persons working part time for economic reasons (slack work, jobs started or terminated during survey week, etc.)

[1] Spouse present

Source: Department of Labor

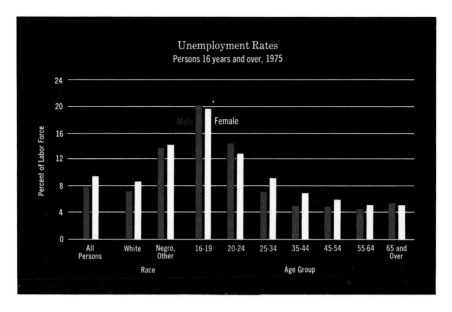

Unemployment Rates
Persons 16 years and over, 1975

CHARACTERISTICS OF THE UNEMPLOYED, 1975

Persons 16 years and over

Characteristic	Number Un-employed (Thou-sands)	Un-employ-ment Rate[1] (Per-cent)	Characteristic	Number Un-employed (Thou-sands)	Un-employ-ment Rate[1] (Per-cent)
TOTAL	7,830	8.5	55-64	216	5.1
			65 and over	52	5.1
Male	4,385	7.9			
Female	3,445	9.3	Occupation[2]		
			Professional, Technical	425	3.2
White	6,371	7.8	Mgrs, Administrators ..	276	3.0
Negro, Other Races ...	1,459	13.9	Clerical...............	1,063	6.6
			Sales	336	5.8
Age: Males			Craft Workers	994	8.3
16-19	957	20.1	Operatives	1,955	13.8
20-24	1,059	14.3	Nonfarm Laborers	756	15.6
25-34	963	7.0	Private Household	67	5.4
35-44	502	4.9	Other Service Workers	1,024	8.9
45-54	501	4.8	Farmers, Farm Labor	108	3.5
55-64	300	4.3			
65 and over	103	5.4			
			Marital Status		
Age: Females			Male: Single	1,939	16.1
16-19	795	19.7	Married[3]	2,044	5.1
20-24	769	12.7	Other	401	11.0
25-34	773	9.1	Female: Single	1,164	13.0
35-44	445	6.9	Married[3]	1,680	7.9
45-54	394	5.9	Other	601	8.9

[1] Percent of civilian labor force
[2] Experienced workers
[3] Spouse present

Source: Department of Labor

Married Women in the Labor Force

Participation
Rate

Married Women
in Labor Force

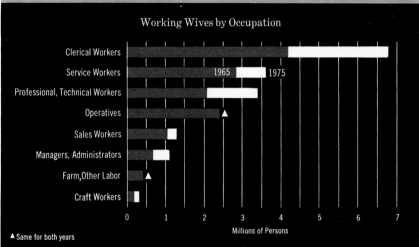

Working Wives by Occupation

Clerical Workers
Service Workers
Professional, Technical Workers
Operatives
Sales Workers
Managers, Administrators
Farm, Other Labor
Craft Workers

1965   1975

▲ Same for both years

Millions of Persons

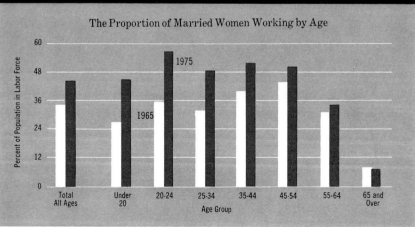

The Proportion of Married Women Working by Age

Percent of Population in Labor Force

1975

1965

| Total All Ages | Under 20 | 20-24 | 25-34 | 35-44 | 45-54 | 55-64 | 65 and Over |

Age Group

MARRIED WOMEN IN THE LABOR FORCE BY PRESENCE OF CHILDREN

Year	Total Married Women[1]	Presence of Children Under 18 Years		
		None Present	6-17 Years Only	Any Under 6 Years
Labor Force (Thousands)				
1950	8,550	4,946	2,205	1,399
1955	10,423	5,227	3,183	2,012
1960	12,253	5,692	4,087	2,474
1965	14,708	6,755	4,836	3,117
1970	18,377	8,174	6,289	3,914
1975	21,111	9,702	6,970	4,439
Participation Rate[2]				
1950	23.8	30.3	28.3	11.9
1955	27.7	32.7	34.7	16.2
1960	30.5	34.7	39.0	18.6
1965	34.7	38.3	42.7	23.3
1970	40.8	42.2	49.2	30.3
1975	44.4	43.9	52.3	36.6

[1] Husband present   [2] Percent of noninstitutional population in the labor force   Source: Department of Labor

MARRIED WOMEN IN THE LABOR FORCE BY AGE

Percent of each age group participating

Age Group	1950	1955	1960	1965	1970	1975
TOTAL, ALL AGES	23.8	27.7	30.5	34.7	40.8	44.4
Under 20	24.0	19.8	25.3	27.0	36.0	45.6
20-24	28.5	29.4	30.0	35.6	47.4	57.1
25-34	23.8	26.0	27.7	32.1	39.3	48.3
35-44	28.5	33.7	36.2	40.6	47.2	52.1
45-64	21.8	29.0	34.2	39.0	44.1	44.1
65 and over	6.4	7.5	5.9	7.6	7.9	7.2

Note: Data refer to married women with husband present. Figures for 1965 and earlier refer to persons 14 years and over; later years relate to the population 16 years and over   Source: Department of Labor

WORKING WIVES BY OCCUPATION

Percent distribution of employed married women, husband present

Occupation	1950	1955	1960	1965	1970	1975
TOTAL (Millions)	8.0	10.0	11.6	14.0	17.5	19.3
PERCENT DISTRIBUTION	100.0	100.0	100.0	100.0	100.0	100.0
Professional, Technical	9.5	10.5	13.0	14.7	15.4	17.6
Managers, Administrators	7.0	4.6	5.0	4.7	4.7	5.6
Clerical Workers	32.4	25.4	28.3	30.2	33.6	35.0
Sales Workers		9.4	8.4	8.1	7.1	6.8
Craft Workers	1.2	1.3	1.0	1.3	1.3	1.6
Operatives	23.1	21.8	18.6	17.5	16.3	12.5
Service Workers	20.2	19.1	22.1	20.6	19.5	18.8
Farm, Other Labor	6.6	7.9	3.6	3.0	2.1	2.0

Source: Department of Labor

POPULATION AND LABOR FORCE BY MARITAL STATUS AND SEX

Thousands of persons, except percent

	Male			Female		
		Labor Force			Labor Force	
Year and Marital Status	Civilian Population	Number	Percent of Population	Civilian Population	Number	Percent of Population
Single						
1950	14,212	8,898	62.6	11,126	5,621	50.5
1955	13,522	8,276	61.2	10,962	5,087	46.4
1960	15,274	8,473	55.5	12,252	5,401	44.1
1965	17,338	8,719	50.3	14,607	5,912	40.5
1970	15,722	9,545	60.7	13,141	6,965	53.0
1975	18,244	12,233	67.1	14,915	8,464	56.7
Married[1]						
1950	35,925	32,912	91.6	35,925	8,550	23.8
1955	37,570	34,064	90.7	37,570	10,423	27.7
1960	40,205	35,757	88.9	40,205	12,253	30.5
1965	42,367	37,140	87.7	42,367	14,708	34.7
1970	45,055	39,138	86.9	45,055	18,377	40.8
1975	47,547	39,516	83.1	47,547	21,111	44.4
Other						
1950	4,149	2,616	63.1	9,584	3,624	37.8
1955	4,902	2,976	60.7	11,718	4,643	39.6
1960	4,794	2,845	59.3	12,150	4,861	40.0
1965	5,438	3,032	55.8	13,717	5,332	38.9
1970	5,416	2,938	54.2	15,065	5,891	39.1
1975	6,270	4,091	65.2	17,015	6,932	40.7

Note: Data for 1965 and earlier refer to persons 14 years and over; later figures are for population 16 years and over
[1] Spouse present   Source: Department of Labor

FAMILIES WITH MEMBERS IN THE LABOR FORCE

Percent distribution of husband-wife families

Year	Total Families[1] (Millions)	Percent With Family Member in Labor Force				No Member in Labor Force
		Total	Wife Only	Wife and Other	Other Only	
1955	34.1	39.9	23.9	4.9	11.2	60.1
1960	35.0	43.0	25.8	6.2	11.1	57.0
1965	36.5	47.4	29.6	7.3	10.5	52.6
1966	36.8	48.7	29.8	8.2	10.7	51.3
1967	37.1	50.4	30.7	8.8	10.9	49.6
1968	37.7	50.7	32.6	8.3	9.8	49.3
1969	38.1	51.8	33.4	8.9	9.4	48.2
1970	38.6	53.1	34.5	9.3	9.3	46.9
1971	38.5	53.5	34.7	9.2	9.6	46.5
1972	39.1	54.6	35.1	9.9	9.6	45.4
1973	39.3	55.7	36.0	9.8	9.9	44.3
1974	39.3	57.2	37.4	9.9	9.8	42.8
1975	39.1	58.5	38.8	10.3	9.5	41.5

[1] With head in the labor force   Source: Department of Labor

MULTIEARNER FAMILIES BY INCOME CLASS, 1974

Family Characteristic	Total Families (Millions)	Percent Distribution by Income Class					
		Under $3,000	$3,000- 5,000	$5,000- 7,000	$7,000- 10,000	$10,000- 15,000	$15,000 and Over
ALL FAMILIES	55.7	5.3	7.7	8.8	13.8	24.3	39.8
No Earners	6.2	22.1	30.5	21.8	13.8	8.1	3.8
One Earner	19.6	6.1	8.7	11.4	17.8	28.5	27.5
Two Earners	22.0	1.6	3.0	5.5	13.2	28.1	48.6
Three Earners	5.3	.7	1.3	2.4	6.6	19.7	69.2
Four Earners or more	2.7	.6	.7	1.5	4.2	10.9	82.2
HUSBAND-WIFE FAMILIES	47.0	3.3	5.9	7.8	13.3	25.7	44.2
No Earners	4.3	13.5	29.0	25.3	16.9	10.3	4.8
One Earner	15.6	3.7	6.3	9.7	17.3	30.9	32.1
Head only	14.0	3.7	5.7	8.9	16.5	31.4	33.9
Two Earners	19.9	1.3	2.4	4.8	12.5	28.4	50.5
Head, Wife only	16.7	1.2	2.5	4.9	13.0	29.1	49.4
Three Earners or more	7.2	.5	.8	1.5	4.9	16.0	76.3

Source: Department of Commerce

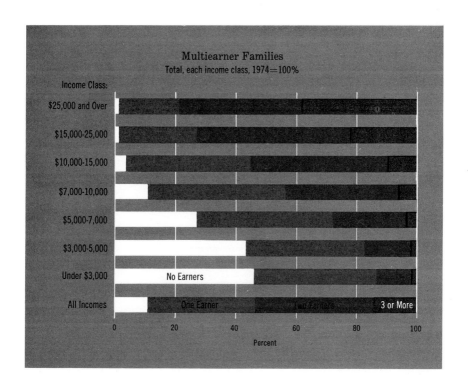

AGE AND RACE OF FAMILIES BY WORK EXPERIENCE OF WIFE, 1974

Race and Age of Head	Husband-Wife Families (Thousands)				Median Family Income (Dollars)	
		Only Husband Worked	Both Spouses Worked		Only Husband Worked	Both Spouses Worked
	Total		Number	Percent		
WHITE, TOTAL	42,969	12,958	20,101	46.8	12,541	16,553
Under 25	3,053	781	2,215	72.6	7,759	10,626
25-34	9,924	3,902	5,776	58.2	12,789	15,228
35-44	8,155	2,598	4,310	52.8	14,463	18,192
45-54	8,792	1,982	4,519	51.4	13,556	19,771
55-64	6,871	2,382	2,691	39.2	12,694	18,157
65 and over	6,175	1,313	590	9.6	8,350	12,763
NEGRO, TOTAL	3,346	824	1,821	54.4	8,555	13,316
Under 25	291	96	179	61.5	6,121	8,989
25-34	784	210	545	69.5	9,093	14,193
35-44	718	182	454	63.2	9,777	13,891
45-54	626	130	353	56.4	10,280	15,411
55-64	502	145	223	44.4	7,697	11,939
65 and over	425	61	68	16.0	[1]	[1]

Note: Wives with work experience are those having any paid civilian employment at any time during the year

[1] Not computed because of insufficient sample

Source: Department of Commerce

EARNINGS OF WIFE BY EARNINGS OF HUSBAND, 1974

Husband-wife families

Earnings of Wife	Total Families	Total with Earnings	Earnings of Husband				
			Under $5,000	$5,000- 7,000	$7,000- 10,000	$10,000- 15,000	$15,000 and Over
TOTAL (Millions) ...	47.0	40.6	5.9	3.7	7.4	12.5	11.1
PERCENT DISTRIBUTION	100.0	100.0	100.0	100.0	100.0	100.0	100.0
No Earnings	49.5	45.3	47.5	38.9	37.2	43.6	53.5
Under $1,000	9.5	10.2	11.4	12.4	10.7	9.8	9.0
$1,000-3,000	10.8	11.7	13.7	14.2	13.1	11.4	9.2
3,000-5,000	9.7	10.6	10.7	14.5	14.1	9.7	7.8
5,000-7,000	8.4	9.1	7.9	11.0	12.0	10.0	6.1
7,000-10,000	7.7	8.4	6.2	6.3	9.6	10.2	7.5
10,000 and over	4.3	4.7	2.6	2.7	3.3	5.2	6.9

Source: Department of Commerce

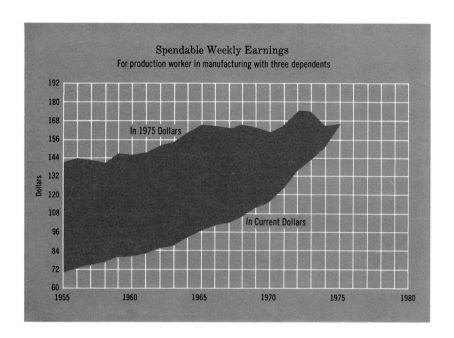

Spendable Weekly Earnings
For production worker in manufacturing with three dependents

GROSS AND SPENDABLE WEEKLY EARNINGS IN MANUFACTURING

In dollars

Year	Gross Average Weekly Earnings		Spendable Average Weekly Earnings[1]	
	Current Dollars	1975 Dollars	Current Dollars	1975 Dollars
1955........................	75.70	152.16	69.79	140.28
1960........................	89.72	163.05	80.11	145.60
1961........................	92.34	166.13	82.18	147.85
1962........................	96.56	171.81	85.53	152.17
1963........................	99.63	175.14	87.58	153.96
1964........................	102.97	178.67	92.18	159.94
1965........................	107.53	183.43	96.78	165.08
1966........................	112.34	186.31	99.45	164.92
1967........................	114.90	185.22	101.26	163.23
1968........................	122.51	189.52	106.75	165.15
1969........................	129.51	190.14	111.44	163.60
1970........................	133.73	185.36	115.90	160.65
1971........................	142.44	189.30	124.24	165.10
1972........................	154.69	199.02	135.56	174.40
1973........................	166.06	201.11	143.20	173.44
1974........................	176.40	192.52	151.25	165.07
1975........................	189.51	189.51	165.33	165.33

[1] Refers to earnings of a production or nonsupervisory worker with three dependents after deduction of social security taxes and federal income taxes

Source: Department of Labor

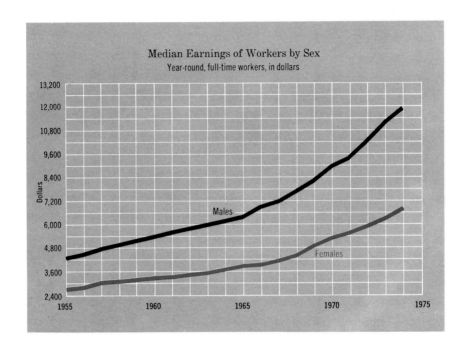

Median Earnings of Workers by Sex
Year-round, full-time workers, in dollars

NONAGRICULTURAL EMPLOYMENT BY INDUSTRY

Thousands of persons

Industry	1950	1960	1965	1970	1974	1975
TOTAL	45,222	54,234	60,815	70,920	78,334	79,985
Mining	901	712	632	623	672	745
Contract Construction	2,333	2,885	3,186	3,536	3,985	3,457
Manufacturing	15,241	16,796	18,062	19,349	20,016	18,347
Durable Goods	8,094	9,459	10,406	11,195	11,837	10,679
Nondurable Goods	7,147	7,336	7,656	8,154	8,179	7,668
Transportation, Public Utilities	4,034	4,004	4,036	4,504	4,699	4,498
Wholesale, Retail Trade	9,386	11,391	12,716	15,040	17,011	16,947
Wholesale Trade	2,518	3,004	3,312	3,816	4,259	4,177
Retail Trade	6,868	8,388	9,404	11,225	12,751	12,771
Finance, Insurance, Real Estate	1,919	2,669	3,023	3,687	4,161	4,223
Services	5,382	7,423	9,087	11,621	13,506	13,995
Government	6,026	8,353	10,074	12,561	14,285	14,773
Federal	1,928	2,270	2,378	2,731	2,724	2,748
State and Local	4,098	6,083	7,696	9,830	11,560	12,025

Source: Department of Labor

MEDIAN EARNINGS OF WORKERS BY SEX

Wage or salary income of year-round, full-time workers, in dollars

Year	Median Earnings Men	Median Earnings Women	Women's Earnings as Percent of Men's	Year	Median Earnings Men	Median Earnings Women	Women's Earnings as Percent of Men's
1955	4,252	2,719	63.9	1965	6,375	3,823	60.0
1956	4,466	2,827	63.3	1966	6,848	3,973	58.0
1957	4,713	3,008	63.8	1967	7,182	4,150	57.8
1958	4,927	3,102	63.0	1968	7,664	4,457	58.2
1959	5,209	3,193	61.3	1969	8,227	4,977	60.5
1960	5,417	3,293	60.8	1970	8,966	5,323	59.4
1961	5,644	3,351	59.4	1971	9,399	5,593	59.5
1962	5,794	3,446	59.5	1972	10,202	5,903	57.9
1963	5,978	3,561	59.6	1973	11,186	6,335	56.6
1964	6,195	3,690	59.6	1974	11,835	6,772	57.2

Note: Data beginning 1970 includes earnings of self-employed persons

Source: Department of Commerce

TOTAL EMPLOYMENT BY SECTOR: ESTIMATES AND PROJECTIONS

Thousands of persons, except percent

Industry	1965	1972	1980	1985	Average Annual Rate of Change 1972-80	Average Annual Rate of Change 1980-85
TOTAL	74,552	86,551	101,861	109,466	2.1	1.5
Agriculture	3,816	3,450	2,750	2,300	−2.5	−3.5
Mining	667	660	785	820	2.2	.9
Contract Construction	4,000	4,694	5,180	5,800	1.2	2.3
Manufacturing	18,452	19,493	21,871	22,530	1.4	.6
Durable Goods	10,624	11,232	13,087	13,599	1.9	.8
Nondurable Goods	7,828	8,261	8,784	8,931	.8	.3
Transportation, Communication, Public Utilities	4,249	4,725	5,219	5,421	1.3	.8
Wholesale, Retail Trade	15,334	18,751	22,504	23,228	2.3	.6
Wholesale Trade	3,596	4,244	5,142	5,221	2.4	.3
Retail Trade	11,738	14,507	17,362	18,007	2.3	.7
Finance, Insurance, Real Estate	3,369	4,310	5,415	5,989	2.9	2.0
Services[1]	14,069	17,106	21,332	24,078	2.8	2.5
Government[2]	10,074	13,340	16,800	19,300	2.9	2.8

Note: Employment data are on a jobs concept (persons holding more than one job are counted in each job held), and include wage and salary workers, the self-employed and unpaid family workers. Projections assume an annual growth in gross national product of 3.92 percent from 1972-1980 and 3.57 percent from 1980-1985. A 4 percent unemployment rate by 1985 (declining from 8.5 percent in 1975) is also an underlying assumption. These projections are part of a revised series to be published in late 1976, and are not consistent with projections shown elsewhere in this chapter

[1] Includes paid household employment
[2] Includes government enterprise employees

Source: Department of Labor

EMPLOYMENT, HOURS AND EARNINGS BY STATES, 1975

State	Employ-ment (Thou-sands)	Average Weekly Hours	Average Hourly Earnings (Dollars)	Average Weekly Earnings (Dollars)
TOTAL U.S.	76,985	39.4	4.81	189.51
Alabama	1,150	39.6	4.13	163.55
Alaska	162	n.a.	n.a.	n.a.
Arizona	724	39.0	4.85	189.15
Arkansas	620	38.8	3.59	139.29
California	7,815	39.5	5.21	205.80
Colorado	948	n.a.	n.a.	n.a.
Connecticut	1,220	40.5	4.78	193.59
Delaware	227	39.5	5.07	200.27
District of Columbia[1]	578	38.5	5.52	212.52
Florida	2,730	39.7	4.04	160.39
Georgia	1,725	39.2	3.88	152.10
Hawaii	339	39.2	4.62	181.10
Idaho	268	38.9	4.72	183.61
Illinois	4,425	39.7	5.40	214.50
Indiana	1,930	39.8	5.49	218.50
Iowa	993	39.7	5.40	214.38
Kansas	797	40.8	4.65	189.98
Kentucky	1,042	38.8	4.65	180.42
Louisiana	1,199	41.1	4.81	197.69
Maine	356	39.9	3.81	152.02
Maryland	1,424	39.1	5.03	196.67
Massachusetts	2,328	39.1	4.47	174.78
Michigan	3,127	40.8	6.15	250.76
Minnesota	1,470	39.3	5.10	200.43
Mississippi	667	39.3	3.55	139.52
Missouri	1,719	39.0	4.75	185.25
Montana	240	36.8	5.32	195.78
Nebraska	554	40.7	4.51	183.68
Nevada	264	38.2	5.26	200.93
New Hampshire	293	39.0	3.95	154.05
New Jersey	2,668	40.5	4.93	199.99
New Mexico	365	39.1	3.67	143.50
New York	6,791	38.9	4.91	191.00
North Carolina	1,996	38.5	3.51	135.14
North Dakota	197	39.6	4.32	171.07
Ohio	4,010	40.3	5.55	223.67
Oklahoma	887	40.1	4.41	176.84
Oregon	831	38.4	5.54	212.74
Pennsylvania	4,416	38.5	4.96	190.96
Rhode Island	343	38.9	3.84	149.04
South Carolina	978	39.4	3.59	141.45
South Dakota	208	41.0	4.20	172.20
Tennessee	1,497	39.8	3.92	156.02
Texas	4,413	40.6	4.57	185.54
Utah	n.a.	38.4	4.05	155.52
Vermont	159	40.4	4.07	164.43
Virginia	1,755	39.2	3.99	156.41
Washington	1,209	38.7	5.79	224.07
West Virginia	561	38.8	4.90	190.12
Wisconsin	1,670	40.4	5.26	212.25
Wyoming	143	40.1	5.11	205.07

Note: Employment figures are for all employees on nonagricultural payrolls while data for hours and earnings refer to production workers on manufacturing payrolls only

[1] Hours and earnings data refer to entire Washington SMSA and employment data include Federal employees in Maryland and Virginia sectors of Washington SMSA

n.a.-Not available

Source: Department of Labor

Hourly Earnings by States
Production workers in manufacturing, 1975

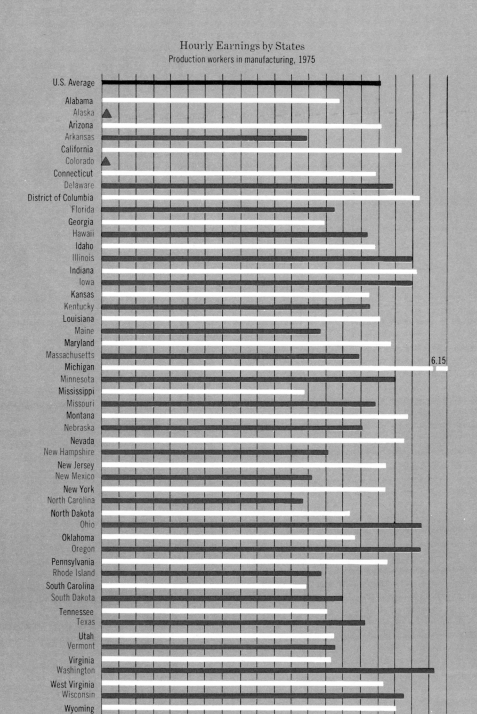

Not available

HOURS AND EARNINGS IN MANUFACTURING

Production workers

Year	Average Weekly Hours	Average Hourly Earnings (Dollars)	Year	Average Weekly Hours	Average Hourly Earnings (Dollars)
1950	40.5	1.44	1963	40.5	2.46
1951	40.6	1.56	1964	40.7	2.53
1952	40.7	1.65			
1953	40.5	1.74	1965	41.2	2.61
1954	39.6	1.78	1966	41.3	2.72
			1967	40.6	2.83
1955	40.7	1.86	1968	40.7	3.01
1956	40.4	1.95	1969	40.6	3.19
1957	39.8	2.05			
1958	39.2	2.11	1970	39.8	3.36
1959	40.3	2.19	1971	39.9	3.57
			1972	40.6	3.81
1960	39.7	2.26	1973	40.7	4.08
1961	39.8	2.32	1974	40.0	4.41
1962	40.4	2.39	1975	39.4	4.81

Source: Department of Labor

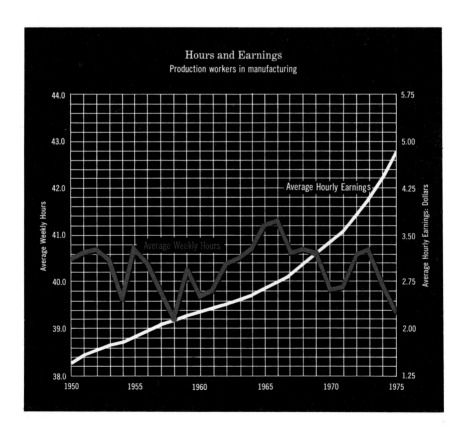

Hours and Earnings
Production workers in manufacturing

EMPLOYMENT, HOURS AND EARNINGS BY INDUSTRY, 1975

Industry	Employment (Thousands)	Average Weekly Hours	Average Hourly Earnings (Dollars)	Average Weekly Earnings (Dollars)
TOTAL	76,985	36.1	4.54	163.89
Mining	745	42.3	5.90	249.57
Contract Construction	3,457	36.6	7.25	265.35
Manufacturing	18,347	39.4	4.81	189.51
Durables	10,679	39.9	5.14	205.09
Ordnance and accessories	171	41.3	5.23	216.00
Lumber and wood products	557	39.1	4.28	167.35
Furniture and fixtures	451	37.9	3.75	142.13
Stone, clay, and glass products	614	40.6	4.89	198.53
Primary metal industries	1,180	40.0	6.17	246.80
Fabricated metal industries	1,336	40.0	5.04	201.60
Machinery, except electrical	2,069	40.9	5.36	219.22
Electrical equipment, supplies	1,761	39.5	4.58	180.91
Transportation equipment	1,649	40.3	6.02	242.61
Instruments, related products	489	39.5	4.56	180.12
Misc. manufacturing industries	404	38.3	3.79	145.16
Nondurables	7,668	38.8	4.35	168.78
Food and kindred products	1,676	40.3	4.57	184.17
Tobacco manufactures	78	38.0	4.51	171.38
Textile mill products	902	39.2	3.40	133.28
Apparel, other textile products	1,235	35.1	3.19	111.97
Paper and allied products	643	41.6	4.99	207.58
Printing and publishing	1,079	37.0	5.36	198.32
Chemicals and allied products	1,012	40.9	5.37	219.63
Petroleum and coal products	197	41.6	6.42	267.07
Rubber and plastics products	588	39.7	4.35	172.70
Leather and leather products	257	37.4	3.23	120.80
Wholesale and Retail Trade	16,947	33.8	3.75	126.75
Wholesale trade	4,177	38.6	4.89	188.75
Retail trade[1]	12,771	32.4	3.34	108.22
Retail general merchandise	2,469	31.1	3.21	99.82
Food stores	1,950	32.3	3.95	127.59
Finance, Insurance, Real Estate[1]	4,223	36.5	4.13	150.75
Banking	1,274	36.3	3.55	128.87
Insurance carriers	1,105	37.0	4.32	159.84
Services[1]	13,995	33.8	4.06	137.23
Hotels, tourist courts, motels[2]	805	31.9	2.81	89.64
Personal services	835	n.a.	n.a.	n.a.
Medical, other health services	4,194	n.a.	n.a.	n.a.
Educational services	1,216	n.a.	n.a.	n.a.
Transportation, Public Utilities	4,498	39.6	5.92	234.43
Government	14,773	- -	- -	- -

Note: Employment figures refer to total nonagricultural payrolls while hours and earnings data are for the private sector only

[1] Total includes categories not separately listed
[2] Earnings represent money payments only; tips not included
n.a.—Not available

Source: Department of Labor

EMPLOYMENT AND EARNINGS IN MAJOR METROPOLITAN AREAS, 1975

Metropolitan Area	Employ-ment (Thou-sands)	Average Weekly Hours	Average Hourly Earnings (Dollars)	Average Weekly Earnings (Dollars)
Albany,-Schenectady-Troy, N.Y...........	305	39.8	5.01	199.40
Anaheim-Santa Ana-Garden Grove, Calif.	572	40.1	4.83	193.68
Atlanta, Ga............................	734	38.8	4.64	180.03
Baltimore, Md.	844	39.3	5.25	206.33
Boston, Mass.	1,301	39.4	4.90	193.06
Buffalo, N. Y..........................	481	40.0	5.91	236.40
Chicago, Ill...........................	2,986	n.a.	n.a.	n.a.
Cincinnati, Ohio	532	40.8	5.17	210.94
Cleveland, Ohio	849	40.3	5.64	227.29
Columbus, Ohio	446	39.5	5.24	206.98
Dallas-Fort Worth, Tex.................	1,077	40.3	4.32	174.10
Dayton, Ohio	319	41.2	5.75	236.90
Denver, Colo.	604	n.a.	n.a.	n.a.
Detroit, Mich..........................	1,567	41.0	6.50	266.66
Greensboro-Winston Salem-etc., N.C.	328	38.5	3.84	147.84
Hartford, Conn.	337	n.a.	n.a.	n.a.
Houston, Tex..........................	997	42.6	5.30	225.78
Indianapolis, Ind.	448	40.2	5.50	221.10
Kansas City, Mo.......................	540	39.5	5.35	211.33
Los Angeles-Long Beach, Calif.	3,047	39.6	4.91	194.44
Louisville, Ky.	349	39.3	5.46	214.58
Memphis, Tenn.	318	40.3	4.64	186.99
Miami, Fla............................	578	39.0	3.67	143.13
Milwaukee, Wis........................	594	40.3	5.75	231.92
Minneapolis-St. Paul, Minn.	895	39.7	5.40	214.38
Nassau-Suffolk, N.Y.	785	39.2	4.77	186.98
New Orleans, La.......................	419	40.5	4.77	193.19
New York, N. Y.[1]	3,666	37.4	4.68	175.03
Newark, N. J...........................	845	41.6	5.01	208.37
Oklahoma City, Okla. ....·...	311	39.6	4.44	175.82
Philadelphia, Pa.-N. J.	1,778	38.9	5.09	198.00
Phoenix, Ariz..........................	429	39.1	4.88	190.81
Pittsburgh, Pa.	880	39.6	5.86	232.06
Portland, Ore.	437	38.4	5.54	212.74
Providence-Warwick -etc., R. I............	354	38.9	3.83	148.92
Riverside-San Bernardino-etc., Calif.	334	39.8	5.23	208.15
Rochester, N. Y.	384	40.6	5.64	228.98
Sacramento, Calif.	313	39.1	5.66	221.31
St. Louis, Mo..........................	894	39.4	5.47	215.56
San Antonio, Tex.	311	41.0	3.51	143.91
San Diego, Calif.	469	38.5	5.09	195.97
San Francisco-Oakland, Calif..............	1,323	38.9	6.22	241.96
San Jose, Calif.........................	469	39.3	5.58	219.29
Seattle-Everett, Wash....................	568	39.3	5.93	233.05
Tampa-St. Petersburg, Fla.	413	40.2	4.32	173.66
Washington, D. C.-Md.-Va.	1,330	38.5	5.52	212.52

Note: Employment figures are for all employees on nonagricultural payrolls while data for hours and earnings refer to production workers on manufacturing payrolls only
[1] Does not include Nassau and Suffolk counties which comprise a separate SMSA
n.a.-Not available   Source: Department of Labor

INCOME

INCOME

GROSS NATIONAL PRODUCT

Year	Billions of Dollars		Percent Real Growth[1]
	Current Dollars	1975 Dollars	
1950	286.2	674.2	8.7
1951	330.2	728.5	8.1
1952	347.2	756.3	3.8
1953	366.1	785.8	3.9
1954	366.3	775.5	−1.3
1955	399.3	827.5	6.7
1956	420.7	845.2	2.1
1957	442.8	860.5	1.8
1958	448.9	858.7	− .2
1959	486.5	910.4	6.0
1960	506.0	931.1	2.3
1961	523.3	954.5	2.5
1962	563.8	1,009.8	5.8
1963	594.7	1,049.8	4.0
1964	635.7	1,105.0	5.3
1965	688.1	1,170.1	5.9
1966	753.0	1,239.7	6.0
1967	796.3	1,273.4	2.7
1968	868.5	1,329.2	4.4
1969	935.5	1,363.3	2.6
1970	982.4	1,358.9	− .3
1971	1,063.4	1,399.5	3.0
1972	1,171.1	1,479.9	5.7
1973	1,306.3	1,558.6	5.3
1974	1,406.9	1,530.0	−1.8
1975	1,498.9	1,498.9	−2.0

[1] From preceding year; based on constant dollars

Source: Department of Commerce

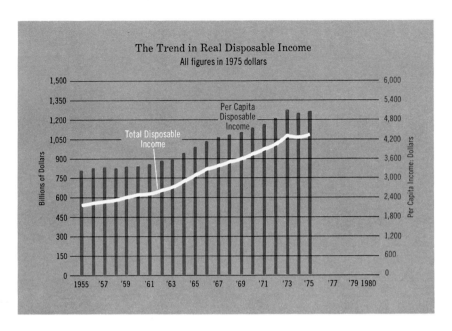

The Trend in Real Disposable Income
All figures in 1975 dollars

PERSONAL AND DISPOSABLE INCOME

Billions of dollars

Year	Personal Income		Disposable Income	
	Current Dollars	1975 Dollars	Current Dollars	1975 Dollars
1950	226.1	500.2	205.5	454.9
1955	308.8	604.3	273.4	535.4
1956	330.9	635.1	291.3	559.2
1957	349.3	649.3	306.9	570.6
1958	359.3	653.2	317.1	577.0
1959	382.1	682.3	336.1	600.1
1960	399.7	701.3	349.4	612.5
1961	415.0	719.2	362.9	629.3
1962	440.7	752.1	383.9	655.7
1963	463.1	779.6	402.8	677.8
1964	495.7	823.3	437.0	725.7
1965	537.0	876.1	472.2	769.8
1966	584.9	926.9	510.4	809.0
1967	626.6	968.5	544.5	841.9
1968	685.2	1,018.2	588.1	873.9
1969	745.8	1,059.4	630.4	895.4
1970	801.3	1,088.7	685.9	932.2
1971	859.1	1,118.6	742.8	966.6
1972	942.5	1,184.1	801.3	1,007.2
1973	1,054.3	1,256.6	903.1	1,076.0
1974	1,154.7	1,244.3	983.6	1,060.3
1975	1,245.9	1,245.9	1,076.7	1,076.7

Source: Department of Commerce

PERSONAL INCOME BY SOURCE

Billions of dollars

Type of Income	1955	1960	1965	1970	1975 Amount	1975 Percent
TOTAL INCOME[1]	308.8	399.7	537.0	801.3	1,245.9	100.0
Wages and Salaries	211.7	271.9	362.0	546.5	801.6	64.3
Other Labor Income	7.0	11.2	17.8	32.0	61.3	4.9
Proprietors' Income[2]	42.5	47.0	56.7	65.1	83.3	6.7
Nonfarm	31.2	35.6	44.1	51.2	58.7	4.7
Farm	11.3	11.4	12.6	13.9	24.6	2.0
Rent[3]	11.3	13.8	17.1	18.6	21.1	1.7
Dividends	10.3	12.9	19.1	22.9	32.8	2.6
Interest......................	13.8	23.3	37.2	64.3	120.5	9.7
Transfer Payments[4]	17.5	28.9	40.4	79.9	175.0	14.0

[1] The difference between the sum of the sources of personal income and total income is equal to personal contributions for social insurance
[2] With inventory valuation and capital consumption adjustments
[3] With capital consumption adjustment
[4] Benefits paid, such as old-age, survivors', disability and health insurance, etc.   Source: Department of Commerce

PER CAPITA PERSONAL INCOME

In dollars

Year	Personal Income Current Dollars	Personal Income 1975 Dollars	Disposable Income Current Dollars	Disposable Income 1975 Dollars
1950	1,491	3,299	1,355	2,999
1955	1,868	3,656	1,654	3,239
1956	1,967	3,775	1,731	3,325
1957	2,039	3,790	1,792	3,331
1958	2,063	3,751	1,821	3,313
1959	2,158	3,854	1,898	3,389
1960	2,212	3,881	1,934	3,390
1961	2,259	3,915	1,976	3,425
1962	2,363	4,032	2,058	3,515
1963	2,447	4,120	2,128	3,581
1964	2,583	4,291	2,278	3,782
1965	2,764	4,509	2,430	3,962
1966	2,976	4,716	2,597	4,115
1967	3,153	4,873	2,740	4,237
1968	3,414	5,073	2,930	4,354
1969	3,680	5,227	3,111	4,418
1970	3,911	5,314	3,348	4,549
1971	4,149	5,402	3,588	4,668
1972	4,513	5,670	3,837	4,823
1973	5,011	5,973	4,292	5,113
1974	5,450	5,873	4,642	5,004
1975	5,833	5,833	5,040	5,040

Source: Department of Commerce

PER CAPITA DISPOSABLE INCOME: NONFARM AND FARM

In dollars

Year	Total	Nonfarm	Farm
1955	1,654	1,773	847
1956	1,731	1,851	876
1957	1,792	1,903	915
1958	1,821	1,917	1,045
1959	1,898	2,002	964
1960	1,934	2,019	1,073
1961	1,976	2,055	1,178
1962	2,058	2,132	1,259
1963	2,128	2,198	1,344
1964	2,278	2,348	1,383
1965	2,430	2,487	1,675
1966	2,597	2,650	1,873
1967	2,740	2,799	1,898
1968	2,930	2,993	2,067
1969	3,111	3,175	2,293
1970	3,348	3,422	2,460
1971	3,588	3,651	2,643
1972	3,837	3,877	3,133
1973	4,292	4,282	4,572
1974	4,642	4,640	4,258
1975	5,040	n.a.	n.a.

Note: Total per capita disposable income figures in the first column are consistent with revised national income and product accounts tables shown elsewhere in this volume, but the farm and nonfarm components are based on unrevised data. Revisions to these figures are scheduled for publication too late for inclusion in this volume
Sources: Departments of Agriculture and Commerce

PERSONAL SAVING

Year	Billions of Dollars	As Percent of Disposable Income
1950	10.8	5.3
1955	14.9	5.4
1956	19.7	6.8
1957	20.6	6.7
1958	21.7	6.8
1959	18.8	5.6
1960	17.1	4.9
1961	20.2	5.6
1962	20.4	5.3
1963	18.8	4.7
1964	26.1	6.0
1965	30.3	6.4
1966	33.0	6.5
1967	40.9	7.5
1968	38.1	6.5
1969	35.1	5.6
1970	50.6	7.4
1971	57.3	7.7
1972	49.4	6.2
1973	72.7	8.0
1974	74.0	7.5
1975	88.9	8.3

Source: Department of Commerce

PERSONAL INCOME BY REGIONS

Region	Billions of Dollars			Percent Distribution		Average Annual Growth (Percent)	
	1960	1970	1975p	1960	1975p	1960-1970	1970-1975
TOTAL U.S.	399.9	808.2	1,243.3	100.0	100.0	7.3	9.0
Northeast	114.1	217.9	311.9	28.5	25.1	6.7	7.4
New England	25.6	51.1	74.2	6.4	6.0	7.1	7.8
Middle Atlantic	88.5	166.8	237.6	22.1	19.1	6.5	7.3
North Central	118.5	228.1	346.6	29.6	27.9	6.8	8.7
East North Central	86.8	166.7	251.3	21.7	20.2	6.7	8.5
West North Central	31.7	61.4	95.4	7.9	7.7	6.8	9.2
South	97.2	215.7	350.6	24.3	28.2	8.3	10.2
South Atlantic	48.1	111.3	182.2	12.0	14.7	8.7	10.4
East South Central	18.1	38.3	61.8	4.5	5.0	7.8	10.0
West South Central	30.9	66.1	106.7	7.7	8.6	7.9	10.1
West	70.1	146.5	234.2	17.5	18.8	7.7	9.8
Mountain	14.4	30.1	51.8	3.6	4.2	7.7	11.5
Pacific	55.7	116.5	182.4	13.9	14.7	7.6	9.4

p-Preliminary
Source: Department of Commerce

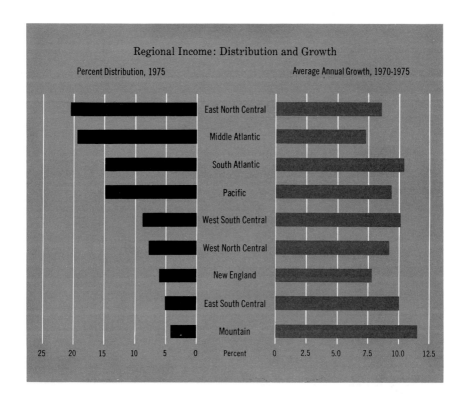

Regional Income: Distribution and Growth

Percent Distribution, 1975

Average Annual Growth, 1970-1975

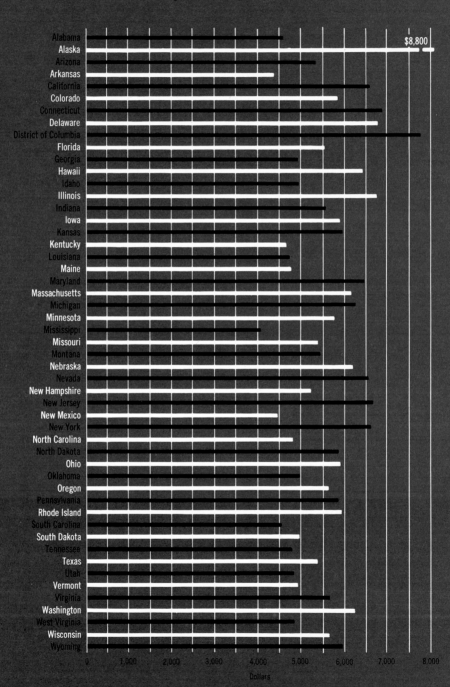

Per Capita Income by States, 1975

Alabama
Alaska — $8,800
Arizona
Arkansas
California
Colorado
Connecticut
Delaware
District of Columbia
Florida
Georgia
Hawaii
Idaho
Illinois
Indiana
Iowa
Kansas
Kentucky
Louisiana
Maine
Maryland
Massachusetts
Michigan
Minnesota
Mississippi
Missouri
Montana
Nebraska
Nevada
New Hampshire
New Jersey
New Mexico
New York
North Carolina
North Dakota
Ohio
Oklahoma
Oregon
Pennsylvania
Rhode Island
South Carolina
South Dakota
Tennessee
Texas
Utah
Vermont
Virginia
Washington
West Virginia
Wisconsin
Wyoming

0   1,000   2,000   3,000   4,000   5,000   6,000   7,000   8,000

Dollars

120

PERSONAL INCOME BY STATES, 1975

State	Total Personal Income (Mil. Dollars)	Per Capita Personal Income	
		Dollars	As Percent of Total U.S.
TOTAL U. S.	1,243,313	5,834	100.0
Alabama.........................	16,469	4,557	78.1
Alaska	3,103	8,815	151.1
Arizona	11,852	5,329	91.3
Arkansas	9,274	4,383	75.1
California.......................	138,874	6,555	112.4
Colorado	14,797	5,839	100.1
Connecticut.....................	21,212	6,854	117.5
Delaware	3,937	6,799	116.5
District of Columbia	5,549	7,751	132.9
Florida	46,105	5,517	94.6
Georgia	24,477	4,969	85.2
Hawaii	5,475	6,426	110.1
Idaho	4,084	4,980	85.4
Illinois	75,230	6,750	115.7
Indiana.........................	29,673	5,587	95.8
Iowa	16,931	5,899	101.1
Kansas	13,530	5,968	102.3
Kentucky	15,852	4,668	80.0
Louisiana.......................	17,928	4,729	81.1
Maine	5,067	4,785	82.0
Maryland	26,378	6,437	110.3
Massachusetts	35,895	6,159	105.6
Michigan	57,142	6,240	107.0
Minnesota	22,591	5,754	98.6
Mississippi......................	9,481	4,041	69.3
Missouri........................	25,659	5,387	92.3
Montana........................	4,065	5,434	93.1
Nebraska	9,546	6,175	105.8
Nevada.........................	3,862	6,524	111.8
New Hampshire..................	4,262	5,210	89.3
New Jersey	48,496	6,629	113.6
New Mexico	5,141	4,482	76.8
New York	119,649	6,603	113.2
North Carolina	26,171	4,801	82.3
North Dakota....................	3,718	5,855	100.4
Ohio	63,290	5,883	100.8
Oklahoma	13,548	4,996	85.6
Oregon	12,837	5,610	96.2
Pennsylvania....................	69,468	5,874	100.7
Rhode Island	5,485	5,917	101.4
South Carolina	12,739	4,521	77.5
South Dakota	3,401	4,980	85.4
Tennessee	19,959	4,766	81.7
Texas	65,919	5,387	92.3
Utah	5,812	4,819	82.6
Vermont........................	2,320	4,925	84.4
Virginia	28,169	5,671	97.2
Washington	22,665	6,226	106.7
West Virginia	8,681	4,815	82.5
Wisconsin	25,922	5,627	96.5
Wyoming	2,222	5,942	101.9

Note: Data are preliminary
Source: Department of Commerce

PROJECTIONS OF PERSONAL INCOME BY STATES
All figures in 1967 dollars

State	Total Income (Million Dollars)			Per Capita Income (Dollars)		
	1970	1980	1990	1970	1980	1990
TOTAL U.S.	708,584	1,068,496	1,517,173	3,476	4,780	6,166
Alabama	8,853	13,408	19,467	2,565	3,579	4,759
Alaska	1,282	1,875	2,795	4,202	5,625	7,145
Arizona	5,718	9,607	14,782	3,191	4,316	5,473
Arkansas	4,871	7,376	10,717	2,529	3,535	4,719
California	78,571	118,504	168,154	3,930	5,290	6,731
Colorado	7,522	12,097	17,410	3,380	4,677	6,024
Connecticut	12,493	18,720	26,255	4,111	5,575	7,077
Delaware	2,175	3,415	4,914	3,954	5,450	6,946
D.C.	3,995	5,378	6,937	5,284	7,170	9,249
Florida	22,153	39,988	63,320	3,236	4,480	5,768
Georgia	13,551	21,182	31,940	2,945	4,115	5,407
Hawaii	3,081	4,555	6,646	4,044	5,374	6,790
Idaho	2,077	2,899	3,954	2,897	4,095	5,360
Illinois	44,179	65,787	91,014	3,967	5,441	6,971
Indiana	17,281	26,577	38,027	3,318	4,595	5,975
Iowa	9,353	13,367	17,845	3,305	4,588	5,963
Kansas	7,569	10,180	13,549	3,367	4,568	5,940
Kentucky	8,871	13,953	20,520	2,752	3,866	5,153
Louisiana	9,844	14,202	19,672	2,701	3,793	4,997
Maine	2,891	3,993	5,371	2,905	4,106	5,415
Maryland	14,535	22,494	34,235	3,692	5,028	6,491
Massachusetts	21,780	33,024	46,443	3,822	5,269	6,755
Michigan	32,628	49,562	69,602	3,666	5,087	6,538
Minnesota	12,987	19,731	28,279	3,398	4,790	6,211
Mississippi	5,108	7,666	10,850	2,305	3,293	4,428
Missouri	15,607	23,224	32,467	3,325	4,580	5,970
Montana	2,115	2,817	3,654	3,035	4,207	5,498
Nebraska	4,999	7,000	9,450	3,355	4,670	6,069
Nevada	1,950	3,230	5,004	3,956	5,247	6,578
New Hampshire	2,368	3,778	5,388	3,191	4,483	5,863
New Jersey	28,245	43,212	60,788	3,926	5,348	6,812
New Mexico	2,816	4,099	5,370	2,766	3,885	5,065
New York	77,643	111,947	153,705	4,252	5,785	7,338
North Carolina	14,468	22,504	33,305	2,842	3,923	5,152
North Dakota	1,679	2,281	2,917	2,717	3,941	5,177
Ohio	37,539	56,489	78,877	3,512	4,849	6,255
Oklahoma	7,623	11,251	16,066	2,964	4,073	5,367
Oregon	6,857	10,466	14,754	3,262	4,483	5,815
Pennsylvania	41,247	60,754	83,363	3,472	4,803	6,214
Rhode Island	3,303	4,982	6,945	3,473	4,829	6,228
South Carolina	6,791	10,322	15,127	2,616	3,662	4,845
South Dakota	1,867	2,609	3,384	2,803	3,986	5,227
Tennessee	10,679	17,179	25,920	2,716	3,770	4,994
Texas	35,536	53,047	77,063	3,158	4,360	5,675
Utah	3,042	4,672	6,900	2,846	4,027	5,269
Vermont	1,360	2,083	3,020	3,042	4,319	5,822
Virginia	14,979	23,402	35,638	3,219	4,419	5,809
Washington	12,032	17,408	24,055	3,524	4,904	6,321
West Virginia	4,711	6,810	9,089	2,698	3,717	4,926
Wisconsin	14,666	21,899	29,921	3,308	4,623	5,969
Wyoming	1,096	1,490	1,947	3,282	4,503	5,828

Note: For a brief descripton of these projections, see *Note* to table on page 123   Source: Department of Commerce

PROJECTIONS OF PERSONAL INCOME BY REGIONS

All figures in 1967 dollars

Region	Billions of Dollars			Percent Distribution		Percent Growth	
	1970	1980	1990	1970	1990	1970-1980	1980-1990
TOTAL U.S.	708.6	1,068.5	1,517.2	100.0	100.0	50.8	42.0
Northeast	191.3	282.5	391.3	27.0	25.8	47.6	38.5
New England	44.2	66.6	93.4	6.2	6.2	50.7	40.3
Middle Atlantic	147.1	215.9	297.9	20.8	19.6	46.7	38.0
North Central	200.4	298.7	415.3	28.3	27.4	49.1	39.0
E. North Central......	146.3	220.3	307.4	20.6	20.3	50.6	39.5
W. North Central	54.1	78.4	107.9	7.6	7.1	45.0	37.6
South	188.7	293.6	434.8	26.6	28.7	55.5	48.1
South Atlantic	97.4	155.5	234.5	13.7	15.5	59.7	50.8
E. South Central	33.5	52.2	76.8	4.7	5.1	55.8	47.0
W. South Central	57.9	85.9	123.5	8.2	8.1	48.4	43.8
West	128.2	193.7	275.8	18.1	18.2	51.2	42.4
Mountain	26.3	40.9	59.4	3.7	3.9	55.3	45.1
Pacific	101.8	152.8	216.4	14.4	14.3	50.1	41.6

Note: The projection, prepared by the Bureau of Economic Analysis, are based on both economic and demographic assumptions. Nationally, they forecast a slow population growth (based on Series E population data), a private output per man-hour of 2.9 percent annually, and a 4 percent unemployment rate

Source: Department of Commerce

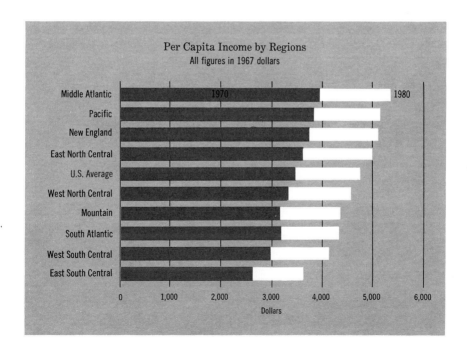

PERSONAL INCOME OF MAJOR METROPOLITAN AREAS, 1974

Standard Metropolitan Statistical Area	Total		Per Capita	
	Millions of Dollars	Avg. Annual Percent Growth 1959-1974	Amount (Dollars)	Percent of Total U.S.
TOTAL U.S.	1,151,721	7.6	5,449	100
Metropolitan	901,739	7.6	5,813	107
Nonmetropolitan	249,982	7.6	4,444	82
Akron, Ohio	3,829	6.9	5,704	105
Albany-Schenectady-Troy, N.Y.	4,433	6.9	5,545	102
Allentown-Bethlehem-Easton, Pa.-N.J.	3,554	7.1	5,764	106
Anaheim-Santa Ana-Garden Grove, Calif.	10,313	10.6	6,210	114
Atlanta, Georgia	10,188	9.7	5,737	105
Baltimore, Md.	12,036	7.8	5,624	103
Birmingham, Ala.	4,066	7.6	5,179	95
Boston-Lowell-Brockton-etc., Mass.-N.H.	23,382	7.0	5,967	109
Bridgeport-Norwalk-Stamford-etc., Conn.	6,155	7.3	7,781	143
Buffalo, N.Y.	7,367	6.0	5,537	101
Charlotte-Gastonia, N.C.	3,186	8.9	5,407	99
Chicago, Ill	47,267	6.7	6,780	124
Cincinnati, Ohio-Ky.-Ind.	7,756	6.4	5,637	103
Cleveland, Ohio	12,698	6.2	6,400	117
Columbus, Ohio	5,677	7.4	5,321	98
Dallas-Fort Worth, Tex.	14,385	8.9	5,758	106
Dayton, Ohio	4,760	6.8	5,633	103
Denver-Boulder, Colo.	8,468	9.1	6,087	112
Detroit, Mich.	29,176	7.5	6,580	121
Fort Lauderdale, Hollywood, Fla.	5,252	14.1	6,510	119
Gary-Hammond-East Chicago, Ind.	3,410	6.6	5,296	97
Grand Rapids, Mich.	3,077	7.5	5,506	101
Greensboro-Winston-Salem-High Point, N.C.	4,143	8.3	5,455	100
Hartford-New Britain-Bristol, Conn.	6,581	7.5	6,216	114
Honolulu, Hawaii	4,321	9.7	6,321	116
Houston, Tex.	13,234	9.6	5,954	109
Indianapolis, Ind.	6,590	7.0	5,762	106
Jacksonville, Fla.	3,504	9.0	5,192	95
Jersey City, N.J.	3,332	5.8	5,715	105
Kansas City, Mo.-Kans.	7,555	7.3	5,805	106
Los Angeles-Long Beach, Calif.	43,932	6.9	6,343	116
Louisville, Ky.-Ind.	4,869	7.6	5,455	100
Memphis, Tenn.-Ark.-Miss.	4,403	8.5	5,162	95
Miami, Fla.	8,872	10.3	6,266	115
Milwaukee, Wis.	8,757	6.6	6,187	113
Minneapolis-St. Paul, Minn.	12,243	7.9	6,089	112
Nashville-Davidson, Tenn.	3,830	8.7	5,143	94
Nassau-Suffolk, N.Y.	18,566	7.7	7,084	130
Newark, N.J.	13,854	6.7	6,861	126
New Brunswick-Perth Amboy-etc., N.J.	3,689	8.1	6,250	115
New Haven-Waterbury-Meriden, Conn.	4,478	6.8	5,894	108
New Orleans, La.	5,480	7.4	5,026	92
New York, N.Y.-N.J.	64,238	5.9	6,668	122
Norfolk-Virginia Beach-Portsmouth, Va.-N.C.	3,834	8.4	5,006	92
Oklahoma City, Okla.	3,792	8.2	4,949	91
Omaha, Nebr.-Iowa	3,111	7.4	5,378	99
Philadelphia, Pa.-N.J.	28,032	6.4	5,828	107
Phoenix, Ariz.	6,547	11.3	5,586	102

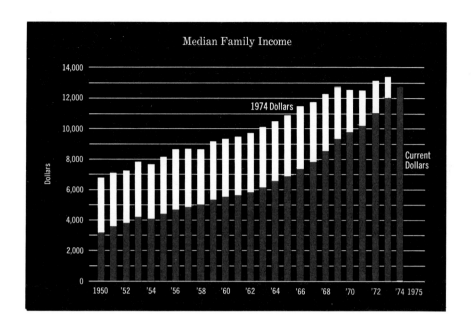

Median Family Income

PERSONAL INCOME OF MAJOR METROPOLITAN AREAS, 1974 (continued)

| | Total | | Per Capita | |
Standard Metropolitan Statistical Area	Millions of Dollars	Avg. Annual Percent Growth 1959-1974	Amount (Dollars)	Percent of Total U.S.
Pittsburgh, Pa.	13,183	6.0	5,649	104
Portland, Oreg.-Wash.	6,390	8.2	5,918	108
Providence-Pawtucket-Warwick, R.I.	4,611	7.0	5,397	99
Richmond, Va.	3,586	8.3	6,222	114
Riverside-San Bernardino-Ontario, Calif.	5,888	8.7	4,851	89
Rochester, N.Y.	5,984	7.3	6,192	114
Sacramento, Calif.	4,681	7.5	5,304	97
St. Louis, Mo.-Ill.	13,494	6.6	5,690	104
Salt Lake City-Ogden, Utah	3,749	7.9	4,897	90
San Antonio, Tex.	4,478	8.8	4,570	84
San Diego, Calif.	8,321	8.7	5,482	101
San Francisco-Oakland, Calif.	22,046	7.3	7,030	129
San Jose, Calif.	7,372	10.2	6,239	114
Seattle-Everett, Wash.	8,628	7.4	6,182	113
Springfield-Chicopee-Holyoke, Mass.	3,096	6.6	5,251	96
Syracuse, N.Y.	3,407	6.5	5,276	97
Tampa-St. Petersburg, Fla.	6,860	10.6	5,146	94
Toledo, Ohio-Mich.	4,454	7.1	5,703	105
Washington, D.C.-Md.-Va.	21,416	8.9	7,102	130
Wilmington, Del.-N.J.-Md.	3,327	7.3	6,482	119
Worcester-Fitchburg-Leominster, Mass.	3,537	16.9	5,455	100

Note: Data based on personal income by place of residence in SMSA's as currently defined, except for New England where data shown here are on a county basis

Source: Department of Commerce

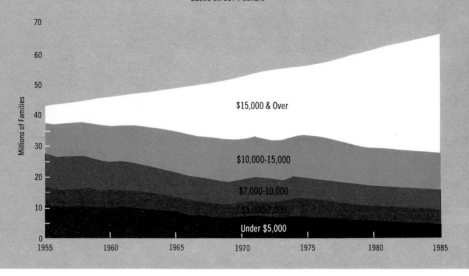

Families by Income Class
Based on 1974 dollars

$15,000 & Over

$10,000-15,000

$7,000-10,000

$5,000-7,000

Under $5,000

MEDIAN FAMILY INCOME BY SELECTED CHARACTERISTICS, 1974

In dollars

Family Characteristic	Median Income	Family Characteristic	Median Income
TOTAL FAMILIES	12,836	Occupation of Employed Head	
		Professional, Technical	19,441
Race		Managers, Administrators	19,707
White	13,356	Clerical Workers	13,325
Negro, Other Races	8,265	Sales Workers	16,593
		Craft Workers	14,838
Age of Head		Operatives	12,894
Under 25	8,618	Farmers, Farm Mgrs.	9,498
25-34	13,000	Service Workers[2]	11,098
35-44	15,117		
45-54	16,709	Residence	
55-64	13,645	Nonfarm	12,934
65 and over	7,298	Farm	10,431
Type of Family		Metropolitan Areas	13,771
Husband-Wife	13,847	1,000,000 or more	14,475
Wife Working	16,461	Central Cities	12,025
Wife not Working	12,082	Outside Central Cities	16,315
Other Male Head	11,737	Under 1,000,000	12,940
Female Head	6,413	Central Cities	12,013
		Outside Central Cities	13,622
Education of Head[1]		Nonmetropolitan	11,045
Elementary, 8 yrs.	9,728		
Some High School	11,384	Region	
H. S. Graduate	13,941	Northeast	13,796
Some College	15,892	North Central	13,736
College Graduate	19,303	South	11,230
Postgraduate	21,082	West.......................	13,160

[1] Family heads 25 years and over
[2] Excluding private household workers

Source: Department of Commerce

FAMILIES BY INCOME CLASS
Millions of families, based on 1974 dollars

Year	Total Families	Income Class					
		Under $3,000	$3,000-5,000	$5,000-7,000	$7,000-10,000	$10,000-15,000	$15,000 and Over
1955	42.9	6.0	4.9	6.4	10.5	10.0	5.1
1956	43.5	5.5	4.7	5.7	10.6	10.8	6.1
1957	43.7	5.5	4.7	5.6	11.0	10.9	5.9
1958	44.2	5.4	5.0	5.9	10.7	10.9	6.3
1959	45.1	5.2	4.8	5.5	10.0	11.8	7.8
1960	45.5	5.2	4.7	5.5	9.7	11.9	8.6
1961	46.4	5.3	4.8	5.5	9.4	12.0	9.3
1962	47.1	4.9	4.8	5.5	9.5	12.3	10.2
1963	47.5	4.6	4.7	5.3	9.1	12.6	11.2
1964	48.0	4.2	4.8	5.2	8.6	12.8	12.4
1965	48.5	4.1	4.5	4.9	8.4	13.2	13.4
1966	49.2	3.4	4.3	4.5	8.2	13.4	15.3
1967	50.1	3.4	4.2	4.4	8.0	13.7	16.4
1968	50.8	3.0	3.9	4.3	7.8	13.9	18.0
1969	51.6	3.0	3.8	4.2	7.4	13.7	19.4
1970	52.2	3.2	3.9	4.5	7.5	13.6	19.5
1971	53.3	3.1	4.2	4.8	7.7	13.6	19.8
1972	54.4	2.9	4.2	4.5	7.5	13.3	22.0
1973	55.1	2.8	4.1	4.6	7.3	13.3	23.0
1974	55.7	3.0	4.3'	5.0	7.7	13.5	22.2
Projections[1]:							
1980	61.2	2.4	3.4	4.3	6.7	12.2	32.1
1985	66.3	2.0	3.0	4.0	6.6	11.6	39.1

[1] Based on an annual average growth in personal income of 4% and Series B (moderate) projections of families

Sources: Department of Commerce; The Conference Board

MEDIAN FAMILY INCOME
In current dollars, except where indicated

Year	All Families		Race of Head	
	Current Dollars	1974 Dollars	White	Negro, Other
1950	3,319	6,800	3,445	1,869
1955	4,418	8,137	4,613	2,544
1960	5,620	9,358	5,835	3,230
1961	5,735	9,454	5,981	3,191
1962	5,956	9,709	6,237	3,328
1963	6,249	10,064	6,548	3,465
1964	6,569	10,444	6,858	3,838
1965	6,957	10,874	7,251	3,993
1966	7,532	11,445	7,825	4,691
1967	7,933	11,717	8,234	5,094
1968	8,632	12,236	8,937	5,590
1969	9,433	12,689	9,794	6,191
1970	9,867	12,531	10,236	6,516
1971	10,285	12,523	10,672	6,714
1972	11,116	13,103	11,549	7,106
1973	12,051	13,373	12,595	7,596
1974	12,836	12,836	13,356	8,265

Source: Department of Commerce

FAMILIES AND INDIVIDUALS BY INCOME CLASS AND RACE

Percent distribution, based on 1974 dollars

Income Class	1950	1960	1965	1970	1974
TOTAL FAMILIES (Millions)	39.9	45.5	48.5	52.2	55.7
(Percent)	100.0	100.0	100.0	100.0	100.0
Under $3,000	17.4	11.5	8.4	6.1	5.3
$3,000- 5,000........................	15.4	10.3	9.3	7.5	7.8
5,000- 7,000........................	19.8	12.0	10.1	8.7	8.9
7,000-10,000........................	23.1	21.2	17.3	14.3	13.8
10,000-15,000........................	} 24.4	{ 26.2	27.3	26.0	24.3
15,000 and over		{ 18.8	27.6	37.4	39.8
Median Income (Dollars)	6,800	9,358	10,874	12,531	12,836
WHITE FAMILIES (Millions)	n.a.	41.1	43.5	46.5	49.5
(Percent)	100.0	100.0	100.0	100.0	100.0
Under $3,000	15.3	9.6	7.2	5.1	4.3
$3,000- 5,000........................	14.5	9.5	8.2	6.7	6.8
5,000- 7,000........................	19.8	11.6	9.3	8.1	8.4
7,000-10,000........................	24.3	21.6	17.2	13.9	13.5
10,000-15,000........................	} 26.1	{ 27.6	28.5	26.7	25.1
15,000 and over		{ 20.1	29.5	39.4	42.0
Median Income (Dollars)	7,057	9,716	11,334	13,000	13,356
NONWHITE FAMILIES (Millions)	n.a.	4.3	4.8	5.4	6.3
(Percent)	100.0	100.0	100.0	100.0	100.0
Under $3,000	39.8	28.9	19.7	14.5	13.5
$3,000- 5,000........................	25.4	17.7	18.9	14.0	16.0
5,000- 7,000........................	19.4	16.3	17.3	13.6	13.1
7,000-10,000........................	9.7	16.9	17.6	17.6	16.1
10,000-15,000........................	} 5.7	{ 13.7	16.4	20.3	19.0
15,000 and over		{ 6.6	10.2	19.9	22.3
Median Income (Dollars)	3,828	5,379	6,242	8,275	8,265
UNRELATED INDIVIDUALS (Millions)	9.4	11.1	12.2	15.5	18.9
(Percent)	100.0	100.0	100.0	100.0	100.0
Under $1,500	40.4	31.0	22.9	16.7	10.2
$1,500- 3,000........................	18.5	20.6	23.5	24.0	24.7
3,000- 5,000........................	17.3	15.3	16.0	17.3	19.6
5,000- 7,000........................	13.5	12.6	11.7	11.8	13.7
7,000-10,000........................	7.5	13.0	13.1	13.3	14.0
10,000 and over	2.8	7.6	12.8	16.8	17.8
Median Income (Dollars)	2,140	2,864	3,365	3,984	4,439

n.a.—Not available

Source: Department of Commerce

INCOME SHARE TO FIFTHS OF FAMILIES RANKED BY INCOME

Percent distribution

Income Rank	1947	1950	1960	1965	1970	1974
ALL FAMILIES	100.0	100.0	100.0	100.0	100.0	100.0
Lowest Fifth	5.1	4.5	4.8	5.2	5.4	5.4
Second Fifth	11.8	11.9	12.2	12.2	12.2	12.0
Third Fifth	16.7	17.4	17.8	17.8	17.6	17.6
Fourth Fifth	23.2	23.6	24.0	23.9	23.8	24.1
Highest Fifth	43.3	42.7	41.3	40.9	40.9	41.0
Top 5 Percent	17.5	17.3	15.9	15.5	15.6	15.3
WHITE FAMILIES	100.0	100.0	100.0	100.0	100.0	100.0
Lowest Fifth	5.5	4.9	5.2	5.6	5.8	5.8
Second Fifth	12.2	12.3	12.7	12.6	12.5	12.3
Third Fifth	16.9	17.2	17.7	17.8	17.7	17.6
Fourth Fifth	22.8	23.5	23.7	23.7	23.6	23.8
Highest Fifth	42.6	42.1	40.7	40.3	40.5	40.5
Top 5 Percent	17.4	17.3	15.7	15.4	15.5	15.1
NONWHITE FAMILIES	100.0	100.0	100.0	100.0	100.0	100.0
Lowest Fifth	4.8	3.8	3.7	4.7	4.5	4.6
Second Fifth	10.2	9.7	9.7	10.8	10.6	10.0
Third Fifth	15.7	17.9	16.5	16.6	16.8	16.2
Fourth Fifth	23.6	25.1	25.2	24.7	24.8	25.0
Highest Fifth	45.8	43.4	44.9	43.2	43.4	44.2
Top 5 Percent	17.0	16.6	16.2	15.1	15.4	15.9

Source: Department of Commerce

The Changing Income Pyramid
Total families each year=100%; based on 1974 dollars

1964	Income Class	1974
25.8%	$15,000 & Over	39.8%
26.6%	$10,000-15,000	24.3%
17.9%	$7,000-10,000	13.8%
10.9%	$5,000-7,000	8.9%
10.1%	$3,000-5,000	7.8%
8.8%	Under $3,000	5.3%

FAMILIES BY INCOME CLASS AND REGION

Percent distribution, based on 1974 dollars

Region and Income Class	1955	1960	1965	1970	1974
U.S. TOTAL	100.0	100.0	100.0	100.0	100.0
Under $3,000	14.1	11.5	8.4	6.1	5.3
$3,000- 5,000......................	11.5	10.3	9.3	7.5	7.8
5,000- 7,000......................	14.9	12.0	10.1	8.7	8.9
7,000-10,000......................	24.5	21.2	17.3	14.3	13.8
10,000-15,000......................	23.2	26.2	27.3	26.0	24.3
15,000 and over	11.9	18.8	27.6	37.4	39.8
Median Income (Dollars).............	8,137	9,358	10,874	12,531	12,836
NORTHEAST, TOTAL	100.0	100.0	100.0	100.0	100.0
Under $3,000	8.8	6.5	5.3	4.3	3.2
$3,000- 5,000......................	9.0	8.2	7.3	6.0	7.3
5,000- 7,000......................	16.0	11.3	8.7	7.7	7.6
7,000-10,000......................	28.0	23.5	17.0	13.2	13.1
10,000-15,000......................	25.7	28.3	29.8	26.8	24.5
15,000 and over	12.5	22.2	31.9	42.0	44.2
Median Income (Dollars).............	8,687	10,086	11,850	13,584	13,796
NORTH CENTRAL, TOTAL	100.0	100.0	100.0	100.0	100.0
Under $3,000	11.7	10.3	6.3	4.9	3.9
$3,000- 5,000......................	10.5	10.1	8.4	7.0	6.2
5,000- 7,000......................	14.2	11.3	9.2	8.0	7.9
7,000-10,000......................	24.6	21.1	17.4	13.3	12.7
10,000-15,000......................	25.4	28.9	29.2	26.9	25.7
15,000 and over	13.6	18.2	29.6	39.9	43.4
Median Income (Dollars).............	8,744	9,636	11,413	13,115	13,736
SOUTH, TOTAL	100.0	100.0	100.0	100.0	100.0
Under $3,000	22.2	19.6	14.7	9.3	8.2
$3,000- 5,000......................	15.3	13.9	12.7	9.2	9.8
5,000- 7,000......................	15.2	14.6	12.3	10.5	10.3
7,000-10,000......................	21.4	19.9	18.3	16.4	15.2
10,000-15,000......................	17.3	20.2	23.3	24.5	24.1
15,000 and over	8.7	11.7	18.8	30.2	32.5
Median Income (Dollars).............	6,602	7,300	8,767	10,861	11,230
WEST, TOTAL	100.0	100.0	100.0	100.0	100.0
Under $3,000	11.3	6.7	5.2	5.0	4.7
$3,000- 5,000......................	9.9	7.3	7.6	7.3	7.2
5,000- 7,000......................	13.7	9.8	9.7	8.0	9.4
7,000-10,000......................	24.7	20.1	15.6	13.5	14.1
10,000-15,000......................	26.4	29.2	27.9	26.2	22.5
15,000 and over	14.0	26.9	34.1	39.9	42.1
Median Income (Dollars).............	8,867	10,899	12,040	13,047	13,160

Source: Department of Commerce

FAMILIES BY INCOME, REGION AND RACE, 1974

Percent distribution

Income Class	Total U.S.	Region			
		North-east	North Central	South	West
ALL FAMILIES[1] (Millions)	55.7	12.6	15.0	18.1	10.0
(Percent)	100.0	100.0	100.0	100.0	100.0
Under $3,000	5.3	3.2	3.9	8.2	4.7
$3,000- 5,000	7.8	7.3	6.2	9.8	7.2
5,000- 7,000	8.9	7.6	7.9	10.3	9.4
7,000-10,000	13.8	13.1	12.7	15.2	14.1
10,000-15,000	24.3	24.5	25.7	24.1	22.5
15,000-25,000	28.3	30.8	31.3	23.4	29.7
25,000 and over	11.5	13.4	12.2	9.0	12.4
Median Income (Dollars)	12,836	13,796	13,736	11,230	13,160
WHITE FAMILIES (Millions)	49.5	11.4	13.8	15.1	9.0
(Percent)	100.0	100.0	100.0	100.0	100.0
Under $3,000	4.3	2.9	3.3	6.0	4.5
$3,000- 5,000	6.8	6.2	5.5	8.2	6.7
5,000- 7,000	8.4	7.0	7.8	9.4	9.0
7,000-10,000	13.5	13.0	12.4	14.7	13.9
10,000-15,000	25.1	25.0	26.0	25.4	23.0
15,000-25,000	29.7	31.7	32.1	25.7	30.0
25,000 and over	12.4	14.2	12.8	10.4	12.7
Median Income (Dollars)	13,356	14,164	14,017	12,050	13,339
NEGRO FAMILIES (Millions)	5.5	1.0	1.1	2.8	.5
(Percent)	100.0	100.0	100.0	100.0	100.0
Under $3,000	14.4	6.6	11.8	19.7	8.0
$3,000- 5,000	17.1	19.3	13.9	18.0	14.9
5,000- 7,000	13.5	14.7	8.9	14.5	15.7
7,000-10,000	16.5	14.5	16.2	17.0	17.7
10,000-15,000	19.1	20.2	22.3	17.7	17.5
15,000-25,000	16.2	19.6	21.7	11.5	23.0
25,000 and over	3.2	5.2	5.1	1.7	3.2
Median Income (Dollars)	7,808	8,788	9,846	6,730	8,585

[1] Includes races other than white and Negro, not shown separately
Source: Department of Commerce

CHARACTERISTICS OF FAMILIES BY INCOME LEVEL, 1974

Family Characteristic	Total Families (Millions)	Percent Distribution by Income Class					
		Under $3,000	$3,000-5,000	$5,000-7,000	$7,000-10,000	$10,000-15,000	$15,000 & Over
TOTAL FAMILIES......	55.7	5.3	7.8	8.9	13.8	24.3	39.8
TOTAL INCOME	807.9a	.5	2.2	3.7	8.0	20.8	64.8
Race of Head							
White..................	49.5	4.3	6.8	8.4	13.5	25.1	42.0
Negro and Other Races.	6.3	13.5	16.0	13.1	16.1	19.0	22.3
Negro	5.5	14.4	17.1	13.5	16.5	19.1	19.4
Age of Head							
Under 25..............	4.2	12.1	11.9	13.7	23.2	26.6	12.3
25-34	12.7	4.6	6.2	6.9	14.1	30.1	38.2
35-44	10.9	3.5	4.7	6.3	10.9	24.3	50.5
45-54	11.2	3.6	3.7	5.1	10.1	21.4	56.0
55-64	8.7	4.8	6.1	7.8	12.7	25.3	43.3
65 and over	8.0	8.3	20.0	19.4	19.0	17.3	16.0
Education of Head[1]							
Elementary, 8 yrs.	5.2	7.0	12.5	14.2	17.7	24.6	23.9
High School Graduate ...	17.2	3.1	4.9	6.7	13.2	28.2	43.9
Some College...........	6.7	2.4	3.1	5.6	10.4	25.2	53.3
College Graduate	8.4	1.5	1.9	3.3	6.1	17.8	69.4
Occupation of Head							
Professional, Tech.	6.3	.8	1.4	2.9	7.0	19.6	68.4
Mgrs., Administrators ...	6.4	1.5	1.5	2.5	6.4	20.5	67.8
Clerical Workers	3.4	2.8	3.8	7.7	16.1	29.3	40.3
Sales Workers	2.5	1.8	2.3	4.0	10.7	25.5	55.6
Craft Workers	8.3	1.2	2.5	4.4	11.4	31.7	48.9
Operatives	6.7	1.7	4.4	7.0	16.9	33.5	36.5
Service Workers[2]	3.2	5.0	8.9	11.4	18.6	26.6	29.3
Type of Family							
Husband-Wife	47.0	3.3	5.9	7.8	13.3	25.7	44.2
Wife Working	20.3	1.3	2.4	4.5	10.8	25.3	55.8
Wife not Working	26.7	4.6	8.7	10.3	15.3	25.8	35.4
Other Male Head	1.5	5.7	9.0	9.8	15.6	24.8	35.2
Female Head	7.2	19.1	19.8	15.8	16.9	16.1	12.3
Residence							
Nonfarm	53.3	5.0	7.7	8.8	13.8	24.6	40.2
Farm	2.4	11.5	9.4	10.9	16.1	20.3	31.7
Metropolitan	37.7	4.6	6.8	8.0	12.6	23.9	44.1
Central Cities	16.0	5.9	9.3	9.9	14.8	23.5	36.6
Outside C. C.	21.7	3.4	4.9	6.6	11.1	24.3	49.7
Nonmetropolitan	18.0	7.1	10.0	10.8	16.3	25.4	30.6
Region							
Northeast	12.6	3.2	7.3	7.6	13.1	24.5	44.2
North Central	15.0	3.9	6.3	7.9	12.7	25.7	43.5
South	18.1	8.3	9.8	10.3	15.2	24.1	32.4
West	10.0	4.8	7.2	9.4	14.1	22.5	42.1

[1] Family heads 25 years and over

[2] Except private household

a—Billions of dollars

Source: Department of Commerce

FAMILY SIZE BY INCOME CLASS, 1974

Income Class	Families	Persons in Families	Children in Families	Average Family Size (Persons)
		Millions		
TOTAL	55.7	190.5	65.8	3.42
Under $3,000	3.0	8.8	3.8	2.96
$3,000- 5,000	4.3	12.8	4.4	2.94
5,000- 7,000	5.0	14.9	5.1	3.00
7,000-10,000	7.7	24.8	8.5	3.21
10,000-15,000	13.6	46.5	16.5	3.42
15,000-25,000	15.8	58.1	20.3	3.68
25,000 and over	6.4	24.8	7.2	3.88
		Percent Distribution		
TOTAL	100.0	100.0	100.0	- -
Under $3,000	5.3	4.6	5.7	- -
$3,000- 5,000	7.8	6.7	6.7	- -
5,000- 7,000	8.9	7.8	7.7	- -
7,000-10,000	13.8	13.0	12.9	- -
10,000-15,000	24.3	24.4	25.1	- -
15,000-25,000	28.3	30.5	30.9	- -
25,000 and over	11.5	13.0	11.0	- -

Source: Department of Commerce

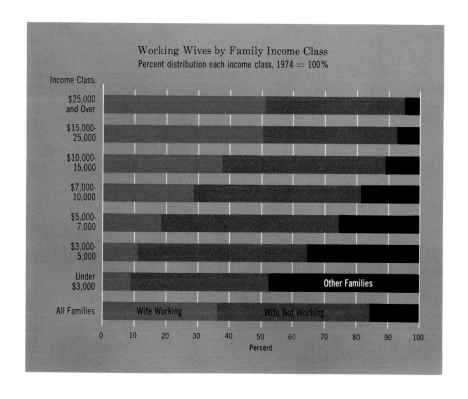

Working Wives by Family Income Class
Percent distribution each income class, 1974 = 100%

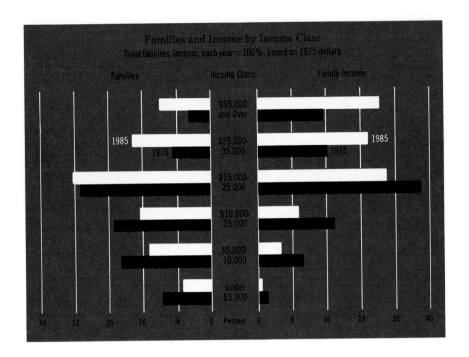

Families and Income by Income Class
Total families, income, each year = 100%; based on 1975 dollars

Families   Income Class: Family Income

$35,000 and Over

$25,000-35,000

$15,000-25,000

$10,000-15,000

$5,000-10,000

Under $5,000

40 32 24 16 8 0 Percent 0 8 16 24 32 40

PROJECTIONS OF FAMILIES AND INCOME BY INCOME CLASS

Percent distribution, based on 1975 dollars

Income Class	1975	1980	1985
FAMILIES (Millions)	56.7	61.2	66.3
Families (Percent)	100.0	100.0	100.0
Under $5,000	11.7	8.5	6.9
$5,000-10,000	21.1	16.2	14.7
10,000-15,000	22.6	18.9	16.3
15,000-20,000	18.5	18.0	17.0
20,000-25,000	12.1	14.4	15.1
25,000-35,000	9.0	15.0	18.2
35,000-50,000	3.6	6.2	8.0
50,000 and over	1.5	2.8	3.9
Income (Percent)	100.0	100.0	100.0
Under $5,000	2.2	1.3	1.0
$5,000-10,000	10.2	6.4	5.2
10,000-15,000	18.0	12.3	9.6
15,000-20,000	20.7	16.4	14.0
20,000-25,000	17.4	16.9	16.0
25,000-35,000	16.1	22.7	25.8
35,000-50,000	9.5	13.1	15.3
50,000 and over	6.0	10.9	13.2

Note: All years are projections and assume an average annual real growth in personal income of 4 percent between 1973 and 1980 and 3.5 percent between 1980 and 1985. Family projections are Series B (moderate growth)

Sources: Department of Commerce; The Conference Board

PROJECTIONS OF FAMILIES BY AGE AND INCOME LEVEL

Percent distributions, based on 1975 dollars

Income Class	Total	Age of Family Head					
		Under 25	25-34	35-44	45-54	55-64	65 and Over
1975—TOTAL:							
Millions	56.7	4.4	13.2	10.8	11.2	8.9	8.2
Percent	100.0	100.0	100.0	100.0	100.0	100.0	100.0
Under $5,000	11.7	22.0	9.5	7.0	6.5	10.0	25.0
$5,000-10,000	21.1	34.0	18.5	15.5	13.5	18.5	39.0
10,000-15,000	22.6	28.0	28.0	21.5	19.0	22.5	17.5
15,000-20,000	18.5	12.0	23.0	22.0	20.0	18.0	8.5
20,000-25,000	12.1	3.0	12.5	16.5	16.0	12.5	4.5
25,000-35,000	9.0	1.0	6.5	11.5	15.5	11.0	3.0
35,000-50,000	3.6	[1]	1.5	4.5	7.0	5.5	1.5
50,000 and over	1.5	[1]	.5	1.5	2.5	2.0	1.0
1985—TOTAL:							
Millions	66.3	4.6	17.1	14.9	10.8	9.7	9.2
Percent	100.0	100.0	100.0	100.0	100.0	100.0	100.0
Under $5,000	6.9	15.0	5.5	4.5	4.5	6.0	12.5
$5,000-10,000	14.7	22.5	12.0	9.5	8.0	12.5	34.5
10,000-15,000	16.3	27.0	16.5	13.0	12.0	15.5	21.5
15,000-20,000	17.0	19.5	20.5	17.0	15.0	16.0	12.5
20,000-25,000	15.1	10.0	19.0	18.0	14.5	14.5	7.0
25,000-35,000	18.2	5.0	19.0	24.0	24.0	19.5	7.0
35,000-50,000	8.0	1.0	6.0	9.5	14.5	10.0	3.0
50,000 and over	3.9	[1]	1.5	4.5	7.5	6.0	2.0

Note: Projections are based on a 4 percent average annual real growth in GNP between 1973 and 1980 and 3.5 percent between 1980 and 1985. Family projections are series B (moderate growth)

[1] Less than .05 percent

Sources: Department of Commerce: The Conference Board

SOURCES OF FAMILY INCOME, 1974

Type of Income	Families with Specified Income		Income		Mean Income (Dollars)
	Thousands	Percent of All Families	Millions of Dollars	Percent Distribution	
TOTAL	55,712	100.0	808,769	100.0	14,502
Earnings	49,531	88.9	696,696	86.1	n.a.
Wage or Salary Income	47,048	84.4	631,794	78.1	13,434
Nonfarm Self-Employment . .	6,539	11.7	52,384	6.5	7,962
Farm Self-Employment	2,576	4.6	12,518	1.5	4,518
Other Income	40,017	71.8	112,073	13.9	2,804
Social Security[1]	12,162	21.8	36,963	4.6	3,043
Dividends, Interest, Rent . . .	27,243	48.9	31,818	3.9	1,169
Public Assistance, Welfare . .	4,359	7.8	8,250	1.0	1,894
Unemployment, etc.[2]	10,296	18.5	21,407	2.6	2,081
Private Pensions, Annuities, etc.	6,581	11.8	13,635	1.7	2,075

Note: Data exclude families reporting net losses, and their negative income, but total includes a small number of families who reported no money income

[1] Includes Government railroad retirement
[2] Includes workmen's compensation, Government employee pensions, and veterans' payments
n.a.—Not available

Source: Department of Commerce

Spending Power by Family Characteristics
Total family income, 1974 = 100%

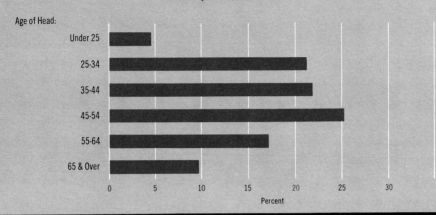

Age of Head:

Under 25	
25-34	
35-44	
45-54	
55-64	
65 & Over	

Percent: 0, 5, 10, 15, 20, 25, 30

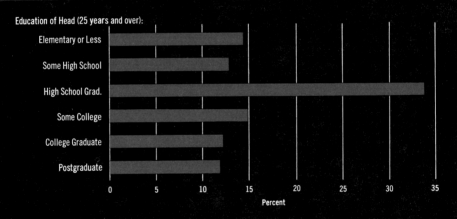

Education of Head (25 years and over):

Elementary or Less	
Some High School	
High School Grad.	
Some College	
College Graduate	
Postgraduate	

Percent: 0, 5, 10, 15, 20, 25, 30, 35

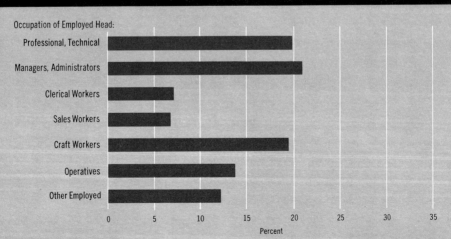

Occupation of Employed Head:

Professional, Technical	
Managers, Administrators	
Clerical Workers	
Sales Workers	
Craft Workers	
Operatives	
Other Employed	

Percent: 0, 5, 10, 15, 20, 25, 30, 35

DISTRIBUTION OF FAMILY SPENDING POWER, 1974

Family Characteristic	Percent Distribution Families	Spending Power[1]	Family Characteristic	Percent Distribution Families	Spending Power[1]
TOTAL	100.0	100.0	Mgrs, Administrators ..	15.7	20.9
			Clerical Workers	8.3	7.2
Age of Head			Sales Workers.........	6.1	6.8
Under 25...........	7.6	4.6	Craft Workers.........	20.6	19.4
25-34	22.8	21.3	Operatives	16.6	13.7
35-44	19.5	21.9	Service Workers[4]	8.0	5.9
45-54	20.2	25.3	Other Employed.......	9.0	6.3
55-64	15.5	17.1			
65 and over	14.4	9.7	Residence		
			Metropolitan Areas	67.7	72.2
Race of Head			1,000,000 or more ...	38.3	42.7
White	88.8	92.1	Central Cities	15.2	14.5
Negro, Other Races ..	11.2	7.9	Outside C. C.	23.1	28.3
Negro	9.9	6.5	Under 1,000,000	29.4	29.5
			Central Cities	13.6	13.0
Education of Head[2]			Outside C. C.	15.9	16.5
Elementary or Less ..	21.8	14.4	Nonmetropolitan Areas	32.3	27.8
Some High School ...	15.4	12.9	Nonfarm	28.8	24.8
High School Graduate	33.4	33.7	Farm	3.5	3.0
Some College........	13.0	14.9			
College Graduate	8.7	12.2	Region		
Postgraduate	7.6	11.9	Northeast.............	22.6	24.0
			North Central	27.0	28.3
Occupation of Head[3]			South	32.5	29.3
Professional, Tech. ..	15.6	19.9	West	18.0	18.4

[1] Total money income accruing to families
[2] Distribution based on family heads 25 years and over
[3] Distribution based on employed civilians only
[4] Except private household

Source: Department of Commerce

WORKING WIVES BY FAMILY INCOME CLASS, 1974

Income Class	Husband-Wife Families Total	Wife Working	Wife Not Working	Percent With Working Wife
TOTAL (Millions)	47.0	20.3	26.7	43.2
(Percent)	100.0	100.0	100.0	--
Under $3,000	3.3	1.3	4.6	17.0
$3,000- 5,000.................	5.9	2.4	8.7	17.6
5,000- 7,000.................	7.8	4.5	10.3	24.9
7,000-10,000.................	13.3	10.8	15.3	35.0
10,000-15,000.................	25.7	25.3	25.8	42.5
15,000-25,000.................	31.2	39.6	24.8	54.8
25,000 and over	13.0	16.2	10.6	53.8
Median Income (Dollars).......	13,847	16,461	12,082	--
Mean Income (Dollars)	15,532	17,492	14,044	--

Note: Data refer to wife in paid labor force

Source: Department of Commerce

FAMILIES BY INCOME AND EDUCATION OF HEAD, 1974

Families with head 25 years and over

Income Class	Total Families	Years of School Completed				
		Elementary or Less	Some High School	High School Graduate	Some College	College Graduate
TOTAL FAMILIES:						
(Millions)	51.5	11.2	7.9	17.2	6.7	8.4
Percent Distribution	100.0	100.0	100.0	100.0	100.0	100.0
Under $3,000	4.7	10.2	5.9	3.2	2.4	1.5
$3,000- 5,000	7.5	16.3	10.3	4.8	3.1	1.9
5,000- 7,000	8.5	15.6	10.4	6.7	5.6	3.2
7,000- 10,000	13.1	17.8	15.7	13.1	10.4	6.2
10,000- 15,000	24.1	21.1	25.8	28.2	25.2	17.8
15,000- 25,000	29.7	15.6	25.7	33.7	37.3	37.9
25,000 and over	12.4	3.4	6.2	10.3	16.0	31.5
TOTAL INCOME:						
(Billion Dollars)	770.4	110.7	99.4	259.3	115.2	185.8
Percent Distribution	100.0	100.0	100.0	100.0	100.0	100.0
Under $3,000	.5	1.8	.7	.2	.2	.1
$3,000- 5,000	2.0	6.6	3.3	1.3	.7	.3
5,000- 7,000	3.4	9.2	4.9	2.6	2.0	.9
7,000- 10,000	7.4	14.9	10.5	7.4	5.1	2.5
10,000- 15,000	20.0	25.8	25.0	22.9	18.2	10.4
15,000- 25,000	37.7	29.7	38.5	42.0	41.1	33.8
25,000 and over	29.0	12.0	17.1	23.6	32.7	52.0

Source: Department of Commerce

FAMILY INCOME BY AGE AND EDUCATIONAL LEVEL, 1974

Income in dollars for family heads 25 years and over

Age Group	Total Families	Years of School Completed				
		Elementary or Less	Some High School	High School Graduate	Some College	College Graduate
MEDIAN INCOME, TOTAL .	13,326	8,241	11,384	13,941	15,892	20,124
Age of Head						
25-34	13,000	7,745	9,418	12,433	14,113	17,462
35-44	15,117	9,819	12,070	14,708	17,335	21,697
45-54	16,709	11,240	13,972	16,959	19,724	24,905
55-64	13,645	9,915	13,272	14,864	18,270	23,383
65 and over	7,298	6,018	7,520	8,499	10,056	12,819
MEAN INCOME, TOTAL ...	14,962	9,867	12,517	15,063	17,187	22,084
Age of Head						
25-34	13,552	8,426	9,875	12,792	14,484	17,738
35-44	16,325	10,738	12,876	15,341	17,985	23,646
45-54	18,204	12,407	15,042	17,764	21,222	27,461
55-64	15,963	10,864	14,422	17,004	19,741	26,410
65 and over	9,739	7,866	9,128	10,786	12,932	16,365

Source: Department of Commerce

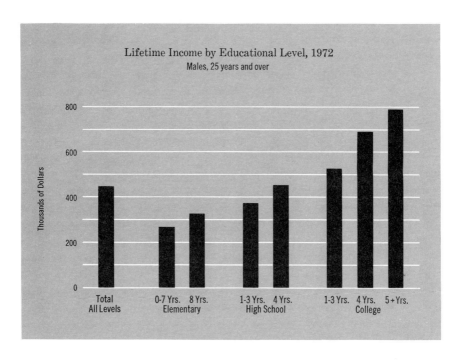

Lifetime Income by Educational Level, 1972
Males, 25 years and over

LIFETIME AND MEAN INCOME BY EDUCATIONAL LEVEL

Figures in 1972 dollars for males 25 years and over

Years of School Completed	1958	1966	1968	1970	1972
LIFETIME INCOME[1]:					
Total	292,776	391,088	408,451	419,488	447,828
Elementary					
Less than 8 Years.........	173,735	223,830	235,594	236,481	260,307
8 Years..................	240,590	294,233	309,495	308,991	323,437
High School					
1-3 Years	277,301	348,446	353,558	357,328	371,023
4 Years..................	328,014	412,576	420,947	425,125	452,086
College					
1-3 Years	400,667	490,606	493,994	516,070	525,343
4 Years or more	558,683	670,550	704,383	687,308	731,315
4 Years.................	501,663	625,803	675,037	634,434	686,227
5 Years or more	621,700	730,095	739,474	751,385	785,778
MEAN INCOME:					
Total	6,711	8,902	9,261	9,525	10,125
Elementary Graduate	5,321	6,272	6,571	6,503	6,756
High School Graduate	7,608	9,657	9,793	9,898	10,433
College Graduate	12,508	15,128	15,550	15,554	16,201

Note: Data for 1958 and 1966 computed from grouped data; subsequent years are derived from ungrouped data

[1] Age 25 to death   Source: Department of Commerce

PROFILE OF POVERTY

Persons and families below poverty level

Characteristic	Thousands			Percent of Total in Group		
	1960	1970	1974	1960	1970	1974
TOTAL PERSONS	39,851	25,420	24,260	22.2	12.6	11.6
Race						
White	28,309	17,484	16,290	17.8	9.9	8.9
Negro, other Races	11,542	7,936	7,970	55.9	32.0	31.4
Residence						
Nonfarm	32,264	n.a.	22,764	19.6	n.a.	11.4
Farm	7,587	n.a.	1,496	51.3	n.a.	16.5
Metropolitan Areas	17,019a	n.a.	14,588	15.3a	n.a.	10.2
Central Cities	10,437a	n.a.	8,796	18.3a	n.a.	14.4
Outside Central Cities	6,582a	n.a.	5,792	12.2a	n.a.	7.1
Nonmetropolitan Areas	21,747a	n.a.	9,672	33.2a	n.a.	14.4
Family Status						
In Families	34,925	20,330	19,440	20.7	10.9	10.2
Head	8,243	5,260	5,109	18.1	10.1	9.2
Related Children	17,288	10,235	10,196	26.5	14.9	15.5
Other Family Members	9,394	4,835	4,135	16.2	7.4	6.0
Unrelated Individuals	4,926	5,090	4,820	45.2	32.9	25.5
TOTAL FAMILIES	8,243	5,260	5,109	18.1	10.1	9.2
Sex of Head						
Male	6,288	3,309	2,757	15.4	7.2	5.7
Female	1,955	1,951	2,351	42.4	32.5	32.5
Age of Head						
Under 25	637	586	733	27.4	15.5	17.3
25-34	1,601	1,078	1,282	17.7	10.2	10.1
35-44	1,618	974	1,051	14.9	8.9	9.7
45-54	1,463	731	701	14.9	6.6	6.2
55-64	1,234	704	581	17.1	8.2	6.7
65 and over	1,690	1,188	760	27.2	16.5	9.5
Family Size						
2 Persons	2,908	1,970	1,705	19.6	10.7	8.2
3 and 4 Persons	2,350	1,601	1,815	12.5	7.7	7.8
5 and 6 Persons	1,657	970	1,028	18.8	9.8	11.0
7 Persons or more	1,328	720	560	46.5	22.9	23.0
Employment Status of Head						
Employed	4,665	2,270	2,048	13.1	5.7	5.1
Unemployed	678	272	449	29.7	16.7	16.1
Not in Civilian Labor Force ...	2,900	2,720	2,611	37.8	26.2	20.9

Note: Poverty statistics, as shown here, are based on revised definitions of poverty adopted as official standards in 1969. Earlier poverty data used the poverty thresholds developed in 1964 by the Social Security Administration. These thresholds provided a range of poverty income cutoffs adjusted by such factors as family size, age and sex of family head, and place of residence. The SSA definition of poverty was described primarily in terms of a nutritionally adequate food plan. Annual revisions of poverty income cutoffs were based on the cost of food in an economy food plan.

In the current definition, the SSA thresholds have been retained for the base year 1963. However, annual adjustments are now made to these base levels in accordance with changes in the consumer price index. In addition, the farm-nonfarm distinction in relative poverty has been reduced, and farm poverty cutoffs have been raised from 70 to 85 per cent of corresponding nonfarm levels. In 1974, the average poverty threshold for a nonfarm family of four persons was $5,950

a—1959 data based on 1-in-1,000 sample of the 1960 census
n.a.—Not available
Source: Department of Commerce

THE LOW-INCOME POPULATION

Persons below the poverty level, in thousands except as indicated

Year	Total Number	Percent of Total Population	White	Negro, Other Races	In Families	Unrelated Individuals[1]
1959.....	39,490	22.4	28,484	11,006	34,562	4,928
1960.....	39,851	22.2	28,309	11,542	34,925	4,926
1961.....	39,628	21.9	27,890	11,738	34,509	5,119
1962.....	38,625	21.0	26,672	11,953	33,623	5,002
1963.....	36,436	19.5	25,238	11,198	31,498	4,938
1964.....	36,055	19.0	24,957	11,098	30,912	5,143
1965.....	33,185	17.3	22,496	10,689	28,358	4,827
1966.....	28,510	14.7	19,290	9,220	23,809	4,701
1967.....	27,769	14.2	18,983	8,786	22,771	4,998
1968.....	25,389	12.8	17,395	7,994	20,695	4,694
1969.....	24,147	12.1	16,659	7,488	19,175	4,972
1970.....	25,420	12.6	17,484	7,936	20,330	5,090
1971.....	25,559	12.5	17,780	7,780	20,405	5,154
1972.....	24,460	11.9	16,203	8,257	19,577	4,883
1973.....	22,973	11.1	15,142	7,831	18,299	4,674
1974.....	24,260	11.6	16,290	7,970	19,440	4,820

Note: Beginning 1966, new series based on revised methodology for processing income data. Beginning 1969, based on 1970 population controls and not strictly comparable with earlier data. For a description of poverty thresholds, see footnote to table on page 140

[1] 14 years and over

Source: Department of Commerce

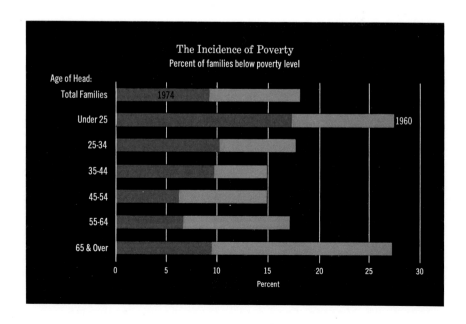

The Incidence of Poverty
Percent of families below poverty level

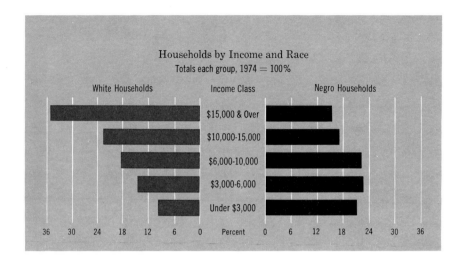

Households by Income and Race
Totals each group, 1974 = 100%

White Households	Income Class	Negro Households
	$15,000 & Over	
	$10,000-15,000	
	$6,000-10,000	
	$3,000-6,000	
	Under $3,000	

36 30 24 18 12 6 0   Percent   0 6 12 18 24 30 36

HOUSEHOLDS BY INCOME AND SELECTED CHARACTERISTICS, 1974

Household Characteristic	Total House- holds (Millions)	Under $3,000	$3,000- 5,000	$5,000- 7,000	$7,000- 10,000	$10,000- 15,000	$15,000 and Over
TOTAL	71.1	10.9	10.2	9.7	13.9	22.0	33.2
Race of Head							
White	62.9	9.7	9.5	9.2	13.7	22.7	35.1
Negro, Other Races	8.2	20.2	16.0	12.8	15.6	17.2	18.3
Negro.................	7.3	21.5	16.7	13.2	15.7	17.1	15.7
Sex of Head							
Male	54.3	5.1	6.9	8.3	13.7	25.0	40.9
Female	16.8	29.7	20.8	13.9	14.9	12.6	8.1
Age of Head							
Under 25	5.8	13.5	13.6	14.8	22.9	23.8	11.3
25-34	14.9	5.1	6.5	7.7	15.5	29.6	35.6
35-44	11.9	4.4	5.1	6.5	11.5	24.4	48.2
45-54	12.9	6.0	5.0	6.2	11.0	21.3	50.6
55-64	11.3	10.3	9.3	9.8	13.3	22.5	34.7
65 and over	14.3	26.2	22.4	15.5	13.8	11.9	10.2
Education of Head[1]							
Elementary, 8 yrs.	7.2	17.7	16.4	13.4	15.0	19.5	18.0
High School Graduate	20.8	6.4	7.3	8.0	14.1	26.2	37.9
Some College	8.4	5.7	5.2	7.2	12.1	24.3	45.5
College Graduate	10.4	3.2	3.3	4.5	8.6	19.1	61.3
Occupation of Employed Head							
Professional, Technical	7.9	2.1	2.8	4.0	9.6	21.4	60.1
Managers, Administrators ..	7.1	2.2	2.1	3.1	7.5	21.4	63.7
Clerical Workers	4.8	4.1	6.5	11.5	20.8	26.6	30.4
Sales Workers	2.9	3.1	5.0	6.1	12.2	24.0	49.6
Craft Workers	8.9	1.6	2.8	4.5	12.0	32.0	47.1
Operatives	7.5	2.2	5.8	8.7	17.8	32.2	33.6
Service Workers	4.6	12.0	13.1	13.2	17.9	21.8	22.0

[1] Head 25 years and over

Source: Department of Commerce

PERSONS BY INCOME, SEX AND RACE, 1974

Percent distribution, except as indicated

Income Class	Total 14 Years and Over	Male			Female		
		Total	White	Negro	Total	White	Negro
All Persons (Millions)	159.9	76.3	67.7	7.5	83.6	73.3	9.0
Percent with Income	81.2	92.5	93.4	84.8	70.8	70.5	74.3
INCOME RECIPIENTS (Millions)	129.8	70.6	63.2	6.4	59.2	51.7	6.7
Percent Distribution..........	100.0	100.0	100.0	100.0	100.0	100.0	100.0
Under $1,000	13.1	8.3	7.9	11.2	19.0	19.3	16.7
$1,000- 3,000	20.3	12.2	11.3	20.6	30.1	29.3	35.6
3,000- 5,000	14.6	11.5	11.1	15.4	18.3	18.0	20.0
5,000- 7,000	12.0	10.8	10.4	14.4	13.2	13.4	12.4
7,000- 10,000	13.8	15.7	15.5	16.8	11.5	11.7	9.8
10,000- 15,000	14.9	22.3	23.1	15.9	6.1	6.3	4.5
15,000 and over	11.4	19.3	20.7	5.7	1.8	1.9	.9
Median Income (Dollars)	5,311	8,379	8,794	5,370	3,093	3,114	2,806
Mean Income (Dollars)	7,175	9,717	10,083	6,210	4,142	4,184	3,738

Source: Department of Commerce

DISCRETIONARY PURCHASING POWER

Billions of dollars

Year	Aggregate Purchasing Power	Discretionary Purchasing Power	Discretionary Saving	Discretionary Spending
1955.................	297.9	124.9	17.3	107.6
1956.................	312.3	128.6	19.1	109.5
1957.................	323.9	128.2	16.9	111.4
1958.................	334.3	128.9	20.0	108.9
1959.................	362.6	145.0	21.2	123.9
1960.................	371.6	143.6	17.0	126.6
1961.................	385.1	149.0	19.5	129.5
1962.................	408.6	158.2	25.0	133.2
1963.................	434.6	169.7	29.6	140.1
1964.................	470.2	191.1	36.6	154.5
1965.................	507.3	208.8	40.6	168.2
1966.................	540.5	218.6	41.4	177.2
1967.................	575.4	235.3	45.8	189.5
1968.................	630.4	265.0	52.6	212.4
1969.................	669.2	270.6	38.9	231.7
1970.................	718.1	286.0	52.6	233.4
1971.................	795.9	326.4	66.5	259.9
1972.................	882.7	374.5	87.7	286.8
1973.................	984.8	425.4	103.7	321.7
1974.................	1,042.1	416.6	87.5	329.1
1975.................	1,140.8	458.1	110.8	347.3

Note: For a description of this series and comparison with *supernumerary income* data, see note to table on following page. Data from 1962 forward are revised based on new estimates of national accounts and flow of funds statistics. Revisions for earlier years were not available at press time   Source: The Conference Board

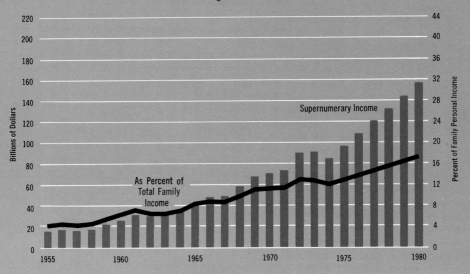

Supernumerary Income
After—tax figures in 1974 dollars

SUPERNUMERARY INCOME

Year	Families with Supernumerary Income		Supernumerary Income (After Taxes)		
	Millions	Percent of All Families	Billion Current Dollars	Billion 1974 Dollars	Percent of All Income
1955...................	2.1	5.0	8.0	14.7	4.2
1960...................	3.6	8.0	15.2	25.3	6.1
1961...................	4.4	9.4	18.6	30.7	7.1
1962...................	4.7	9.9	18.4	30.0	6.7
1963...................	5.2	11.0	19.4	31.2	6.7
1964...................	5.6	11.7	21.3	33.9	6.9
1965...................	6.0	12.3	26.7	41.7	8.1
1966...................	7.4	15.0	31.0	47.1	8.6
1967...................	7.8	15.5	32.4	47.9	8.5
1968...................	9.4	18.5	41.1	58.2	9.7
1969...................	10.3	20.0	51.1	68.7	11.1
1970...................	10.4	20.0	55.4	70.4	11.2
1971...................	10.9	20.5	60.2	73.3	11.3
1972...................	12.8	23.6	75.3	88.7	12.9
1973...................	12.9	23.5	81.0	89.9	12.6
1974...................	12.1	21.8	82.6	82.6	12.0
Projection:					
1980...................	20.5	33.5	- -	156.3	17.0

Note: Data are preliminary. The term *supernumerary income,* as used here, refers to that share of consumer income which is not needed for the essentials and is available for optional spending. Specifically, it consists of all income in excess of $20,000 a year flowing to each family unit. The supernumerary income series represents a general measure of rising consumer affluence. Projections are based on a 4 percent annual growth in real personal income.

The *discretionary purchasing power* series, which is shown on the preceding page, is based on an entirely different concept. Briefly, it is computed by combining disposable income, net borrowing, and several minor credits, and subtracting from the total all expenditures for essential goods and services, and fixed commitments (e.g., instalment debt). In effect, discretionary purchasing power represents "uncommitted" consumer income. Throughout the postwar period this series has been running at about 40% of aggregate consumer purchasing power. But with substantial variation around cyclical turning points. Because discretionary purchasing power is based on a sliding scale of essentials and fixed outlays, it principally measures short-term fluctuations rather than long-run secular growth

Sources: Department of Commerce; The Conference Board

FINANCIAL ASSETS AND LIABILITIES OF INDIVIDUALS

End of year; billions of dollars

Item	1964	1966	1968	1970	1972	1974
FINANCIAL ASSETS, TOTAL	1,329.4	1,460.0	1,910.3	1,918.9	2,405.8	2,183.2
Currency, Demand Deposits	86.5	98.1	121.7	134.5	157.3	173.9
Savings Accounts	259.5	306.8	371.7	422.3	567.9	694.7
U.S. Government Securities	79.3	89.5	96.6	99.7	85.9	118.2
Corporate Stock[1]	566.5	576.9	865.1	733.6	959.1	525.2
Insurance, Pension Reserves	238.6	274.2	326.4	367.9	457.5	471.2
Other Assets	99.0	114.6	128.8	161.0	177.9	200.0
LIABILITIES, TOTAL	319.1	370.7	428.4	480.0	591.9	702.2
Mortgage Debt	204.2	234.5	261.8	293.0	357.9	437.1
Consumer Credit	80.3	96.2	110.7	127.2	157.5	190.1
Other Liabilities	34.6	39.9	55.8	59.8	76.4	75.0
NET EQUITY	1,010.3	1,089.3	1,481.9	1,438.9	1,813.9	1,481.0

Note: Data refer to households, personal trusts and nonprofit organizations. Revisions to these figures were being processed at press time and are scheduled for release in fall 1976

[1] At market value

Source: Federal Reserve

SAVING BY INDIVIDUALS

Billions of dollars

Item	1965	1970	1971	1972	1973	1974	1975
Increase in Financial Assets ..	58.2	80.7	99.8	124.6	138.2	133.9	161.4
Currency, Demand Deposits	7.8	11.3	11.1	12.1	13.1	8.6	8.2
Savings Accounts	28.0	44.4	70.3	75.4	67.7	59.6	91.1
Securities	3.1	-2.9	-14.4	3.1	21.1	21.3	13.9
Insurance, Pension Reserves	17.0	24.3	27.8	30.4	31.6	38.9	41.4
Misc. Financial Assets	2.3	3.6	5.1	3.7	4.8	5.5	6.9
Net Investment In:							
Nonfarm Homes	12.3	10.6	17.6	25.3	27.4	18.2	14.8
Consumer Durables	11.3	7.9	13.9	21.5	24.4	11.2	3.5
Noncorp. Plant & Equipment	10.1	10.0	10.6	15.0	17.0	11.8	2.8
Inventories	1.8	-1.3	1.1	-1.3	2.0	-.9	[1]
Less: Increase in Debt	38.6	32.2	57.3	85.8	87.6	58.2	58.5
Home Mortgages	15.2	12.5	24.2	38.4	44.2	32.6	34.6
Consumer Credit	9.6	6.0	11.2	19.2	22.9	9.6	5.3
Other Debt	13.7	13.6	21.9	28.2	20.4	15.9	18.5
Equals: Individuals' Saving ...	55.1	75.7	85.7	99.3	121.4	116.0	124.0
Personal Saving[2]	38.1	58.2	61.9	65.2	84.2	88.9	104.6

Note: Refers to households, private trust funds, nonprofit institutions, farms and other non-corporate business

[1] Less than .05

[2] Individuals' saving minus Government insurance and pension reserves, net investment in consumer durables, capital gains dividends from investment companies, and net saving by farm corporations. Personal saving as shown here, is measured by acquisitions of assets less borrowing. Figures shown on page 118 measures personal saving as income less taxes and consumption

Source: Federal Reserve

STOCK OWNERSHIP: CHARACTERISTICS OF SHAREOWNERS

Millions of persons

Item	1965	1970	1975	Item	1965	1970	1975
TOTAL	20.1	30.8	25.3	Minors	1.3	2.2	1.8
Sex[1]				**Household Income[3]**			
Male	9.1	14.3	11.6	Under $5,000	3.2	2.4	.8
Female	9.4	14.3	11.6	$5,000- 8,000	4.5	2.9	1.3
Age[2]				8,000-10,000	3.1	2.9	1.4
Under 21	1.2	2.2	1.8	10,000-15,000	5.2	8.3	4.6
21-34	2.6	4.5	6.8	15,000-25,000	2.6	7.7	8.8
35-44	4.2	5.8	6.8	25,000 and over	1.1	4.1	6.6
45-54	4.8	7.6	10.8				
55-64	3.5	6.1	10.8	**Residence (SMSA Size)**			
65 and over	3.3	4.3	5.8	Metropolitan	15.3	23.7	20.2
				1,000,000 and over	9.9	14.9	11.9
Education[2]				500,000-1,000,000	2.2	3.7	3.3
Less than H.S. Grad	3.1	3.6	1.6	250,000-500,000	1.9	2.7	2.7
H. S. Graduate	5.3	8.7	6.6	100,000-250,000	1.3	2.2	2.1
Some College	4.0	5.9	5.3	Under 100,000	.1	.2	.3
College Graduate	6.0	10.0	9.9	Nonmetropolitan	4.6	6.9	5.0

[1] Adults residing in conterminous United States
[2] Excludes small number not classified

Source: New York Stock Exchange

THE STRUCTURE OF INSTALMENT CREDIT

End of year, billions of dollars

Year	Total Instalment Credit	Automobile Paper	Home Improvement Loans	Other Consumer Goods	Personal Loans
1955	28.9	13.5	1.7	7.6	6.1
1956	31.7	14.4	1.9	8.6	6.8
1957	33.9	15.3	2.1	8.8	7.6
1958	33.6	14.2	2.3	9.0	8.1
1959	39.2	16.4	2.8	10.6	9.4
1960	43.0	17.7	3.1	11.5	10.6
1961	43.9	17.1	3.2	11.9	11.7
1962	48.7	19.4	3.3	12.6	13.4
1963	55.5	22.3	3.4	14.2	15.6
1964	62.7	24.9	3.6	16.3	17.8
1965	70.9	28.4	3.7	18.5	20.2
1966	76.2	30.0	3.8	20.7	21.7
1967	79.4	29.8	4.0	22.4	23.2
1968	87.7	32.9	4.2	24.6	25.9
1969	97.1	35.5	4.6	28.3	28.7
1970	102.1	35.2	5.1	31.5	30.3
1971	111.7	38.8	5.4	34.6	32.8
1972	127.4	44.3	6.3	39.8	37.1
1973	148.3	51.3	7.5	47.3	42.2
1974	158.1	52.2	8.4	52.0	45.4
1975	161.8	53.6	8.3	52.7e	47.2e

e—Estimate. The Federal Reserve no longer publishes separate data for personal loans, except for commercial banks and finance companies

Source: Federal Reserve

CONSUMER CREDIT OUTSTANDING

End of year, billions of dollars

Year	Total Consumer Credit	Instalment Credit	Noninstalment Credit			
			Total	Charge Accounts[1]	Single Payment Loans	Service Credit
1955	38.8	28.9	9.9	4.8	3.0	2.1
1956	42.3	31.7	10.6	5.0	3.3	2.4
1957	45.0	33.9	11.1	5.1	3.4	2.6
1958	45.1	33.6	11.5	5.1	3.6	2.8
1959	51.5	39.2	12.3	5.1	4.1	3.1
1960	56.1	43.0	13.2	5.3	4.5	3.3
1961	58.0	43.9	14.1	5.3	5.1	3.6
1962	63.8	48.7	15.1	5.7	5.5	4.0
1963	71.7	55.5	16.3	5.9	6.1	4.2
1964	80.3	62.7	17.6	6.2	6.9	4.5
1965	89.9	70.9	19.0	6.4	7.7	4.9
1966	96.2	76.2	20.0	6.7	8.0	5.3
1967	100.8	79.4	21.4	7.1	8.6	5.7
1968	110.8	87.7	23.0	7.2	9.5	6.3
1969	121.1	97.1	24.0	7.4	9.7	6.9
1970	127.2	102.1	25.1	8.0	9.7	7.5
1971	139.1	111.7	27.4	8.4	10.9	8.2
1972	157.9	127.4	30.5	8.8	12.6	9.0
1973	180.8	148.3	32.5	9.2	13.4	10.0
1974	191.5	158.1	33.4	9.5	13.0	10.9
1975	196.7	161.8	34.9	10.4	12.5	12.0

[1] In addition to retail charge accounts, includes service station and miscellaneous credit card accounts and home heating oil accounts

Source: Federal Reserve

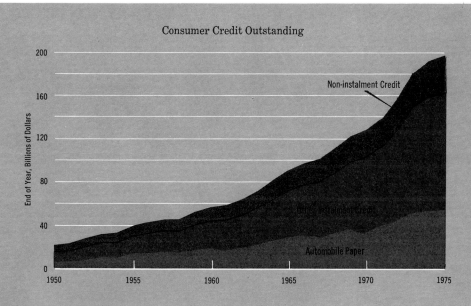

Consumer Credit Outstanding

INSTALMENT CREDIT EXTENDED AND LIQUIDATED

Billions of dollars

Year	Extensions	Liquidations	Net Change
1955	39.0	33.6	5.3
1956	39.9	37.1	2.8
1957	42.0	39.9	2.1
1958	40.1	40.3	− .2
1959	48.0	42.6	5.4
1960	49.8	46.1	3.7
1961	49.0	48.1	.9
1962	56.2	51.4	4.8
1963	63.6	56.8	6.8
1964	70.7	63.5	7.2
1965	78.7	70.5	8.2
1966	82.8	77.5	5.4
1967	87.2	84.0	3.2
1968	100.0	91.7	8.3
1969	109.1	99.8	9.4
1970	112.2	107.2	5.0
1971	124.7	115.1	9.6
1972	142.9	127.1	15.8
1973	164.5	143.7	20.8
1974	166.2	156.3	9.8
1975	166.8	163.1	3.7

Source: Federal Reserve

DISPOSABLE INCOME AND CONSUMER CREDIT

Year	Disposable Personal Income (Billion Dollars)	As Percent of Disposable Income	
		Total Credit	Instalment Credit
1960	349.4	16.1	12.3
1961	362.9	16.0	12.1
1962	383.9	16.6	12.7
1963	402.8	17.8	13.8
1964	437.0	18.4	14.3
1965	472.2	19.0	15.0
1966	510.4	18.9	14.9
1967	544.5	18.5	14.6
1968	588.1	18.8	14.9
1969	630.4	19.2	15.4
1970	685.9	18.5	14.9
1971	742.8	18.7	15.0
1972	801.3	19.7	15.9
1973	903.1	20.0	16.4
1974	983.6	19.5	16.1
1975	1,076.7	18.3	15.0

Sources: Department of Commerce; Federal Reserve

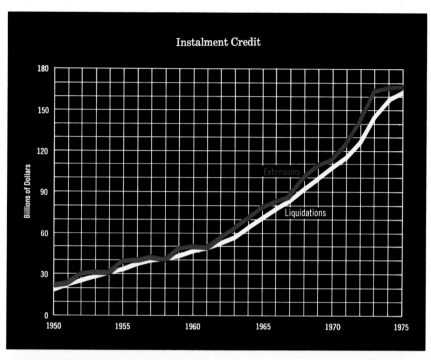

Instalment Credit

Billions of Dollars

Extensions

Liquidations

180 150 120 90 60 30 0

1950   1955   1960   1965   1970   1975

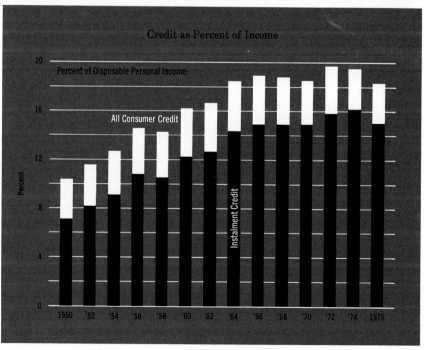

Credit as Percent of Income

Percent of Disposable Personal Income:

All Consumer Credit

Instalment Credit

Percent

20   16   12   8   4   0

1950 '52 '54 '56 '58 '60 '62 '64 '66 '68 '70 '72 '74 1975

INSTALMENT CREDIT AT COMMERCIAL BANKS

End of year; millions of dollars.

Type of Credit	1970	1971	1972	1973	1974	1975
TOTAL	45,398	51,606	60,870	71,871	75,846	75,710
Automobile	20,806	23,252	27,305	31,502	30,994	30,198
Mobile Homes[1]	- -	4,634	6,408	8,340	8,972	8,420
Home Improvements	3,071	3,231	3,601	4,083	4,694	4,813
Revolving Credit:						
Bank Credit Cards...........	3,792	4,490	5,408	6,838	8,281	9,078
Bank Check Credit	1,336	1,462	1,775	2,254	2,797	2,883
All Other	16,393	14,538	16,373	18,854	20,108	20,318
Personal Loans..............	9,280	10,064	11,380	12,873	13,771	14,035
Other[1]	7,113	4,474	4,993	5,981	6,337	6,283

Note: Data for 1970 not strictly comparable with figures for later years
[1] Mobile homes included in "Other" in 1970

Source: Federal Reserve

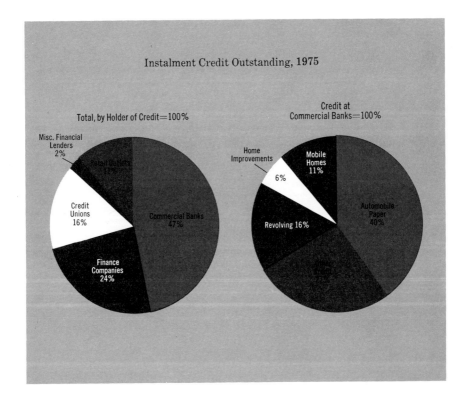

Instalment Credit Outstanding, 1975

Total, by Holder of Credit=100%

Misc. Financial Lenders 2%

Retail Outlets

Credit Unions 16%

Commercial Banks 47%

Finance Companies 24%

Credit at Commercial Banks=100%

Home Improvements 6%

Mobile Homes 11%

Automobile Paper 40%

Revolving 16%

CHARACTERISTICS OF FIRST MORTGAGE LOANS

Item and Year	Contract Interest Rate (Percent)	Term to Maturity (Years)	Loans to Price Ratio (Percent)	Purchase Price (Thousand Dollars)
New Homes				
1965—April	5.74	24.9	73.7	24.9
1967—April	6.31	24.8	73.2	27.0
1968—April	6.57	25.3	73.4	30.3
1969—April	7.47	25.4	72.6	34.4
1970—April	8.24	24.8	71.3	34.9
1971—April	7.37	26.3	73.6	36.0
1972—April	7.38	27.2	76.0	38.3
1973—April[1]	7.53	26.6	78.2	36.9
1974—April	8.47	26.1	77.3	38.5
1975—April	8.71	26.5	76.4	44.5
October	8.75	27.3	77.5	43.9
1976—April p	8.72	27.1	74.6	48.6
Existing Homes				
1965—April	5.89	20.4	71.8	19.6
1967—April	6.34	22.3	72.6	23.7
1968—April	6.64	22.6	72.8	25.1
1969—April	7.46	23.0	71.8	28.2
1970—April	8.19	22.7	70.2	29.6
1971—April	7.34	24.2	73.6	31.8
1972—April	7.30	25.2	75.3	33.6
1973—April[1]	7.55	23.9	77.3	30.1
1974—April	8.43	22.9	73.2	32.7
1975—April	8.92	23.9	73.5	37.5
October	8.97	24.3	74.3	38.6
1976—April p	8.85	24.5	73.3	39.6

Note: Data refer to loans originated directly by savings and loan associations, life insurance companies, mortgage companies, commercial banks and mutual savings banks
[1] New series, not strictly comparable with earlier data   Source: Federal Home Loan Bank Board
p-Preliminary

INSTALMENT CREDIT OUTSTANDING BY HOLDER

End of year; billions of dollars, except percent

Credit Holder	1955	1960	1965	1970	1975 Amount	1975 Percent
TOTAL	28.9	43.0	70.9	102.1	161.8	100.0
Financial Institutions ...	24.4	36.7	61.1	88.2	143.5	88.7
Commercial Banks ...	10.6	16.7	29.0	45.4	75.7	46.8
Finance Companies[1] .	11.8	15.4	23.9	27.7	38.9	24.1
Credit Unions	1.7	3.9	7.3	13.0	25.4	15.7
Misc. Lenders[2]	.3	.6	1.0	2.1	3.5	2.2
Retail Outlets[3]	4.5	6.3	9.8	13.9	18.3	11.3

[1] Sales finance, consumer finance and other finance companies
[2] Savings and loan associations and mutual savings banks and auto dealers
[3] Excludes 30-day charge credit held by retailers, oil and gas companies, and travel and entertainment companies
Source: Federal Reserve

MORTGAGE DEBT OUTSTANDING ON NONFARM HOMES

Debt as of year-end on 1-4 family homes; billions of dollars, except percent

Mortgage Holder	1955	1960	1965	1970	1975p Amount	1975p Percent
TOTAL DEBT OUTSTANDING .	88.2	141.3	212.9	280.2	447.6	100.0
Savings, Loan Associations	30.0	55.4	94.2	125.0	225.3	50.3
Mutual Savings Banks	11.1	18.4	30.1	37.3	46.0	10.3
Commercial Banks	15.1	19.2	30.4	42.3	76.6	17.1
Life Insurance Companies	17.7	24.9	29.6	26.7	17.7	4.0
Federal Government Agencies ...	3.0	7.1	6.4	22.0	58.4	13.1
Individuals and Others	11.4	16.3	22.3	26.9	23.5	5.3

p—Preliminary

Sources: Federal Home Loan Bank Board; Federal Reserve (compiled from data from Government agencies and private organizations)

LIFE INSURANCE IN FORCE

End of year, billions of dollars

Year	Total	Ordinary	Group	Industrial	Credit
1950..................	234.2	149.1	47.8	33.4	3.8
1951..................	253.1	159.1	54.4	34.9	4.8
1952..................	276.6	170.9	62.9	36.4	6.4
1953..................	304.3	185.0	72.9	37.8	8.6
1954..................	333.7	198.6	86.4	38.7	10.0
1955..................	372.3	216.8	101.3	39.7	14.5
1956..................	412.6	238.3	117.4	40.1	16.8
1957..................	458.4	264.9	133.9	40.1	19.4
1958..................	493.6	288.6	144.8	39.6	20.5
1959..................	542.1	317.2	160.2	39.8	25.0
1960..................	586.4	341.9	175.9	39.6	29.1
1961..................	629.5	366.1	192.8	39.5	31.1
1962..................	676.0	391.0	210.0	39.6	35.3
1963..................	730.6	420.8	229.5	39.7	40.7
1964..................	797.8	457.9	253.6	39.8	46.5
1965..................	900.6	499.6	308.1	39.8	53.0
1966..................	984.7	541.0	345.9	39.7	58.1
1967..................	1,079.8	584.6	394.5	39.2	61.5
1968..................	1,183.4	633.4	442.8	38.8	68.4
1969..................	1,284.5	682.5	488.9	38.6	74.6
1970..................	1,402.1	734.7	551.4	38.6	77.4
1971..................	1,503.3	792.3	590.0	39.2	81.9
1972..................	1,628.0	853.9	640.7	40.0	93.4
1973..................	1,778.3	928.2	708.3	40.6	101.2
1974..................	1,985.7	1,009.0	827.6	39.4	109.6
1975..................	2,139.6	1,083.4	904.7	39.4	112.0

Note: Credit life insurance is limited to life insurance loans of ten years or less. "Ordinary" and "Group" include credit life insurance on loans of more than ten years

Source: Institute of Life Insurance

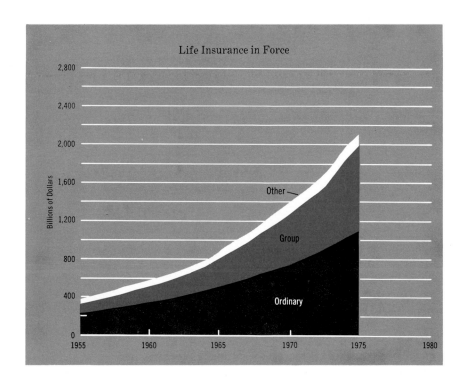

Life Insurance in Force

Billions of Dollars

Other

Group

Ordinary

HOME MORTGAGE DEBT AND DISPOSABLE INCOME

Billions of dollars, except percent

Year	Home Mortgage Debt[1]	Disposable Personal Income	Debt as Percent of Income
1960	141.3	349.4	40.4
1961	153.1	362.9	42.2
1962	166.5	383.9	43.4
1963	182.2	402.8	45.2
1964	197.6	437.0	45.2
1965	212.9	472.2	45.1
1966	223.6	510.4	43.8
1967	236.1	544.5	43.4
1968	251.2	588.1	42.7
1969	266.5	630.4	42.3
1970	280.3	685.9	40.9
1971	307.2	742.8	41.4
1972	345.3	801.3	43.1
1973	384.6	903.1	42.6
1974	411.6	983.6	41.8
1975p	447.6	1,076.7	41.6

[1] Debt outstanding on one- to four-family nonfarm dwellings, as of year-end
p—Preliminary

Sources: Department of Commerce; Federal Home Loan Bank Board; Federal Reserve

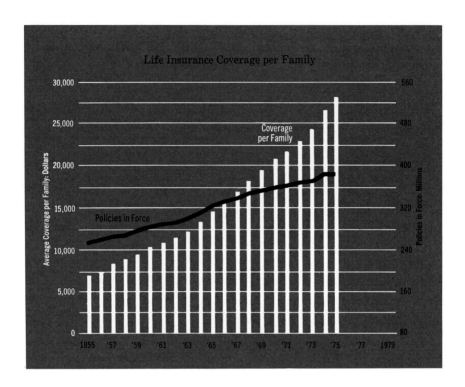

Life Insurance Coverage per Family

LIFE INSURANCE SALES

Billions of dollars

Year	Total	Ordinary	Group[1]	Industrial
1960	74.4	52.9	14.6	6.9
1961	79.0	55.0	17.0	7.0
1962	79.6	57.0	15.5	7.0
1963	89.6	64.3	18.2	7.2
1964	105.0	74.0	23.7	7.3
1965	142.2b	83.5	51.4b	7.3
1966	122.0	88.7	26.2	7.1
1967	140.9a	94.7	39.1a	7.1
1968	150.5a	103.9	39.9a	6.7
1969	159.3	113.5	39.3	6.5
1970	193.1b	122.8	63.7b	6.6
1971	188.8	132.1	49.4	7.3
1972	208.7	145.5	55.9	7.4
1973	234.2	162.5	64.5	7.2
1974p	298.2b	182.3	108.9b	7.0
1975p	283.1b	185.2	90.9b	7.0

Note: Data refer to new paid-for insurance and are estimates of all sales, excluding credit life insurance
[1] Includes sales of mass-marketed ordinary beginning 1966
a—Includes Federal Employees Government Life Insurance
b—Includes Servicemen's Group Life Insurance, amounting to $27.8 billion in 1965, $17.1 billion in 1970, $907 million in 1974 and $1,694 million in 1975

p—Preliminary

Sources: Life Insurance Agency Management Association; Institute of Life Insurance

LIFE INSURANCE IN FORCE AND DISPOSABLE INCOME

Year	Life Insurance Policies in Force[1] (Millions)	Life Insurance Coverage per Family (Dollars)	Disposable Income per Family (Dollars)	Premiums[2] as Percent of Disposable Income	Average Size of Policy in Force (Dollars) Ordinary	Average Size of Policy in Force (Dollars) Group
1950 ...	202	4,600	4,000	3.50	2,320	2,480
1955 ...	252	6,900	5,100	3.73	2,720	3,200
1960 ...	282	10,200	6,100	3.82	3,600	4,030
1965 ...	320	14,600	7,700	3.88	4,660	5,060
1966 ...	331	15,800	8,200	3.84	4,940	5,360
1967 ...	336	17,100	8,600	3.81	5,150	5,730
1968 ...	345	18,300	9,100	3.80	5,450	6,070
1969 ...	351	19,400	9,500	3.85	5,770	6,470
1970 ...	355	20,700	10,100	3.70	6,110	6,910
1971 ...	357	21,700	10,700	3.75	6,440	7,170
1972 ...	365	22,900	11,300	3.77	6,790	7,530
1973 ...	369	24,400	12,400	3.67	7,230	8,010
1974 ...	380	26,500	13,100	3.61	7,690	8,840
1975 ...	380	28,100	14,100	3.67	8,090	9,360

Note: Data are revised. See *note* to table page 152 for decription of revisions

[1] Ordinary, group, industrial and credit life insurance policies
[2] Premiums paid for life insurance and annuities

Sources: Institute of Life Insurance; Department of Commerce

INDIVIDUAL INCOME TAX RETURNS BY INCOME CLASS, 1974

Income Class	Returns (Millions)	Adjusted Gross Income[1] (Mil. Dollars)	Total Income Tax[2] Total (Mil. Dollars)	Total Income Tax[2] As Percent of Income	Total Income Tax[2] Avg. Tax Per Return (Dollars)
Total Returns	83.3	906.1	123.7	13.7	1,484
Taxable Returns	67.2	880.2	123.7	14.1	1,839
Percent Distribution					
Taxable Returns	100.0	100.0	100.0	14.1	1,839
Under 3,000	5.3	1.0	.2	2.8	67
$3,000- 5,000	12.2	3.8	1.6	6.1	245
$5,000- 7,000	12.4	5.7	3.3	8.2	492
7,000- 10,000	16.9	11.0	7.7	9.9	838
10,000- 15,000	23.1	21.9	17.3	11.1	1,380
15,000- 20,000	14.9	19.6	17.8	12.7	2,197
20,000- 30,000	10.7	19.4	20.7	15.0	3,562
30,000- 50,000	3.2	9.1	12.3	18.9	6,959
50,000-100,000	1.0	5.2	9.9	26.5	17,506
100,000 and over	.2	3.3	9.1	38.4	68,172

[1] Less deficit
[2] Income tax after credits plus additional tax for tax preferences
Source: Treasury Department

INDIVIDUAL INCOME TAX BY STATES, 1974

State	Taxable Returns (Thousands)	Average Tax per Taxable Return (Dollars)	State	Taxable Returns (Thousands)	Average Tax per Taxable Return (Dollars)
TOTAL U.S.[1]	67,629	1,829	Missouri	1,443	1,749
			Montana	218	1,592
Alabama	944	1,526	Nebraska	499	1,720
Alaska	114	2,613	Nevada	230	1,857
Arizona	698	1,617	New Hampshire ...	268	1,637
Arkansas	558	1,427	New Jersey	2,546	2,128
California	6,945	1,867	New Mexico	304	1,526
Colorado	848	1,781	New York	5,957	1,978
Connecticut	1,120	2,166	North Carolina	1,621	1,485
Delaware	202	2,054			
District of			North Dakota	192	1,646
Columbia	217	2,191	Ohio	3,537	1,827
Florida	2,638	1,818	Oklahoma	737	1,761
Georgia	1,445	1,582	Oregon	755	1,728
Hawaii	284	1,895	Pennsylvania	3,922	1,774
Idaho	233	1,579	Rhode Island	314	1,676
Illinois	3,820	2,132	South Carolina	833	1,382
Indiana	1,679	1,886	South Dakota	187	1,522
Iowa	879	1,841	Tennessee	1,215	1,584
Kansas	717	1,832			
Kentucky	903	1,705	Texas	3,577	1,900
Louisiana	988	1,710	Utah	336	1,511
Maine	323	1,361	Vermont	139	1,393
Maryland	1,470	2,045	Virginia	1,635	1,816
Massachusetts	1,937	1,811	Washington	1,153	1,854
Michigan	2,882	1,963	West Virginia	492	1,658
Minnesota	1,235	1,679	Wisconsin	1,417	1,683
Mississippi	541	1,405	Wyoming	119	2,023

[1] Includes data for Puerto Rico and U.S. citizens residing in Panama Canal Zone, Virgin Islands, and abroad

Source: Treasury Department

EXPENDITURES

EXPENDITURES

PERSONAL CONSUMPTION EXPENDITURES

Year	Total	Durable Goods	Nondurable Goods	Services
Billions of Dollars				
1950	192.0	30.8	98.2	63.0
1955	253.7	38.6	122.9	92.1
1960	324.9	43.1	151.1	130.7
1965	430.2	62.8	188.6	178.7
1966	464.8	67.7	204.7	192.4
1967	490.4	69.6	212.6	208.1
1968	535.9	80.0	230.4	225.6
1969	579.7	85.5	247.0	247.2
1970	618.8	84.9	264.7	269.1
1971	668.2	97.1	277.7	293.4
1972	733.0	111.2	299.3	322.4
1973	808.5	122.9	334.4	351.3
1974	885.9	121.9	375.7	388.3
1975	963.8	128.1	409.8	426.0
Billions of 1975 Dollars				
1950	425.0	50.7	216.2	161.4
1955	496.6	61.0	247.7	191.4
1960	569.4	61.4	278.2	233.6
1965	701.5	85.8	326.0	292.5
1966	736.7	92.4	341.3	305.7
1967	758.2	93.2	346.7	320.8
1968	796.2	103.1	361.0	334.1
1969	823.8	107.4	369.3	348.9
1970	840.8	103.9	377.7	361.2
1971	869.7	114.7	384.1	372.2
1972	921.4	130.0	399.9	391.7
1973	963.2	141.3	413.6	408.0
1974	955.1	131.5	404.8	418.4
1975	963.8	128.1	409.8	426.0

Note: Components do not add to totals because of rounding

Source: Department of Commerce

PER CAPITA REAL SPENDING

All per capita figures in 1975 dollars

Year	Personal Income	Personal Consumption Expenditures[1]			
		Total	Durables	Nondurables	Services
1960	3,881	3,151	340	1,540	1,293
1965	4,059	3,610	442	1,678	1,505
1966	4,716	3,748	470	1,736	1,555
1967	4,873	3,815	469	1,745	1,614
1968	5,073	3,967	514	1,799	1,665
1969	5,227	4,065	530	1,822	1,722
1970	5,314	4,104	507	1,844	1,763
1971	5,402	4,201	554	1,855	1,798
1972	5,670	4,412	622	1,915	1,876
1973	5,973	4,578	672	1,966	1,939
1974	5,873	4,508	621	1,910	1,975
1975	5,833	4,513	600	1,918	1,994

[1] Components do not add to totals because of rounding   Source: Department of Commerce

COMPONENTS OF CONSUMER EXPENDITURES

Year	Total[1]	Food, Beverages	Clothing, Shoes	Housing	Household Operation	Furniture, Equipment	Motor Vehicles, Parts	Gasoline, Oil
				Billions of Dollars				
1960	324.9	81.1	26.7	48.1	20.1	17.7	19.7	12.0
1961	335.0	83.2	27.4	51.2	21.0	17.9	17.8	12.0
1962	355.2	85.5	28.7	54.7	22.2	18.9	21.5	12.6
1963	374.6	87.8	29.5	58.0	23.4	20.3	24.4	12.9
1964	400.4	92.7	31.9	61.4	24.8	22.8	26.0	13.5
1965	430.2	98.9	33.5	65.5	26.3	24.7	29.8	14.7
1966	464.8	106.6	36.6	69.5	28.0	27.7	30.1	16.0
1967	490.4	109.6	38.2	74.1	30.6	29.5	29.7	17.0
1968	535.9	118.3	41.8	79.9	32.7	32.6	35.8	18.4
1969	579.7	126.1	45.1	86.8	35.5	35.0	37.7	20.4
1970	618.8	136.3	46.6	94.0	38.3	36.7	34.9	22.0
1971	668.2	140.6	50.5	102.7	41.6	39.4	43.8	23.4
1972	733.0	150.4	55.1	112.3	45.9	44.8	50.6	24.9
1973	808.5	168.0	61.4	123.1	50.3	50.7	54.4	28.3
1974	885.9	189.4	65.2	136.0	56.4	54.7	48.0	36.4
1975	963.8	209.1	69.9	148.8	63.3	57.4	49.5	40.3
				Billions of 1975 Dollars				
1950	425.0	127.2	35.1	44.5	23.3	19.8	25.2	12.6
1955	496.6	145.6	38.4	58.8	28.8	22.1	31.4	17.6
1960	569.4	160.9	41.8	74.8	35.4	23.0	29.8	22.1
1965	701.5	182.2	50.5	95.3	43.4	32.4	41.6	26.1
1970	840.8	205.0	56.2	119.3	55.0	43.9	43.3	35.0
1975	963.8	209.1	69.9	148.8	63.3	57.4	49.5	40.3

[1] Total includes items not shown separately   Source: Department of Commerce

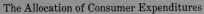

The Allocation of Consumer Expenditures

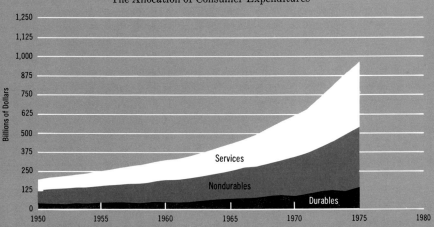

Services

Nondurables

Durables

Personal Consumption Expenditures

1975 Dollars

Current Dollars

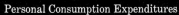

The Rise in Per Capita Spending

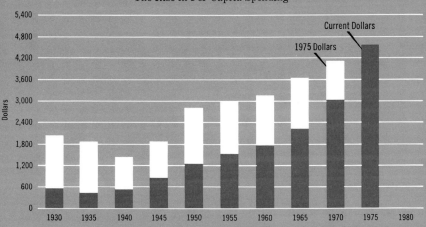

Current Dollars

1975 Dollars

PATTERNS OF CONSUMER SPENDING
Billions of dollars

Type of Product	1960	1970	1974 Amount	1974 Percent
TOTAL CONSUMPTION EXPENDITURES.......	324.9	618.8	885.9	100.0
Food, Beverages, Tobacco[1,2]	88.0	147.1	203.1	22.9
Food for Home Consumption[1]	61.6	102.0	141.5	16.0
Purchased Meals, Beverages[1]	17.2	31.5	44.3	5.0
Food (excl. Alcoholic Beverages)	70.5	118.6	166.4	18.8
Alcoholic Beverages	10.6	17.7	22.9	2.6
Tobacco	6.9	10.8	13.8	1.6
Clothing, Accessories, Jewelry[3]	32.2	55.6	76.4	8.6
Women's, Children's Clothing	14.4	25.1	35.8	4.0
Men's, Boys' Clothing	7.7	13.6	19.2	2.2
Jewelry, Watches	1.9	4.1	5.8	.7
Shoes, Other Footwear	4.5	7.7	10.2	1.1
Clothing Services[4]	3.6	4.9	5.3	.6
Personal Care..............................	5.2	10.9	13.4	1.5
Toilet Articles, Preparations	2.9	6.9	9.2	1.0
Personal Care Services.....................	2.3	4.0	4.2	.5
Housing	48.1	94.0	136.0	15.3
Household Operations and Furnishings[3]	46.1	87.8	130.5	14.7
Furniture, Bedding	4.6	8.2	12.0	1.4
Household Appliances	4.2	6.9	10.0	1.1
Other Housefurnishings	8.5	18.4	27.9	3.2
Household Supplies.......................	3.7	8.6	12.0	1.4
Household Utilities, Telephone, Telegraph	18.0	33.9	53.5	6.0
Medical Care	20.0	49.9	75.8	8.6
Drugs, Supplies, Equipment	4.6	8.4	10.7	1.2
Medical Care Services	15.4	41.5	65.1	7.4
Personal Business	14.2	31.3	44.5	5.0
Transportation	42.4	78.0	115.3	13.0
User-Operated Transportation[3]	39.1	72.5	108.0	12.2
Automobile Purchase[5]	17.2	30.3	41.0	4.6
Gasoline, Oil	12.0	22.0	36.4	4.1
Tires, Accessories, Repairs, etc.	7.6	15.8	24.7	2.8
Public Transportation	3.3	5.5	7.4	.8
Recreation[3]	17.9	41.0	60.5	6.8
Radio, TV, Records, Musical Instruments	3.0	8.9	13.3	1.5
Toys, Sporting Goods.....................	4.5	11.0	16.8	1.9
Books, Magazines, Newspapers.............	3.3	6.3	10.1	11.4
Paid Admissions, Spectator Amusements	1.7	3.1	4.0	.5
Private Education, Research..................	3.7	9.9	13.5	1.5
Religious, Welfare Activities..................	4.9	8.5	11.7	1.3
Foreign Travel and Other, Net	2.1	4.7	5.1	.6

Note: This table summarizes major series of personal consumption expenditures that are shown in greater detail in tables on pages 163 through 168

[1] Includes alcoholic beverages
[2] Components below do not add to total because of overlapping
[3] Includes items not shown separately
[4] Cleaning, laundering, alteration, storage of clothing; shoe repair and cleaning; watch and jewelry repair and miscellaneous services
[5] Includes other motor vehicles

Source: Department of Commerce

CONSUMER SPENDING FOR FOOD, BEVERAGES AND TOBACCO

Millions of dollars

Year	Food, Alcoholic Beverages		Food Only[1]	Alcoholic Beverages	Tobacco
	At Home	Away from Home			
1960	61,559	17,214	70,476	10,640	6,863
1961	62,798	18,111	72,364	10,875	7,134
1962	63,838	19,345	73,913	11,553	7,215
1963	65,159	20,446	75,764	12,070	7,494
1964	68,958	21,580	80,154	12,559	7,559
1965	73,910	22,705	85,775	13,105	8,086
1966	80,028	23,994	92,605	13,980	8,523
1967	82,039	24,914	94,955	14,652	8,923
1968	88,320	27,345	102,647	15,684	9,373
1969	94,230	29,074	109,553	16,509	9,751
1970	102,035	31,520	118,617	17,728	10,795
1971	105,237	32,678	122,024	18,587	11,322
1972	112,111	35,490	130,626	19,790	12,204
1973	124,929	39,903	146,756	21,283	13,065
1974	146,457	44,340	166,446	22,905	13,780

[1] Includes food furnished military and other Government and commercial employees, not included in first two columns

Source: Department of Commerce

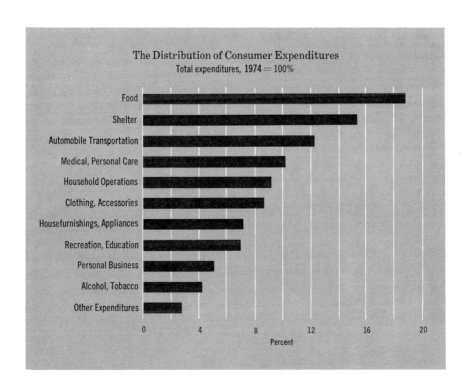

The Distribution of Consumer Expenditures
Total expenditures, 1974 = 100%

CONSUMER SPENDING FOR APPAREL

Millions of dollars

Year	Total[1]	Clothing, Accessories		Shoes, Other Footwear	Clothing Care Services[2]	Jewelry and Watches
		Men's, Boys'	Women's, Children's			
1960	32,219	7,741	14,443	4,479	3,155	1,904
1961	32,904	7,935	14,859	4,537	3,169	1,876
1962	34,416	8,229	15,673	4,738	3,230	2,017
1963	35,402	8,422	16,232	4,791	3,273	2,132
1964	38,277	9,186	17,537	5,154	3,421	2,382
1965	40,304	9,720	18,363	5,316	3,585	2,639
1966	44,091	10,674	19,884	5,866	3,728	3,114
1967	46,149	11,362	20,481	6,177	3,845	3,354
1968	50,276	12,300	22,410	6,892	3,952	3,678
1969	54,009	13,253	24,010	7,669	4,008	3,982
1970	55,619	13,639	25,067	7,733	3,907	4,146
1971	59,618	14,697	27,528	8,162	3,759	4,326
1972	64,809	16,262	29,893	8,915	3,798	4,694
1973	71,955	18,031	33,306	10,005	3,749	5,415
1974	76,365	19,195	35,775	10,169	3,781	5,830

[1] Includes standard clothing issued to military personnel, watch and jewelry repair, and miscellaneous services related to clothing, not shown separately
[2] Cleaning, laundering, alterations, repair of garments; shoe cleaning and repair

Source: Department of Commerce

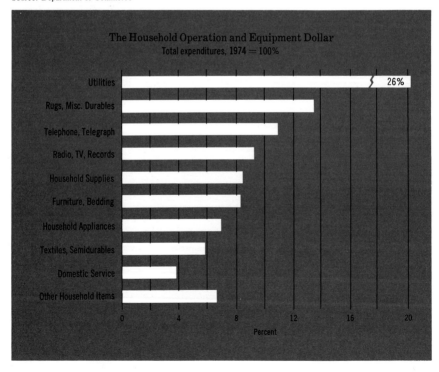

CONSUMER SPENDING FOR HOUSING AND HOUSEHOLD OPERATION

Millions of dollars

Year	Housing[1]	Household Operations Total[2]	Household Supplies	Utilities	Telephone, Telegraph	Domestic Service
1960	48,117	28,747	3,743	13,496	4,515	3,797
1961	51,160	29,974	4,164	13,997	4,827	3,734
1962	54,726	31,689	4,561	14,758	5,110	3,807
1963	57,971	33,551	4,869	15,639	5,524	3,831
1964	61,394	35,589	5,284	16,395	5,951	3,916
1965	65,469	37,891	5,719	17,289	6,488	3,969
1966	69,522	40,754	6,328	18,258	7,007	4,021
1967	74,144	43,773	6,660	19,185	7,668	4,701
1968	79,927	46,828	7,326	20,403	8,329	4,853
1969	86,816	50,617	7,970	21,962	9,258	4,913
1970	93,986	54,257	8,575	23,796	10,060	5,053
1971	102,690	58,285	9,078	25,854	11,005	5,174
1972	112,277	64,299	9,856	28,763	12,386	5,348
1973	123,097	71,545	10,980	32,308	14,167	5,390
1974	135,955	80,661	12,023	37,900	15,649	5,465

[1] Space-rental value
[2] Includes household operations such as writing supplies, service on appliances and homefurnishings, premiums for fire and theft insurance, postage and moving expenses that are not shown separately
Source: Department of Commerce

CONSUMER SPENDING FOR HOUSEFURNISHINGS AND EQUIPMENT

Millions of dollars

Year	Total[1]	Furniture and Bedding	Rugs and Other Household Durables	Tableware and Utensils	Household Textiles, Other Semi-durables	Household Appliances	Radio, TV[2]
1960	20,382	4,586	4,081	1,739	2,727	4,246	3,003
1961	20,808	4,597	4,188	1,756	2,870	4,237	3,160
1962	22,036	4,925	4,513	1,859	3,116	4,274	3,349
1963	23,509	5,309	4,958	1,900	3,223	4,457	3,662
1964	26,347	5,937	5,661	2,125	3,555	4,810	4,259
1965	28,472	6,294	6,117	2,371	3,818	4,831	5,041
1966	31,921	6,804	6,714	2,738	4,194	5,264	6,207
1967	33,862	7,032	7,074	2,947	4,408	5,449	6,952
1968	37,501	7,596	8,045	3,275	4,942	6,050	7,593
1969	40,390	8,110	8,642	3,543	5,347	6,583	8,165
1970	42,421	8,213	8,954	3,762	5,689	6,918	8,885
1971	45,686	8,787	9,685	4,048	6,244	7,388	9,534
1972	51,820	9,920	11,007	4,498	6,981	8,450	10,964
1973	58,558	11,210	12,621	5,092	7,867	9,480	12,288
1974	63,127	11,970	13,946	5,506	8,470	9,965	13,270

[1] Total of items shown
[2] Includes musical instruments and records

Source: Department of Commerce

CONSUMER SPENDING FOR AUTOMOBILE TRANSPORTATION

Millions of dollars

Year	Total	Auto-mobile Purchase[1]	Tires, Tubes Acces-sories, Parts	Auto Repairs, Parking, Rental, etc.	Gasoline and Oil	Tolls	Auto Insur-ance[2]
1960	39,058	17,192	2,485	5,065	11,977	310	2,029
1961	37,640	15,269	2,567	5,360	11,981	330	2,133
1962	42,293	18,706	2,823	5,701	12,567	356	2,140
1963	45,964	21,425	3,010	6,100	12,920	379	2,130
1964	48,510	22,833	3,118	6,492	13,530	421	2,116
1965	54,240	26,578	3,223	6,901	14,696	463	2,379
1966	56,759	26,636	3,434	7,393	15,962	495	2,839
1967	58,259	26,128	3,568	8,004	17,014	517	3,028
1968	66,671	31,861	3,944	8,864	18,422	563	3,017
1969	71,628	33,403	4,304	9,945	20,371	603	3,002
1970	72,503	30,343	4,587	11,248	21,997	643	3,685
1971	85,116	38,631	5,119	12,532	23,396	689	4,749
1972	95,345	44,860	5,691	13,922	24,879	745	5,248
1973	103,959	47,958	6,424	15,380	28,295	786	5,116
1974	107,967	41,030	6,942	17,735	36,447	748	5,065

[1] New cars, net purchases of used cars and purchases of other motor vehicles
[2] Auto insurance premiums less claims paid

Source: Department of Commerce

CONSUMER SPENDING FOR PUBLIC TRANSPORTATION

Millions of dollars

Year	Total	Local	Intercity			
			Total[1]	Railway[2]	Bus	Airline
1960	3,333	2,026	1,307	306	290	676
1961	3,370	1,992	1,378	291	288	760
1962	3,540	2,032	1,508	284	298	882
1963	3,562	2,040	1,522	264	290	924
1964	3,749	2,042	1,707	280	335	1,044
1965	3,965	2,061	1,904	284	375	1,191
1966	4,249	2,121	2,128	297	429	1,329
1967	4,661	2,236	2,425	270	466	1,582
1968	4,956	2,293	2,663	227	475	1,838
1969	5,314	2,407	2,907	206	470	2,086
1970	5,529	2,521	3,008	185	496	2,166
1971	5,799	2,600	3,199	155	525	2,347
1972	6,093	2,604	3,489	176	523	2,637
1973	6,544	2,632	3,912	204	545	2,988
1974	7,363	2,812	4,551	259	616	3,484

[1] Includes inland water and other transportation not shown separately
[2] Excluding commutation

Source: Department of Commerce

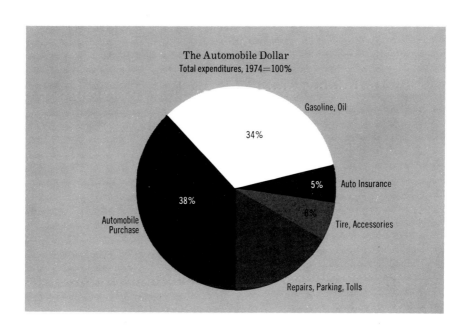

The Automobile Dollar
Total expenditures, 1974=100%

Gasoline, Oil

34%

5% Auto Insurance

38%

8%

Automobile
Purchase

Tire, Accessories

Repairs, Parking, Tolls

CONSUMER SPENDING FOR RECREATION

Millions of dollars

Year	Total[1]	Reading Materials		Toys, Sport Equipment		Spectator Admissions
		Books, Maps	Magazines, News-papers	Wheel Goods, Durables	Non-durables	
1960	17,855	1,139	2,164	1,976	2,477	1,652
1961	18,573	1,212	2,026	1,944	2,663	1,685
1962	20,042	1,287	2,305	2,015	2,889	1,757
1963	21,655	1,413	2,468	2,180	3,113	1,820
1964	23,698	1,612	2,498	2,520	3,375	1,922
1965	25,907	1,648	2,662	2,888	3,585	2,123
1966	29,794	1,840	3,130	3,620	4,039	2,310
1967	31,942	1,847	3,206	4,085	4,272	2,404
1968	35,159	1,941	3,537	4,706	4,650	2,653
1969	38,130	2,082	3,552	5,359	5,102	2,903
1970	40,999	2,356	3,900	5,511	5,477	3,141
1971	43,664	2,461	4,240	5,902	5,839	3,359
1972	49,100	2,530	4,685	7,315	6,542	3,487
1973	54,945	2,784	5,802	8,197	7,305	3,659
1974	60,544	3,049	7,078	8,853	7,993	4,016

[1] Includes radio and TV, shown with housefurnishings and equipment on page 165, and other recreational expenditures not separately listed

Source: Department of Commerce

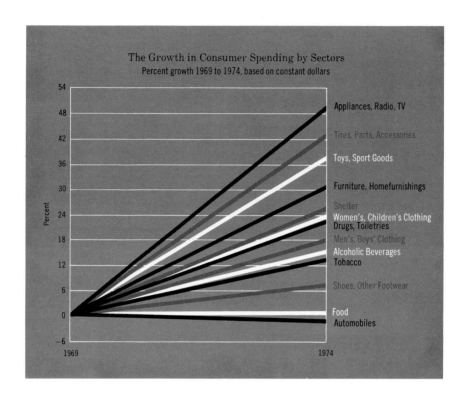

The Growth in Consumer Spending by Sectors
Percent growth 1969 to 1974, based on constant dollars

Appliances, Radio, TV
Tires, Parts, Accessories
Toys, Sport Goods
Furniture, Homefurnishings
Shelter
Women's, Children's Clothing
Drugs, Toiletries
Men's, Boys' Clothing
Alcoholic Beverages
Tobacco
Shoes, Other Footwear
Food
Automobiles

CONSUMER SPENDING FOR MEDICAL AND PERSONAL CARE

Millions of dollars

Year	Medical Care			Personal Care		
	Total	Drug Items, Other Medical Products	Professional Services, Insurance	Total	Toiletries, Preparations	Services
1960	20,002	4,613	15,389	5,242	2,938	2,304
1961	21,328	4,955	16,373	5,783	3,254	2,529
1962	23,383	5,423	17,960	6,351	3,595	2,756
1963	25,174	5,668	19,506	6,656	3,829	2,827
1964	28,183	5,876	22,307	7,106	4,128	2,978
1965	30,053	6,152	23,901	7,617	4,504	3,113
1966	32,554	6,530	26,024	8,455	4,992	3,463
1967	35,091	6,709	28,382	9,082	5,375	3,707
1968	38,766	7,323	31,443	9,545	5,943	3,602
1969	44,596	7,812	36,784	10,265	6,481	3,784
1970	49,853	8,360	41,493	10,920	6,947	3,973
1971	54,671	8,521	46,150	11,096	7,325	3,771
1972	61,188	9,093	52,095	11,749	7,869	3,880
1973	67,468	9,803	57,665	12,616	8,557	4,059
1974	75,771	10,659	65,112	13,418	9,238	4,180

Source: Department of Commerce

THE REAL GROWTH IN CONSUMPTION EXPENDITURES
Index numbers, 1960 = 100; based on constant dollars

Year	Food[1]	Alcoholic Beverages	Tobacco	Women's, Children's Clothing	Men's, Boys' Clothing	Footwear
1960 (Billion 1974 dollars)...	133.7	15.6	11.7	21.3	12.0	7.3
1960 (Index numbers)	100	100	100	100	100	100
1965	113	117	106	124	119	112
1966	116	122	107	131	128	117
1967	118	123	108	130	132	117
1968	122	127	107	134	135	124
1969	124	127	105	136	136	130
1970	127	130	107	137	135	124
1971	127	129	108	145	140	127
1972	129	135	112	154	152	135
1973	128	145	117	166	164	145
1974	124	146	118	168	161	139

	Housing	Household Services	Furniture, Bedding	Other Household furnishings	Household Supplies	Household Appliances
1960 (Billion 1974 dollars)...	70.9	32.1	6.8	11.5	5.5	4.4
1960 (Index numbers)	100	100	100	100	100	100
1965	128	123	133	139	153	124
1966	133	129	141	153	167	138
1967	139	138	139	158	171	143
1968	146	143	144	171	184	155
1969	153	150	144	180	198	164
1970	160	155	141	185	202	169
1971	166	158	146	200	204	176
1972	175	166	162	221	220	202
1973	184	175	177	245	238	226
1974	192	175	175	242	220	226

	Radio, TV	Autos (New & Used)	Tires, Parts, Accessories	Gasoline, Oil	Drugs, Toiletries	Medical, Personal Care Services
1960 (Billion 1974 dollars)...	2.6	23.7	3.2	21.0	8.0	34.4
1960 (Index numbers)	100	100	100	100	100	100
1965	192	139	129	118	143	133
1966	248	139	132	125	154	139
1967	280	133	135	130	164	141
1968	304	153	142	138	176	146
1969	328	155	152	148	186	158
1970	356	137	155	158	197	168
1971	380	162	168	167	200	174
1972	440	182	184	175	212	185
1973	492	191	213	182	224	195
1974	520	153	216	173	228	202

[1] Excludes alcoholic beverages

Source: Department of Commerce

THE PATTERN OF GROWTH IN CONSUMER SPENDING, 1960-1974

Average annual growth rates and income elasticity ratios, selected items,
based on constant dollars

Item	Average Annual Growth Rates		Income Elasticity Ratios[1]	
	1960-1974	1967-1974	1960-1974	1967-1974
DISPOSABLE PERSONAL INCOME	4.2	3.6	1.00	1.00
PERSONAL CONSUMPTION EXPENDITURES .	4.0	3.5	.95	.97
Durable Goods[2]	6.2	5.5	1.48	1.53
Automobile Purchase	4.5	3.3	1.07	.90
Tires, Tubes, Accessories, Parts	4.9	7.1	1.17	1.96
Furniture, Bedding	4.0	3.6	.95	.99
Kitchen, Other Household Appliances	6.2	6.9	1.49	1.90
China, Glassware, Other Durable Hsfgs ...	7.0	6.7	1.67	1.86
Radios, TV, Records, Instruments	12.5	9.2	2.99	2.53
Wheel Goods, Durable Toys, Sport Equip. .	10.0	8.1	2.39	2.25
Nondurable Goods[2]	3.0	2.4	.71	.66
Food, Beverages at Home	2.2	.9	.53	.26
Purchased Meals, Beverages.............	2.0	2.0	.49	.55
Food Only (excl. Alcoholic Beverages)	2.0	.9	.48	.25
Alcoholic Beverages	2.6	2.4	.62	.67
Tobacco	.9	1.5	.22	.42
Shoes, Other Footwear	2.7	2.6	.64	.71
Women's Children's Clothing	3.6	3.9	.85	1.09
Men's, Boys' Clothing (incl. Military)	3.6	3.3	.86	.90
Gasoline, Oil	4.7	4.7	1.13	1.31
Toilet Articles, Preparations	6.3	3.8	1.50	1.05
Semidurable Housefurnishings	6.2	6.1	1.46	1.68
Household Supplies, Preparations	5.9	4.0	1.40	1.10
Drug Preparations, Sundries	5.5	5.6	1.31	1.55
Services[2]	4.3	3.9	1.02	1.06
Housing: Owner-Occupied (Nonfarm)	5.0	5.0	1.18	1.39
Housing: Renter-Occupied (Nonfarm)	4.7	4.4	1.11	1.21
Household Operation Services, Total	4.3	3.6	1.02	.99
Electricity	6.0	5.9	1.43	1.64
Gas	3.3	1.6	.78	.45
Telephone	7.9	7.2	1.87	1.99
Auto Transportation Services	4.9	4.9	1.18	1.36
Purchased Local Transportation	−2.8	−3.1	−.67	.87
Purchased Intercity Transportation	6.0	2.7	1.43	.75
Medical Care Services	5.5	6.1	1.31	1.68
Personal Care Services..................	− .1	−3.4	−.02	.93
Admissions to Spectator Amusements	1.0	1.5	.21	.41
Higher Education.......................	5.0	2.9	1.18	.80
Foreign Travel, U.S. Residents	5.7	3.6	1.37	.99

Note: Growth rates are based on exponential trend growth
[1] Percentage change in personal consumption expenditures for each 1% rise in real disposable personal income
[2] Includes items not separately listed   Sources: Department of Commerce; The Conference Board

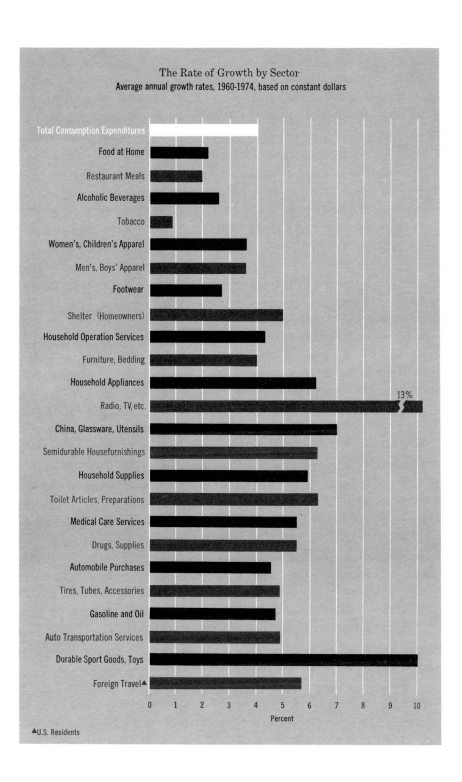

The Rate of Growth by Sector

Average annual growth rates, 1960-1974, based on constant dollars

Total Consumption Expenditures
Food at Home
Restaurant Meals
Alcoholic Beverages
Tobacco
Women's, Children's Apparel
Men's, Boys' Apparel
Footwear
Shelter (Homeowners)
Household Operation Services
Furniture, Bedding
Household Appliances
Radio, TV, etc.
13%
China, Glassware, Utensils
Semidurable Housefurnishings
Household Supplies
Toilet Articles, Preparations
Medical Care Services
Drugs, Supplies
Automobile Purchases
Tires, Tubes, Accessories
Gasoline and Oil
Auto Transportation Services
Durable Sport Goods, Toys
Foreign Travel▲

0   1   2   3   4   5   6   7   8   9   10

Percent

▲U.S. Residents

171

FAMILY SPENDING PATTERNS BY AGE OF HEAD, 1960-1961

Average annual expenditures, all nonfarm families and single consumers

		Age of Head					
Item	Total	Under 25	25-34	35-44	45-54	55-64	65 and Over
PERCENT DISTRIBUTION:							
All Families[1]	100.0	5.0	19.1	22.2	19.3	15.5	19.0
All Persons	100.0	4.3	22.9	29.5	20.7	11.8	10.8
Total Expenditures[2]	100.0	4.2	20.4	27.4	22.8	14.2	11.0
AVERAGE FAMILY SIZE	3.2	2.6	3.8	4.2	3.4	2.4	1.8
				Dollars			
TOTAL EXPENDITURES[2]	5,152	4,310	5,521	6,364	6,092	4,734	2,983
Food	1,259	928	1,298	1,589	1,471	1,174	778
Prepared at Home	1,006	685	1,029	1,269	1,171	927	660
Away from Home	253	243	269	319	301	248	118
Alcoholic Beverages	81	56	88	105	105	74	37
Tobacco	93	85	107	116	114	84	40
Housing, Household Operations	1,236	1,031	1,377	1,449	1,352	1,132	869
Shelter	688	657	798	803	743	612	460
Fuel, Light, etc.	250	137	241	292	283	249	209
Other Operations	298	236	339	353	326	271	200
Housefurnishings, Equipment	269	285	332	346	296	225	120
Appliances	76	94	100	95	76	60	35
Furniture	78	102	106	102	83	57	28
Other Furnishings	115	89	126	149	137	108	57
Clothing and Accessories	525	396	540	716	687	454	213
Men's and Boys'	190	133	205	277	249	150	61
Women's, Girls, etc.	266	211	258	353	352	242	121
Materials, Services	68	53	77	85	86	61	31
Transportation	781	842	879	960	942	711	350
Automobile	700	782	814	869	848	617	285
Other	81	60	65	91	94	94	65
Medical Care	342	252	331	367	369	362	303
Services	269	212	263	292	295	283	225
Supplies	81	40	68	76	74	79	80
Personal Care	148	120	153	186	181	138	81
Services	67	45	60	80	85	72	42
Supplies	81	75	93	106	96	66	38
Recreation, Equipment	205	192	248	277	244	167	74
Reading, Education	100	78	87	123	165	82	42
Other Expenditures	113	45	81	130	166	131	76

[1] Includes single consumers
[2] For current consumption

Sources: Department of Labor; The Conference Board

FAMILY SPENDING PATTERNS BY INCOME CLASS, 1960-1961

Average annual expenditures, all nonfarm families and single consumers

Item	Total	Family Income					
		Under $3,000	$3,000- 5,000	5,000- 7,500	$7,500- 10,000	$10,000- 15,000	$15,000 & Over
PERCENT							
DISTRIBUTION	100.0	22.4	20.8	26.2	16.1	10.7	3.7
All Persons	100.0	14.9	19.7	29.0	18.8	13.2	4.4
Total Expenditures[2]	100.0	8.9	15.6	27.1	21.2	18.0	9.1
AVERAGE FAMILY							
SIZE	3.2	2.1	3.0	3.5	3.7	3.9	3.8
				Dollars			
TOTAL							
EXPENDITURES[2] . . .	5,152	2,043	3,859	5,315	6,788	8,679	12,687
Food	1,259	600	1,015	1,318	1,624	1,970	2,550
Prepared at Home	1,006	511	835	1,088	1,290	1,484	1,762
Away from Home	253	89	180	230	333	486	788
Alcoholic Beverages	81	21	55	81	117	152	242
Tobacco	93	42	84	105	123	126	134
Housing, Household							
Operations	1,236	620	968	1,263	1,552	1,889	3,002
Shelter	688	349	543	710	866	1,040	1,595
Fuel, Light, etc.	250	153	208	263	311	348	448
Other Operations	298	118	216	290	375	502	959
Housefurnishings,							
Equipment	269	83	185	284	376	476	690
Appliances	76	27	60	90	100	117	126
Furniture	78	19	53	81	116	146	192
Other Furnishings	115	37	72	113	160	213	372
Clothing and Accessories .	525	145	348	528	720	1,001	1,550
Men's and Boys'	190	45	123	199	270	366	526
Women's, Girls', etc. . .	266	81	177	259	358	509	833
Materials, Services	68	19	48	70	93	127	189
Transportation	781	176	560	848	1,093	1,450	1,891
Automobile	700	143	501	783	1,005	1,293	1,541
Other	81	33	59	65	89	157	350
Medical Care	342	174	269	350	425	539	771
Services	269	128	208	274	335	436	652
Supplies	73	47	60	77	90	104	119
Personal Care	148	61	118	156	194	241	312
Services	67	26	50	66	86	119	179
Supplies	81	36	68	90	107	121	133
Recreation, Equipment . . .	205	48	133	201	291	419	597
Reading, Education	100	26	55	88	126	215	440
Other Expenditures	113	47	69	93	147	201	508

[1] Includes single consumers
[2] For current consumption

Sources: Department of Labor; The Conference Board

AVERAGE FAMILY EXPENDITURES: SELECTED ITEMS BY AGE AND INCOME
Average annual expenditures, all urban and rural families and single consumers

Year and Characteristic	Families[1] (millions)	Average Annual Expenditures: Dollars					
		Food at Home	Fuel and Utilities	House-furnishings, Equipment	Clothing and Services	Vehicle Purchase, Operation	Reading and Education
1972-TOTAL ...	70.8	1,232	378	391	622	1,387	143
Income Class[2]							
Under $5,000 ...	18.6	724	230	143	248	492	31
$5,000-10,000....	16.8	1,080	327	305	475	1,148	69
10,000-15,000....	15.0	1,395	424	466	680	1,716	123
15,000-20,000....	9.1	1,634	496	617	903	2,096	221
20,000-25,000....	4.4	1,841	547	674	1,137	2,390	352
25,000 and over .	3.6	1,966	630	847	1,551	2,576	635
Age of Head:							
Under 25	6.5	468	152	323	453	1,403	80
25-34	13.5	1,061	340	501	689	1,472	107
35-44	12.1	1,725	479	514	865	1,759	178
45-54	13.0	1,629	471	499	862	1,871	283
55-64	11.3	1,277	409	329	554	1,353	147
65 and over	14.4	929	321	167	269	576	46
1973-TOTAL ...	71.7	1,378	429	460	670	1,503	154
Income Class[2]:							
Under $5,000 ...	16.2	798	248	169	257	520	37
$5,000-10,000....	16.5	1,148	349	316	468	1,106	64
10,000-15,000....	14.1	1,471	450	468	659	1,706	117
15,000-20,000....	10.0	1,746	533	631	867	2,108	198
20,000-25,000....	5.2	1,973	643	795	1,081	2,492	336
25,000 and over .	5.4	2,218	691	1,029	1,565	2,955	533
Age of Head:							
Under 25	6.2	566	194	373	483	1,396	65
25-34	14.8	1,158	388	579	740	1,593	118
35-44	12.0	1,929	525	632	939	1,808	186
45-54	12.9	1,831	526	530	875	2,044	320
55-64	11.6	1,436	479	385	608	1,565	166
65 and over	14.1	1,038	362	225	313	650	41

Note: These data represent preliminary figures from the Bureau of Labor Statistics Consumer Expenditure Survey of 1972 and 1973. For each year about 10,000 families and single consumers were interviewed. More extensive data from this survey will become available in late 1976 and early 1977 and will be included in the 1977/78 *Guide*
[1] Total families and single consumers in universe. Percent reporting expenditures varies
[2] Families and single consumers not reporting income are excluded   Source: Department of Labor

PER CAPITA CONSUMPTION OF ALCOHOLIC BEVERAGES

Year	Beer (Gallons)		Distilled Spirits (Tax Gal.)		Wines (Wine Gal.)[1]	
	Domestic	Imported	Domestic	Imported	Domestic	Imported
1950.....	24.97	.02	1.33	.15	1.31	.03
1955.....	23.83	.05	1.36	.22	1.24	.06
1960.....	23.91	.11	1.54	.33	1.31	.09
1965.....	25.29	.17	1.66	.47	1.37	.13
1970.....	28.45	.21	1.91	.71	1.66	.20
1971.....	28.16	.21	1.89	.76	1.86	.23
1972.....	29.23	.20	2.02	.82	2.03	.29
1973.....	29.45	.23	2.00	.81	2.09	.37
1974.....	30.75	.27	2.04	.86	2.04	.36
1975.....	31.14	.32	2.02	.83	2.08	.33

Note: For years ending June 30; per capita figures based on population 18 years and over as of January 1, including Armed Forces overseas
[1] Refers to both still and effervescent wines   Sources: Departments of Commerce and the Treasury

HOUSEHOLD FOOD CONSUMPTION

Average weekly consumption per household

Item	Quantity (Pounds)		Money Value (Dollars)[1]	
	1955	1965	1955	1965
TOTAL FOOD	- -	- -	24.43	27.82
Meat	10.10	11.05	6.04	7.66
Poultry	2.36	2.81	1.23	1.08
Fish and Shellfish	1.32	1.21	.72	.73
Eggs (shell-equivalent)	2.81	2.69	1.00	.85
Dairy Products[2]	31.86	28.78	3.80	3.63
Fats and Oils[2]	2.97	2.70	1.09	.99
Fruits	14.21	13.37	1.98	2.14
Vegetables	12.93	11.79	2.24	2.49
Potatoes and Sweet Potatoes	6.23	5.37	.53	.76
Flour and Cereals	5.87	4.69	.92	1.04
Bakery Products	6.70	7.64	1.65	2.33
Sugar and Sweets	4.15	3.70	.80	.89
Beverages (non-alcoholic)	- -	- -	1.38	1.76
Soup, Other Mixtures	1.53	1.95	.50	.79
Other Foods	- -	- -	.55	.68

[1] Includes money value of food federally donated, home-produced, and received as gift or pay, valued at retail prices
[2] Butter included with fats and oils

Source: Department of Agriculture

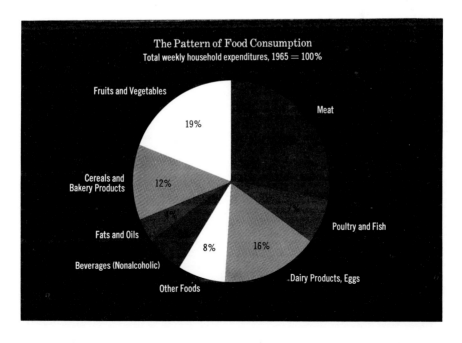

AVERAGE SHOPPER'S GROCERY PURCHASES FOR $20

Purchases made in supermarkets and grocery stores, in dollars

Item	1970	1974	Item	1970	1974
TOTAL	20.00	20.00	Dried Foods[4]	.21	.24
			Jams, Jellies, Preserves	.07	.08
Perishables	10.08	10.05	Pasta Products	.08	.09
Baked Goods, Snacks	1.24	1.17	Soft Drinks	.44	.51
Dairy Products[1]	1.26	1.31	Sugar	.16	.29
Frozen Foods	1.03	1.01	Other Edibles	1.26	1.20
Meat, Fish, Poultry	4.53	4.40			
Produce	2.02	2.16	Other Groceries	2.48	2.39
			Paper Goods	.32	.46
Dry Groceries	5.63	5.72	Soaps, Detergents[5]	.47	.44
Beer, Wine, Spirits	1.00	1.01	Other Household Prod.	.49	.34
Baby Foods[2]	.15	.12	Pet Foods	.25	.29
Cereals, Rice	.25	.31	Tobacco Products	.80	.71
Confectionery	.22	.21	Other	.14	.15
Canned Foods	1.23	1.13			
Fruits, Juices, Drinks.	.40	.36	General Merchandise	1.81	1.84
Meat, Poultry, Seafood	.38	.34	Health, Beauty Aids[6]	.74	.82
Vegetables, Soups	.45	.43	Housewares	.20	.19
Coffee, Tea[3]	.56	.53	Other Merchandise	.87	.83

[1] Includes eggs, margarine
[2] Includes canned milk
[3] Includes instants
[4] Dried fruits, vegetables, milk
[5] Includes other laundry products
[6] Includes prescriptions

Source: *Supermarketing* (Gralla Publications)

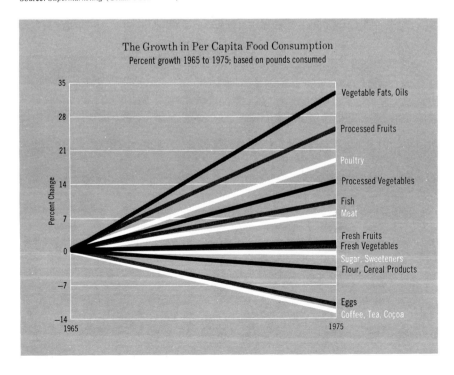

The Growth in Per Capita Food Consumption
Percent growth 1965 to 1975; based on pounds consumed

PER CAPITA FOOD CONSUMPTION INDEX

Index numbers, 1967 = 100

Commodity	1940	1950	1960	1965	1970	1975p
TOTAL FOODS[1]	90.9	95.3	96.4	97.2	102.8	101.3
ANIMAL PRODUCTS	87.4	93.8	95.7	96.9	102.5	99.9
CROP PRODUCTS	96.4	98.1	97.1	97.6	103.1	103.0
Meat, Poultry, Fish, Total ..	76.5	82.3	89.5	93.6	105.0	n.a.
Meat	84.5	86.0	92.3	93.9	104.2	101.0
Poultry	37.9	53.6	74.5	89.2	107.8	106.0
Fish	99.6	108.3	95.3	101.0	108.6	111.0
Eggs	94.3	118.5	103.6	97.0	98.5	86.0
Dairy Products						
Including Butter	107.2	110.3	105.7	103.4	99.2	100.0
Excluding Butter	91.4	104.2	103.7	102.5	99.5	n.a.
Fats and Oils						
Excluding Butter	63.2	79.5	84.9	93.7	110.5	n.a.
Including Butter	110.8	100.2	95.6	98.6	107.1	106.0
Animal	228.0	162.2	122.6	111.1	90.3	76.0
Vegetable	50.6	67.4	80.7	91.9	116.3	122.0
Fruits, Total	108.8	103.0	102.8	94.7	102.4	107.0
Fresh	176.3	138.0	111.3	100.5	101.3	102.0
Processed	53.5	73.4	95.3	89.7	103.5	112.0
Melons	147.0	120.6	112.2	102.9	105.7	n.a.
Vegetables, Total	105.1	102.4	98.9	97.8	101.2	102.0
Fresh	139.8	122.2	106.8	99.6	99.5	100.0
Processed, Total	47.1	66.3	84.3	94.6	104.4	108.0
Canned	62.8	77.7	85.6	94.8	104.2	n.a.
Frozen	6.2	35.1	80.1	94.2	105.3	n.a.
Potatoes, Sweet Potatoes	91.8	76.2	79.0	92.4	112.0	n.a.
Fresh	n.a.	n.a.	129.0	105.0	n.a.	86.0
Processed	n.a.	n.a.	56.0	86.0	n.a.	130.0
Beans, Peas, Nuts, Soya	112.2	111.9	97.3	103.0	99.6	n.a.
Flour and Cereal Products ..	123.7	115.4	102.6	100.9	98.1	97.0
Sugar, Sweeteners	82.6	97.3	98.2	99.3	106.1	99.0
Coffee, Tea, Cocoa	100.3	102.2	100.5	99.3	93.8	87.0

Note: Civilian consumption only after 1940. Quantities of individual foods, measured in pounds equivalent to the form sold at retail stores, are combined into indexes using 1947-1949 average retail prices for 1940 and 1950 and 1957-1959 average retail prices for later years. Includes Alaska and Hawaii beginning 1960
[1] Includes soup, baby food, not shown separately
p - Preliminary
n.a. - Not available

Source: Department of Agriculture

PER CAPITA CONSUMPTION OF TOBACCO PRODUCTS

Year or Average	Pounds[1]			Units		Population 18 Yrs. & Over[3] (Millions)
	All Tobacco Products	Ciga-rettes	Cigars, Ciga-rillos[2]	Ciga-rettes	Cigars, Ciga-rillos[2]	
Average:						
1950-1954	12.61	9.98	2.63	3,695	112	107.1
1955-1959	11.71	9.39	2.48	3,806	116	112.5
1960	11.82	9.64	2.42	4,171	125	116.1
1961	12.00	9.84	2.43	4,266	123	117.8
1962	11.80	9.69	2.40	4,265	122	119.2
1963	11.78	9.70	2.39	4,345	125	120.6
1964	11.54	9.21	2.69	4,194	154	121.9
1965	11.51	9.37	2.57	4,258	144	124.2
1966	11.12	9.08	2.41	4,287	136	126.3
1967	10.80	8.86	2.28	4,280	131	128.3
1968	10.59	8.69	2.15	4,186	126	130.4
1969	10.04	8.11	2.11	3,993	125	132.5
1970	9.68	7.77	2.08	3,985	125	135.2
1971	9.52	7.75	1.94	4,037	119	137.5
1972	9.65	7.95	1.74	4,043	109	139.8
1973	9.53	7.92	1.61	4,148	102	142.2
1974	9.40	7.90	1.47	4,141	92	144.6
1975p	9.14	7.75	1.32	4,121	82	147.3

Note: Per capita figures are based on estimates as of July 1 for the population 18 years and over including Armed Forces overseas

[1] Unstemmed processing weight
[2] Per male 18 years and over
[3] Including Armed Forces overseas

p—Preliminary

Sources: Departments of Agriculture, Commerce, and the Treasury

PRIVATE HEALTH INSURANCE COVERAGE

Millions of dollars, except percent

Year	Private Consumer Expenditures			Percent Met by Insurance[1]		
	Total Health Care[2]	Hospital Care	Physicians' Services	Total Health Care[2]	Hospital Care	Physicians' Services
1950	8,125	1,832	2,597	12.2	37.1	12.0
1955	11,668	2,997	3,433	21.7	56.0	25.0
1960	17,986	5,108	5,309	27.8	64.7	30.0
1965	26,782	8,136	8,179	32.6	71.2	32.8
1966	28,307	8,685	8,358	32.3	69.0	33.9
1967	28,508	8,369	8,248	33.5	73.3	35.9
1968	31,228	9,532	8,546	36.3	76.9	40.7
1969	35,698	11,250	9,797	36.6	74.3	41.2
1970	40,881	12,840	11,201	38.5	77.9	43.8
1971	44,522	13,674	12,361	39.8	82.5	43.9
1972	48,691	15,673	13,263	40.1	78.1	45.9
1973	53,849	17,444	14,590	41.6	79.2	48.2
1974p	58,358	19,492	15,417	44.2	80.6	53.1

[1] Private health insurance benefit payments
[2] Excludes expenses for prepayment, but includes other expenditures not shown separately

p-Preliminary
Source: Department of Health, Education and Welfare

PRIVATE CONSUMER EXPENDITURES FOR HEALTH CARE

Millions of dollars, except as indicated

Item	1960	1965	1970	1974p Amount	1974p Percent	1974p Per Capita (Dollars)
TOTAL EXPENDITURES	18,831	28,050	42,322	61,205	100.0	283.99
Percent of DPI[1]	5.4	5.9	6.1	6.2	- -	- -
Hospital Care	5,108	8,136	12,840	19,492	31.8	90.44
Physicians' Services	5,309	8,179	11,201	15,417	25.2	71.54
Dentists' Services	1,974	2,772	4,517	6,734	11.0	31.25
Other Professional Services	826	978	1,181	1,566	2.6	7.27
Drugs and Drug Sundries	3,598	4,708	6,925	9,331	15.2	43.30
Eyeglasses, Appliances	760	1,200	1,725	2,159	3.5	10.02
Nursing-Home Care	411	805	2,492	3,660	6.0	16.98
Health Insurance, Net Cost	845	1,272	1,441	2,846	4.6	13.21

Note: Per capita figures based on total population including Armed Forces and civilians abroad
[1] Disposable personal income
p—Preliminary
Source: Department of Health, Education and Welfare

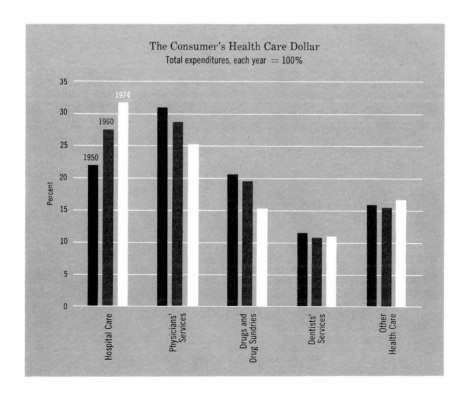

The Consumer's Health Care Dollar
Total expenditures, each year = 100%

CONSUMER CONFIDENCE AND PLANS TO BUY

Seasonally adjusted index numbers, 1969-1970 = 100

Index and Year	January-February	March-April	May-June	July-August	September-October	November-December
Consumer Confidence:						
1967	115.4	120.3	120.3	119.8	120.0	121.2
1968	119.3	115.8	116.8	120.9	126.1	122.3
1969	123.4	121.6	122.9	117.3	112.6	112.0
1970	90.9	88.3	80.1	83.5	76.9	70.6
1971	72.4	70.5	76.9	76.6	74.9	79.4
1972	86.6	87.6	90.5	95.0	101.7	105.1
1973	99.4	92.3	93.4	83.3	96.2	61.5
1974	56.0	85.9	83.3	69.1	48.9	39.9
1975	50.9	62.5	68.0	77.3	72.1	86.8
1976	93.3	82.2	86.7	- -	- -	- -
Consumer Buying Plans:						
1967	97.3	101.9	108.6	107.6	108.8	107.5
1968	109.3	98.9	96.3	95.9	101.5	105.2
1969	104.8	112.8	114.1	108.2	101.3	99.2
1970	99.8	98.0	88.9	93.5	91.3	87.0
1971	101.5	112.6	109.3	112.3	109.7	109.3
1972	113.3	107.1	106.6	102.5	111.0	111.8
1973	102.7	125.2	111.1	111.6	103.2	93.7
1974	89.2	87.6	97.5	81.1	93.6	76.8
1975	80.0	88.0	100.3	104.6	105.8	108.7
1976	126.3	96.7	105.9	- -	- -	- -

Sources: The Conference Board; National Family Opinion, Inc.

THE TREND IN NEW HOUSING STARTS

Thousands of units, including farm housing

Year	Total	Privately Owned		Publicly Owned
		Total	One-Family	
1960	1,296	1,252	995	44
1961	1,365	1,313	974	52
1962	1,492	1,463	991	30
1963	1,635	1,603	1,012	32
1964	1,561	1,529	970	32
1965	1,510	1,473	964	37
1966	1,196	1,165	779	31
1967	1,322	1,292	844	30
1968	1,545	1,508	899	38
1969	1,500	1,467	811	33
1970	1,469	1,434	813	35
1971	2,084	2,052	1,151	32
1972	2,378	2,357	1,309	22
1973	2,058	2,045	1,132	12
1974	1,352	1,338	888	15
1975	1,171	1,160	892	11

Source: Department of Commerce

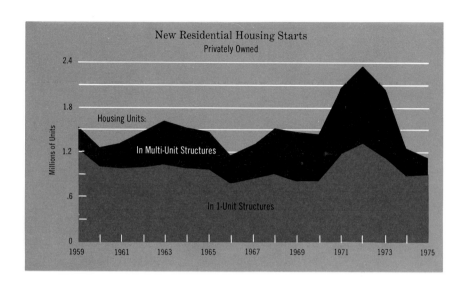

New Residential Housing Starts
Privately Owned

Housing Units:

In Multi-Unit Structures

In 1-Unit Structures

Millions of Units

2.4

1.8

1.2

.6

0

1959   1961   1963   1965   1967   1969   1971   1973   1975

HOUSING VACANCY RATES

Item and Year	Total U.S.	Inside SMSA's			Outside SMSA's
		Total	Central Cities	Outside C.C.	
Homeowner Vacancy Rate					
1960	1.3	1.3	n.a.	n.a.	1.4
1962	1.4	1.3	n.a.	n.a.	1.6
1964	1.5	1.7	n.a.	n.a.	1.4
1966	1.4	1.6	1.5	1.4	1.3
1968	1.1	1.0	1.2	.9	1.3
1970	1.0	1.0	1.1	.9	1.1
1971	1.0	1.0	1.i	.9	1.0
1972	1.0	1.0	1.3	.8	1.0
1973	1.0	1.1	1.2	1.0	1.0
1974	1.2	1.2	1.3	1.2	1.1
1975	1.2	1.3	1.4	1.3	1.1
Rental Vacancy Rate					
1960	8.1	7.0	n.a.	n.a.	10.3
1962	8.1	7.5	n.a.	n.a.	9.7
1964	8.3	8.1	n.a.	n.a.	8.1
1966	7.7	7.0	7.1	6.8	9.2
1968	5.9	5.1	5.5	4.5	7.7
1970	5.3	4.9	5.3	4.3	6.4
1971	5.4	5.1	5.4	4.5	6.4
1972	5.6	5.4	5.7	4.8	6.1
1973	5.8	5.7	6.2	5.0	6.1
1974	6.2	6.2	6.8	5.2	6.2
1975	6.0	6.1	6.6	5.4	5.7

Note: Vacancy rates are ratios showing the relationship between vacant units and the total housing supply
n.a.-Not available
Source: Department of Commerce

CHARACTERISTICS OF NEW HOUSING STARTS

Thousands

Characteristic	1960	1965	1970	1973	1974	1975
TOTAL HOUSING UNITS	1,296	1,510	1,469	2,058	1,352	1,171
Ownership						
Private......................	1,252	1,473	1,434	2,045	1,338	1,160
Public	44	37	35	12	15	11
Type of Structure						
1 Unit	1,009	965	815	1,133	889	896
2-4 Units .... } 288 {		101	96	124	76	68
5 Units or more		444	558	800	387	208
Location						
Inside SMSA's	889	1,035	1,034	1,502	932	767
Outside SMSA's..............	407	475	435	556	420	405
Region						
Northeast	237	281	224	278	183	150
North Central	304	369	301	442	320	295
South	441	588	629	906	561	448
West	314	271	314	431	288	278

Source: Department of Commerce

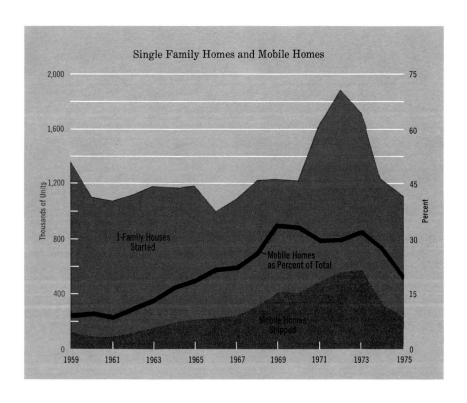

Single Family Homes and Mobile Homes

HOUSING STARTS AND MOBILE HOMES

Thousands of units

Year	Total, All Units[1]	1-Family Private Housing Starts	Mobile Home[2] Shipments	Mobile Home[2] Percent of Total
1959	1,355	1,234	121	8.9
1960	1,099	995	104	9.5
1961	1,064	974	90	8.5
1962	1,109	991	118	10.6
1963	1,163	1,012	151	13.0
1964	1,161	970	191	16.5
1965	1,180	964	216	18.3
1966	996	779	217	21.8
1967	1,084	844	240	22.1
1968	1,217	899	318	26.1
1969	1,223	811	413	33.8
1970	1,214	813	401	33.0
1971	1,648	1,151	497	30.2
1972	1,885	1,309	576	30.6
1973	1,712	1,132	580	33.9
1974	1,217	888	329	27.0
1975	1,108	892	216	19.5

[1] Total new privately owned single-family housing starts plus manufacturers' shipments of mobile homes
[2] Manufacturers' shipments; a mobile home is defined as a portable housing structure built on a chassis and designed to be used without permanent foundation as a year-round dwelling when connected to utilities. A mobile home must be 29 feet or longer and weigh over 4,500 lbs.

Sources: Department of Commerce; Mobile Homes Manufacturers' Association

SPENDING FOR RESIDENTIAL IMPROVEMENTS AND UPKEEP

Percent distribution, except as indicated

Expenditure	1965	1969	1971	1973	1975
TOTAL RESIDENTIAL PROPERTIES (Million Dollars)	11,442	13,535	16,299	18,512	25,239
1-UNIT, OWNER-OCCUPIED (Million Dollars)	7,033	8,594	10,234	11,297	15,684
Percent Distribution	100.0	100.0	100.0	100.0	100.0
Maintenance and Repairs	33.9	28.7	27.9	32.0	28.9
Construction Improvements	66.1	71.3	72.1	68.0	71.0
Additions and Alterations	52.0	55.2	52.4	50.3	53.9
Residential Additions	13.0	10.7	12.5	9.5	10.7
Residential Alterations	28.2	31.1	28.2	31.4	31.5
Property Outside Res. Structure	10.8	13.3	11.7	9.5	11.7
Major Replacements	14.1	16.1	19.7	17.6	17.1

Source: Department of Commerce

THE PRICE OF NEW HOMES

In dollars, except as indicated

Item	1965	1967	1969	1971	1973	1974	1975p
TOTAL HOMES SOLD (Thousands)[1]	575	487	448	656	620	501	545
Median Sales Price:							
All Locations	20,000	22,700	25,600	25,200	32,500	35,900	39,200
Inside SMSA's	21,300	23,800	27,200	26,600	34,200	37,300	n.a.
Outside SMSA's	16,900	19,800	21,300	20,900	27,900	31,400	n.a.
Northeast	21,500	25,400	31,600	30,600	37,100	40,100	44,000
North Central	21,600	25,100	27,600	27,200	32,900	36,100	39,600
South	17,500	19,400	22,800	22,500	30,900	34,500	37,200
West	21,600	24,100	25,300	25,500	32,400	35,800	40,500

Note: For national and regional price indexes of new one-family homes sold, see table on page 254
[1] New one-family homes sold
n.a.—Not available
p—Preliminary

Sources: Departments of Commerce and Housing and Urban Development

DISTRIBUTION OF NEW HOMES SOLD BY SALES PRICE, 1974

Sales Price	Total Homes Sold[1]	Location		Region			
		Inside SMSA's	Outside SMSA's	North-east	North Central	South	West
TOTAL (Thousands)	501	398	103	69	97	196	139
TOTAL REPORTING (Thous.)[2] . . .	489	390	100	65	94	192	138
Percent Distribution	100	100	100	100	100	100	100
Under $20,000	5	3	10	[3]	2	9	1
20,000-25,000	8	7	14	4	8	10	8
25,000-30,000	15	14	20	12	16	14	17
30,000-35,000	19	18	23	17	21	17	21
35,000-40,000	16	17	15	16	18	15	17
40,000-50,000	19	21	13	23	18	19	19
50,000 and over	17	20	7	28	17	14	17

[1] Data refer to new one-family homes sold
[2] Reporting sales price
[3] Less than 0.5 percent

Sources: Departments of Commerce and Housing and Urban Development

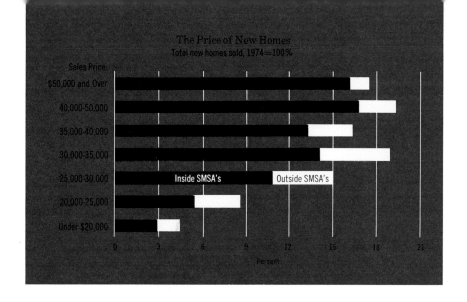

The Price of New Homes
Total new homes sold, 1974=100%

Sales Price:
$50,000 and Over
40,000-50,000
35,000-40,000
30,000-35,000
25,000-30,000   Inside SMSA's   Outside SMSA's
20,000-25,000
Under $20,000

0   3   6   9   12   15   18   21
Percent

CHARACTERISTICS OF NEW ONE-FAMILY HOMES SOLD

Percent distribution, except as indicated

Characteristic	1965	1967	1969	1971	1973	1974
TOTAL HOMES SOLD (Thous.)	575	487	448	656	620	501
Median Square Feet	1,495	1,570	1,585	1,415	1,540	1,565
PERCENT DISTRIBUTION	100	100	100	100	100	100
Location						
Inside SMSA's....................	75	77	76	76	77	79
Outside SMSA's	25	23	24	24	23	21
Region						
Northeast........................	16	16	14	12	15	14
North Central	25	23	22	19	19	19
South	36	37	39	41	40	39
West	22	25	26	27	26	28
Bedrooms						
2 or less	6	6	8	8	9	9
3................................	67	63	61	62	64	65
4 or more	27	31	31	30	27	26
Bathrooms						
1................................	21	17	16	24	17	17
1½	25	24	21	21	18	17
2................................	35	36	40	38	43	44
2½ or more	18	23	24	18	21	22
Stories						
1................................	68	64	65	69	61	60
2 or more	20	23	22	20	28	27
Split	13	13	13	11	11	13
Equipment: Percent Having						
Central Air Conditioning	25	29	39	40	50	51
Stove	84	86	89	88	89	88
Refrigerator......................	5	6	9	11	16	13
Dishwasher	35	45	51	48	65	73

Sources: Departments of Commerce and Housing and Urban Development

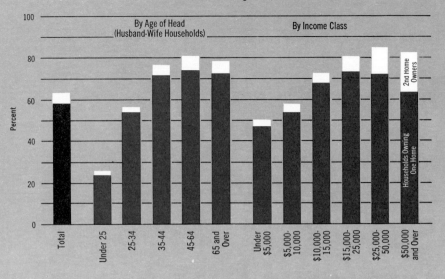

The Incidence of Home Ownership
Percent of households owning homes, 1970

By Age of Head (Husband-Wife Households) — By Income Class

OCCUPIED HOUSING UNITS BY TENURE
Millions of units

Year	Occupied Units			Percent Owner-Occupied	Population per Occupied Unit
	Total	Owner-Occupied	Renter-Occupied		
Total					
1900	16.0	7.5	8.5	46.7	4.8
1910	20.3	9.3	11.0	45.9	4.5
1920	24.4	11.1	13.2	45.6	4.3
1930	29.9	14.3	15.6	47.8	4.1
1940	34.9	15.2	19.7	43.6	3.8
1950	42.8	23.6	19.3	55.0	3.5
1960	53.0	32.8	20.2	61.9	3.4
1970	63.4	39.9	23.6	62.9	3.1
1973	69.3	44.7	24.7	64.4	n.a.
White[1]					
1900	14.1	7.0	7.1	49.8	4.8
1910	n.a.	n.a.	n.a.	n.a.	n.a.
1920	21.8	10.5	11.3	48.2	4.3
1930	27.0	13.5	13.4	50.2	4.1
1940	31.6	14.4	17.1	45.7	3.7
1950	39.0	22.2	16.8	57.0	3.5
1960	47.9	30.8	17.1	64.4	3.3
1970	56.5	37.0	19.5	65.4	n.a.
1973	61.5	41.2	20.2	67.1	n.a.
Nonwhite[1]					
1900	1.9	.4	1.5	23.6	4.8
1910	n.a.	n.a.	n.a.	n.a.	n.a.
1920	2.5	.6	1.9	23.9	4.3
1930	2.9	.7	2.2	25.2	4.3
1940	3.3	.8	2.5	23.6	4.1
1950	3.8	1.3	2.5	34.9	4.2
1960	5.1	2.0	3.2	38.4	4.0
1970	6.9	2.9	4.0	42.0	n.a.
1973	7.9	3.4	4.5	43.4	n.a.

[1] Refers to household head
n.a.—Not available

Source: Department of Commerce

CHARACTERISTICS OF HOME OWNERS: FIRST AND SECOND HOMES: 1970

Thousands of units, except percent

Characteristic	Total Occupied Units[1]	Households Owning		Percent Home-Owners	Percent Owning Second Home
		First Home	Second Home		
TOTAL U.S.	63,447	39,882	2,890	62.9	4.6
Household Type and Age:					
Multiperson Households	52,296	35,119	2,503	67.2	4.8
Husband-Wife[2]	43,596	30,818	2,162	70.7	5.0
Head under 25 years ...	3,072	789	44	25.7	1.4
25-34	9,128	5,182	223	56.8	2.4
35-44	9,232	7,091	434	76.8	4.7
45-64	16,418	13,262	1,123	80.8	6.8
65 and over	5,745	4,495	338	78.2	5.9
Other Male Head	2,452	1,302	139	53.1	5.7
Female Head	6,248	2,998	202	48.0	3.2
One-Person Households	11,151	4,763	387	42.7	3.5
Male	3,968	1,351	178	34.1	4.5
Female	7,183	3,412	209	47.5	2.9
Household Income:					
Under $5,000	18,617	9,318	552	50.1	3.0
$5,000-10,000	19,548	11,264	703	57.6	3.6
10,000-15,000	14,329	10,392	685	72.5	4.8
15,000-25,000	8,427	6,782	608	80.5	7.2
25,000-50,000	2,062	1,745	254	84.7	12.3
50,000 and over	464	381	88	82.1	18.9
Region of Residence:					
Northeast	15,480	8,917	781	57.6	5.0
New England	3,645	2,222	237	61.0	6.5
Middle Atlantic	11,834	6,694	544	56.6	4.6
North Central	17,537	11,922	759	68.0	4.3
East North Central	12,383	8,353	538	67.5	4.3
West North Central	5,154	3,569	221	69.2	4.3
South	19,258	12,456	827	64.7	4.3
South Atlantic	9,438	5,992	430	63.5	4.6
East South Central	3,868	2,578	134	66.6	3.5
West South Central	5,952	3,885	263	65.3	4.4
West	11,172	6,590	523	59.0	4.7
Mountain	2,518	1,649	146	65.5	5.8
Pacific	8,653	4,942	377	57.1	4.4

Note: Figures for occupied units differ slightly from data in table on page 189 because they are based on different samples of the 1970 Census

[1] Occupied housing units equal total number of households
[2] No nonrelatives present

Source: Department of Commerce

HOUSEHOLDS WITH SECOND HOME

In thousands, except percent

Item	1967	1970	1973
TOTAL HOUSEHOLDS	58,845	63,447	69,337
No Second Home	57,169	60,557	66,326
With Second Home	1,676	2,890	3,011
Percent of Total	2.9	4.6	4.3

Source: Department of Commerce

HOUSING UNITS BY AGE OF STRUCTURE, 1973

Thousands of occupied units

| Year Structure Built | Total Units | Metropolitan Areas | | | Outside Metro- politan Areas |
		Total	Inside Central Cities	Outside Central Cities	
Owner-Occupied	44,653	28,942	11,087	17,854	15,711
April 1970 or later	4,685	2,634	635	1,998	2,051
1965-March 1970	6,017	3,815	1,003	2,812	2,202
1960-1964	5,275	3,659	1,162	2,498	1,616
1950-1959	9,785	7,212	2,505	4,706	2,573
1940-1949	4,879	3,334	1,408	1,926	1,544
1939 or earlier	14,013	8,288	4,374	3,914	5,726
Renter-Occupied	24,684	18,783	11,406	7,377	5,901
April 1970 or later	2,421	2,014	921	1,094	407
1965-March 1970	3,271	2,662	1,270	1,393	609
1960-1964	2,173	1,786	896	891	387
1950-1959	3,055	2,263	1,222	1,041	792
1940-1949	2,575	1,861	1,188	673	714
1939 or earlier	11,189	8,196	5,910	2,286	2,994

Source: Department of Commerce

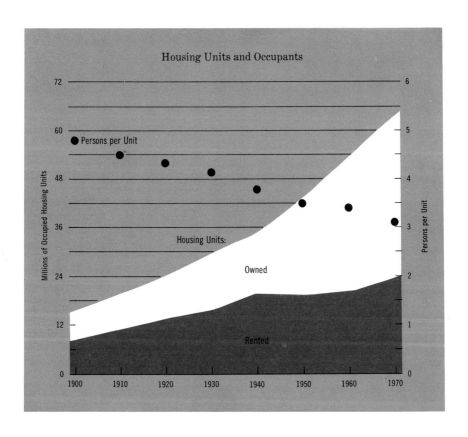

Housing Units and Occupants

188

OCCUPIED HOUSING UNITS BY LOCATION AND TENURE

			Metropolitan		
Item	Total, All Areas	Total	Inside Central Cities	Outside Central Cities	Non-Metro-politan
OCCUPIED UNITS, 1973 (Thous.):					
Total U.S.	69,337	47,725	22,493	25,231	21,612
Northeast.........................	16,152	12,943	6,001	6,942	3,209
North Central	18,742	12,368	5,715	6,653	6,374
South	21,806	12,349	6,265	6,084	9,456
West	12,638	10,064	4,513	5,552	2,574
PERCENT GROWTH, 1970-73:					
Total U.S.	9.3	8.8	5.1	12.3	10.3
Northeast.........................	4.3	3.5	.6	6.1	7.8
North Central	6.9	6.5	1.3	11.4	7.7
South	13.2	13.8	9.0	19.1	12.6
West	13.2	13.3	11.7	14.8	12.4
PERCENT OWNER-OCCUPIED:					
Total U.S. — 1970..............	62.9	59.5	48.1	70.3	70.4
1973..............	64.4	60.6	49.3	70.8	72.7
Northeast — 1970..............	57.6	54.3	36.0	70.9	71.6
1973..............	59.2	55.7	37.5	71.4	73.1
North Central — 1970..............	68.0	64.9	53.0	76.1	74.1
1973..............	69.1	66.0	54.2	76.1	75.1
South — 1970..............	64.7	61.5	54.4	69.5	68.7
1973..............	66.5	62.0	53.8	70.4	72.4
West — 1970..............	59.0	57.3	50.2	63.2	65.6
1973..............	60.6	58.8	52.5	63.9	67.5

Source: Department of Commerce

HOUSING UNITS BY TYPE AND LOCATION, 1973

Thousands of year-round units

		Metropolitan Areas			Outside Metro-politan Areas
Type of Structure	Total U.S.	Total	Inside Central Cities	Outside Central Cities	
1970—TOTAL.....................	67,699	46,083	22,584	23,499	21,616
Single Family, Detached	44,801	27,219 }	11,430	17,603	{ 17,582
Single Family, Attached..............	1,990	1,814			176
Multi-family, 2-4 Units	9,007	7,184	4,753	2,431	1,823
Multi-family, 5 or more Units	9,829	8,934	6,225	2,709	895
Mobile Home, Trailer	2,073	933	176	757	1,140
1973—TOTAL.....................	75,293	51,002	24,099	26,903	24,292
Single Family, Detached	47,953	28,900	10,424	18,476	19,053
Single Family, Attached..............	3,334	2,845	1,736	1,109	489
Multi-family, 2-4 Units	9,639	7,880	5,145	2,736	1,759
Multi-family, 5 or more Units	11,089	10,088	6,580	3,508	1,001
Mobile Home, Trailer	3,278	1,288	214	1,074	1,990

Source: Department of Commerce

The Demand for Household Durables, 1974
Percent distribution of households and their expenditures for selected durable goods ▲

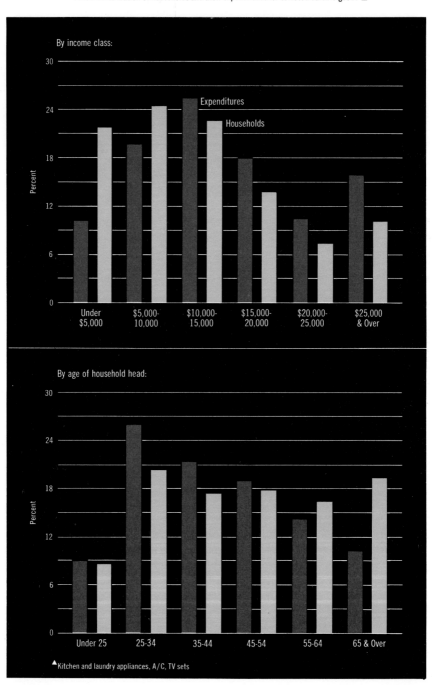

By income class:

By age of household head:

▲Kitchen and laundry appliances, A/C, TV sets

190

HOUSEHOLD EXPENDITURES FOR SELECTED DURABLE GOODS, 1974

Average expenditures per household, for new purchases, in dollars

Item	Income Class					
	Under $5,000	$5,000-10,000	$10,000-15,000	$15,000-20,000	$20,000-25,000	$25,000-and Over
TOTAL EXPENDITURES[1]	76	131	184	212	231	255
Washing Machine..............	10	19	26	29	33	32
Clothes Dryer.................	5	9	16	18	22	22
Dishwasher	2	3	10	18	19	24
Refrigerator	17	25	36	37	47	51
Home Food Freezer	4	8	14	13	17	16
Kitchen Range	9	15	19	25	26	28
Black and White TV	7	7	7	8	7	7
Color TV.....................	16	37	45	54	50	64
Room Air Conditioner	6	8	11	10	10	11

Item	Age of Head					
	Under 25	25-34	35-44	45-54	55-64	65 and Over
TOTAL EXPENDITURES[1]	171	209	202	174	141	87
Washing Machine..............	27	29	28	23	20	10
Clothes Dryer.................	18	19	17	14	9	5
Dishwasher	3	15	15	13	7	3
Refrigerator	32	42	38	33	27	18
Home Food Freezer	7	15	14	12	10	5
Kitchen Range	19	23	23	20	15	10
Black and White TV	9	6	9	8	7	5
Color TV.....................	47	49	49	41	38	24
Room Air Conditioner	9	11	9	10	8	7

Item	Race of Head		Residence			
				Metropolitan Areas		
	White	Negro	Total	Central Cities	Outside Central Cities	Non-metro-politan
TOTAL EXPENDITURES[1]	166	125	153	124	177	186
Washing Machine..............	23	19	20	16	24	27
Clothes Dryer.................	14	7	12	9	14	17
Dishwasher	11	2	10	6	14	9
Refrigerator	32	28	30	25	34	36
Home Food Freezer	11	7	9	6	11	15
Kitchen Range	18	15	16	10	21	23
Black and White TV	7	12	7	7	7	8
Color TV.....................	41	29	40	36	43	42
Room Air Conditioner	9	6	9	9	9	9

Note: For the number of households by each characteristic, see table on page 192. Average household expenditures for each item can be found on page 196. Data as of autumn

[1] Total expenditures for household items listed

Source: Department of Commerce

HOUSEHOLD AVAILABILITY OF DURABLES BY SELECTED CHARACTERISTICS, 1974

Percent of households in each group having indicated items available

Item	Income Class[1]					
	Under $5,000	$5,000-10,000	$10,000-15,000	$15,000-20,000	$20,000-25,000	$25,000-and Over
TOTAL HOUSEHOLDS (Mil.)	15.4	17.2	15.9	9.7	5.2	7.1
Percent Having:						
Washing Machine	53.0	65.4	77.2	85.3	86.0	89.2
Clothes Dryer	23.6	40.6	60.9	72.1	76.3	82.2
Dishwasher	7.7	14.9	27.6	42.9	52.8	69.8
Refrigerator	97.6	98.9	99.4	99.5	99.7	99.7
Home Food Freezer	21.6	28.4	37.0	40.6	44.2	48.4
Kitchen Range	96.6	98.3	99.0	99.5	99.6	99.5
Any TV	92.0	96.5	97.9	99.0	99.0	98.7
Color TV	35.9	54.0	67.4	78.1	80.2	84.4
Room Air Conditioner	24.2	32.8	35.5	36.1	34.3	30.4
Central Air Conditioning	9.2	13.3	18.2	24.4	28.7	38.6

Item	Age of Head					
	Under 25	25-34	35-44	45-54	55-64	65 and Over
TOTAL HOUSEHOLDS (Mil.)	6.1	14.4	12.3	12.6	11.6	13.7
Percent Having:						
Washing Machine	44.1	69.0	83.3	81.7	77.1	63.8
Clothes Dryer	39.1	57.0	67.5	64.3	53.5	32.3
Dishwasher	14.1	31.8	41.4	38.1	25.5	12.8
Refrigerator	98.5	99.3	99.2	98.8	98.9	98.7
Home Food Freezer	8.9	26.0	45.9	44.0	39.5	27.6
Kitchen Range	98.0	99.0	98.8	97.9	98.8	98.1
Any TV	93.0	96.8	97.9	97.3	97.2	95.7
Color TV	41.5	64.3	71.0	68.4	63.8	49.8
Room Air Conditioner	28.9	34.1	30.2	33.2	33.6	29.5
Central Air Conditioning	17.4	21.3	21.6	21.0	16.2	13.9

Item	Race of Head		Residence			
				Metropolitan Areas		
	White	Negro	Total	Central Cities	Outside Central Cities	Non-Metropolitan
TOTAL HOUSEHOLDS (Mil.)	62.6	7.3	48.5	22.3	26.2	22.3
Percent Having:						
Washing Machine	74.5	51.4	69.2	60.0	77.0	77.9
Clothes Dryer	56.8	18.2	51.5	39.6	61.6	55.0
Dishwasher	30.8	7.2	31.6	23.5	38.5	21.2
Refrigerator	99.1	97.5	98.8	98.4	99.1	99.2
Home Food Freezer	35.0	24.1	27.6	20.3	33.9	47.0
Kitchen Range	98.7	96.8	98.3	97.8	98.8	98.8
Any TV	96.9	93.7	96.7	95.6	97.7	96.3
Color TV	64.2	37.8	63.3	56.1	69.4	57.0
Room Air Conditioning	33.2	21.9	32.6	33.1	32.2	30.1
Central Air Conditioner	20.0	8.5	20.6	17.3	23.4	14.5

Note: Availability ratios for total households are given in table on page 193. Data as of autumn

[1] Households not reporting income level are excluded

Source: Department of Commerce

Household Availability of Appliances
Percent of all households having indicated appliances available, 1974

Washing Machine
Clothes Dryer
Dishwasher
Refrigerator
Home Food Freezer
Kitchen Range
Any TV
Color TV
Central Air Conditioning
Room Air Conditioner

0   20   40   60   80   100
Percent

DOMESTIC INTERCITY PASSENGER TRAFFIC BY VOLUME

Billions of passenger miles

Year	Total Volume	Private Auto-mobiles	Airways[1]	Com-mercial Motor Carriers	Rail-roads	Inland Water-ways[2]
1950	508.5	438.3	10.1	26.4	32.5	1.2
1955	716.1	637.4	22.7	25.5	28.7	1.7
1960	783.6	706.1	34.0	19.3	21.6	2.7
1961	791.4	713.6	34.6	20.3	20.5	2.3
1962	818.1	735.9	37.5	21.8	20.2	2.7
1963	852.6	765.9	42.8	22.5	18.6	2.8
1964	895.5	801.8	49.2	23.3	18.4	2.8
1965	920.2	817.7	58.1	23.8	17.6	3.1
1966	971.0	856.4	69.4	24.6	17.3	3.4
1967	1,020.6	889.8	87.2	24.9	15.3	3.4
1968	1,078.9	936.4	101.2	24.5	13.3	3.5
1969	1,137.9	977.0	119.9	24.9	12.3	3.8
1970	1,184.8	1,026.0	118.6	25.3	10.9	4.0
1971	1,229.4	1,071.0	119.9	25.5	8.9	4.1
1972	1,300.3	1,129.0	133.0	25.6	8.7	4.0
1973p	1,356.8	1,174.0	143.1	26.4	9.4	4.0

[1] Includes domestic commercial revenue service, private pleasure and business flying
[2] Includes Great Lakes

p—Preliminary

Source: Interstate Commerce Commission

AUTOMOBILE REGISTRATIONS BY STATES
Thousands

State	1974	1975e	State	1974	1975e
TOTAL U.S. . . .	104,901	107,371	Mississippi	965	983
			Missouri	2,142	2,180
Alabama	1,854	1,876	Montana	363	370
Alaska	126	135	Nebraska	807	826
Arizona	1,082	1,109	Nevada	338	348
Arkansas	848	875	New Hampshire . . .	404	418
California	11,162	11,392	New Jersey	3,753	3,839
Colorado	1,395	1,429	New Mexico	532	552
Connecticut	1,829	1,870	New York	6,663	6,772
Delaware	285	289	North Carolina	2,773	2,844
District of			North Dakota	321	332
Columbia	246	249	Ohio	6,098	6,206
Florida	4,705	4,855	Oklahoma	1,395	1,425
Georgia	2,534	2,609	Oregon	1,282	1,331
Hawaii	421	428	Pennsylvania	6,167	6,354
Idaho	405	419	Rhode Island	500	510
Illinois	5,277	5,406	South Carolina	1,334	1,384
Indiana	2,542	2,572	South Dakota	331	337
Iowa	1,506	1,528	Tennessee	1,988	2,029
Kansas	1,252	1,271	Texas	6,007	6,165
Kentucky	1,626	1,653	Utah	589	608
Louisiana	1,616	1,635	Vermont	230	235
Maine	498	520	Virginia	2,656	2,785
Maryland	2,000	2,055	Washington	1,826	1,883
Massachusetts	2,726	2,787	West Virginia	703	720
Michigan	4,536	4,619	Wisconsin	2,132	2,194
Minnesota	1,942	1,967	Wyoming	188	193

Note: Registrations include private and publicly owned automobiles and taxicabs, except vehicles owned by the military services

e-Estimate made by Federal Highway Administration based on partial data for 1974 and information available on current trends, vehicle production, etc.

Source: Department of Transportation

PASSENGER CAR MILEAGE

Year	Vehicle-Miles (Millions)		Passenger Mileage as Percent of Total	Average Miles per Passenger Car
	All Motor Vehicles	Passenger Cars[1]		
1940	302.2	249.6	82.6	9,080
1950	458.2	363.6	79.3	9,020
1955	603.4	487.5	80.8	9,359
1960	718.8	588.1	81.8	9,446
1965	887.8	711.6	80.2	9,286
1970	1,120.7	901.0	80.4	9,783
1971	1,186.3	954.2	80.4	9,926
1972	1,268.3	1,003.5	79.1	9,969
1973	1,308.6	1,036.5	79.2	9,767
1974	1,289.6	1,017.9	78.9	9,494

[1] Includes taxicabs and motorcycles

Source: Department of Transportation

PASSENGER CAR REGISTRATIONS

Millions

Year	Registrations Total[1]	New Cars	Year	Registrations Total[1]	New Cars
1940	27.5	3.4	1964	72.0	8.1
1945	25.8	--			
1950	40.3	6.3	1965	75.3	9.3
			1966	78.1	9.0
			1967	80.4	8.4
1955	52.1	7.2	1968	83.6	9.4
1956	54.2	6.0	1969	86.9	9.4
1957	55.9	6.0			
1958	56.9	4.7	1970	89.3	8.4
1959	59.5	6.0	1971	92.8	9.8a
			1972	96.9	10.5a
1960	61.7	6.6	1973	101.8	11.4a
1961	63.4	5.9	1974	104.9	8.7a
1962	66.1	6.9			
1963	69.1	7.6	1975	107.4	8.3a

[1] Includes private and commercially owned passenger cars
a - Excludes data for Oklahoma

Sources: Department of Transportation; R. L. Polk & Co.

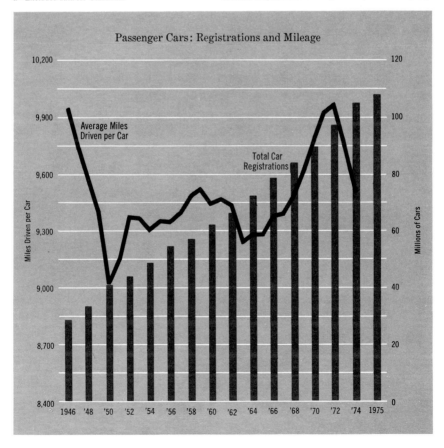

Passenger Cars: Registrations and Mileage

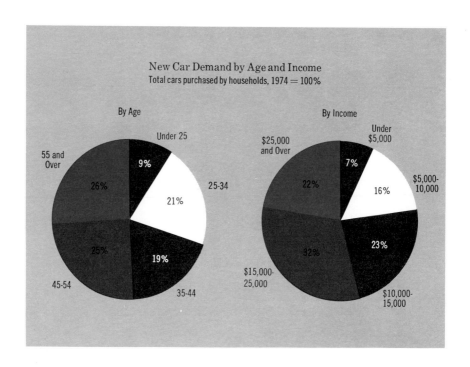

New Car Demand by Age and Income
Total cars purchased by households, 1974 = 100%

By Age

Under 25 9%
25-34 21%
35-44 19%
45-54 25%
55 and Over 26%

By Income

Under $5,000 7%
$5,000-10,000 16%
$10,000-15,000 23%
$15,000-25,000 32%
$25,000 and Over 22%

HOUSEHOLD AVAILABILITY AND PURCHASES OF SELECTED DURABLES

Autumn 1974

Item	Households with Item Available (Percent)	Purchases and Expenditures[1]		
		Number Purchased per 100 Households	Average Price Paid (Dollars)	Average Household Expenditure (Dollars)
Television Sets, Total	96.6	- -	- -	- -
Black and White Sets only	35.3	5.7	126	7
Color Sets	61.3	8.9	455	40
Air Conditioners:				
Central System	18.7	- -	- -	- -
Room-size	31.8	3.7	242	9
Household Appliances:				
Washing Machine	71.9	8.9	254	23
Clothes Dryer	52.6	6.5	204	13
Dishwasher	28.4	3.8	259	10
Refrigerator	98.9	8.5	375	32
Home Food Freezer	33.7	3.9	276	11
Kitchen Range	98.5	6.0	300	18

[1] Purchases of and expenditures for new merchandise made within preceding 12 months and owned at time of survey

Source: Department of Commerce

HOUSEHOLD PURCHASES OF NEW AND USED CARS, 1974

Household Characteristic	Households (Millions)	Number Purchased per 100 Households	
		New Cars	Used Cars
TOTAL	70.8	12.0	19.4
Income[1]			
Under $3,000	8.0	2.7	9.7
$3,000- 5,000	7.4	4.7	15.4
5,000- 7,500	8.9	6.3	20.1
7,500-10,000	8.3	9.2	22.0
10,000-15,000	15.9	12.5	23.2
15,000-20,000	9.7	16.7	21.4
20,000-25,000	5.2	21.6	22.1
25,000 and over	7.1	26.2	17.7
Age of Head			
Under 25	6.1	12.5	33.8
25-34	14.4	12.5	24.6
35-44	12.3	13.2	24.7
45-54	12.6	16.7	21.0
55-64	11.6	11.9	13.4
65 and over	13.7	6.2	6.4
Region			
Northeast	16.6	12.3	16.2
North Central	18.9	13.0	21.3
South	22.5	12.0	20.3
West	12.8	10.3	19.1
Race			
White	62.6	12.6	19.9
Negro	7.3	6.6	16.0

Note: Survey data are as of autumn
[1] Households not reporting income level are excluded

Source: Department of Commerce

MOTOR FUEL CONSUMPTION

Millions of gallons, except averages

Year	All Motor Vehicles			Passenger Cars[1]		
	Total Fuel Consumption	Average Gallons per Vehicle	Average Mileage per Gallon	Total Fuel Consumption	Average Gallons per Vehicle	Average Mileage per Gallon
1940	24,404	678	13.80	16,323	594	15.29
1950	40,280	728	12.87	24,305	603	14.95
1955	53,116	759	12.67	33,548	644	14.53
1960	63,714	777	12.42	41,169	661	14.28
1965	71,104	775	12.49	50,275	656	14.15
1970	92,328	830	12.14	65,784	714	13.70
1971	97,547	838	12.16	69,514	723	13.73
1972	105,062	859	12.07	73,463	730	13.67
1973	110,473	851	11.85	78,011	736	13.29
1974	106,301	788	12.13	74,244	676	13.71

[1] Includes taxicabs and motorcycles

Source: Department of Transportation

HOUSEHOLD OWNERSHIP OF CARS, 1974

Household Characteristic	Total Households (Millions)	Percent of Households Owning:			Total Cars Owned by Households[1] (Millions)	Percent Households Owning Current Model Car[2]
		One Car	Two Cars	Three or More Cars		
TOTAL	70.8	48.8	26.8	5.9	85.0	10.8
Income[3]						
Under $3,000	8.0	37.0	5.5	.7	4.2	4.7
$3,000- 5,000	7.4	51.9	8.0	.8	5.2	4.8
5,000- 7,500	8.9	60.4	13.6	2.0	8.4	6.8
7,500-10,000	8.3	61.9	20.9	2.2	9.1	7.2
10,000-15,000	15.9	54.9	32.4	4.4	21.2	10.7
15,000-20,000	9.7	45.4	42.3	7.8	14.9	13.0
20,000-25,000	5.2	36.8	46.9	13.2	8.9	15.7
25,000 and over	7.1	29.5	45.7	21.5	13.4	19.4
Income Quartile[3]						
Lowest	17.7	45.7	7.3	.9	11.3	5.2
Second Lowest	17.7	62.1	18.8	2.1	18.7	7.6
Second Highest	17.7	51.7	36.2	5.0	24.5	11.1
Highest	17.7	36.0	45.2	15.5	30.7	16.6
Age of Head						
Under 25	6.1	56.9	23.2	1.8	6.6	12.7
25-34	14.4	55.5	29.7	2.1	17.4	11.7
35-44	12.3	45.4	35.8	7.4	17.1	10.7
45-54	12.6	39.4	33.6	14.5	19.2	13.4
55-64	11.6	48.5	27.5	7.2	14.6	10.1
65 and over	13.7	50.2	10.5	1.2	10.4	6.1
Race of Head						
White	62.6	50.1	28.1	6.2	78.3	11.0
Negro	7.3	39.2	15.6	2.6	5.8	8.0
Spanish Origin	2.9	44.2	22.2	2.6	2.7	8.6
Tenure						
Owner-occupied	45.9	48.6	33.0	8.0	63.9	11.2
Renter-occupied	24.9	49.2	15.4	1.9	21.4	9.9
Regions						
Northeast	16.6	44.3	24.8	5.7	18.6	11.4
North Central	18.9	49.5	28.4	6.5	24.1	11.6
South	22.6	50.1	27.0	5.5	27.2	10.9
West	12.8	51.4	27.0	5.7	15.6	8.9
Residence						
Metropolitan	48.5	46.2	28.0	6.3	59.2	11.4
Central Cities	22.3	44.9	21.9	4.5	23.0	10.2
Outside Cent. Cities .	26.2	47.2	33.2	7.9	36.2	12.4
Nonmetropolitan	22.3	54.7	24.2	4.9	26.0	9.5

[1] Differences between total cars owned by all households and sums by individual characteristics are due to rounding
[2] 1974-1975 model year
[3] Households not reporting income level are excluded
Source: Department of Commerce

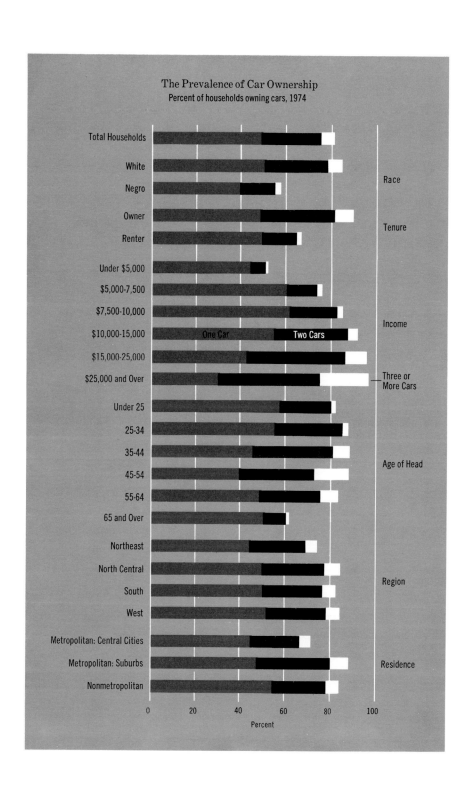

The Prevalence of Car Ownership
Percent of households owning cars, 1974

	Race
Total Households	
White	
Negro	

Tenure
Owner
Renter

Income
Under $5,000
$5,000-7,500
$7,500-10,000
$10,000-15,000
$15,000-25,000
$25,000 and Over

Three or More Cars

One Car   Two Cars

Age of Head
Under 25
25-34
35-44
45-54
55-64
65 and Over

Region
Northeast
North Central
South
West

Residence
Metropolitan: Central Cities
Metropolitan: Suburbs
Nonmetropolitan

0   20   40   60   80   100
Percent

199

HOUSEHOLD EXPENDITURES FOR AUTOS AND OTHER VEHICLES, 1974

Average annual expenditures and prices paid per household, in dollars

Characteristic	Average Expenditure[2]			Average Price Paid[2]	
	All Vehicles[1]	New Cars	Used Cars	New Cars	Used Cars
TOTAL HOUSEHOLDS.......	860	458	249	3,806	1,284
Income					
Under $3,000	219	103	76	3,780	786
$3,000- 5,000...............	387	164	160	3,488	1,039
5,000- 7,500...............	527	228	209	3,587	1,036
7,500-10,000...............	698	322	258	3,486	1,074
10,000-15,000...............	967	465	297	3,715	1,281
15,000-20,000...............	1,151	640	303	3,841	1,414
20,000-25,000...............	1,377	832	324	3,850	1,465
25,000 and over	1,656	1,074	345	4,097	1,951
Age of Head					
Under 25	940	436	363	3,495	1,073
25-34	1,006	486	301	3,894	1,226
35-44	1,015	506	295	3,843	1,192
45-54	1,107	650	281	3,887	1,340
55-64	815	445	240	3,747	1,782
65 and over	345	232	82	3,745	1,286
Race of Head					
White	901	478	256	3,782	1,290
Negro	492	272	194	4,130	1,213
Residence					
Metropolitan	846	482	240	3,843	1,306
Central Cities	684	389	217	3,826	1,317
Outside Central Cities	984	561	260	3,858	1,296
Nonmetropolitan	891	408	267	3,707	1,245

Note: Data as of autumn, based on vehicles owned at time of survey and purchased within preceding 12 months
[1] Includes household expenditures for trucks and recreational vehicles, not shown separately
[2] Net average expenditure or price (after trade-in allowance) per household   Source: Department of Commerce

AIR TRAVEL

Year	Passenger-Miles Flown (Billions)[1]			Revenue Passenger Enplanements (Millions)
	Total	Domestic	International	
1960.......................	38.9	30.6	8.3	57.9
1965.......................	68.7	51.9	16.8	94.7
1966.......................	79.9	60.6	19.3	109.4
1967.......................	98.7	75.5	23.3	132.1
1968.......................	114.0	87.5	26.5	150.2
1969.......................	125.4	95.9	29.5	159.2
New Series:				
1969.......................	125.4	102.7	22.7	171.9
1970.......................	131.7	104.1	27.6	169.9
1971.......................	135.7	106.4	29.2	173.7
1972.......................	152.4	118.1	34.3	191.3
1973.......................	162.0	126.3	35.6	202.2
1974.......................	162.9	129.7	33.2	207.4
1975.......................	162.8	131.7	31.1	205.1

[1] Revenue passengers, scheduled service. Beginning 1969 (new series) domestic flights include Alaska and Hawaii formerly shown as international service
Source: Civil Aeronautics Board

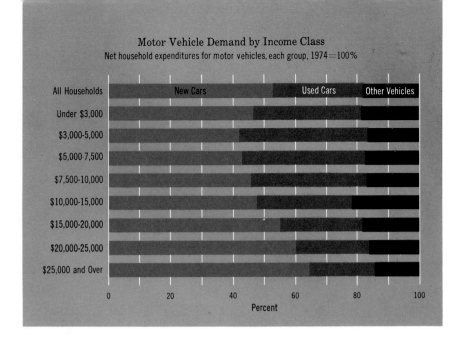

Motor Vehicle Demand by Income Class
Net household expenditures for motor vehicles, each group, 1974=100%

All Households	New Cars		Used Cars	Other Vehicles
Under $3,000				
$3,000-5,000				
$5,000-7,500				
$7,500-10,000				
$10,000-15,000				
$15,000-20,000				
$20,000-25,000				
$25,000 and Over				

Percent: 0   20   40   60   80   100

FOREIGN TRAVEL: TRAVELERS AND EXPENDITURES

Item	1950	1960	1970	1974	1975
	Thousands				
TOTAL OVERSEAS TRAVELERS[1]	676	1,634	5,260	6,467	6,354
Means of Transport from U.S.:					
Sea	298	317	120	47	36
Air.............................	378	1,317	5,140	6,420	6,318
Destination:					
Europe and Mediterranean	302	832	2,898	3,325	3,185
West Indies and Central America ...	323	641	1,663	2,147	2,065
South America	38	71	249	423	447
Other	13	90	450	572	657
	Millions of Dollars				
TOTAL EXPENDITURES[2]	1,022	2,623	6,180	9,406	10,143
Transportation[3]:					
Foreign Flag Carriers	145	513	1,215	2,095	2,380
U.S. Flag Carriers	123	360	985	1,331	1,346
Expenditures Abroad	754	1,750	3,980	5,980	6,417
Canada	261	380	1,018	1,359	1,306
Mexico	172	383	778	1,475	1,637
Total Overseas Travel	321	987	2,184	3,146	3,474
Europe and Mediterranean	225	692	1,425	1,802	1,918
West Indies and Central America .	61	166	390	685	787
South America	22	45	90	209	242
Other	13	84	279	450	527

Note: Data refer to residents of the U.S. and Puerto Rico

[1] Excludes travel to Canada and Mexico, cruise travelers, military and other Government personnel stationed abroad, and U.S. citizens residing abroad
[2] Includes shore expenditures of cruise travelers; excludes travel expenditures of military and other Government employees and dependents stationed abroad, and U.S. citizens residing abroad
[3] Excludes passenger fares of emigrant aliens

Source: Department of Commerce

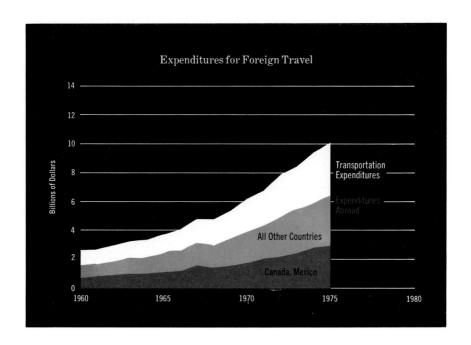

Expenditures for Foreign Travel

Billions of Dollars

Transportation Expenditures

Expenditures Abroad

All Other Countries

Canada, Mexico

1960   1965   1970   1975   1980

VISITS TO NATIONAL AND STATE PARKS

In millions

Item	1950	1955	1960	1965	1970	1974
NATIONAL PARK SYSTEM:						
Visits, Total[1]	33.3	56.6	79.2	121.3	172.0	217.4
National Parks	13.9	18.8	26.6	36.6	45.9	53.1
Other Areas[2]	19.3	37.7	52.6	84.7	126.1	164.3
Overnight Stays, Total[3]	4.5	5.4	9.4	13.0	16.2	15.4
Camper Days[4]	2.2	3.3	4.8	8.1	9.0	8.4
In Commercial Lodgings ..	2.3	2.2	2.8	3.3	4.9	3.7
Other	n.a.	n.a.	1.8	1.6	2.2	3.3
STATE PARK SYSTEMS:						
Day Visits, Total	108.2	169.1	238.4	354.8a	432.0	n.a.
Overnight Visits, Total	6.1	11.1	20.6	36.2a	50.6	n.a.
Cabins and Hotels	1.2	1.6	1.7	2.4a	2.9	n.a.
Organized Camps	1.5	1.7	2.2	2.1a	1.9	n.a.
Tent, Trailer Camps	3.4	7.6	16.2	31.8a	45.7	n.a.

[1] Data for 1950 are not strictly comparable with later figures. Includes White House visits beginning 1965
[2] Visits to National monuments, historical and military areas, seashores, etc.
[3] Excludes ''other'' overnight stays in 1950 and 1955
[4] Excludes National Capital Parks in 1950

a—Data for 1967
n.a.—Not available

Sources: Department of the Interior; National Recreation and Park Association

TRAVEL PROFILE, 1972

Percent distribution, except as indicated

Household Characteristic	House-holds Taking Trips	Persons Taking Trips	Trips (of One or More Persons)	Person-Trips[2]
TOTAL (Millions)	41.3	114.1	236.9	458.5
PERCENT DISTRIBUTION	100.0	100.0	100.0	100.0
Family Income				
Under $5,000	16.5	11.4	9.6	8.3
$5,000- 7,500...............	15.9	14.9	12.0	12.6
7,000-10,000...............	17.5	18.6	14.7	16.2
10,000-15,000...............	27.4	30.6	31.1	32.5
15,000 and over............	17.6	20.1	27.9	26.2
Not reported	5.1	4.4	4.7	4.2
Occupation of Household Head				
Professional, Managers	27.5	30.9	40.9	39.2
Clerical, Sales	14.0	13.7	16.8	15.5
Craftsmen, Operatives, Labor	28.8	32.1	21.8	26.3
Retired Persons.............	12.0	7.6	7.5	6.3
Other[3]	17.7	15.7	13.0	12.7
Residence				
Metropolitan	66.6	65.7	68.2	66.7
Central Cities.............	18.1	16.3	17.8	16.8
Outside Central Cities.....	48.5	49.4	50.4	49.9
Nonmetropolitan	33.4	34.3	31.8	33.3
Sex of Traveler				
Male	- -	46.0	- -	52.6
Female	- -	49.1	- -	43.2
Not reported	- -	4.8	- -	4.1
Age of Traveler				
Under 18 years	- -	31.6	- -	24.1
18-24	- -	9.1	- -	8.4
25-34	- -	13.9	- -	16.7
35-44	- -	13.0	- -	15.9
45-54	- -	12.9	- -	16.8
55-64	- -	9.1	- -	9.8
65 and over	- -	6.5	- -	4.9
Not reported	- -	3.9	- -	3.4
Education of Traveler				
Less than High School	- -	10.3	- -	7.5
Any High School	- -	39.0	- -	36.1
College	- -	23.4	- -	34.9
Not Reported...............	- -	27.4	- -	21.5

[1] About 38 per cent of all households and 45 per cent of all persons took no trips during the survey year
[2] A person on a trip. A person is counted each time he takes a trip, and several persons on one trip are counted separately
[3] Includes unemployed persons, non-military travel of military personnel, as well as occupations not reported

Source: Department of Commerce

UNITED STATES: PASSENGER ARRIVALS AND DEPARTURES

Thousands of persons

	1960		1970		1975	
Item	Passengers Arriving	Passengers Departing	Passengers Arriving	Passengers Departing	Passengers Arriving	Passengers Departing
TOTAL	3,112	2,939	10,039	9,354	14,240	13,099
Citizenship:						
Aliens	1,191	1,004	3,831	3,247	6,094	5,130
Citizens	1,921	1,935	6,208	6,107	8,146	7,969
Mode of Travel:						
By Sea	754	720	867	859	923	864
By Air	2,358	2,219	9,172	8,495	13,317	12,236
Flag of Carrier:						
United States	1,472	1,378	5,106	4,612	6,972	6,226
Foreign	1,640	1,561	4,933	4,742	7,268	6,874
Area:						
Europe[1]	1,256	1,231	4,087	3,907	5,251	4,827
Asia[1]	197	169	893	808	1,765	1,592
Africa	14	13	30	33	56	58
Oceania	55	47	225	221	402	389
Canada[2]	23	23	79	55	393	248
Mexico	257	246	880	846	1,613	1,522
West Indies . .	847	805	2,481	2,157	2,718	2,463
Cent. America	93	84	264	243	411	389
So. America . .	194	175	531	490	847	829
Cruise	175	146	569	594	784	782

Note: Data are for years ending June 30
[1] Turkey included with Europe through 1970 and with Asia thereafter
[2] Includes Newfoundland and Greenland

Source: Department of Justice

PRODUCTION AND DISTRIBUTION

PRODUCTION AND DISTRIBUTION

TOTAL INDUSTRIAL PRODUCTION

Index numbers, 1967 = 100

| Year | Total Industrial Production | Final Products | | Materials |
		Total	Consumer Goods	
1950	44.9	43.4	50.0	45.2
1951	48.7	46.8	49.5	50.0
1952	50.6	50.3	50.6	50.7
1953	54.8	53.7	53.7	56.3
1954	51.9	50.8	53.3	52.0
1955	58.5	54.9	59.5	61.5
1956	61.1	58.2	61.7	63.1
1957	61.9	59.9	63.2	63.1
1958	57.9	57.1	62.6	56.8
1959	64.8	62.7	68.7	65.5
1960	66.2	64.8	71.3	66.4
1961	66.7	65.3	72.8	66.4
1962	72.2	70.8	77.7	72.4
1963	76.5	74.9	82.0	77.0
1964	81.7	79.6	86.8	82.6
1965	89.2	86.8	93.0	91.0
1966	97.9	96.1	98.6	99.8
1967	100.0	100.0	100.0	100.0
1968	105.7	105.8	106.6	105.7
1969	110.7	109.0	111.1	112.4
1970	106.6	104.5	110.3	107.7
1971	106.8	104.7	115.7	107.4
1972	115.2	111.9	123.6	117.4
1973	129.8	124.4	131.5	133.9
1974p	129.3	125.1	128.9	132.4
1975p	117.8	118.2	124.0	115.5

Note: Revisions to all series of the industrial production index were in progress at press time and will be available in late 1976, too late for inclusion in this volume. Figures for 1973-1975 shown on this page are revised. Data for tables on pages 208 and 209 will be revised at a later date, as will earlier years series

p-Preliminary
Source: Federal Reserve

OUTPUT OF CONSUMER GOODS: CONSUMER STAPLES

Industrial production index numbers, 1967 = 100

Year	Total Consumer Staples	Consumer Foods, Tobacco	Nonfood Consumer Staples			
			Total	Chemical Products	Paper Products	Fuel and Lighting
1955	54.7	66.6	43.8	32.8	56.4	47.3
1960	70.8	79.2	62.6	53.0	72.1	66.1
1961	73.4	81.3	65.8	56.9	73.1	69.5
1962	76.9	83.8	70.1	61.9	74.9	74.4
1963	80.6	86.6	74.7	67.8	76.7	79.0
1964	85.0	90.3	79.8	72.6	82.4	84.1
1965	88.8	92.4	85.3	80.3	87.3	88.1
1966	95.5	96.9	94.1	92.6	95.8	94.1
1967	100.0	100.0	100.0	100.0	100.0	100.0
1968	105.2	103.6	106.9	108.2	103.0	108.0
1969	111.4	107.3	115.6	122.0	104.6	116.8
1970	115.4	110.6	120.4	126.1	104.0	125.2
1971	119.8	113.6	126.3	133.8	107.9	130.8
1972	126.2	117.5	135.3	144.6	114.8	139.5
1973	132.4	122.1	143.2	153.3	121.3	147.5
1974p	134.5	125.4	144.0	158.8	125.2	143.5
1975p	136.2	125.3	147.7	161.3	125.1	149.9

Note: See note to table page 207

p—Preliminary

Source: Federal Reserve

OUTPUT OF CONSUMER GOODS: AUTOMOTIVE PRODUCTS

Industrial production index numbers, 1967 = 100

Year	Total Automotive Products	Autos	Auto Parts, Allied Goods
1955	77.7	98.1	51.2
1960	76.4	83.6	63.5
1961	69.8	71.0	66.3
1962	84.5	91.1	72.3
1963	92.5	101.4	76.5
1964	96.8	103.3	84.7
1965	112.3	125.4	89.3
1966	108.8	116.4	94.5
1967	100.0	100.0	100.0
1968	117.9	120.0	113.9
1969	117.4	111.4	128.9
1970	99.9	86.5	125.6
1971	119.5	108.3	140.9
1972	127.7	112.7	156.5
1973	136.6	125.4	158.2
1974p	110.0	94.9	139.0
1975p	99.1	86.9	122.3

Note: See note to table page 207

p—Preliminary

Source: Federal Reserve

OUTPUT OF CONSUMER GOODS: HOME GOODS AND APPAREL

Industrial production index numbers, 1967 = 100

		Home Goods				
Year	Total	Appli-ances and A/C	TV and Home Audio	Carpets, Furniture	Misc. Home Goods	Clothing
1955	55.2	51.2	59.4	62.9	53.2	74.5
1960	62.0	58.2	67.1	69.2	59.9	81.8
1961	63.9	59.3	74.2	67.9	62.5	83.2
1962	69.4	66.0	81.0	75.9	66.2	86.7
1963	74.9	74.2	83.3	81.5	71.0	89.7
1964	81.7	82.4	93.1	88.1	76.8	94.2
1965	91.4	90.1	111.2	95.2	87.1	99.0
1966	100.7	100.7	111.0	101.7	98.4	101.6
1967	100.0	99.9	100.0	100.0	100.0	100.0
1968	106.9	108.8	96.7	110.4	106.6	104.4
1969	111.6	118.2	87.9	115.7	112.1	105.6
1970	107.6	122.1	68.2	108.4	109.7	101.3
1971	112.6	127.6	81.4	117.2	111.2	101.4
1972	124.5	144.5	87.5	132.6	121.0	109.7
1973	140.1	157.8	119.8	149.8	133.5	116.2
1974p	138.0	148.6	100.3	153.5	134.8	109.0
1975p	120.1	118.3	n.a.	133.8	124.5	99.0

Note: See note to table page 207
p—Preliminary

Source: Federal Reserve

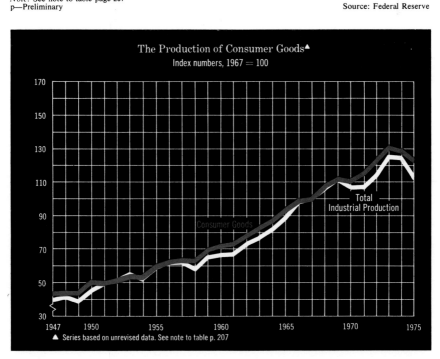

The Production of Consumer Goods▲
Index numbers, 1967 = 100

Total Industrial Production

Consumer Goods

▲ Series based on unrevised data. See note to table p. 207

RETAIL SALES: TOTAL AND MULTIUNIT FIRMS
Billions of dollars, except percent

Year	All Retail Stores			Multiunit Firms[1]	
	Total	Durable Goods	Non-durable Goods	Total	As Percent of All Stores
1960	219.5	70.6	149.0	50.7	23.1
1961	219.0	67.3	151.7	52.5	24.0
1962	235.6	74.9	160.7	55.6	23.6
1963	246.7	79.9	166.7	58.3	23.6
1964	261.9	84.6	177.3	68.3	26.1
1965	284.1	94.2	189.9	73.4	25.8
1966	304.0	98.3	205.7	80.3	26.4
1967	313.8	100.2	213.6	85.2	27.2
1968	341.9	111.2	230.7	94.2	27.8
1969	357.9	115.5	242.4	103.1	29.3
1970	375.5	114.3	261.2	117.2	31.2
1971	408.8	131.8	277.0	125.6	30.7
1972	448.4	149.7	298.7	137.6	30.7
1973	503.3	170.3	333.0	154.5	30.7
1974	537.8	167.3	370.5	169.4	31.5
1975	584.4	180.7	403.7	183.1	31.3

Note: Data based on new samples beginning 1961, and again beginning 1968. Revision of sample based on the 1967 census of business took place in 1971

[1] Firms operating 11 or more stores. Data prior to 1964 not comparable with later years. See also *Note* above

Source: Department of Commerce

THE TREND IN TOTAL RETAIL SALES

Year	Retail Sales		Total Sales as Percent of PCE[2]
	Total (Bil. Dollars)	Per Capita[1] (Dollars)	
1960	219.5	1,232	67.5
1961	219.0	1,209	65.3
1962	235.6	1,283	66.3
1963	246.7	1,323	65.8
1964	261.9	1,375	65.3
1965	284.1	1,483	65.6
1966	304.0	1,572	65.2
1967	313.8	1,608	63.7
1968	341.9	1,735	63.8
1969	357.9	1,798	61.8
1970	375.5	1,862	60.8
1971	408.8	2,002	61.3
1972	448.4	2,172	61.7
1973	503.3	2,419	62.6
1974	537.8	2,565	61.3
1975	584.4	2,764	60.6

Note: Data based on new samples beginning 1961, and again beginning 1968. Revision of sample based on the 1967 census of business took place in 1971

[1] Based on total civilian resident population as of July 1

[2] Personal consumption expenditures

Source: Department of Commerce

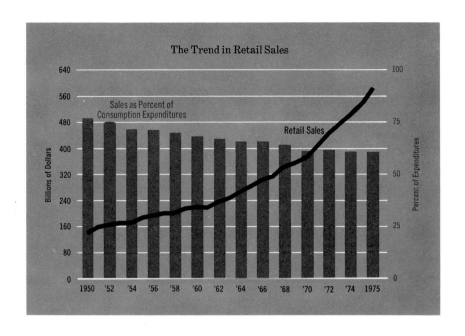

The Trend in Retail Sales

Sales as Percent of
Consumption Expenditures

Retail Sales

Billions of Dollars

Percent of Expenditures

1950 '52 '54 '56 '58 '60 '62 '64 '66 '68 '70 '72 '74 1975

PATTERNS OF RETAIL SALES, 1975

Kind of Business	Retail Sales		Kind of Business	Retail Sales	
	Billions of Dollars	Per-cent Distri-bution		Billions of Dollars	Per-cent Distri-bution
TOTAL RETAIL TRADE ..	584.4	100.0	Furniture, Appliances	26.1	4.5
			Furniture, Hfgs. Stores ..	15.3	2.6
Food Group	131.7	22.5	Furniture Stores	11.1	1.9
Grocery Stores	122.7	21:0	Appliances, TV, Radio ..	8.4	1.4
Meat, Fish Markets	3.1	.5	Appliance Dealers	5.1	.9
Bakery Products Stores ..	1.5	.2			
			Lumber, Bldg., Hardware[3]	34.2	5.9
Eating and Drinking Places	47.5	8.1	Lumber, Bldg. Materials .	18.2	3.1
Eating Places	39.5	6.8	Hardware Stores	5.8	1.0
Restaurants, Cafeterias .	31.4	5.4			
Drinking Places	8.0	1.4	Automotive Group Dealers .	102.1	17.5
			Passenger Car, Other Auto	93.0	15.9
Gen'l. Merchandise Group[1]	95.4	16.3	Pass. Car Dealers	85.6	14.6
Dept. Stores, Dry Goods	73.4	12.6	Franchised Dealers .	80.0	13.7
Department Stores	60.7	10.4	Tire, Battery, Accessories	9.1	1.5
Variety Stores	9.1	1.6			
Mail Order Houses[2]	6.0	1.0	Gasoline Service Stations ..	43.9	7.5
Apparel Group	26.7	4.6	Drug, Proprietary Stores ..	18.1	3.1
Men's, Boys' Wear Stores	6.1	1.0			
Women's Apparel, etc. ..	10.4	1.8	Liquor Stores	11.0	1.9
Family Clothing Stores ..	4.7	.8			
Shoe Stores	4.1	.7	Other Stores	47.6	8.2

[1] Includes nonstores
[2] Department store merchandise
[3] Includes farm equipment

Source: Department of Commerce

RETAIL SALES BY REGIONS, 1975

Billions of dollars, except as indicated

Region	Total Retail Sales			Durable Goods Stores	Nondurable Goods Stores
	Amount	Percent	Per Capita (Dollars)		
TOTAL U.S.	584.4	100.0	2,764	180.7	403.7
Northeast	126.3	21.6	2,560	33.5	92.9
New England	32.1	5.5	2,646	8.5	23.7
Middle Atlantic	94.2	16.1	2,532	25.0	69.2
North Central	170.6	29.2	2,966	54.2	116.3
East North Central	117.4	20.1	2,870	35.2	82.2
West North Central	53.2	9.1	3,202	19.0	34.1
South	177.2	30.3	2,635	58.7	118.6
South Atlantic	88.0	15.1	2,651	26.8	61.2
East South Central	32.4	5.5	2,410	11.7e	20.7
West South Central	56.9	9.7	2,757	20.2	36.7
West	110.3	18.9	2,954	34.4	75.9
Mountain	27.5	4.7	2,890	9.9e	17.6
Pacific	82.7	14.2	2,976	24.4	58.3

Note: Per capita figures are based on civilian population as of July 1

e—Estimate

Source: Department of Commerce

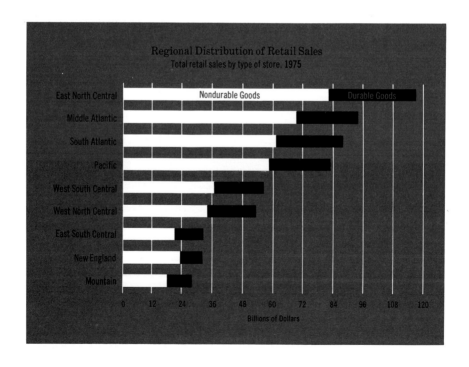

Regional Distribution of Retail Sales
Total retail sales by type of store, 1975

RETAIL SALES: FOOD STORES AND RESTAURANTS
Billions of dollars

Year	Food Stores		Grocery Stores, Multiunit[2]	Eating and Drinking Places
	Total	Grocery Stores[1]		
1960	54.0	48.6	21.4	16.1
1961	53.4	49.0	22.1	15.5
1962	55.6	51.4	23.0	16.4
1963	57.3	53.0	23.7	17.2
1964	60.2	55.7	26.2	18.5
1965	64.0	59.3	27.6	20.2
1966	68.1	63.3	29.9	22.1
1967	69.1	64.4	31.2	23.5
1968	74.1	69.0	36.8	25.7
1969	78.3	72.9	39.4	27.0
1970	86.1	79.8	43.2	29.7
1971	89.2	82.8	45.2	31.1
1972	95.0	88.3	49.2	33.9
1973	105.7	98.4	55.2	37.9
1974	119.8	111.3	62.6	41.8
1975	131.7	122.7	68.4	47.5

Note: Data based on new samples beginning 1961, and again beginning 1968. Revision of sample based on the 1967 census of business took place in 1971
[1] Data for years 1961-1969 estimated, using ratio of new samples to old samples
[2] Firms operating 11 or more stores. Data prior to 1964 not comparable with later years

Source: Department of Commerce

RETAIL SALES: AUTOMOTIVE GROUP

Billions of dollars

Year	Automotive Group, Total	Passenger Car, Other Auto Dealers	Tire, Battery Accessory Dealers
1960	39.6	37.0	2.5
1961	37.5	34.7	2.8
1962	43.5	40.5	3.0
1963	46.7	43.6	3.1
1964	49.3	46.0	3.3
1965	56.9	53.5	3.4
1966	58.1	54.1	3.9
1967	58.3	54.0	4.3
1968	65.7	61.0	4.7
1969	68.2	63.1	5.1
1970	65.0	59.4	5.6
1971	78.9	72.5	6.4
1972	88.6	81.5	7.1
1973	100.7	92.8	7.9
1974	93.1	84.8	8.3
1975	102.1	93.0	9.1

Note: Data based on the new samples beginning 1961, and again beginning 1968. Revision of the sample based on the 1967 census of business took place in 1971

Source: Department of Commerce

RETAIL SALES: GENERAL MERCHANDISE, FURNISHINGS, APPAREL

Billions of dollars

Year	General Merchandise		Apparel Group Stores	Furniture, Appliance Group Stores
	Total, with Nonstores	Department Stores		
1960	24.1	- -	13.6	10.6
1961	29.9	- -	13.6	10.1
1962	32.5	- -	14.2	10.5
1963	34.2	- -	14.2	11.3
1964	38.3	22.2	15.3	12.7
1965	42.3	25.0	15.8	13.4
1966	47.0	27.9	17.3	14.6
1967	49.8	29.6	18.1	15.3
1968	54.1	33.1	19.2	16.7
1969	57.6	35.7	19.9	17.3
1970	61.3	37.3	19.8	17.8
1971	68.1	42.0	20.8	18.6
1972	74.9	46.3	22.0	21.3
1973	83.3	52.3	24.1	24.0
1974	89.3	55.9	24.9	25.5
1975	95.4	60.7	26.7	26.1

Note: Data based on new samples beginning 1961, and again beginning 1968. Revision of the sample based on the 1967 census of business took place in 1971
Source: Department of Commerce

THE DEPARTMENT STORE'S COMPETITIVE POSITION BY REGIONS

Region	Dept. Store Sales (Mil. Dollars)		Percent of GAF Sales[1]	
	1967	1972	1967	1972
TOTAL U.S.	32,344	51,084	39.3	45.5
Northeast	8,523	12,730	38.1	45.1
New England	1,919	2,968	37.8	44.4
Middle Atlantic	6,603	9,763	38.3	45.4
North Central	9,828	14,956	41.2	48.8
East North Central	7,520	11,321	42.5	50.4
West North Central	2,308	3,635	37.2	44.5
South	7,984	13,877	36.3	41.3
South Atlantic	4,246	7,609	38.2	43.3
East South Central	1,165	2,275	29.7	38.9
West South Central	2,574	3,992	36.8	39.2
West	6,008	9,520	42.5	47.8
Mountain	1,030	1,965	37.2	42.7
Pacific	4,979	7,555	43.8	49.4

[1] Stores in the general merchandise (including all nonstores), apparel, and furniture and equipment groups

Source: Department of Commerce

DEPARTMENT STORES AND SALES IN METROPOLITAN AREAS, 1975

Standard Metropolitan Statistical Area	Number of Stores[1]	Millions of Dollars	Standard Metropolitan Statistical Area	Number of Stores[1]	Millions of Dollars
Anaheim-Santa Ana-Garden Grove, Calif. ..	70	760.8	Milwaukee, Wis.	50	558.9
Atlanta, Ga.	65	811.5	Minneapolis-St. Paul, Minn............	61	939.8
Baltimore, Md...........	70	653.7	Nassau-Suffolk, N.Y.....	64	981.4
Boston, Mass.	93	820.8	New York N.Y.[2]	81	2,111.1
Buffalo, N.Y.	64	452.5	Newark, N.J.	33	455.5
Chicago, Ill.	223	2,554.5	Paterson-Clifton-Passaic, N.J...........	34	588.3
Cincinnati, Ohio-Ky.-Ind...............	57	536.5	Philadelphia, Pa.-N.J...............	133	1,457.0
Cleveland, Ohio	78	769.9			
Columbus, Ohio	42	443.9	Pittsburgh, Pa.	73	870.3
Dallas, Tex.	76	652.7	St. Louis, Mo.-Ill.	75	860.6
Denver, Colo.	60	536.1	San Francisco-Oakland, Calif.........	89	1,217.3
Detroit, Mich.	96	1,557.1	San Jose, Calif.	38	491.8
Houston, Tex.	85	1,071.3			
Indianapolis, Ind.	58	454.6	Seattle-Everett, Wash.	37	499.3
Kansas City, Mo.-Kans.	53	439.7	Tampa-St. Petersburg, Fla.............	61	470.0
Los Angeles-Long Beach, Calif...........	220	2,639.9	Washington, D.C.-Md.-Va..............	88	1,230.7
Miami, Fla.............	53	546.0			

Note: SMSA's as defined prior to 1970 unless otherwise indicated. Data exclude sales by mail order catalog desks within department stores

[1]As of January 1976
[2]Includes New York City, Rockland and Westchester Counties, N.Y.   Source: Department of Commerce

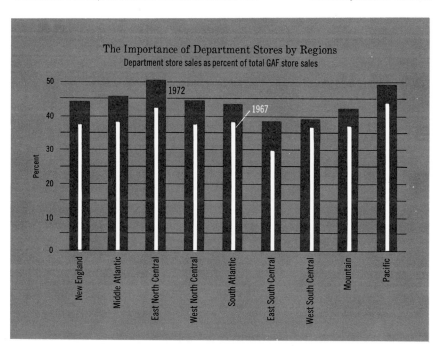

215

DEPARTMENT STORE SALES BY MERCHANDISE LINES

Merchandise Line	1972 Dollars (Millions)	1972 Per-cent	As Percent of Total Retail Sales 1967	As Percent of Total Retail Sales 1972
TOTAL SALES	51,084	100.0	11.0	11.6
Food, Beverages Tobacco	1,918	3.8	1.3	1.4
Men's, Boys' Clothing	6,129	12.0	39.1	40.9
Women's, Girls' Clothing	12,004	23.5	44.5	46.3
Footwear	2,256	4.4	26.8	29.4
Furniture, Bedding, Floor Coverings	2,341	4.6	20.1	16.5
Major Appliances, Radio, TV	4,179	8.2	26.0	26.9
Kitchenware, Homefurnishings	2,415	4.7	39.8	40.0
Curtains, Draperies, Dry Goods	3,528	6.9	48.2	43.2
Cosmetics, Drugs[1]	1,817	3.6	[2]	11.6
Jewelry, Optical Goods	977	1.9	19.8	19.6
Hardware, Gardening Equip., Lumber	3,043	6.0	11.2	12.5
Auto Fuels, Tires, Accessories	2,243	4.4	3.7	5.1
Sporting, Recreation Equipment	1,232	2.4	23.8	17.0
Toys, Games, Wheel Goods	1,138	2.2 }		
Books, Stationery, Photo Equipment	1,221	2.4 }	[2]	15.0
All Other Merchandise[1]	876	1.7 }		
Nonmerchandise Receipts[3]	3,767	7.4	--	19.6

Note: Data refer only to establishments with payroll

[1] Household cleaners included with cosmetics and drugs, in 1967, with all other merchandise in 1972
[2] Comparable data not available
[3] Service receipts

Source: Department of Commerce

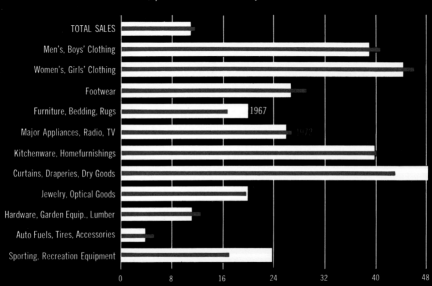

The Department Store's Share of Market
Sales as percent of total retail sales by selected lines

TOTAL SALES
Men's, Boys' Clothing
Women's, Girls' Clothing
Footwear
Furniture, Bedding, Rugs
Major Appliances, Radio, TV
Kitchenware, Homefurnishings
Curtains, Draperies, Dry Goods
Jewelry, Optical Goods
Hardware, Garden Equip., Lumber
Auto Fuels, Tires, Accessories
Sporting, Recreation Equipment

0   8   16   24   32   40   48

Percent

RETAIL SALES: OTHER STORES
Billions of dollars

Year	Drug, Proprietary Stores	Liquor Stores	Lumber, Building, Hardware[1]	
			Total Stores	Hardware Stores
1960................	7.5	4.9	11.2	2.7
1965................	9.2	5.7	12.4	2.7
1966................	10.0	6.1	12.6	2.8
1967................	10.7	6.4	12.7	2.9
1968................	11.6	7.0	14.3	3.2
1969................	12.2	7.4	15.0	3.4
1970................	13.4	8.0	15.3	3.4
1971................	13.7	8.8	17.4	3.6
1972................	14.5	9.2	20.1	4.1
1973................	15.5	9.6	22.8	4.7
1974................	16.8	10.3	32.5	5.2
1975................	18.1	11.0	34.2	5.8

Note: Data based on new samples beginning 1961, and again beginning 1968. Revision of the sample based on the the 1967 census of business took place in 1971
[1]Also includes farm equipment

Source: Department of Commerce

RETAIL TRADE: ESTABLISHMENTS AND SALES
Establishments in thousands; sales in million dollars

Item	1958	1963	1967	1972
TOTAL ESTABLISHMENTS	1,795	1,708	1,763	1,934
Building Materials, Hardware, Farm Equip.	108	93	86	77
General Merchandise Group Stores	87	62	67	76
Food Stores	357	319	294	267
Automotive Dealers	94	99	106	132
Gasoline Service Stations	207	211	216	226
Apparel and Accessory Stores	119	116	110	129
Furniture, Homefurnishings, Equip. Stores	104	94	99	117
Eating and Drinking Places	346	334	348	360
Drug and Proprietary Stores	56	55	54	52
Liquor Stores	37	40	40	42
Other Retail Stores	204	205	249	295
Nonstore Retailers	75	80	94	162
TOTAL SALES	200,365	244,202	310,214	470,806
Building Materials, Hardware, Farm Equip.	14,326	14,606	17,200	25,575
General Merchandise Group Stores	21,971	30,003	43,537	66,676
Food Stores	49,225	57,079	70,251	100,719
Automotive Dealers	31,905	45,376	55,631	93,774
Gasoline Service Stations	14,228	17,760	22,709	33,655
Apparel and Accessory Stores	12,569	14,040	16,672	24,741
Furniture, Homefurnishings, Equip. Stores .	10,110	10,926	14,542	22,533
Eating and Drinking Places	15,290	18,412	23,843	36,868
Drug and Proprietary Stores	6,803	8,487	10,930	15,599
Liquor Stores	4,202	5,189	6,663	9,874
Other Retail Stores	14,323	16,120	20,611	29,223
Nonstore Retailers	5,413	6,204	7,623	11,568

Note: Data based on 1967 Standard Industrial Classification. See note to table page 219

Source: Department of Commerce

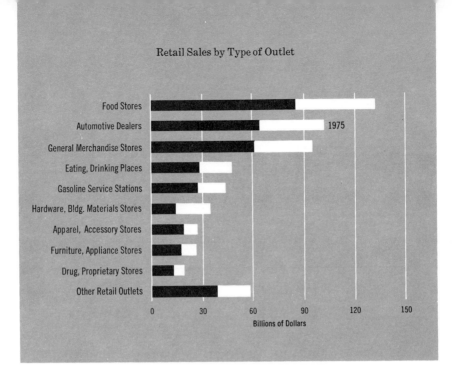

Retail Sales by Type of Outlet

Food Stores
Automotive Dealers
General Merchandise Stores
Eating, Drinking Places
Gasoline Service Stations
Hardware, Bldg. Materials Stores
Apparel, Accessory Stores
Furniture, Appliance Stores
Drug, Proprietary Stores
Other Retail Outlets

1975

0   30   60   90   120   150
Billions of Dollars

THE CHANGING PATTERN OF RETAIL TRADE

Percent distribution

Item	1958	1963	1967	1972
TOTAL ESTABLISHMENTS	100.0	100.0	100.0	100.0
Building Materials, Hardware, Farm Equipment .	6.0	5.4	4.9	4.0
General Merchandise Group Stores	4.9	3.6	3.8	3.9
Food Stores	19.9	18.7	16.7	13.8
Automotive Dealers	5.2	5.8	6.0	6.8
Gasoline Service Stations	11.5	12.4	12.3	11.7
Apparel and Accessory Stores	6.6	6.8	6.2	6.7
Furniture, Homefurnishings, Equipment Stores .	5.8	5.5	5.6	6.0
Eating and Drinking Places	19.3	19.6	19.7	18.6
Drug and Proprietary Stores	3.1	3.2	3.0	2.7
Liquor Stores	2.1	2.4	2.3	2.2
Other Retail Stores	11.4	12.0	14.1	15.2
Nonstore Retailers	4.2	4.7	5.4	8.4
TOTAL SALES	100.0	100.0	100.0	100.0
Building Materials, Hardware, Farm Equipment .	7.1	6.0	5.5	5.4
General Merchandise Group Stores	11.0	12.3	14.0	14.2
Food Stores	24.6	23.4	22.6	21.4
Automotive Dealers	15.9	18.6	17.9	19.9
Gasoline Service Stations	7.1	7.3	7.3	7.1
Apparel and Accessory Stores	6.3	5.7	5.4	5.3
Furniture, Homefurnishings, Equipment Stores .	5.0	4.5	4.7	4.8
Eating and Drinking Places	7.6	7.5	7.7	7.8
Drug and Proprietary Stores	3.4	3.5	3.5	3.3
Liquor Stores	2.1	2.1	2.1	2.1
Other Retail Stores	7.1	6.6	6.6	6.2
Nonstore Retailers	2.7	2.5	2.5	2.5

Note: See note to table page 219

Source: Department of Commerce

RETAIL TRADE BY KIND OF BUSINESS, 1972

Kind of Business	All Establishments		Establishments with Payroll		
	Number (Thousands)	Sales (Mil. Dollars)	Number (Thousands)	Sales (Mil. Dollars)	Payroll Entire Year (Mil. Dollars)
TOTAL RETAIL TRADE	1,912.9	459,040	1264.9	440,222	55,372
Food Stores[1]	267.4	100,719	173.1	96,375	8,820
Grocery Stores	194.3	93,328	128.1	90,048	7,846
Eating and Drinking Places	359.5	36,868	287.2	35,048	8,735
Eating Places	253.1	30,385	208.9	29,313	7,620
Drinking Places	106.4	6,482	78.4	5,735	1,114
General Merchandise Stores[1] ...	56.2	65,091	44.4	64,669	9,037
Department Stores	7.7	51,084	7.7	51,084	7,226
Variety Stores	21.9	7,344	18.4	7,220	1,113
Apparel Stores[1]	129.2	24,741	105.7	24,115	3,602
Men's, Boys' Apparel	23.2	5,584	21.0	5,497	860
Women's Apparel, Accessories	49.6	9,397	40.6	9,173	1,363
Shoe Stores	26.8	4,075	23.4	3,972	605
Furniture and Equipment Stores[1]	116.9	22,533	82.5	21,505	3,113
Furniture Stores	38.7	10,443	30.0	10,128	1,514
Household Appliance Stores .	20.3	3,824	14.6	3,627	473
Radio, TV, Music Stores	29.9	4,645	20.2	4,365	580
Lumber, Building, Hardware, etc. Stores	83.8	23,844	62.0	22,958	2,675
Automotive Dealers[1]	121.4	90,030	85.1	88,491	8,622
Motor Vehicle Dealers[1]	64.2	77,833	44.3	76,817	7,099
New Car Dealers	32.5	73,309	31.6	73,254	6,843
Tire, Battery, Accessory Dealers	n.a.	n.a.	22.4	5,526	885
Gasoline Service Stations	226.5	33,655	183.4	31,440	2,974
Drug, Proprietary Stores	51.5	15,599	47.6	15,420	2,202
Liquor Stores	42.0	9,874	33.7	9,342	632
Jewelry Stores	25.3	3,118	16.0	2,904	473
Other Retail Stores	271.1	21,399	124.6	18,251	2,811
Nonstore Retailers	162.1	11,568	19.7	9,705	1,675
Mail Order Houses	8.0	4,574	5.4	4,528	737
Automatic Merchandising Machine Operators	12.8	3,011	5.4	2,829	455
Direct Selling Establishments .	141.3	3,984	8.9	2,349	484

Note: Data based on revised Standard Industrial Classification of 1972. The principal difference lies in the elimination of farm equipment stores and sales from retail trade statistics. Figures shown here differ, therefore, from 1972 data shown on pages 217, 221, 226 and 229 where the figures have been adjusted for comparability with earlier censuses

[1] Includes kinds of business not shown separately

n.a.—Not available

Source: Department of Commerce

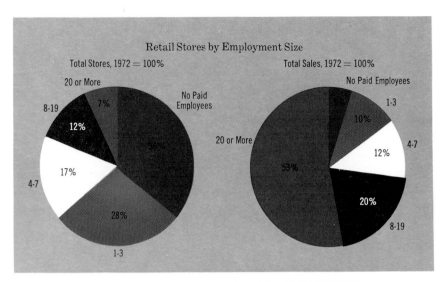

Retail Stores by Employment Size

Total Stores, 1972 = 100%

20 or More
8-19
7%
12%
17%
4-7
28%
1-3
36%
No Paid Employees

Total Sales, 1972 = 100%

No Paid Employees
1-3
10%
4-7
12%
20 or More
53%
20%
8-19

RETAIL ESTABLISHMENTS AND SALES BY SIZE
Percent distribution

Item	1963 Estab-lishments	1963 Sales	1967 Estab-lishments	1967 Sales	1972 Estab-lishments	1972 Sales
TOTAL RETAIL TRADE	100.0	100.0	100.0	100.0	100.0	100.0
Sales Size[1]						
Less than $30,000	33.7	3.2	34.9	2.7	30.2	1.6
$ 30,000- 50,000	15.9	4.1	13.6	2.9	11.0	1.7
50,000- 100,000	21.5	10.1	19.3	7.6	17.8	5.1
100,000- 300,000	20.0	21.8	21.5	20.1	26.3	18.2
300,000- 500,000	3.8	9.5	4.4	9.4	6.2	9.5
500,000-1,000,000	2.8	13.0	3.3	12.8	4.1	11.4
1,000,000 or more	2.4	38.4	3.0	44.4	4.3	52.5
Employment Size[1] [2]						
Less than 4 Employees	69.6	20.7	68.9	18.9	64.6	14.9
4-7	16.1	14.9	14.8	12.5	16.5	12.4
8-19	9.7	20.7	10.9	20.4	12.4	19.8
20 or more	4.6	43.7	5.4	48.2	6.5	52.9
Number of Units Operated[3]						
Single Units	87.1	63.4	87.5	60.2	84.8	54.8
Multiunits	12.9	36.6	12.5	39.8	15.2	45.2
Legal Form or Organization						
Individual Proprietorships	65.9	26.9	n.a.	n.a.	51.6	15.3
Partnerships	12.4	9.8	n.a.	n.a.	7.8	5.2
Corporations	21.0	61.9	25.6	67.4	29.6	74.7
Other Legal Forms[4]	.8	1.4	74.4	32.6	10.9	4.8

[1] Refers only to firms operated entire year
[2] Number of employees as of workweek nearest Nov. 15 for 1963, and workweek including March 12 for 1967 and 1972. Includes those with no paid employees.
[3] Sales data for 1972 based on firms in business at end of year
[4] For 1967, data refer to individual proprietorships, partnerships, as well as other legal forms of organization
n.a.—Not available

Source: Department of Commerce

RETAIL TRADE BY EMPLOYMENT SIZE, 1972

Kind of Business	Total[1]	Percent Distribution by Number of Paid Employees[2]				
		None	1-3	4-7	8-19	20 or More
TOTAL ESTABLISHMENTS	1,710	36.2	28.4	16.5	12.4	6.5
Building Materials, Hardware, etc. ..	78	28.2	32.8	20.0	14.5	4.5
Gen'l Merchandise Group Stores	52	22.1	20.7	14.8	18.0	24.5
Food Stores	244	37.3	27.1	14.7	11.1	9.8
Automotive Dealers	111	31.6	22.9	15.7	16.9	13.0
Gasoline Service Stations	197	23.8	43.0	23.1	9.1	1.0
Apparel and Accessory Stores	118	19.8	33.6	24.7	16.0	5.9
Furniture and Equipment Stores	107	31.5	33.3	19.3	12.8	3.0
Eating and Drinking Places	316	26.0	29.8	16.4	17.1	10.7
Drug and Proprietary Stores	49	8.8	21.2	28.1	32.2	9.7
Liquor Stores	38	22.2	46.4	22.4	8.4	.6
Other Retail Stores	398	65.4	18.7	8.9	5.4	1.5
Nonstore Retailers	134	87.1	5.5	2.7	2.9	1.9
TOTAL SALES	427,640	4.9	10.0	12.4	19.8	52.9
Building Materials, Hardware, etc. ..	22,412	4.7	13.5	19.4	31.6	30.8
Gen'l Merchandise Group Stores	62,155	.7	1.4	2.1	5.3	90.5
Food Stores	94,070	4.7	7.5	8.1	16.4	63.3
Automotive Dealers	85,932	2.2	4.3	6.7	18.6	68.3
Gasoline Service Stations	29,136	9.0	31.4	32.7	21.4	5.5
Apparel and Accessory Stores	22,776	3.4	12.9	20.4	27.6	35.7
Furniture and Equipment Stores	21,002	5.6	16.3	22.4	32.0	23.7
Eating and Drinking Places	33,139	7.3	11.9	12.3	23.9	44.6
Drug and Proprietary Stores	14,742	1.6	6.6	16.4	38.9	36.5
Liquor Stores	9,156	6.5	29.2	33.3	26.3	4.6
Other Retail Stores	33,120	15.3	15.6	17.3	22.9	29.0
Nonstore Retailers	10,558	15.6	6.7	7.9	17.6	52.2

[1] Stores in thousands, sales in millions of dollars. Data only for stores operated entire year
[2] Number of employees as of March 12

Source: Department of Commerce

SALES SIZE: FOOD STORES AND RESTAURANTS, 1972

Annual Sales Volume	Food Stores		Eating and Drinking Places	
	Establish-ments	Sales	Establish-ments	Sales
ALL ESTABLISHMENTS[1]	267.4	100,719	359.5	36,868
No. Operated All Year[1]	243.5	94,070	316.3	33,139
PERCENT DISTRIBUTION	100.0	100.0	100.0	100.0
Under $30,000	21.3	.8	30.0	4.5
$ 30,000- 50,000	11.3	1.1	18.9	7.0
50,000- 100,000	18.2	3.4	22.9	15.4
100,000- 300,000	28.2	12.4	20.9	33.2
300,000- 500,000	5.8	5.7	4.3	15.8
500,000-1,000,000	4.8	8.8	2.4	15.2
1,000,000-2,000,000	5.0	18.8	.5	5.9
2,000,000 or more	5.4	48.9	.1	3.0

Note: Distributions based on establishments operated entire year

[1] Establishments in thousands; sales in millions of dollars

Source: Department of Commerce

SALES SIZE: GENERAL MERCHANDISE, APPAREL AND HOMEFURNISHINGS STORES, 1972

Annual Sales Volume	General Merchandise Group		Department Stores		Variety Stores	
	Estab-lishments	Sales	Estab-lishments	Sales	Estab-lishments	Sales
ALL ESTABLISHMENTS[1]	56.2	65,091	7.7	51,083	21.9	7,344
No. Operated All Year[1]	52.4	62,155	7.3	49,076	20.4	6,949
PERCENT DISTRIBUTION	100.0	100.0	100.0	100.0	100.0	100.0
Under $30,000	16.9	.2	--	--	14.2	.6
$ 30,000- 50,000	8.1	.3	--	--	7.5	.9
50,000-100,000	14.2	.9	--	--	15.4	3.3
100,000-300,000	25.8	3.9	--	--	32.1	17.3
300,000-500,000	9.2	3.0	.4	[2]	12.9	14.6
500,000-1,000,000	7.6	4.5	4.2	.5	10.4	21.2
1,000,000-2,000,000	5.5	6.7	16.7	3.8	4.9	20.3
2,000,000 or more	12.8	80.6	78.6	95.7	2.6	21.7

Annual Sales Volume	Apparel, Accessories, Total		Women's Clothing, Specialty		Men's Boys' Clothing	
	Estab-lishments	Sales	Estab-lishments	Sales	Estab-lishments	Sales
ALL ESTABLISHMENTS[1]	129.2	24,741	49.6	9,397	23.2	5,584
No. Operated All Year[1]	118.5	22,776	45.6	8,692	21.4	5,189
PERCENT DISTRIBUTION	100.0	100.0	100.0	100.0	100.0	100.0
Under $30,000	19.4	1.4	21.2	1.5	9.9	.6
$ 30,000- 50,000	9.8	2.0	11.4	2.3	6.7	1.1
50,000-100,000	21.6	8.3	23.0	8.7	19.1	5.9
100,000-300,000	33.9	30.3	30.5	27.0	41.5	30.7
300,000-500,000	7.9	15.5	6.7	13.4	12.5	19.5
500,000-1,000,000	5.0	17.6	4.7	16.7	7.6	21.4
1,000,000-2,000,000	1.7	12.4	1.9	13.2	2.2	20.8
2,000,000 or more	.6	12.5	.8	17.1	.6	

Annual Sales Volume	Furniture, Hfgs., Equip., Total		Furniture, Homefurnishings		Appliances, Radio, TV	
	Estab-lishments	Sales	Estab-lishments	Sales	Estab-lishments	Sales
ALL ESTABLISHMENTS[1]	116.9	22,533	66.7	14,064	50.2	8,469
No. Operated All Year[1]	107.4	21,002	61.2	13,066	46.2	7,936
PERCENT DISTRIBUTION	100.0	100.0	100.0	100.0	100.0	100.0
Under $30,000	26.8	1.9	26.2	1.6	27.6	2.2
$ 30,000- 50,000	10.0	2.0	9.6	1.8	10.6	2.4
50,000-100,000	16.5	6.2	15.9	5.4	17.3	7.4
100,000-300,000	29.2	26.6	28.8	24.2	29.6	30.3
300,000-500,000	9.0	17.5	9.6	17.2	8.1	18.0
500,000-1,000,000	6.1	21.1	6.9	22.3	4.9	19.1
1,000,000-2,000,000	1.9	12.7	2.2	13.7	1.4	11.1
2,000,000 or more	.6	12.1	.7	13.7	.4	9.4

Note: Distributions based on establishments operated entire year

[1] Establishments in thousands; sales in millions of dollars
[2] Less than 0.5 percent
Source: Department of Commerce

SALES SIZE: AUTOMOTIVE GROUP, 1972

Annual Sales Volume	Automotive Dealers		Tire, Battery, Accessory Dlrs.		Gasoline Service Stations	
	Estab-lishments	Sales	Estab-lishments	Sales	Estab-lishments	Sales
ALL ESTABLISHMENTS[1]	121.3	90,030	22.4	5,526	226.5	33,655
No. Operated All Year[1]	111.3	85,932	20.8	5,181	197.2	29,136
PERCENT DISTRIBUTION	100.0	100.0	100.0	100.0	100.0	100.0
Under $30,000	20.1	.3	6.0	.4	14.0	1.5
$ 30,000- 50,000	6.5	.3	5.6	.9	8.2	2.3
50,000- 100,000	11.8	1.1	15.9	4.7	22.8	11.5
100,000- 300,000	24.5	5.8	45.7	34.4	45.1	52.5
300,000- 500,000	9.6	4.8	16.8	25.6	7.3	18.2
500,000-1,000,000	9.5	8.8	8.0	21.4	2.2	9.7
1,000,000-2,000,000	7.9	14.6	1.6	8.5	.3	2.9
2,000,000 or more	10.0	64.2	.4	4.1	.1	1.3

Note: Distributions based on establishments operated entire year

[1] Establishments in thousands; sales in millions of dollars

Source: Department of Commerce

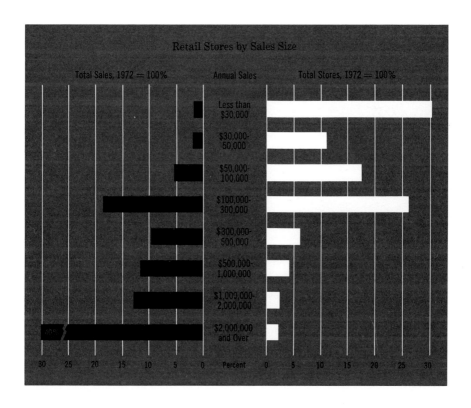

SALES SIZE: OTHER RETAIL STORES, 1972

Annual Sales Volume	Drug, Proprietary Stores		Liquor Stores		Hardware, Building Materials[1]	
	Estab-lishments	Sales	Estab-lishments	Sales	Estab-lishments	Sales
ALL ESTABLISHMENTS[2]	51.5	15,599	42.0	9,874	83.8	23,844
No. Operated All Year[2]	48.9	14,742	38.4	9,156	77.8	22,412
PERCENT DISTRIBUTION	100.0	100.0	100.0	100.0	100.0	100.0
Under $30,000	6.0	.3	9.6	.7	20.0	.9
$ 30,000- 50,000	4.4	.6	7.4	1.2	8.2	1.1
50,000- 100,000	14.1	3.5	18.9	5.8	17.0	4.3
100,000- 300,000	46.9	28.4	42.0	31.4	30.6	18.9
300,000- 500,000	14.4	18.1	11.7	18.5	10.0	13.4
500,000-1,000,000	9.6	22.1	7.1	20.4	8.4	20.3
1,000,000-2,000,000	3.7	16.3	2.7	15.4	3.9	18.8
2,000,000 or more	1.0	10.6	.5	6.6	1.9	22.2

Note: Distributions based on establishments operated entire year

[1] Also includes garden supply and mobile home dealers
[2] Establishments in thousands; sales in millions of dollars

Source: Department of Commerce

RETAIL TRADE: SINGLE UNITS AND MULTIUNITS, 1972

Kind of Business	Single Units		Multiunits		
	Firms/ Estab-lishments[1] (Thous.)	Sales (Million Dollars)	Firms (Thous.)	Estab-lishments (Thous.)	Sales (Million Dollars)
TOTAL RETAIL TRADE	1,621.4	245,168	43.6	291.5	201,838
Bldg. Materials, Hardware, etc.[1]	69.7	15,260	2.8	14.1	7,892
General Merchandise Group Stores ..	31.7	5,191	1.5	24.5	59,576
Food Stores	213.3	34,919	5.0	54.0	63,686
Automotive Dealers	109.7	79,457	2.3	11.7	8,692
Gasoline Service Stations	197.8	24,776	3.8	28.7	6,602
Apparel and Accessory Stores	88.8	10,710	6.6	40.4	13,367
Furniture, Hfgs., Equip. Stores	98.7	14,592	4.2	18.1	7,254
Eating and Drinking Places	320.6	25,886	6.6	39.0	9,367
Drug and Proprietary Stores	39.6	7,835	1.9	11.9	7,509
Other Retail Stores	301.6	23,215	7.2	36.8	10,055
Nonstore Retailers	156.3	5,880	.6	5.8	5,167

Note: Data based on firms in business at end of year. A small number of firms operate establishments under more than one kind-of-business classification and may be classified variously as single or multiunits. Figures, therefore, are not additive to totals shown

[1] Includes garden equipment and mobile home dealers

Source: Department of Commerce

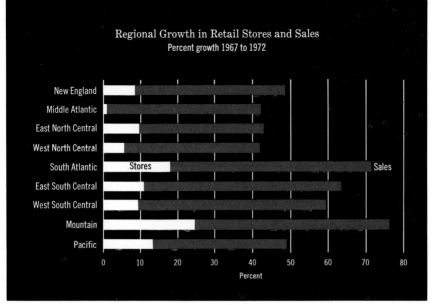

Regional Growth in Retail Stores and Sales
Percent growth 1967 to 1972

RETAIL TRADE BY MERCHANDISE LINES, 1972

	Establishments		Sales	
Merchandise Line	Number (Thousands)	As Percent of Total[1]	Millions of Dollars	Percent Distribution
TOTAL	1,264.9	100.0	440,222	100.0
Groceries, Other Foods	255.2	20.2	86,391	19.6
Meals, Snacks	302.1	23.9	29,297	6.7
Alcoholic Drinks	131.5	10.4	7,306	1.7
Packaged Alcoholic Beverages	113.4	9.0	11,286	2.6
Cigars, Cigarettes, Tobacco	224.9	17.8	6,110	1.4
Men's Boys' Clothing	97.0	7.7	14,995	3.4
Women's, Girls' Clothing[2]	131.0	10.4	25,933	5.9
Footwear (exc. Infants', Toddlers')	93.6	7.4	7,673	1.7
Furniture and Bedding....................	69.2	5.5	10,252	2.3
Floor Coverings	63.2	5.0	3,947	.9
Curtains, Draperies, Dry Goods	82.7	6.5	8,164	1.9
Kitchenware, Homefurnishings	117.3	9.3	6,039	1.4
Major Household Appliances	76.9	6.1	7,339	1.7
Radios, TV's, Musical Instruments	99.6	7.9	8,176	1.9
Automobiles, Trucks	53.0	4.2	66,486	15.1
Auto Fuels, Lubricants	236.0	18.7	27,306	6.2
Tires, Batteries, Accessories	235.1	18.6	16,465	3.7
Hardware, Electrical Supplies	88.7	7.0	4,576	1.0
Lawn, Garden Supplies...................	80.2	6.3	3,959	.9
Lumber, Building Materials	77.7	6.1	15,723	3.6
Drugs, Health Aids	133.4	10.5	11,170	2.5
Toiletries	139.7	11.0	4,485	1.0
Jewelry, Optical Goods...................	95.1	7.5	4,979	1.1
Sporting, Recreational Equipment	74.6	5.9	7,244	1.6
Household Fuels, Ice	27.0	2.1	4,138	.9
All Other Merchandise	261.0	20.6	21,548	4.9
Nonmerchandise Receipts[3]...............	661.0	52.3	19,236	4.4

Note: Data based only on establishments with payroll

[1] The sum of the details will exceed 100 percent since many establishments handle more than one line of merchandise
[2] Includes infants' and toddlers' clothing and footwear
[3] Service receipts, such as repair, storage, rental, installation of merchandise, and carrying charges, credit, sales and excise taxes

Source: Department of Commerce

REGIONAL DISTRIBUTION OF RETAIL TRADE

Region	1958	1963	1967	1972		
				Number	Percent Distribution	Percent Change 1967-72
Establishments (Thousands)						
TOTAL U.S.	1,795	1,708	1,763	1,934	100.0	9.7
Northeast	485	439	432	443	22.9	2.4
New England	113	103	103	111	5.8	8.6
Middle Atlantic	372	337	330	331	17.1	.4
North Central	529	492	488	529	27.4	8.4
East North Central	356	334	321	353	18.2	9.8
West North Central	174	158	167	176	9.1	5.6
South	520	513	552	626	32.4	13.4
South Atlantic	237	239	249	293	15.1	17.8
East South Central	108	112	113	124	6.4	10.4
West South Central	174	162	191	209	10.8	9.5
West	260	264	290	336	17.4	15.8
Mountain	67	69	75	93	4.8	24.3
Pacific	193	194	215	243	12.6	12.9
Sales (Million Dollars)						
TOTAL U.S.	200,365	244,202	310,214	470,806	100.0	51.8
Northeast	52,842	62,036	76,903	110,727	23.5	44.0
New England	12,452	15,088	18,952	28,192	6.0	48.8
Middle Atlantic	40,390	46,948	57,951	82,535	17.5	42.4
North Central	60,385	71,665	91,216	130,211	27.7	42.8
East North Central	42,177	50,611	64,625	92,421	19.6	43.0
West North Central	18,208	21,054	26,591	37,790	8.0	42.1
South	52,992	65,707	86,089	143,018	30.4	66.1
South Atlantic	25,493	32,365	42,789	73,275	15.6	71.2
East South Central	9,829	12,351	15,909	26,027	5.5	63.6
West South Central	17,670	20,991	27,391	43,716	9.3	59.6
West	34,146	44,794	56,006	86,850	18.4	55.1
Mountain	7,924	10,147	12,210	21,542	4.6	76.4
Pacific	26,222	34,646	43,797	65,308	13.9	49.1

Note: See note to table page 219

Source: Department of Commerce

RETAIL SALES BY TYPE AND REGION, 1972

Millions of dollars

Region		Sales by Kind of Business				
	Total Retail Sales[1]	Food Stores	Eating and Drinking Places	Department Stores	Apparel, Access. Stores	Furniture, Equipment Stores
TOTAL U.S.	459,040	100,719	36,868	51,084	24,741	22,533
Northeast..............	109,096	25,423	9,408	12,70	6,896	5,547
New England	27,909	6,285	2,268	2,968	1,573	1,338
Middle Atlantic	81,187	19,139	7,140	9,763	5,323	4,208
North Central	125,253	26,402	10,302	14,956	6,113	5,958
East North Central	90,201	19,384	7,615	11,321	4,480	4,331
West North Central	35,052	7,018	2,687	3,635	1,633	1,627
South	139,487	30,398	9,381	13,877	7,529	6,920
South Atlantic	71,829	15,281	5,071	7,609	3,744	3,764
East South Central	25,172	5,686	1,441	2,275	1,307	1,165
West South Central	42,486	9,431	2,869	3,992	2,478	1,992
West	85,205	18,495	7,777	9,520	4,203	4,109
Mountain	20,989	4,307	1,728	1,965	923	1,005
Pacific	64,216	14,188	6,049	7,555	3,280	3,103

	Sales by Kind of Business					
	Lumber, Bldg. Hardware etc. Stores	Automotive Dealers	Gasoline Service Stations	Drug, Proprietary Stores	Liquor Stores	Non-store Retailers
TOTAL U.S.	23,844	90,030	33,655	15,599	9,874	11,568
Northeast..............	4,532	17,550	6,716	3,244	2,925	3,136
New England	1,407	4,699	1,814	817	877	727
Middle Atlantic	3,125	12,851	4,902	2,427	2,047	2,409
North Central	6,817	25,209	9,965	4,260	2,154	3,999
East North Central	4,513	18,024	6,730	3,128	1,492	2,926
West North Central	2,304	7,184	3,235	1,132	662	1,073
South	8,007	30,323	10,671	4,768	2,859	2,871
South Atlantic	4,138	15,019	5,396	2,630	1,709	1,555
East South Central	1,596	5,704	1,990	835	480	487
West South Central	2,273	9,600	3,285	1,303	670	829
West	4,487	16,949	6,302	3,327	1,937	1,562
Mountain	1,528	4,438	1,730	801	360	374
Pacific	2,959	12,511	4,572	2,526	1,577	1,188

Note: See note to table page 219

[1] Includes kinds of business not shown separately

Source: Department of Commerce

Retail Sales by States, 1972

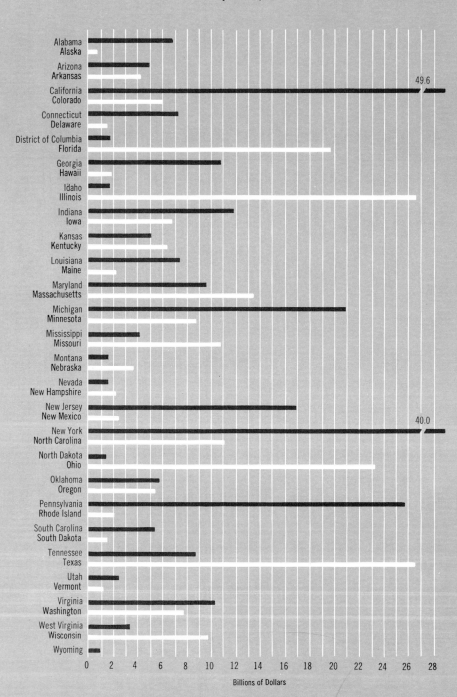

Billions of Dollars

Alabama
Alaska
Arizona
Arkansas
California — 49.6
Colorado
Connecticut
Delaware
District of Columbia
Florida
Georgia
Hawaii
Idaho
Illinois
Indiana
Iowa
Kansas
Kentucky
Louisiana
Maine
Maryland
Massachusetts
Michigan
Minnesota
Mississippi
Missouri
Montana
Nebraska
Nevada
New Hampshire
New Jersey
New Mexico
New York — 40.0
North Carolina
North Dakota
Ohio
Oklahoma
Oregon
Pennsylvania
Rhode Island
South Carolina
South Dakota
Tennessee
Texas
Utah
Vermont
Virginia
Washington
West Virginia
Wisconsin
Wyoming

0 2 4 6 8 10 12 14 16 18 20 22 24 26 28

RETAIL ESTABLISHMENTS AND SALES BY STATES

State	Establishments (Thousands)		Sales (Million Dollars)		Percent Change, 1967-1972	
	1967	1972	1967	1972	Establish-ments	Sales
TOTAL U.S.	1,763.3	1,934.5	310,214	470,806	9.7	51.8
Alabama	28.8	32.7	4,120	6,736	13.8	63.5
Alaska	2.0	3.0	403	772	52.1	91.8
Arizona	14.3	18.6	2,473	4,839	30.2	95.7
Arkansas	21.1	22.5	2,535	4,135	6.3	63.2
California	162.4	179.2	33,498	49,633	10.4	48.2
Colorado	19.8	24.6	3,281	5,988	24.2	82.5
Connecticut	25.3	27.9	5,043	7,274	10.4	44.2
Delaware	4.1	5.4	917	1,499	32.1	63.4
District of Columbia	4.9	4.6	1,603	1,799	− 4.9	12.2
Florida	58.7	76.6	10,280	19,761	30.4	92.2
Georgia	39.0	46.4	6,175	10,735	19.0	73.9
Hawaii	5.2	6.4	1,083	1,892	23.1	74.6
Idaho	7.6	8.9	1,149	1,801	17.2	56.8
Illinois	89.2	95.4	19,252	26,597	6.9	38.2
Indiana	42.4	46.6	8,329	11,870	9.8	42.5
Iowa	31.3	32.8	5,017	6,804	4.6	35.6
Kansas	25.0	26.4	3,447	5,072	5.6	47.1
Kentucky	28.9	30.1	3,983	6,369	4.1	59.9
Louisiana	30.6	32.9	4,760	7,418	7.7	55.9
Maine	10.3	11.0	1,471	2,290	6.4	55.7
Maryland	25.0	31.6	5,805	9,619	26.2	65.7
Massachusetts	46.9	50.0	9,167	13,385	6.8	46.0
Michigan	63.6	72.4	14,114	20,938	13.9	48.3
Minnesota	32.9	37.0	5,980	8,742	12.6	46.2
Mississippi	20.5	22.6	2,524	4,197	10.1	66.3
Missouri	45.6	46.9	7,561	10,706	2.9	41.6
Montana	7.5	9.0	1,137	1,696	20.4	49.2
Nebraska	16.9	17.6	2,555	3,589	3.9	40.5
Nevada	4.1	5.7	894	1,610	39.6	80.1
New Hampshire	7.2	8.3	1,180	2,071	16.2	75.5
New Jersey	61.3	58.7	11,362	16,934	− 4.3	49.0
New Mexico	9.4	11.3	1,359	2,343	21.2	72.4
New York	162.2	159.2	29,091	39,975	− 1.9	37.4
North Carolina	45.4	50.2	6,648	10,972	10.4	65.0
North Dakota	7.1	7.2	1,001	1,429	.7	42.7
Ohio	81.2	91.5	16,295	23,272	12.6	42.8
Oklahoma	28.7	29.7	3,648	5,682	3.3	55.8
Oregon	18.8	22.8	3,347	5,323	21.1	59.1
Pennsylvania	106.4	113.5	17,497	25,627	6.7	46.5
Rhode Island	8.3	8.8	1,382	2,026	5.7	46.6
South Carolina	23.5	26.6	3,104	5,302	13.4	70.8
South Dakota	8.1	8.5	1,028	1,448	4.5	40.9
Tennessee	34.3	38.8	5,283	8,725	13.1	65.1
Texas	110.8	124.3	16,449	26,480	12.1	61.0
Utah	7.8	10.0	1,399	2,417	28.0	72.8
Vermont	4.6	5.3	708	1,146	14.8	61.8
Virginia	32.3	35.6	6,150	10,239	10.3	66.5
Washington	27.1	31.9	5,466	7,687	17.8	40.7
West Virginia	15.6	15.8	2,107	3,350	1.2	59.0
Wisconsin	45.1	47.2	6,634	9,744	4.6	46.9
Wyoming	4.1	4.6	520	850	11.2	63.6

Note: See footnote to table page 219

Source: Department of Commerce

SELECTED RETAIL SALES BY STATES, 1972

State	Total Retail Sales[1] (Mil. Dollars)	Sales as Percent of Total		
		Food Stores	GAF Stores[2]	Automotive Dealers
TOTAL U.S.	459,040	21.9	24.5	19.6
Alabama	6,584	22.3	24.1	23.3
Alaska	772	22.6	21.6	13.1
Arizona	4,763	21.6	23.7	20.3
Arkansas	3,912	22.5	21.2	24.0
California	48,894	21.8	24.4	19.6
Colorado	5,869	19.6	23.5	20.8
Connecticut	7,217	22.7	24.8	16.9
Delaware	1,480	21.6	27.4	16.7
District of Columbia	1,797	16.5	26.9	10.0
Florida	19,498	20.6	24.5	21.7
Georgia	10,412	19.8	24.3	22.3
Hawaii	1,865	22.2	28.2	14.5
Idaho	1,660	20.9	17.5	23.8
Illinois	25,923	20.1	25.2	18.7
Indiana	11,468	20.9	23.7	21.1
Iowa	5,877	21.0	21.9	21.0
Kansas	4,766	20.4	22.9	22.9
Kentucky	6,161	23.3	22.1	20.4
Louisiana	7,214	25.2	24.3	20.5
Maine	2,233	24.5	19.7	19.8
Maryland	9,480	21.9	25.9	18.8
Massachusetts	13,299	21.8	25.1	15.9
Michigan	20,630	22.8	24.4	21.4
Minnesota	8,352	19.0	23.8	18.0
Mississippi	3,961	24.1	22.0	24.3
Missouri	10,272	20.7	24.2	21.1
Montana	1,614	22.2	17.8	21.1
Nebraska	3,195	19.2	24.5	19.7
Nevada	1,600	20.4	23.0	19.2
New Hampshire	2,038	24.4	19.8	18.9
New Jersey	16,831	23.5	26.5	16.4
New Mexico	2,300	20.5	21.5	22.2
New York	39,173	24.3	27.5	13.9
North Carolina	10,650	21.7	22.9	22.2
North Dakota	1,275	18.1	21.0	22.7
Ohio	22,890	22.2	26.5	20.0
Oklahoma	5,527	21.7	23.4	23.6
Oregon	5,191	23.2	19.4	21.8
Pennsylvania	25,182	22.5	25.0	18.4
Rhode Island	2,018	21.5	25.7	16.4
South Carolina	5,174	23.2	22.8	21.6
South Dakota	1,316	19.7	19.8	20.6
Tennessee	8,466	21.6	23.9	23.0
Texas	25,833	21.4	24.5	22.7
Utah	2,367	19.9	21.3	22.4
Vermont	1,103	23.7	17.8	18.8
Virginia	10,030	22.1	25.0	21.0
Washington	7,495	23.2	22.2	19.2
West Virginia	3,307	24.0	24.8	20.5
Wisconsin	9,290	21.5	23.1	19.0
Wyoming	816	19.0	19.1	20.2

Note: See note to table page 219

[1] Totals include items not shown separately
[2] Includes general merchandise group stores with nonstores, apparel stores, and furniture and equipment stores
Source: Department of Commerce

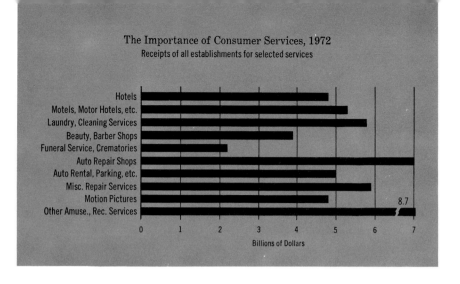

The Importance of Consumer Services, 1972
Receipts of all establishments for selected services

Hotels
Motels, Motor Hotels, etc.
Laundry, Cleaning Services
Beauty, Barber Shops
Funeral Service, Crematories
Auto Repair Shops
Auto Rental, Parking, etc.
Misc. Repair Services
Motion Pictures
Other Amuse., Rec. Services

8.7

0   1   2   3   4   5   6   7
Billions of Dollars

SELECTED SERVICES BY KIND OF BUSINESS, 1972

Kind of Business	Establish- ments (Thousands)	Sales	
		Millions of Dollars	Percent Change 1967 to 1972[1]
TOTAL SELECTED SERVICES	1,370.6	92,815	52.6
Hotels, Motels, Tourist Courts, Camps[2]	79.7	10,638	51.3
Hotels.......................................	14.0	4,794	26.0
Motels, Motor Hotels, Courts	44.7	5,294	97.7
Personal Services[2]	506.4	14,361	19.9
Laundry, Cleaning...........................	94.1	5,562	2.0
Beauty Shops	189.1	3,025	24.2
Barber Shops	91.8	885	−34.7
Photographic Studios	33.0	1,079	41.5
Funeral Service, Crematories	20.9	2,218	48.5
Misc. Business Services[2]	320.7	36,355	58.9
Advertising	28.4	10,605	26.1
Business, Consulting........................	92.3	7,470	135.8
Services to Dwellings, etc.	51.3	2,529	78.8
Auto Repair, Other Services..................	169.0	12,081	71.6
Auto Repair Shops	127.2	7,045	75.0
Auto Parking	10.5	725	50.3
Car, Truck Rental & Leasing[3]	31.3	4,311	68.6
Misc. Repair Services[2]	149.0	5,941	59.3
Electrical Repair Shops	53.5	2,228	72.9
Motion Pictures	21.5	4,804	36.8
Production, Distribution	8.8	2,971	34.0
Theaters...................................	12.7	1,833	41.5
Other Amusements[2]	124.3	8,635	78.3
Producers, Orchestras, Entertainers	47.7	1,436	46.4
Bowling Alleys, Billiards, etc.	14.3	1,204	17.4

Note: Data are based on 1967 Standard Industrial Classification
[1] Data refer to establishments with payroll only
[2] Includes kinds of business not separately listed
[3] Rental and leasing not elsewhere classified

Source: Department of Commerce

RETAIL SALES OF MAJOR METROPOLITAN AREAS, 1972

Standard Metropolitan Statistical Area	Total Sales, All Establishments			Per Capita Sales	
	Millions of Dollars	Percent Change 1967-1972	Percent in Central Cities	Dollars	As Percent of U.S.
TOTAL U.S., ALL AREAS	459,040	48.0	n.a.	2,204	100.0
Albany-Schenectady-Troy, N.Y.	1,762	41.7	36.2	2,200	99.8
Anaheim-Santa Ana-etc., Calif.	3,926	77.2	31.2	2,566	116.4
Atlanta, Ga.	4,490	78.9	40.4	2,664	120.9
Baltimore, Md.	4,676	53.3	38.7	2,212	100.4
Birmingham, Ala.	1,726	62.3	54.9	2,217	100.6
Boston, Mass.[1]	7,964	40.7	27.5	2,328	105.6
Bridgeport, Conn.[1]	2,054	47.7	51.3	2,600	118.0
Buffalo, N.Y.	2,781	35.7	30.7	2,051	93.1
Chicago, Ill.	17,231	38.2	43.5	2,443	110.8
Cincinnati, Ohio-Ky.-Ind.	2,974	41.2	34.6	2,152	97.6
Cleveland, Ohio	4,479	32.9	31.2	2,219	100.7
Columbus, Ohio	2,534	55.8	60.8	2,419	109.8
Dallas-Fort Worth, Tex.	6,095	60.1	58.6	2,521	114.4
Dayton, Ohio	1,869	39.8	30.0	2,193	99.5
Denver-Boulder, Colo.	3,530	82.2	45.6	2,673	121.3
Detroit, Mich.....................	10,471	42.4	26.0	2,349	106.6
Fort Lauderdale-Hollywood, Fla.	2,191	119.8	47.7	3,166	143.6
Hartford, Conn.[1]	2,010	36.8	32.0	2,436	110.5
Houston, Tex.	5,291	74.9	71.1	2,517	114.2
Indianapolis, Ind.................	2,721	42.3	73.9	2,411	109.4
Kansas City, Mo.-Kans.............	3,136	42.4	42.8	2,425	110.0
Los Angeles-Long Beach, Calif.......	17,162	34.0	44.9	2,461	111.7
Louisville, Ky.-Ind................	2,017	54.9	44.2	2,298	104.3
Memphis, Tenn.-Ark.-Miss.	1,960	59.7	83.4	2,279	103.4
Miami, Fla.	3,801	74.8	30.6	2,836	128.7
Milwaukee, Wis.	3,086	41.4	46.2	2,160	98.0
Minneapolis-St. Paul, Minn.-Wis.	4,634	44.8	37.7	2,329	105.7
Nashville-Davidson, Tenn.	1,727	65.5	74.3	2,376	107.8
Nassau-Suffolk, N.Y.	6,831	51.1	[2]	2,620	118.9
New Orleans, La.	2,366	50.2	51.0	2,186	99.2
New York, N.Y.-N.J.	20,401	29.3	73.6	2,056	93.3
Newark, N.J.	4,603	37.7	13.8	2,210	100.3
Oklahoma City, Okla...............	1,838	67.1	61.2	2,506	113.7
Philadelphia, Pa.-N.J.	10,549	42.1	33.9	2,178	98.8
Phoenix, Ariz.	2,766	94.1	59.0	2,595	117.7
Pittsburgh, Pa.	4,898	38.2	23.2	2,052	93.1
Portland, Oreg.-Wash.	2,569	55.8	48.5	2,433	110.4
Providence-Warwick-etc., R.I.-Mass. .	1,989	n.a.	41.5	n.a.	--
Riverside-San Bernardino-etc., Calif. .	2,598	57.8	37.9	2,208	100.2
Rochester, N.Y...................	2,233	36.5	32.8	2,303	104.5
Sacramento, Calif.	2,015	51.2	34.5	2,368	107.4
St. Louis, Mo.-Ill.	5,190	39.3	23.1	2,158	97.9
San Antonio, Tex.	1,853	63.9	83.7	1,981	89.9
San Diego, Calif.	3,290	75.0	50.1	2,312	104.9
San Francisco-Oakland, Calif.	7,737	38.5	36.9	2,478	112.4
San Jose, Calif....................	2,762	59.7	40.3	2,439	110.7
Seattle-Everett, Wash.	3,322	32.6	48.7	2,387	108.3
Tampa-St. Petersburg, Fla.	3,254	104.7	57.1	2,711	123.0
Toledo, Ohio-Mich.................	1,764	45.4	51.3	2,269	102.9
Washington, D.C.-Md.-Va.	7,550	57.5	23.8	2,507	113.7

Note: Standard metropolitan statistical areas as defined in August 1973

[1]State Economic Area
[2]No central city in SMSA

n.a.—Not available
Source: Department of Commerce

SELECTED SERVICES: ESTABLISHMENTS AND SALES

Year and Kind of Business[1]	All Establishments		Establishments with Payroll		
	Number (Thousands)	Sales (Mil. Dollars)	Number (Thousands)	Sales (Mil. Dollars)	Payroll (Mil. Dollars)[2]
1967—TOTAL SELECTED SERVICES	1,188	60,542	521	55,527	17,524
Hotels, Motels, Tourist Courts, Camps	87	7,039	54	6,738	1,990
Personal Services...................	499	11,750	205	10,003	3,923
Miscellaneous Business Services	212	22,595	85	21,427	6,699
Auto Repair, Auto Services, Garages ..	139	7,028	77	6,368	1,468
Miscellaneous Repair Services	138	3,827	42	3,089	1,046
Motion Pictures, Other Amusements, Recreation Services...............	113	8,303	59	7,901	2,398
1972—TOTAL SELECTED SERVICES	1,371	92,815	570	84,754	27,002
Hotels, Motels, Tourist Courts, Camps	80	10,638	47	10,197	2,971
Personal Services...................	506	14,361	200	11,994	4,428
Miscellaneous Business Services	321	36,355	121	34,058	11,578
Auto Repair, Auto Services, Garages ..	169	12,081	91	10,929	2,553
Miscellaneous Repair Services	149	5,941	47	4,922	1,628
Motion Pictures, Other Amusements, Recreation Services	146	13,439	66	12,654	3,845

[1] Based on 1967 standard industrial classification
[2] Entire year

Source: Department of Commerce

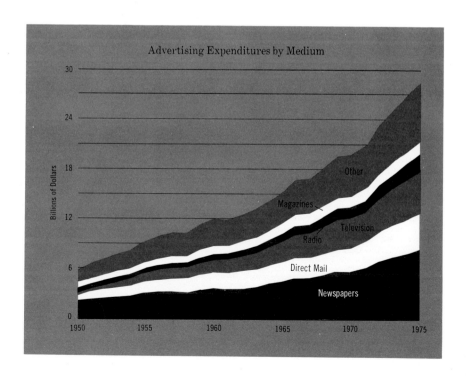

SELECTED SERVICES: SALES BY TYPE

Millions of dollars

Year	Hotels, Motels, Courts, etc.	Personal Services	Business Services	Automotive Services	Misc. Repair Services	Motion Pictures, Amusements
1966.....	6,501	10,981	18,567	6,516	3,939	7,498
1967.....	6,813	11,168	18,356	7,023	4,085	7,159
1968.....	7,010	11,827	23,367	8,109	3,687	8,689
1969.....	6,823	11,481	25,406	8,647	3,885	8,677
1970.....	7,417	12,746	31,082	10,040	4,602	10,256
1971.....	7,856	12,965	31,398	11,113	5,368	10,529
1972.....	8,548	12,965	34,165	12,266	6,190	11,876
1973.....	9,491	13,561	37,857	13,891	7,625	12,270
1974.....	10,236	13,785	42,364	15,187	8,465	14,211
1975.....	11,755	15,090	46,114	17,313	9,255	15,583

Note: Data based on new samples beginning 1968 and again beginning 1970

Source: Department of Commerce

THE TREND IN ADVERTISING EXPENDITURES

Billions of dollars, except percent

Year	Total Expenditures		National	Local
	Amount	Percent of GNP		
1950.........................	5.70	2.00	3.26	2.45
1955.........................	9.15	2.29	5.41	3.79
1956.........................	9.91	2.36	5.93	3.98
1957.........................	10.27	2.32	6.25	4.06
1958.........................	10.31	2.30	6.33	3.97
1959.........................	11.27	2.32	6.84	4.42
1960.........................	11.96	2.36	7.30	4.64
1961.........................	11.86	2.27	7.25	4.59
1962.........................	12.43	2.20	7.66	4.72
1963.........................	13.10	2.20	8.12	4.98
1964.........................	14.15	2.23	8.71	5.44
1965.........................	15.25	2.22	9.36	5.89
1966.........................	16.63	2.21	10.18	6.49
1967.........................	16.87	2.12	10.25	6.62
1968.........................	18.09	2.08	10.88	7.24
1969.........................	19.42	2.08	11.52	7.96
1970.........................	19.55	1.99	11.46	8.14
1971.........................	20.74	1.95	11.78	8.96
1972.........................	23.30	1.99	13.03	10.27
1973.........................	25.11	1.92	13.78	11.34
1974.........................	26.73	1.90	14.72	12.00
1975p	28.27	1.89	15.40	12.87

Note: Revisions made to total expenditures for years shown are not reflected in components

p—Preliminary

Sources: McCann-Erickson, Inc.; Department of Commerce

ADVERTISING: EXPENDITURES BY MEDIUM

Billions of dollars

Year	Total	News-papers	Maga-zines[1]	Tele-vision	Radio	Direct Mail	Other[1]
1950	5.70	2.08	.51	.17	.61	.80	1.54
1955	9.15	3.09	.73	1.03	.54	1.30	2.51
1960	11.96	3.70	.94	1.59	.69	1.83	3.18
1965	15.25	4.46	1.20	2.52	.92	2.32	3.84
1966	16.63	4.90	1.29	2.82	1.01	2.46	4.19
1967	16.87	4.94	1.28	2.91	1.03	2.49	4.22
1968	18.09	5.27	1.32	3.23	1.19	2.61	4.51
1969	19.42	5.75	1.38	3.58	1.26	2.67	4.83
1970	19.55	5.74	1.32	3.60	1.31	2.77	4.86
1971	20.74	6.20	1.37	3.53	1.44	3.07	5.13
1972	23.30	7.01	1.44	4.09	1.61	3.42	5.73
1973	25.11	7.60	1.45	4.46	1.72	3.70	6.20
1974	26.73	8.00	1.50	4.85	1.84	3.99	6.55
1975p	28.27	8.44	1.46	5.27	2.02	4.16	6.91

Note: Revisions made to total expenditures for years shown are not reflected in components

[1] Beginning in 1972 farm national magazines are grouped under "Farm Publications", included in "Other" here

p—Preliminary

Source: McCann-Erickson, Inc.

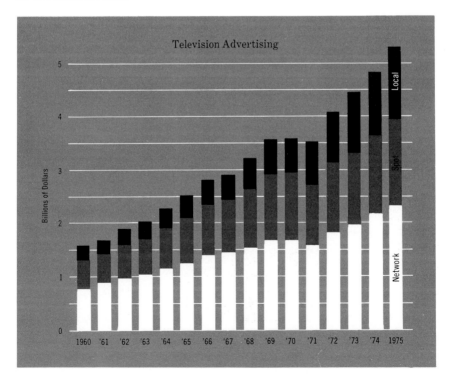

ADVERTISING EXPENDITURES AS PERCENT OF SALES, 1972

Industry	Advertising Expenditures		Industry	Advertising Expenditures	
	Millions of Dollars	Per-cent of Sales		Millions of Dollars	Per-cent of Sales
ALL MANUFACTURING ..	10,474	1.2	General Merchandise	1,970	2.7
			Apparel, Accessories	378	2.0
Tobacco	398	4.2	Food	760	1.0
Chemical	2,476	3.5	Automotive, Gasoline....	823	.9
Professional Instruments ...	341	2.3			
Food, Beverages	2,532	2.2	TOTAL SERVICES	1,275	1.5
Leather Products	112	1.6			
Rubber, Plastic Products...	234	1.3			
Furniture, Fixtures	105	1.1	Motion Pictures	162	3.7
Publishing, Printing	265	.9	Other Amusements	136	2.3
Motor Vehicles, Equipment	567	.6	Hotels, Lodging	159	2.0
Apparel	207	.7	Business	483	2.0
			Personal	103	1.5
TOTAL RETAIL TRADE ...	5,399	1.5	Auto, Other Repairs	79	.9

Source: Treasury Department

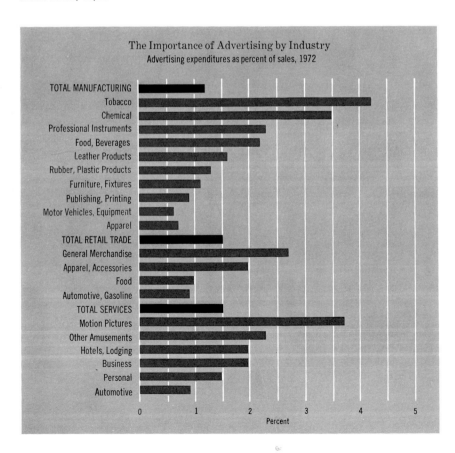

THE IMPORTANCE OF THE MEDIA, 1975

Medium	Advertising Expenditures Millions of Dollars	Percent Distri- bution	Medium	Advertising Expenditures Millions of Dollars	Percent Distri- bution
TOTAL	28,270	100.0	Radio	2,025	7.2
			Network	85	.3
NATIONAL	15,400	54.5	Spot	440	1.6
LOCAL	12,870	45.5	Local	1,500	5.3
Newspapers	8,442	29.9			
National	1,221	4.3	Farm Publications	74	.3
Local	7,221	25.6			
Magazines	1,465	5.2	Direct Mail	4,155	14.7
Weeklies	612	2.2			
Women's	368	1.3	Business Papers	919	3.2
Monthlies	485	1.7			
			Outdoor	335	1.2
Television	5,272	18.6			
Network	2,310	8.2	Miscellaneous	5,583	19.7
Spot	1,630	5.7	National	2,881	10.2
Local	1,332	4.7	Local	2,702	9.5

Source: McCann-Erickson, Inc.

THE VOLUME OF TELEVISION ADVERTISING

Millions of dollars

Year	Total	Advertising Expenditures in: Network TV	Spot TV	Local TV
1950	171	85	31	55
1955	1,025	540	260	225
1960	1,590	783	527	280
1961	1,691	887	533	270
1962	1,897	976	611	310
1963	2,032	1,025	679	328
1964	2,289	1,132	780	377
1965	2,515	1,237	866	412
1966	2,824	1,393	960	471
1967	2,909	1,455	988	466
1968	3,231	1,523	1,131	577
1969	3,585	1,678	1,253	654
1970	3,596	1,658	1,234	704
1971	3,534	1,593	1,145	796
1972	4,091	1,804	1,318	969
1973	4,460	1,968	1,377	1,115
1974	4,851	2,145	1,495	1,211
1975p	5,272	2,310	1,630	1,332

Note: See note to table page 235

Source: McCann-Erickson, Inc.

p —Preliminary

TELEVISION ADVERTISING BY MERCHANDISE LINE, 1975

Percent distribution

Item	Total TV[1]	Network TV	Spot TV
TOTAL EXPENDITURES (Percent)	100.0	58.8	41.2
Food, Beverages	24.4	11.8	12.7
Household Items	15.5	8.7	6.8
Toiletries	13.9	10.0	3.8
Automotive Products	11.1	7.1	3.9
Drug Items	9.0	6.6	2.4
Consumer Services, Insurance	4.0	2.2	1.8
Beer, Wine	3.4	1.7	1.7
Sporting Goods, Toys	3.2	1.2	2.0
Apparel, Footwear	2.8	1.7	1.1
Pet Foods, Supplies	2.8	1.6	1.2
Travel, Hotels, Resorts	1.6	.5	1.1
Other	8.3	5.6	2.8

[1] National television
Source: Television Bureau of Advertising

THE VOLUME OF MAGAZINE ADVERTISING

Millions of dollars

Year	Total[1]	Type of Magazine		
		Monthlies	Women's	Weeklies
1950	515	88	129	261
1955	729	133	161	396
1960	941	200	184	525
1961	924	200	187	508
1962	973	223	200	519
1963	1,034	244	218	540
1964	1,108	260	231	583
1965	1,199	282	269	610
1966	1,291	316	280	658
1967	1,280	312	282	651
1968	1,318	342	284	657
1969	1,376	374	308	662
1970	1,323	374	301	617
1971	1,370	404	340	626
1972	1,440	462	368	610
1973	1,448	503	362	583
1974	1,504	502	372	630
1975p	1,465	485	368	612

Note: See note to table page 235

[1] Total includes farm national magazines from 1950-1971. Beginning in 1972 these magazines are included with "Farm Publications". See table on page 237

p—Preliminary

Source: McCann-Erickson, Inc.

PRICES

PRICES

THE TREND IN CONSUMER PRICES

Index numbers, 1967 = 100

Year	All Items	Commodities			Commodities Less Food	Services	
		Total	Dura-bles	Nondu-rables		Total	Less Rent
1950	72.1	78.8	88.4	75.4	81.4	58.7	56.0
1951	77.8	85.9	95.1	82.5	87.5	61.8	59.3
1952	79.5	87.0	96.4	83.4	88.3	64.5	62.2
1953	80.1	86.7	95.7	83.2	88.5	67.3	64.8
1954	80.5	85.9	93.3	83.2	87.5	69.5	66.7
1955	80.2	85.1	91.5	82.5	86.9	70.9	68.2
1956	81.4	85.9	91.5	83.7	87.8	72.7	70.1
1957	84.3	88.6	94.4	86.3	90.5	75.6	73.3
1958	86.6	90.6	95.9	88.6	91.5	78.5	76.4
1959	87.3	90.7	97.3	88.2	92.7	80.8	79.0
1960	88.7	91.5	96.7	89.4	93.1	83.5	81.9
1961	89.6	92.0	96.6	90.2	93.4	85.2	83.9
1962	90.6	92.8	97.6	90.9	94.1	86.8	85.5
1963	91.7	93.6	97.9	92.0	94.8	88.5	87.3
1964	92.9	94.6	98.8	93.0	95.6	90.2	89.2
1965	94.5	95.7	98.4	94.6	96.2	92.2	91.5
1966	97.2	98.2	98.5	98.1	97.5	95.8	95.3
1967	100.0	100.0	100.0	100.0	100.0	100.0	100.0
1968	104.2	103.7	103.1	103.9	103.7	105.2	105.7
1969	109.8	108.4	107.0	108.9	108.1	112.5	113.8
1970	116.3	113.5	111.8	114.0	112.5	121.6	123.7
1971	121.3	117.4	116.5	117.7	116.8	128.4	130.8
1972	125.3	120.9	118.9	121.7	119.4	133.3	135.9
1973	133.1	129.9	121.9	132.8	123.5	139.1	141.8
1974	147.7	145.5	130.6	151.0	136.6	152.0	156.0
1975	161.2	158.4	145.5	163.2	149.1	166.6	171.9

Source: Department of Labor

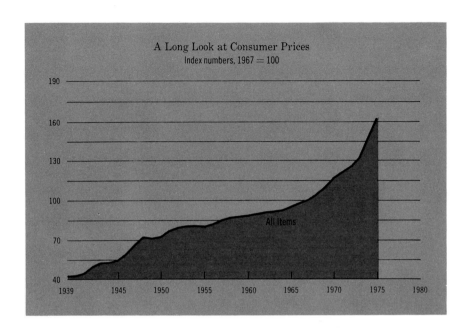

A Long Look at Consumer Prices
Index numbers, 1967 = 100

All Items

CONSUMER PRICE INDEX: MAJOR COMPONENTS

Index numbers, 1967 = 100

Year	All Items	Food	Housing	Apparel and Upkeep	Trans- portation	Health and Rec- reation
1955	80.2	81.6	82.3	84.1	77.4	73.8
1956	81.4	82.2	83.6	85.8	78.8	75.6
1957	84.3	84.9	86.2	87.3	83.3	78.4
1958	86.6	88.5	87.7	87.5	86.0	81.0
1959	87.3	87.1	88.6	88.2	89.6	83.0
1960	88.7	88.0	90.2	89.6	89.6	85.1
1961	89.6	89.1	90.9	90.4	90.6	86.7
1962	90.6	89.9	91.7	90.9	92.5	88.4
1963	91.7	91.2	92.7	91.9	93.0	90.0
1964	92.9	92.4	93.8	92.7	94.3	91.8
1965	94.5	94.4	94.9	93.7	95.9	93.4
1966	97.2	99.1	97.2	96.1	97.2	96.1
1967	100.0	100.0	100.0	100.0	100.0	100.0
1968	104.2	103.6	104.2	105.4	103.2	105.0
1969	109.8	108.9	110.8	111.5	107.2	110.3
1970	116.3	114.9	118.9	116.1	112.7	116.2
1971	121.3	118.4	124.3	119.8	118.6	122.2
1972	125.3	123.5	129.2	122.3	119.9	126.1
1973	133.1	141.4	135.0	126.8	123.8	130.2
1974	147.7	161.7	150.6	136.2	137.7	140.3
1975	161.2	175.4	166.8	142.3	150.6	153.5

Source: Department of Labor

CONSUMER PRICES: FOOD

Index numbers, 1967 = 100

Year	Total Food	Food At Home						Food Away from Home
		Total	Cereals, Bakery Products	Meats, Poultry, Fish	Dairy Products	Fruits, Vege-tables	Other	
1955	81.6	84.1	78.8	82.8	80.2	78.1	99.0	70.8
1960	88.0	89.6	87.1	89.1	88.4	88.3	94.9	81.4
1961	89.1	90.4	88.9	89.3	89.8	88.7	95.8	83.2
1962	89.9	91.0	90.8	91.5	89.2	89.4	94.3	85.4
1963	91.2	92.2	92.1	90.1	88.9	94.5	96.0	87.3
1964	92.4	93.2	92.5	88.7	89.7	98.1	99.7	88.9
1965	94.4	95.5	93.8	94.5	90.0	98.0	99.9	90.9
1966	99.1	100.3	97.7	102.6	95.8	100.1	102.0	95.1
1967	100.0	100.0	100.0	100.0	100.0	100.0	100.0	100.0
1968	103.6	103.2	100.4	102.2	103.3	107.9	102.6	105.2
1969	108.9	108.2	103.3	110.8	106.7	109.3	107.9	111.6
1970	114.9	113.7	108.9	116.5	111.8	113.4	114.1	119.9
1971	118.4	116.4	113.9	116.9	115.3	119.1	115.9	126.1
1972	123.5	121.6	114.7	128.0	117.1	125.0	116.7	131.1
1973	141.4	141.4	127.7	160.4	127.9	142.5	130.3	141.4
1974	161.7	162.4	166.1	163.9	151.9	165.8	162.8	159.4
1975	175.4	175.8	184.8	178.0	156.6	171.0	184.8	174.3

Source: Department of Labor

CONSUMER PRICES: HOUSING

Index Numbers, 1967 = 100

Year	Total Housing	Shelter		Fuel and Utilities	House-furnishings, Operation
		Homeowner-ship Costs	Rent		
1955	82.3	77.0	84.3	85.1	89.9
1960	90.2	86.3	91.7	95.9	93.8
1961	90.9	86.9	92.9	97.1	93.7
1962	91.7	87.9	94.0	97.3	93.8
1963	92.7	89.0	95.0	98.2	94.6
1964	93.8	90.8	95.9	98.4	95.0
1965	94.9	92.7	96.9	98.3	95.3
1966	97.2	96.3	98.2	98.8	97.0
1967	100.0	100.0	100.0	100.0	100.0
1968	104.2	105.7	102.4	101.3	104.4
1969	110.8	116.0	105.7	103.6	109.0
1970	118.9	128.5	110.1	107.6	113.4
1971	124.3	133.7	115.2	115.0	118.1
1972	129.2	140.1	119.2	120.1	121.0
1973	135.0	146.7	124.3	126.9	124.9
1974	150.6	163.2	130.2	150.2	140.5
1975	166.8	181.7	137.3	167.8	158.1

Source: Department of Labor

CONSUMER PRICES: HOUSEFURNISHINGS

Index numbers, 1967 = 100

Year	Total House-furnishings	Textiles	Furniture, Bedding	Floor Coverings	Appliances, Radio, TV
1955	99.2	91.9	88.9	91.6	126.4
1960	99.3	94.5	91.5	98.7	117.9
1961	98.7	95.0	92.4	98.4	115.2
1962	98.1	94.9	92.9	98.3	111.6
1963	97.7	95.0	93.3	99.0	109.2
1964	97.6	95.3	93.4	100.6	107.4
1965	97.1	96.0	94.0	99.5	103.9
1966	98.0	97.3	96.3	99.8	100.7
1967	100.0	100.0	100.0	100.0	100.0
1968	103.9	103.7	105.0	102.4	101.2
1969	108.1	106.9	111.1	104.3	102.4
1970	111.4	109.2	115.5	105.0	104.1
1971	114.3	111.6	119.1	106.3	105.5
1972	116.2	113.6	121.1	106.5	105.8
1973	119.0	116.2	125.3	108.2	105.5
1974	130.8	131.5	136.1	118.9	109.7
1975	144.4	141.4	147.0	129.8	118.4

Source: Department of Labor

CONSUMER PRICES: APPAREL AND UPKEEP

Index numbers, 1967 = 100

Year	Total Apparel, Upkeep	Apparel Commodities				
		Total	Total, Less Foot-wear	Men's and Boys'	Women's and Girls'	Foot-wear
1955	84.1	85.8	88.9	85.0	89.8	71.6
1960	89.6	90.3	91.5	88.9	91.6	85.1
1961	90.4	90.8	92.0	89.9	91.9	85.9
1962	90.9	91.2	92.1	90.4	91.8	87.1
1963	91.9	92.0	93.0	91.6	92.5	88.0
1964	92.7	92.8	93.8	92.8	93.1	88.4
1965	93.7	93.6	94.5	94.0	93.8	90.0
1966	96.1	96.0	96.2	96.5	95.6	95.3
1967	100.0	100.0	100.0	100.0	100.0	100.0
1968	105.4	105.6	105.7	105.7	105.9	105.3
1969	111.5	111.9	111.9	112.4	111.7	111.8
1970	116.1	116.5	116.3	117.1	116.0	117.7
1971	119.8	120.1	119.9	120.3	120.1	121.5
1972	122.3	122.7	122.3	121.9	123.0	124.9
1973	126.8	127.1	126.5	126.4	127.3	130.2
1974	136.2	136.1	135.7	136.4	134.9	138.1
1975	142.3	141.2	140.6	142.2	138.1	144.2

Source: Department of Labor

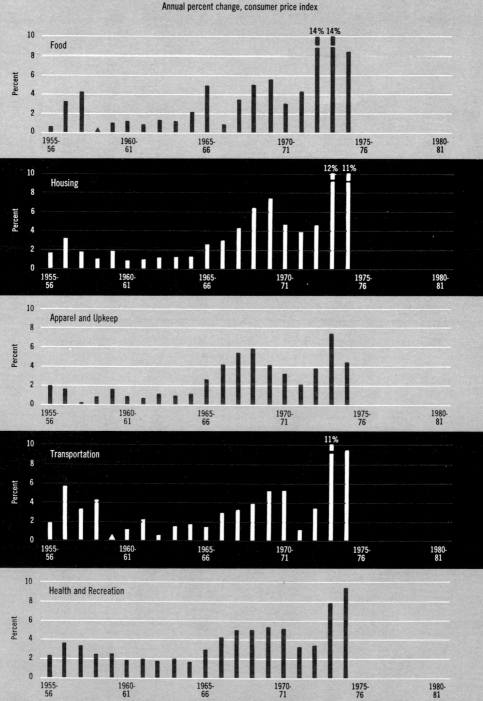

The Components of Price Change
Annual percent change, consumer price index

Food

14% 14%

Housing

12% 11%

Apparel and Upkeep

Transportation

11%

Health and Recreation

▲ −1.6%
△ No change

245

CONSUMER PRICES: PRIVATE TRANSPORTATION

Index numbers, 1967 = 100

Year	Automobiles		Gasoline	New Tires, Tubeless	Repairs, Mainte- nance	Auto Insurance Rates
	New	Used				
1955	90.9	71.8	83.6	89.8	76.5	58.9
1960	104.5	83.6	92.5	87.4	87.2	77.5
1961	104.5	86.9	91.4	83.2	89.3	78.2
1962	104.1	94.8	91.9	87.4	90.4	77.5
1963	103.5	96.0	91.8	91.5	91.6	78.8
1964	103.2	100.1	91.4	92.0	92.8	82.9
1965	100.9	99.4	94.9	94.2	94.5	90.8
1966	99.1	97.0	97.0	96.4	96.2	97.3
1967	100.0	100.0	100.0	100.0	100.0	100.0
1968	102.8	n.a.	101.4	105.6	105.5	102.3
1969	104.4	103.1	104.7	109.7	112.2	111.4
1970	107.6	104.3	105.6	113.1	120.6	126.7
1971	112.0	110.2	106.3	116.3	129.2	141.4
1972	111.0	110.5	107.6	115.9	135.1	140.5
1973	111.1	117.6	118.1	110.6	142.2	138.0
1974	117.5	122.6	159.9	118.4	156.8	138.1
1975	127.6	146.4	170.8	126.3	176.6	145.9

n.a.—Not available

Source: Department of Labor

CONSUMER PRICES: TRANSPORTATION

Index numbers, 1967 = 100

Year	Total Transportation	Private Transportation	Public Transportation
1955	77.4	78.9	67.4
1960	89.6	90.6	81.0
1961	90.6	91.3	84.6
1962	92.5	93.0	87.4
1963	93.0	93.4	88.5
1964	94.3	94.7	90.1
1965	95.9	96.3	91.9
1966	97.2	97.5	95.2
1967	100.0	100.0	100.0
1968	103.2	103.0	104.6
1969	107.2	106.5	112.7
1970	112.7	111.1	128.5
1971	118.6	116.6	137.7
1972	119.9	117.5	143.4
1973	123.8	121.5	144.8
1974	137.7	136.6	148.0
1975	150.6	149.8	158.6

Source: Department of Labor

CONSUMER PRICES: MEDICAL AND PERSONAL CARE

Index numbers, 1967 = 100

Year	Medical Care			Personal Care		
	Total	Drugs, Prescrip- tions	Services	Total	Toilet Goods	Services
1955	64.8	94.7	60.4	77.9	89.6	67.3
1960	79.1	104.5	74.9	90.1	98.9	81.4
1961	81.4	103.3	77.7	90.6	98.5	82.7
1962	83.5	101.7	80.2	92.2	99.5	84.6
1963	85.6	100.8	82.6	93.4	99.9	86.7
1964	87.3	100.5	84.6	94.5	100.0	88.9
1965	89.5	100.2	87.3	95.2	99.4	91.5
1966	93.4	100.5	92.0	97.1	98.3	95.7
1967	100.0	100.0	100.0	100.0	100.0	100.0
1968	106.1	100.2	107.3	104.2	103.0	105.3
1969	113.4	101.3	116.0	109.3	107.6	110.9
1970	120.6	103.6	124.2	113.2	110.4	116.0
1971	128.4	105.4	133.3	116.8	113.8	120.0
1972	132.5	105.6	138.2	119.8	116.9	122.9
1973	137.7	105.9	144.3	125.2	120.0	130.6
1974	150.5	109.6	159.1	137.3	133.3	141.5
1975	168.6	118.8	179.1	150.7	150.0	151.4

Source: Department of Labor

CONSUMER PRICES: OTHER ITEMS

Index numbers, 1967 = 100

Year	Reading and Recreation	Tobacco Products	Alcoholic Beverages
1955	76.7	70.4	87.3
1960	87.3	81.8	92.9
1961	89.3	82.5	93.3
1962	91.3	83.1	93.6
1963	92.8	85.7	94.5
1964	95.0	87.7	95.3
1965	95.9	91.8	96.3
1966	97.5	96.3	98.0
1967	100.0	100.0	100.0
1968	104.7	106.3	103.5
1969	108.7	111.9	107.2
1970	113.4	121.2	112.3
1971	119.3	126.4	116.9
1972	122.8	133.3	119.6
1973	125.9	137.0	122.5
1974	133.8	143.8	131.8
1975	144.4	153.9	142.1

Source: Department of Labor

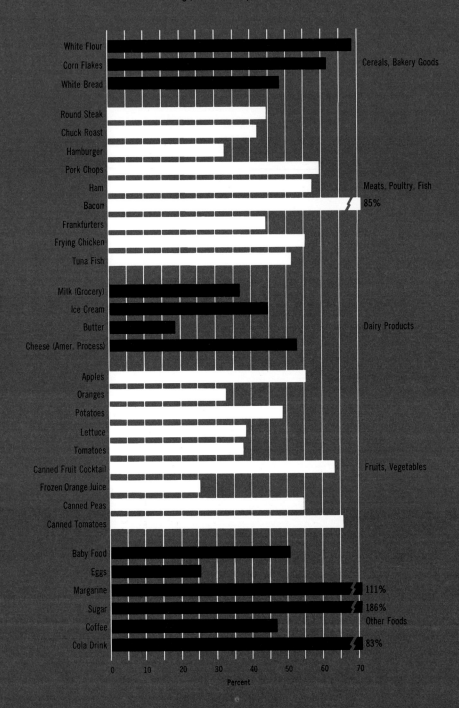

Inflation in the Food Sector
Percent change, selected retail prices, 1970 to 1975

White Flour
Corn Flakes — Cereals, Bakery Goods
White Bread

Round Steak
Chuck Roast
Hamburger
Pork Chops
Ham — Meats, Poultry, Fish
Bacon 85%
Frankfurters
Frying Chicken
Tuna Fish

Milk (Grocery)
Ice Cream
Butter — Dairy Products
Cheese (Amer. Process)

Apples
Oranges
Potatoes
Lettuce
Tomatoes
Canned Fruit Cocktail — Fruits, Vegetables
Frozen Orange Juice
Canned Peas
Canned Tomatoes

Baby Food
Eggs
Margarine 111%
Sugar 186% — Other Foods
Coffee
Cola Drink 83%

0 10 20 30 40 50 60 70
Percent

SELECTED FOODS: AVERAGE RETAIL PRICES

Cents per pound, except as indicated

Commodity	1960	1965	1970	1974	1975
CEREALS, BAKERY PRODUCTS:					
Flour, white, all-purpose	11.1	11.6	11.8	20.5	19.9
Corn flakes (12 oz.).................	25.8	28.9	32.2	41.5	51.9
Bread, white	20.3	20.9	24.3	34.5	36.0
MEATS, POULTRY, FISH:					
Steak, round	105.5	108.4	130.2	179.8	188.5
Chuck roast........................	61.6	59.5	72.5	102.1	102.8
Hamburger	52.4	50.8	66.2	97.2	87.8
Pork chops, center cut	85.8	97.3	116.2	156.5	185.6
Ham, whole	60.4	66.6	78.6	105.4	123.9
Bacon, sliced	65.5	81.3	94.9	132.0	175.6
Frankfurters	62.3	66.2	82.7	114.5	119.3
Frying chickens	42.7	39.0	40.8	56.0	63.3
Tuna fish (6½ oz. can)	32.5	32.0	39.8	57.7	60.3
DAIRY PRODUCTS:					
Milk, fresh (grocery)[1]	24.7	47.3	57.4	78.4	78.5
Ice cream (½ gallon)	86.8	78.7	84.5	107.6	122.3
Butter............................	74.9	75.4	86.6	94.6	102.5
Cheese, American process[2]	34.3	37.7	50.4	72.9	76.8
FRUITS, VEGETABLES:					
Apples	16.2	17.8	21.9	34.3	34.0
Bananas	15.9	16.0	15.9	18.4	23.2
Oranges, size 200 (dozen)	74.8	77.8	86.4	111.4	114.8
Potatoes..........................	7.2	9.4	9.0	16.6	13.4
Lettuce (head)[3]	17.3	25.5	29.9	42.3	41.5
Tomatoes.........................	31.6	34.3	42.0	54.8	57.8
Fruit cocktail (No. 303 can)	27.0	26.1	28.3	40.8	46.2
Frozen orange juice (6 oz. can)	22.5	23.7	22.5	25.8	28.2
Peas, green (No. 303 can)	20.7	23.7	25.3	32.2	39.2
Tomatoes (No. 303 can).............	15.9	16.1	21.3	29.8	35.3
OTHER FOODS:					
Eggs, grade A, large (dozen).........	57.3	52.7	61.4	78.3	77.0
Margarine	26.9	27.9	29.8	57.4	62.9
Sugar	11.6	11.8	13.0	32.3	37.2
Coffee, vacuum can	75.3	83.3	91.1	122.9	133.4
Cola drink, carton[4]	29.8	54.8	72.6	108.9	132.8
Chicken soup (10½ oz. can)	n.a.	18.2	18.4	22.3	23.2
Baby food (4½ oz. can)	10.2	10.4	10.9	14.1	16.4

[1] One quart in 1960; one-half gallon in later years
[2] One-half pound
[3] Size 60 head in 1960; size 24 head in later years
[4] 36 oz. in 1960; 72 oz. in later years

n.a.—Not available

Source: Department of Labor

CONSUMER PRICE INDEX: SELECTED AREAS

All items index numbers, 1967 = 100

Area	1965	1970	1972	1973	1974	1975
UNITED STATES	94.5	116.3	125.3	133.1	147.7	161.2
REGION[1]:						
Northeast............................	--	117.6	128.5	136.7	151.8	164.0
North Central	--	116.1	124.0	131.5	145.7	158.5
South	--	116.4	124.8	133.0	149.0	163.7
West	--	114.3	122.1	129.3	142.9	157.7
POPULATION SIZE GROUP[2]:						
3.5 Million or more	--	117.4	127.5	135.6	150.2	162.5
1.4–3.5 Million	--	116.6	125.5	133.0	147.0	160.4
250,000–1.4 Million	--	116.2	124.7	132.4	146.7	160.3
50,000–250,000	--	115.5	123.9	131.7	146.8	160.7
2,500–50,000	--	114.9	122.9	130.7	146.7	161.3
SMSA/CITY[3]:						
Atlanta, Ga.	94.0	116.5	125.5	133.7	148.5	161.7
Baltimore, Md.........................	94.4	117.0	126.3	134.9	152.4	165.2
Boston, Mass.	94.5	116.7	127.1	134.7	148.7	162.1
Buffalo, N.Y.	94.2	116.1	126.6	134.8	149.5	161.8
Chicago, Ill.-Northwestern Ind.	94.7	116.3	124.3	132.0	146.1	157.6
Cincinnati, Ohio-Ky.	94.4	115.7	124.7	132.1	146.3	160.4
Cleveland, Ohio	94.7	119.3	126.5	134.1	147.8	160.9
Dallas, Tex.	93.8	117.8	124.9	132.0	145.3	158.2
Detroit, Mich.	92.6	117.4	126.2	134.5	149.1	160.3
Honolulu, Hawaii	94.6	114.2	122.8	128.3	141.8	154.4
Houston, Tex.	94.8	116.8	125.2	132.3	147.8	164.9
Kansas City, Mo.-Kans.	95.5	115.8	124.0	130.4	144.2	157.9
Los Angeles-Long Beach, Calif.	95.7	114.3	122.3	129.2	142.5	157.6
Milwaukee, Wis.	95.8	115.8	123.7	131.5	144.1	157.0
Minneapolis-St. Paul, Minn.	94.5	117.5	125.5	133.0	148.3	160.9
New York, N.Y.- Northeastern N.J.	94.3	119.0	131.4	139.7	154.7	166.6
Philadelphia, Pa.-N.J...................	94.7	117.8	127.0	135.5	151.6	164.2
Pittsburgh, Pa.	95.8	116.4	125.3	132.9	147.3	160.0
St. Louis, Mo.-Ill.	94.1	115.2	122.3	129.3	142.2	156.1
San Diego, Calif.	95.2	115.3	124.4	132.5	147.2	160.8
San Francisco-Oakland, Calif.	94.7	115.8	124.3	131.5	144.4	159.1
Seattle, Wash.	94.5	114.0	119.7	127.5	141.5	155.8
Washington, D.C.-Md.-Va..............	94.1	117.6	126.9	135.0	150.0	161.6

Note: Indexes measure time-to-time changes in prices within stated area

[1] Regional data exclude Anchorage, Alaska and Honolulu, Hawaii
[2] Based on 1960 census of population
[3] Data refer to entire urban portion of metropolitan areas shown, as defined in 1960

Source: Department of Labor

PURCHASING POWER OF THE DOLLAR

As measured by consumer prices

Year	1967 = $1.00	1975 = $1.00	Year	1967 = $1.00	1975 = $1.00
1950	1.39	2.23	1963	1.09	1.76
1951	1.29	2.07	1964	1.08	1.73
1952	1.26	2.03			
1953	1.25	2.01	1965	1.06	1.70
1954	1.24	2.00	1966	1.03	1.66
			1967	1.00	1.61
1955	1.25	2.01	1968	.96	1.55
1956	1.23	1.98	1969	.91	1.47
1957	1.19	1.91			
1958	1.16	1.86	1970	.86	1.38
1959	1.15	1.84	1971	.82	1.33
			1972	.80	1.29
1960	1.13	1.81	1973	.75	1.21
1961	1.12	1.80	1974	.68	1.09
1962	1.10	1.78	1975	.62	1.00

Source: Department of Labor

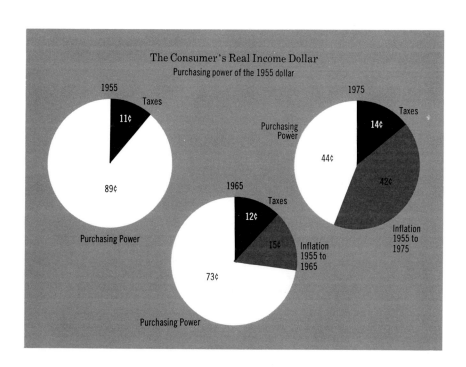

The Consumer's Real Income Dollar
Purchasing power of the 1955 dollar

1955
Taxes
11¢
89¢
Purchasing Power

1965
Taxes
12¢
15¢ Inflation 1955 to 1965
73¢
Purchasing Power

1975
Taxes
14¢
42¢
Purchasing Power
44¢
Inflation 1955 to 1975

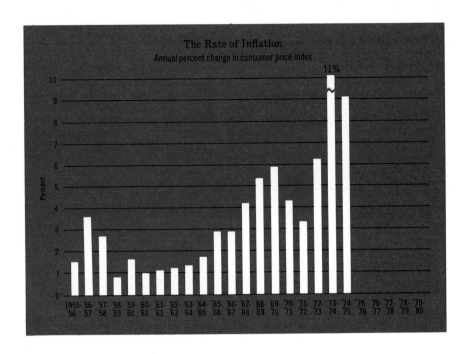

The Rate of Inflation

Annual percent change in consumer price index

PRICE CHANGES BY SECTOR

Consumer price index, selected items

Item	Percent Change 1965-70	Percent Change 1970-75	Item	Percent Change 1965-70	Percent Change 1970-75
ALL ITEMS	23.1	38.6	Women's and Girls'	23.7	19.1
			Footwear	30.8	22.5
Food	21.7	52.7			
Food at Home	19.1	54.6	Transportation	17.5	33.6
Cereals, Bakery Prod. .	16.1	69.7	New Cars	6.6	18.6
Meats, Poultry, Fish ...	23.3	52.8	Used Cars	4.9	40.4
Dairy Products	24.2	40.1	Gasoline	11.3	61.7
Fruits, Vegetables	15.7	50.8	Public Transportation ...	39.8	23.4
Other Foods	14.2	62.0			
Food Away From Home	31.9	45.4	Medical Care	34.7	39.8
			Drugs, Prescriptions	3.4	14.7
Housing	25.3	40.3	Services	42.3	44.2
Rent	13.6	24.7			
Homeownership Costs ..	38.6	41.4	Personal Care	18.9	33.1
Fuel, Utilities	9.5	55.9	Toilet Goods	11.1	35.9
Household Textiles	13.8	29.5	Services	26.8	30.5
Furniture, Bedding	22.9	27.3			
Floor Coverings	5.5	23.6	Reading and Recreation ..	18.2	27.3
Appliances[1]	.2	13.7			
			Tobacco	32.0	27.0
Apparel and Upkeep	23.9	22.6			
Men's and Boys'	24.6	21.4	Alcoholic Beverages	16.6	26.5

[1] Includes radio and TV

Source: Department of Labor

CONSUMER PRICE INDEX FOR SELECTED AREAS BY MAJOR GROUPS, 1975

Index numbers, 1967 = 100

Area	All Items	Food	Housing	Apparel and Upkeep	Trans- portation	Health and Recreation
UNITED STATES	161.2	175.4	166.8	142.3	150.6	153.5
REGION[1]:						
Northeast	164.0	177.0	170.3	143.0	154.6	155.8
North Central	158.5	173.3	160.0	142.2	149.3	154.1
South	163.7	178.7	171.8	144.0	149.2	154.7
West	157.7	169.9	165.5	139.2	148.6	147.1
POPULATION SIZE GROUP[2]:						
3.5 Million or more	162.5	176.4	166.8	139.2	155.9	156.3
1.4-3.5 Million	160.4	175.1	163.6	143.8	150.2	153.5
250,000-1.4 Million	160.3	174.8	165.7	144.0	147.7	152.9
50,000-250,000	160.7	173.5	167.9	145.4	148.9	150.9
2,500-50,000	161.3	174.4	169.1	143.3	148.1	151.2
SMSA/CITY[3]:						
Atlanta, Ga.	161.7	181.7	167.0	138.7	142.9	158.7
Baltimore, Md.	165.2	178.2	176.1	147.6	146.4	156.3
Boston, Mass.	162.1	175.2	166.2	146.8	153.3	151.9
Buffalo, N.Y.	161.8	173.6	169.9	154.1	147.4	149.7
Chicago, Ill.-Northwestern Ind.	157.6	175.1	156.2	136.6	151.8	154.1
Cincinnati, Ohio-Ky.	160.4	177.4	162.3	143.6	144.1	156.5
Cleveland, Ohio	160.9	175.8	157.8	145.1	153.5	163.6
Dallas, Tex.	158.2	172.5	158.0	141.4	156.5	153.5
Detroit, Mich.	160.3	171.6	163.8	137.9	149.1	161.1
Honolulu, Hawaii	154.4	176.7	147.3	141.2	146.8	148.8
Houston, Tex.	164.9	181.2	172.3	152.1	144.1	158.9
Kansas City, Mo.-Kans.	157.9	177.8	159.2	145.7	148.5	150.5
Los Angeles-Long Beach, Calif.	157.6	170.1	163.7	136.4	152.7	147.6
Milwaukee, Wis.	157.0	171.9	154.5	152.7	151.6	150.4
Minneapolis-St. Paul, Minn.	160.9	178.9	168.4	139.5	142.9	152.5
New York, N.Y.- Northeastern N.J.	166.6	179.6	172.5	141.1	161.4	159.1
Philadelphia, Pa.-N.J.	164.2	179.6	171.2	135.9	152.7	158.6
Pittsburgh, Pa.	160.0	177.4	163.4	141.6	148.7	152.7
St. Louis, Mo.-Ill.	156.1	174.3	156.2	135.2	146.0	150.8
San Diego, Calif.	160.8	173.9	171.9	140.6	152.9	145.9
San Francisco-Oakland, Calif.	159.1	171.2	165.6	141.7	151.8	149.7
Seattle, Wash.	155.8	169.6	164.0	139.2	136.2	146.2
Washington, D.C.-Md.-Va.	161.6	180.7	161.4	144.8	151.9	156.9

Note: Indexes measure relative price movements within stated area and do not indicate differences in price levels between areas

[1] Regional data exclude Anchorage, Alaska and Honolulu, Hawaii
[2] Based on 1960 census of population
[3] Data refer to entire urban portion of metropolitan areas shown, as defined in 1960

Source: Department of Labor

PRICE INDEXES: NEW ONE-FAMILY HOMES SOLD

Index numbers, 1967=100

Year	United States	Region			
		North-east	North Central	South	West
1963	90.2	90.7	89.4	91.6	91.1
1965	93.2	91.3	91.4	94.6	94.0
1966	96.6	95.2	96.0	97.0	97.4
1967	100.0	100.0	100.0	100.0	100.0
1968	105.1	108.2	105.7	104.0	103.4
1969	113.6	117.7	115.7	111.4	111.6
1970	117.4	124.1	116.2	116.7	114.9
1971	123.2	134.4	119.8	124.6	117.4
1972	131.0	143.8	126.6	131.1	125.5
1973	144.8	154.7	138.9	142.9	142.4
1974	158.1	167.6	150.5	154.4	157.4
1975	174.3	183.5	166.9	165.2	179.7

Note: Price indexes include value of lot. These indexes measure time to time changes in sales prices of new homes which are the same with respect to floor area, number of stories, number of bathrooms, air conditioning, type of parking facility, type of foundation, geographic division within region, and metropolitan area location, as homes sold in each region in 1967

Source: Department of Commerce

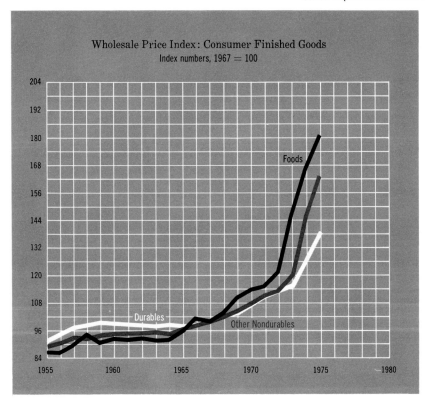

254

THE TREND IN WHOLESALE PRICES

Index numbers, 1967 = 100

Year	All Commodities	Farm Products	Processed Foods and Feeds	Industrial Commodities
1950	81.8	106.7	83.4	78.0
1955	87.8	98.2	85.0	86.9
1956	90.7	96.9	84.9	90.8
1957	93.3	99.5	87.4	93.3
1958	94.6	103.9	91.8	93.6
1959	94.8	97.5	89.4	95.3
1960	94.9	97.2	89.5	95.3
1961	94.5	96.3	91.0	94.8
1962	94.8	98.0	91.9	94.8
1963	94.5	96.0	92.5	94.7
1964	94.7	94.6	92.3	95.2
1965	96.6	98.7	95.5	96.4
1966	99.8	105.9	101.2	98.5
1967	100.0	100.0	100.0	100.0
1968	102.5	102.5	102.2	102.5
1969	106.5	109.1	107.3	106.0
1970	110.4	111.0	112.0	110.0
1971	113.9	112.9	114.3	114.0
1972	119.1	125.0	120.8	117.9
1973	134.7	176.3	148.1	125.9
1974	160.1	187.7	170.9	153.8
1975	174.9	186.7	182.6	171.5

Source: Department of Labor

WHOLESALE PRICES: AUTOMOTIVE GOODS

Index numbers, 1967 = 100

Year	Motor Vehicles, Equipment	Tires, Tubes	Year	Motor Vehicles, Equipment	Tires, Tubes
1950	75.3	79.5	1965	98.5	93.8
			1966	98.6	97.2
1955	86.3	101.5	1967	100.0	100.0
1956	91.2	106.6	1968	102.8	102.8
1957	95.1	105.5	1969	104.8	102.3
1958	98.1	106.7			
1959	100.3	100.3	1970	108.5	109.0
			1971	114.7	109.2
1960	98.8	96.9	1972	118.0	109.2
1961	98.6	96.3	1973	119.2	111.4
1962	98.6	90.7	1974	129.2	133.4
1963	97.8	93.9			
1964	98.3	92.7	1975	144.6	148.5

Source: Department of Labor

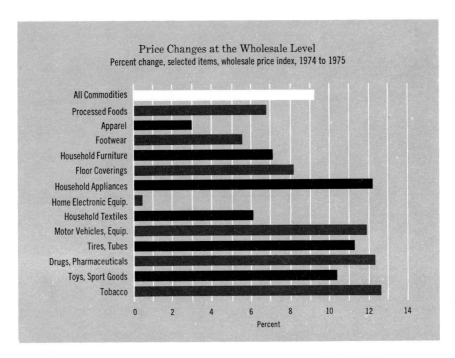

Price Changes at the Wholesale Level
Percent change, selected items, wholesale price index, 1974 to 1975

All Commodities
Processed Foods
Apparel
Footwear
Household Furniture
Floor Coverings
Household Appliances
Home Electronic Equip.
Household Textiles
Motor Vehicles, Equip.
Tires, Tubes
Drugs, Pharmaceuticals
Toys, Sport Goods
Tobacco

0   2   4   6   8   10   12   14
Percent

WHOLESALE PRICES: CONSUMER FINISHED GOODS

Index numbers, 1967 = 100

Year	Consumer Finished Goods: Total	Nondurable Goods		Durable Goods
		Foods	Other	
1955	88.5	86.5	89.4	91.2
1956	89.8	86.3	91.1	94.3
1957	92.4	89.3	93.2	97.1
1958	94.4	94.5	92.6	98.4
1959	93.6	90.1	94.0	99.6
1960	94.5	92.1	94.7	99.2
1961	94.3	91.7	94.7	98.8
1962	94.6	92.5	94.8	98.3
1963	94.1	91.4	95.1	97.8
1964	94.3	91.9	94.8	98.2
1965	96.1	95.4	95.9	97.9
1966	99.4	101.6	97.8	98.5
1967	100.0	100.0	100.0	100.0
1968	102.7	103.7	102.2	102.2
1969	106.5	110.0	105.0	104.0
1970	109.9	113.5	108.3	107.0
1971	112.7	115.2	111.3	110.9
1972	116.6	121.7	113.6	113.2
1973	129.2	146.4	120.5	115.8
1974	149.3	166.9	146.8	126.3
1975	163.6	181.0	163.0	138.2

Source: Department of Labor

WHOLESALE PRICES: PROCESSED FOODS

Index numbers, 1967=100

Year	Processed Foods, Feeds, Total	Cereal, Bakery Products	Meats, Poultry, Fish	Dairy Products	Processed Fruits, Vegetables	Sugar, Con- fectionery	Beverages, Beverage Materials[1]
1950	83.4	71.6	97.7	68.9	86.6	75.3	78.4
1955	85.0	84.1	81.6	77.1	91.5	85.2	93.1
1956	84.9	83.3	78.6	78.9	93.7	84.7	95.3
1957	87.4	84.6	88.5	81.1	90.1	87.5	95.4
1958	91.8	85.3	102.8	81.9	95.1	89.2	93.3
1959	89.4	86.3	94.5	83.1	94.6	88.8	93.0
1960	89.5	88.1	93.1	86.1	92.8	90.1	92.8
1961	91.0	89.8	90.9	88.2	94.9	89.6	92.6
1962	91.9	91.9	94.4	87.7	91.4	90.4	93.0
1963	92.5	91.6	88.9	88.2	96.9	104.8	94.7
1964	92.3	92.1	86.5	88.4	97.8	98.9	99.7
1965	95.5	93.1	96.2	89.0	95.2	96.5	99.2
1966	101.2	98.5	105.0	97.2	97.8	97.8	99.3
1967	100.0	100.0	100.0	100.0	100.0	100.0	100.0
1968	102.2	100.9	103.1	104.8	106.5	102.8	102.8
1969	107.3	102.7	113.8	108.2	108.1	109.9	106.0
1970	112.0	107.6	115.8	111.2	110.4	115.9	112.9
1971	114.3	111.4	116.0	115.4	114.3	119.2	115.8
1972	120.8	114.7	130.0	118.6	119.7	121.6	118.0
1973	148.1	134.4	167.5	131.1	129.6	132.3	121.7
1974	170.9	171.2	163.5	146.4	154.6	258.9	140.7
1975	182.6	178.0	191.0	155.8	169.8	254.3	162.4

[1] Refers to both alcoholic and nonalcoholic beverages

Source: Department of Labor

WHOLESALE PRICES: APPAREL AND FOOTWEAR

Index numbers, 1967=100

Year	Apparel	Footwear	Year	Apparel	Footwear
1950	90.5	70.2	1965	97.1	90.7
			1966	98.3	96.8
1955	92.6	74.0	1967	100.0	100.0
1956	93.6	78.7	1968	103.6	104.8
1957	93.6	79.9	1969	107.4	109.5
1958	93.4	80.5			
1959	94.0	85.4	1970	111.0	113.0
			1971	112.9	116.8
1960	94.9	87.6	1972	114.8	124.5
1961	94.6	88.0	1973	119.0	130.5
1962	95.0	88.9	1974	129.5	140.0
1963	95.4	88.7			
1964	96.3	88.9	1975	133.4	147.8

Source: Department of Labor

WHOLESALE PRICES: HOUSEHOLD GOODS

Index numbers, 1967=100

Year	Total[1]	Furniture and Household Durables				
		Household Furniture	Floor Coverings	Household Appliances	Home Electronic Equipment	Textile House-furnishings
1955	93.3	81.9	104.3	112.9	120.0	94.9
1960	99.0	90.0	107.5	107.5	117.8	96.1
1961	98.4	91.1	106.2	105.5	115.4	96.6
1962	97.7	91.9	103.7	104.2	110.3	98.3
1963	97.0	92.6	103.3	101.8	107.3	97.1
1964	97.4	93.3	106.3	101.2	105.6	97.6
1965	96.9	94.1	104.5	98.9	103.1	97.3
1966	98.0	96.6	103.7	98.8	101.2	98.5
1967	100.0	100.0	100.0	100.0	100.0	100.0
1968	102.8	103.9	101.3	101.8	98.1	104.2
1969	104.9	108.4	100.4	102.9	94.6	100.8
1970	107.5	111.6	99.5	105.3	93.6	103.6
1971	109.9	114.8	98.8	107.2	93.8	104.2
1972	111.4	117.3	98.6	107.6	92.7	109.2
1973	115.2	123.0	102.2	108.5	91.9	113.3
1974	127.9	136.6	115.4	117.9	93.1	143.1
1975	139.7	146.3	124.9	132.3	93.5	151.9

[1] Also includes other household durables and commercial furniture, not separately listed

Source: Department of Labor

ESTIMATED BUDGETS FOR URBAN FAMILIES BY TYPE

Annual cost of living standards based on Autumn 1975 prices, in dollars

Type of Family	Budgets for Current Consumption		
	Lower	Intermediate	Higher
Single person, under 35 yrs.	2,730	4,100	5,650
Husband-wife, under 35 yrs.			
No children	3,820	5,740	7,910
1 Child under 6 yrs.	4,830	7,270	10,010
2 Children under 6 yrs	5,610	8,440	11,620
Husband-wife, 35-54 yrs.			
1 Child, 6-15 yrs.	6,390	9,610	13,230
2 Children, older 6-15 yrs	7,795	11,725	16,141
3 Children, oldest 6-15 yrs.	9,040	13,600	18,720
Single person, 65 and over	2,180	3,280	4,520
Husband-wife, 65 and over...............	3,980	5,980	8,230

Note: These budgets, developed by the Bureau of Labor Statistics, describe three levels of living standards for the family types listed above. Each budget contains a distinct market basket of goods and services, priced in 1975 dollars, required to maintain the indicated living standard. The budgets shown here are for current consumption only and exclude allowances for life insurance, occupational expenses, gifts and contributions, social security and disability payments, and personal taxes

Source: Department of Labor

WHOLESALE PRICES: OTHER CONSUMER GOODS

Index numbers, 1967=100

Year	Drugs, Pharma-ceuticals	Toys, Sporting Goods[1]	Tobacco Products	Photo Equipment, Supplies
1955	105.6	90.9	82.7	82.3
1960	106.6	94.7	90.3	93.4
1961	104.6	95.4	90.3	94.6
1962	102.1	95.3	90.4	96.9
1963	101.2	95.5	92.6	96.8
1964	101.1	95.5	93.9	97.5
1965	100.4	97.1	94.1	98.2
1966	100.5	98.4	97.1	97.9
1967	100.0	100.0	100.0	100.0
1968	99.3	102.4	102.0	102.2
1969	99.9	105.3	107.1	102.4
1970	101.1	109.4	114.0	104.9
1971	102.4	112.6	116.7	106.1
1972	103.0	114.4	117.5	106.7
1973	104.3	117.9	121.9	108.4
1974	112.7	132.3	132.8	116.8
1975	126.6	146.0	149.6	130.6

[1] Includes small arms and ammunition

Source: Department of Labor

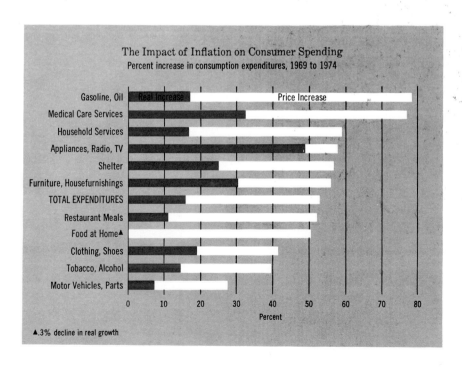

The Impact of Inflation on Consumer Spending
Percent increase in consumption expenditures, 1969 to 1974

▲.3% decline in real growth

ESTIMATED WEEKLY FOOD COSTS FOR FAMILIES AT THREE LEVELS
Cost of food at home, March 1976, in dollars

Family Composition	Total U.S.	Region			
		North-east	North Central	South	West
LOW-COST PLAN					
Couple, 20-54 years	28.90	30.60	28.80	28.70	28.20
Couple, 55 years and over	25.60	27.10	25.50	25.30	25.10
Family of 4:					
Preschool children[1]	40.80	43.00	40.50	40.20	39.70
School children[2]	49.30	51.90	49.10	48.80	48.20
MODERATE-COST PLAN					
Couple, 20-54 years	36.30	39.30	35.50	35.40	35.60
Couple, 55 years and over	31.80	34.30	31.10	30.90	31.10
Family of 4:					
Preschool children[1]	50.90	54.80	49.80	49.50	49.90
School children[2]	61.80	66.50	60.60	60.40	60.80
LIBERAL PLAN					
Couple, 20-54 years	43.70	47.30	42.90	41.10	43.10
Couple, 55 years and over	38.20	41.20	37.40	35.70	37.60
Family of 4:					
Preschool children[1]	61.20	66.00	60.00	57.60	60.50
School children[2]	74.40	80.10	73.10	70.00	73.70

Note: Costs of food plans were estimated by using average price per pound of each food group paid by urban survey families at three income levels in 1965. These prices were adjusted to current levels using retail food prices for cities released by the Bureau of Labor Statistics

[1] Man and woman, 20-54 years; children 1-2 years and 3-5 years
[2] Man and woman, 20-54 years; child 6-8 years and boy 9-11 years   Source: Department of Agriculture

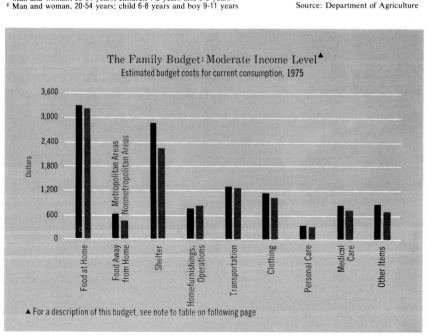

The Family Budget: Moderate Income Level▲
Estimated budget costs for current consumption, 1975

▲ For a description of this budget, see note to table on following page

ESTIMATED FAMILY BUDGETS AT THREE INCOME LEVELS

Annual cost of living standards based on Autumn 1975 prices, in dollars

Item	Urban United States		
	Total	Metropolitan Areas	Nonmetro-politan Areas[1]
HIGHER BUDGET—TOTAL COST[2]	22,294	22,940	19,412
Total Consumption	16,141	16,551	14,312
Food	4,819	4,914	4,393
Food at Home	3,874	3,895	3,784
Food away from Home	945	1,020	609
Housing	5,353	5,535	4,540
Shelter	3,687	3,858	2,922
Homefurnishings, Operations	1,508	1,497	1,554
Transportation[3]	1,658	1,685	1,540
Clothing	1,613	1,633	1,522
Personal Care	470	474	448
Medical Care	857	884	739
Other Consumption	1,371	1,426	1,130
Personal Income Taxes	4,130	4,343	3,178
INTERMEDIATE BUDGET—TOTAL COST[2]	15,318	15,800	14,046
Total Consumption	11,725	11,951	10,715
Food	3,827	3,875	3,610
Food at Home	3,242	3,260	3,165
Food away from Home	584	615	445
Housing	3,533	3,633	3,089
Shelter	2,737	2,848	2,241
Homefurnishings, Operations	797	785	848
Transportation	1,279	1,283	1,262
Clothing	1,102	1,114	1,044
Personal Care	331	337	307
Medical Care	822	848	707
Other Consumption	831	861	695
Personal Income Taxes	2,057	2,136	1,703
LOWER BUDGET—TOTAL COST[2]	9,588	9,720	9,002
Total Consumption	7,795	7,883	7,400
Food	2,952	2,987	2,793
Food at Home	2,563	2,583	2,474
Food away from Home	389	404	319
Housing[4]	1,857	1,886	1,728
Shelter	1,391	1,427	1,227
Homefurnishings, Operations	467	459	501
Transportation	702	666	860
Clothing	771	778	738
Personal Care	248	255	216
Medical Care	818	844	703
Other Consumption	447	467	362
Personal Income Taxes	781	811	645

Note: The budgets, developed by the Bureau of Labor Statistics, describe three levels of living standards for an urban family of four persons. Each budget contains a distinct market basket of goods and services, priced in 1975 dollars, required to maintain the indicated living standard. The family consists of an employed husband, age 38, a wife not employed full-time outside the home, an 8-year old girl and a 13-year old boy. Metropolitan areas are defined as of 1960-1961.
[1] Places with a population of 2,500 to 50,000
[2] The total budget cost also includes allowances for gifts and contributions, life insurance, occupational expenses, and social security, disability and unemployment compensation taxes, in addition to items specifically cited
[3] All families are assumed to be automobile owners
[4] All families are assumed to be renters

Source: Department of Labor

INTERCITY COMPARISONS OF LIVING COSTS

Index numbers, urban United States, Autumn 1975 = 100

Area	Total Budget[1]	Food	Hous-ing	Trans-porta-tion	Cloth-ing	Med-ical Care	Per-sonal Income Taxes
				Cost of Family Consumption[1]			
U. S. URBAN AVERAGE (DOLLARS) .	15,318	3,827	3,533	1,279	1,102	822	2,057
URBAN UNITED STATES (INDEX) ...	100	100	100	100	100	100	100
Metropolitan Areas	102	101	103	100	101	103	104
Nonmetropolitan Areas[2]	91	94	87	99	95	86	83
Northeast							
Boston, Mass.....................	118	108	138	104	104	96	145
Buffalo, N.Y.	106	102	107	108	116	86	119
Hartford, Conn.	107	108	117	110	104	93	90
New York, N.Y.-Northeastern N.J.	114	113	123	92	99	110	135
Philadelphia, Pa.-N.J.	102	111	96	94	93	104	110
Pittsburgh, Pa.	95	103	84	96	98	87	96
Portland, Me.	102	109	104	102	105	91	93
Nonmetropolitan Areas[2]	99	102	104	101	94	88	99
North Central							
Chicago, Ill.-Northwestern Ind.	103	100	107	103	100	107	99
Cincinnati, Ohio-Ky.-Ind.	96	98	93	102	100	87	90
Cleveland, Ohio	102	99	106	103	104	98	95
Detroit, Mich....................	103	99	104	98	103	108	108
Indianapolis, Ind.	99	97	99	109	98	98	91
Kansas City, Mo.-Kans.............	97	100	89	106	102	93	93
Milwaukee, Wis.	106	93	112	100	112	94	136
Minneapolis-St. Paul, Minn.	103	98	98	98	101	92	128
St. Louis, Mo.-Ill.	97	101	92	106	94	88	92
Nonmetropolitan Areas[2]	92	92	90	97	100	82	87
South							
Atlanta, Ga.	92	98	83	97	98	97	82
Austin, Tex.	88	89	81	102	103	95	64
Baltimore, Md.	99	97	90	98	100	107	118
Baton Rouge, La.................	90	99	79	99	101	83	72
Dallas, Tex.	91	92	86	104	93	112	69
Houston, Tex.	92	97	83	101	99	108	69
Nashville, Tenn..................	91	93	90	101	105	87	69
Orlando, Fla.	89	89	89	100	90	103	67
Washington, D.C.-Md.-Va.	104	102	103	103	92	102	118
Nonmetropolitan Areas[2]	87	93	79	99	91	85	72
West							
Denver, Colo....................	96	95	88	100	119	94	96
Los Angeles-Long Beach, Calif.....	99	96	97	104	101	122	92
San Diego, Calif.	98	93	97	106	101	119	90
San Francisco-Oakland, Calif.	107	100	114	105	108	115	106
Seattle-Everett, Wash.	102	103	109	102	109	106	84
Nonmetropolitan Areas[2]	90	89	86	96	101	90	87

Note: Data are based on the cost of a budget for a four-person family at a moderate living standard, autumn 1975. The family consists of an employed husband, age 38, a wife not employed full-time outside the home, an 8-year old girl, and a 13-year old boy. The top line of the table shows actual dollar costs estimated for the total urban United States. Indexes given below denote the relative average cost of this budget for the indicated cities

[1] The difference between the total budget and the sum of the remaining columns is accounted for by the cost of recreation, tobacco, alcoholic beverages, life insurance, gifts and contributions, and other items
[2] Places with a population of 2,500 to 50,000

Source: Department of Labor

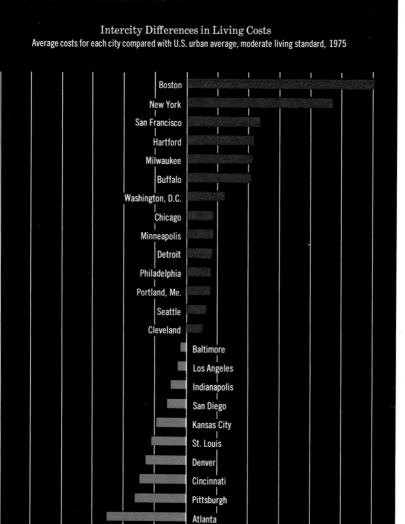

Intercity Differences in Living Costs
Average costs for each city compared with U.S. urban average, moderate living standard, 1975

Boston
New York
San Francisco
Hartford
Milwaukee
Buffalo
Washington, D.C.
Chicago
Minneapolis
Detroit
Philadelphia
Portland, Me.
Seattle
Cleveland
Baltimore
Los Angeles
Indianapolis
San Diego
Kansas City
St. Louis
Denver
Cincinnati
Pittsburgh
Atlanta
Houston
Nashville
Dallas
Baton Rouge
Orlando
Austin

−18   −15   −12   −9   −6   −3   0   3   6   9   12   15   18

Percent

ESTIMATED BUDGETS FOR AN URBAN RETIRED COUPLE

Annual cost of living standards based on Autumn 1974 prices, in dollars

Item	Total Budget[1]	Cost of Family Consumption				
		Food	Housing	Trans- portation	Clothing, Pers. Care	Medical Care[3]
HIGHER BUDGET						
Urban United States	8,969	2,210	3,199	971	764	540
Metropolitan Areas	9,379	2,251	3,469	989	762	544
Nonmetropolitan Areas[2]	7,743	2,088	2,390	915	768	529
INTERMEDIATE BUDGET						
Urban United States	6,041	1,766	2,043	527	504	537
Metropolitan Areas	6,278	1,796	2,198	532	509	541
Nonmetropolitan Areas[2]	5,331	1,677	1,579	512	488	525
LOWER BUDGET						
Urban United States	4,228	1,334	1,410	272	315	534
Metropolitan Areas	4,332	1,349	1,499	246	319	538
Nonmetropolitan Areas[2]	3,916	1,287	1,145	351	306	521

Note: These budgets, developed by the Bureau of Labor Statistics, describe three levels of living standards for an urban retired couple (husband age 65 or over). Each budget contains a distinct market basket of goods and services, priced in 1974 dollars, required to maintain the indicated living standard

[1] The difference between the total budget cost and the sum of the remaining columns is accounted for by other items of current consumption, gifts and contributions. In addition, an allowance for personal taxes is included in the higher and intermediate budgets

[2] Places with a population of 2,500 to 50,000

[3] Preliminary estimates

Source: Department of Labor

DEFINITIONS

DEFINITIONS

Annual Rate—The expansion of a figure pertaining to a period shorter than one year into its annual equivalent, *e.g.,* quarterly data are multiplied by 4; monthly data, by 12.

Arithmetic Mean—The sum of values of a series of items divided by the number of items.

Average—The typical or characteristic value of a group of numbers. Often "average" is used interchangeably with "arithmetic mean," but strictly the term "average" includes a whole group of measures of central tendency such as the median, mode and various means.

Base Periods—Time intervals used as reference points for business and economic data. In the computation of index numbers the figures for a base period are usually averaged and the average is adopted as 100. The base period of an index number is sometimes erroneously regarded as a "normal" period.

Constant Dollars—A series is said to be expressed in "constant dollars" when the effect of changes in the purchasing power of the dollar has been removed. Usually the data are expressed in terms of dollars of some selected year or the average of some set of years.

Consumer Credit—Credit granted to individuals for use in purchasing consumer goods and services; principally credit extended by commercial banks, retail merchants, cash-lending agencies, finance companies and the service industries. The credit is granted for relatively short periods and is repaid either in instalments or in one payment.

Consumer Price Index—A measure of the time-to-time fluctuations in the prices of a quantitatively constant market basket of goods and services, selected as representative of a specific level of living. Hence, it can be thought of as the cost of maintaining a fixed scale of living.

Cost of Living—Amount of expenditure required to pay for goods and services deemed to make up a given level of living, taking into account both changes in the quantities bought as well as the price paid. The term is often misleadingly used to describe a consumer price index which only measures price change, keeping the quantities constant over time.

Crude Birth Rate—The total number of births during a specified period of time per 1,000 persons in the population.

Current Dollars—Dollars current at the time designated or at which transactions listed took place. In most contexts about the same meaning would be conveyed by the simple term "dollars." See also Constant Dollars.

Deposits: Demand, Time—Money in depositors' accounts of a bank. *Demand* deposits are subject to immediate withdrawal (by checks). *Time* deposits are withdrawable at a specified future date or upon lapse of a specific period after an advance notice. *Savings* deposits are special kinds of time deposits. Commercial banks usually have both demand and time deposit claims against them. Savings banks handle only time deposits.

Discretionary Purchasing Power—The dollar magnitude that measures the household sector's ability to exercise discretion over the specific direction of spending and saving. This series, computed quarterly by THE CONFERENCE BOARD, is calculated by subtracting from aggregate consumer purchasing power various items of a nondiscretionary character. These nondiscretionary items are classified into four broad groups—net contractual saving, imputed income, fixed commitments and essential outlays.

Throughout the postwar period this series has been running at about 40% of aggregate consumer purchasing power, but with some variation around cyclical turning points. Because discretionary purchasing power is based on a sliding scale of essentials and fixed outlays, it principally measures short-term fluctuations rather than long-term secular growth. See also Supernumerary Income.

Discretionary Spending—That part of discretionary purchasing power spent on items such as homes and home furnishings, recreation, education, foreign travel, liquor, personal business, personal care, and a portion of total spending for food, clothing and transportation.

Disposable Personal Income—The income remaining to persons after deduction of personal tax and other payments (such as fines and penalties) to general government.

Durable Goods—Generally, any producers' or consumers' goods whose continuous service-ability is likely to exceed three years, such as machinery, trucks, passenger cars, homes, furniture, refrigerators, etc.

Family—As currently defined by the Bureau of the Census, refers to a group of two or more persons related by blood, marriage or adoption and residing together. A "sub-family" consists of a married couple or a parent-child group sharing the living quarters of the family head. A "household" includes all of the persons who occupy a house, room, group of rooms, or an apartment that constitutes a housing unit. A household may contain more than one family, or may be a single person.

Farm—In the 1959, 1964 and 1969 Censuses, places of 10 or more acres were counted as farms if annual sales of farm products amounted to $50 or more. Less than 10 acres were counted as farms only if the annual value of farm products sold amounted to $250 or more.
In the 1950 and 1954 Censuses, places of 3 or more acres were counted as farms if the annual value of agricultural products, exclusive of home gardens, amounted to $150 or more. Places of less than 3 acres were counted as farms only if the annual value of sales of agricultural products amounted to $150 or more.

Fertility Rate—The number of live births per 1,000 females age 15-44 years.

Gross National Product or Expenditure (Often called GNP)—Total value at market prices of all goods and services produced by the nation's economy. As calculated quarterly by the Department of Commerce, gross national product is the broadest available measure of economic activity.

Hourly Earnings, Average—Average monetary compensation for each hour actually worked or paid for. Obtained by dividing gross compensation (with no allowance for payments in kind or for deductions) by total hours worked or paid for. Hourly earnings differ from hourly wage rates because they include overtime premium pay for late shift, recurrent bonuses and other monetary compensation.

Household—As defined for the 1960 and 1970 Censuses, includes all persons who occupy a Housing Unit. The current definition excludes persons living in group quarters (such as boarding homes and college dormitories), whereas the 1950 Census definition partly included such persons.

Housing Starts—Represent the number of new housing units in housekeeping residential buildings on which construction has been started. A construction start is defined as the beginning of the excavation for footings or the foundation. All housing units in an apartment building are individually counted as started when excavation for the building is begun. See also Housing Unit.

Housing Unit—A group of rooms or a single room occupied or intended for occupancy by persons who do not live and eat with any other persons in the structure. It must have either (1) direct access from the outside or through a common hall, or (2) a kitchen or cooking equipment for the exclusive use of the occupants.

Implicit Price Deflator—A measure of the general price level of goods and services. This index is a by-product of stating gross national product (GNP) in two ways—in *current* dollars and in *constant* dollars—and not the result of a direct calculation of a price index.
The general statistical procedure for obtaining constant-dollar GNP (is to divide the current-dollar estimates of GNP, *in as fine a product detail as possible*, by appropriate price indexes. The resulting figures, in turn, are then combined into designated subtotals and then to a total GNP. (This seemingly roundabout method is necessary because there is no suitable price index for aggregates composed of many different products, each having its own particular price fluctuation.) When the deflated subtotals and total are compared with corresponding figures expressed in current dollars, an average price relationship emerges or is "implied."

Imputed Income—Value assigned to goods and services received in kind; most commonly, estimated rental value of owner-occupied homes.

Income Distribution—Refers to the distribution of families and individuals by income classes as well as to the distribution of total income by such classes.

Index Number—A magnitude expressed as a percentage of the corresponding magnitude in some "base" period. The base is usually designated as equal to 100.

Instalment Credit—The credit extended to consumers by retailers or financial institutions usually to purchase cars, appliances, home furnishings and other durable goods. Such credit is usually repayable in three years or less in accordance with a prearranged schedule of payments. Revolving credit and budget and coupon accounts are considered by the Federal Reserve to be instalment credit rather than charge accounts because they involve scheduled repayments on a periodic basis.

Labor Force—The civilian labor force (current BLS definition) includes those of the civilian noninstitutional population sixteen years of age and over who are classified as employed or unemployed in accordance with the following definitions:

Employed—Persons who, during the survey week, were either (a) "At work"—those who did any work for pay or profit, or worked without pay for 15 hours or more on a family farm or business; or (b) "With a job but not at work"—those who did not work and were not looking for work but had a job or business from which they were temporarily absent because of vacation, illness, industrial dispute, bad weather, or because they were taking time off for various other reasons. Prior to 1957, the statistics also included in group (b) persons on layoff who had definite instructions to return to work within 30 days of the date of layoff—now classified as unemployed—and persons waiting to report to new jobs to which they were scheduled to report within 30 days. This latter group is now classified either as unemployed or, if in school during the survey week, as not in the labor force.

Unemployed—Persons who did not work at all during the survey week, and who were looking for work. Also included as unemployed are persons who have been (a) engaged in some specific jobseeking activity (going to the Employment Service, applying to an employer, etc.) within the past four weeks, (b) waiting to start a new job within 30 days, (c) waiting to be recalled from layoff. In all cases the individual must be currently available for work. Prior to 1957, part of group (b)—those whose layoffs were for definite periods of less than 30 days—were classified as employed ("with a job, but not at work") rather than as unemployed.

Members of the Armed Forces are added to the civilian labor force to get total labor force.

Median—That value in any array which divides the number of items in half; i.e., an equal number of items lie above and below this value.

Money Income—Money income statistics are based on data collected in various field surveys where representative samples of the population are interviewed with respect to income received during the previous year. The income here referred to is consumer money income for the calendar year and is before deduction of income taxes or social security taxes. Nonmoney items of income are not covered. See also Personal Income.

Nondurable Goods—Producers' and consumers' goods whose serviceability is generally limited to a period of less than three years. Consists of "perishable" and "semidurable" goods.

Nonproduction Workers—As used by the BLS, everybody who is not a Production Worker. The difference between the total number employed and the number of production workers is referred to as "nonproduction workers." Specifically *excluded* from production workers and therefore automatically *included* as nonproduction workers, are employees engaged in the following activities: executive, accounting, professional, technical, legal, medical, finance, credit, collections, routine office functions, sales, sales delivery, purchasing, advertising, personnel, cafeteria, factory supervisors (above foremen), force-account construction and installation and servicing of firms' own products.

Passenger Mile—A statistical term, defined as one passenger carried one mile, or its equivalent, as for example, two passengers carried one half mile.

Personal Consumption Expenditures—As used in the national accounts, the market value of purchases of goods and services by individuals and nonprofit institutions and the value of food, clothing, housing and financial services received by them as income in kind. It includes the rental value of owner-occupied houses, but excludes purchases of dwellings, which are classified as capital goods.

Personal Income—Current income received by individuals, unincorporated businesses, and nonprofit institutions from all sources. Most of the income is in monetary form but also included is some imputed income. Capital gains and losses are excluded. Personal income is the total of wage and salary receipts, other labor income, proprietors' and rental income, interest, dividends and transfer payments.

Personal Saving—As used in the national accounts, the excess of personal income over personal consumption expenditures and personal taxes and other payments to general government. Consists of the current savings of individuals (including owners of unincorporated businesses), nonprofit institutions, and private pension welfare and trust funds. It may take such forms as changes in cash and deposits, security holdings, indebtedness, reserves of life insurance companies, deposits of mutual savings institutions, the net investment of unincorporated enterprises and the acquisition of real property net of depreciation.

Personal Tax and Nontax Payments—Taxes levied against individuals, their income and their property that are not deductible as expenses of business operation, and of other general government revenues from individuals in their personal capacity. It includes payments for such specific services as are provided within the framework of general government activity but excludes purchases from government enterprises, *e.g.*, post office. Tax refunds are deducted from payments at time of refund.

Population—As defined by the Bureau of the Census, the *Total Population* includes members of the Armed Forces overseas; the *Resident Population* refers to all persons residing in the 50 States; the *Civilian Resident Population* is the resident population excluding all members of the Armed Forces.

Poverty Level—An income level deemed inadequate for providing a family or individual with the basic essentials of life. Revised definitions of poverty were adopted as official standards in 1969, and are based on poverty thresholds developed in 1964 by the Social Security Administration. These thresholds provided a range of poverty income cutoffs adjusted by such factors as family size, age and sex of family head and place of residence (farm-nonfarm). Annual adjustments are made to these base levels in accordance with changes in the consumer price index.

Production and Related Workers—Working foremen and all nonsupervisory workers (including lead men and trainees) engaged in fabricating, processing, assembling, inspection, receiving, storage, handling, packing, warehousing, shipping, maintenance, repair, janitorial, watchman services, product development, auxiliary production for plant's own use (*e.g.*, power plant), and record keeping, and other services closely associated with the above production operations. Embraces craft workers, operatives, unskilled laborers and most service workers. Excludes supervisory employees (above the working foremen level) and their clerical staffs. (This definition was adopted, as of January, 1945, by all Federal Government agencies as a replacement for Wage Earner.)

Productivity—Generally, a ratio of output to input. The number of units of output divided by the number of units of input is called *average* productivity. The number of units of output obtained by employing one additional unit of input (starting from a given situation) is called *marginal* productivity.

Indexes of production, number of physical units produced, or the "real" value of products are among the more commonly used measures of output. Labor input may be measured by the number of persons employed, or more usually by the number of man-hours worked, and the capital input by the "real" value of the stock of tangible capital in use. The choice of definitions in a specific situation depends on the nature of the problem studied. The ratio of output to any particular input is sometimes termed a *partial* productivity measure, in contrast to *total factor* productivity which relates output to a combined measure of all the inputs.

Productivity *trends* are analyzed by comparing productivity ratios for two or more periods in time.

Projection—When a series or any set of magnitudes is extended beyond the range of the observed data it is said to be "projected." The term is also applied to a single figure whose validity depends solely upon relationships existing in some other range of observations.

Purchasing Power of the Dollar—A measurement of the quantity of commodities and services that can be purchased with a dollar in a given period as compared with another period. (Statistically, it is usually the reciprocal of a price index.)

"Real" Earnings or Wages—The purchasing power of money earnings or the amount of goods and services that can be acquired with the money earnings; usually money earnings adjusted for changes in the Consumer Price Index.

Regions—The Department of Commerce defines "regions" by combinations of states as shown below.
Population, labor force, and *retail trade* figures are presented by the Bureau of the Census in nine geographical areas:
New England—Maine, N. H., Vt., Mass., R. I., Conn.
Middle Atlantic—N. Y., N. J., Pa.
East North Central—Ohio, Ind., Ill., Mich., Wis.
West North Central—Minn., Iowa, Mo., N. Dak., S. Dak., Nebr., Kans.
South Atlantic—Del., Md., D. C., Va., W. Va., N. C., S. C., Ga., Fla.
East South Central—Ky., Tenn., Ala., Miss.
West South Central—Ark., La., Okla., Tex.
Mountain—Mont., Idaho, Wyo., Colo., N. Mex., Ariz., Utah, Nev.
Pacific—Wash., Oreg., Calif., Alaska, Hawaii
Population, employment and personal income data, published by the Bureau of Economic Analysis, employs eight regions:
New England—Same as above
Mideast—N. Y., N. J., Pa., Del., Md., D. C.
Great Lakes—Same as East North Central above
Plains—Same as West North Central above
Southeast—Va., W. Va., Ky., Tenn., N. C., S. C., Ga., Fla., Ala., Miss., La., Ark.
Southwest—Okla., Tex., N. Mex., Ariz.
Rocky Mountain—Mont., Idaho, Wyo., Colo., Utah
Far West—Wash., Oreg., Nev., Calif.
(Alaska and Hawaii shown separately)
Where possible, the Bureau of the Census definition is used in this book.

Rental Value of Owner-Occupied Homes (Imputed Rent)—Value ascribed to the housing services homeowners receive from their property. It is presumably equal to the amount obtainable if the property were rented to others.

Retail Sales—Sales of retail stores include merchandise sold and also receipts for repairs and other similar services. Businesses are considered as retail if they are primarily engaged in selling merchandise for personal, household or farm consumption. They are further classified by kind of retail business, primarily on the basis of principal commodities sold.

Scheduled Airlines—Those common carriers which operate flights on a timetable of projected operations.

Seasonal Variation—That movement in many economic series which tends to repeat itself within periods of a year. This movement is induced by periodic climatic conditions and social convention, such as holidays.

Semidurable Goods—Goods ordinarily employed in their ultimate use from six months to three years (clothing, tires, shoes, etc.).

Services—When work is performed by business entities or individuals on behalf of other persons, no goods or commodities being transferred, the firms or individuals so engaged are said to be providing "services." Service organizations include financial firms, most areas of government and the utilities supplying electricity, gas and telephone service.

Social Security Taxes—Contributions by employees, employers and self-employed persons for old-age, survivors' and disability insurance; taxes on carriers and their employees for the railroad retirement program; state unemployment contributions by employers in all states, and employees in two states; state sickness insurance contributions by employees in four states, two of which also have employer contributions; and railroad unemployment and sickness insurance contributions by carriers.

Standard of Living—The kind and quantities of goods and services which are considered essential by an individual or group. Technically, standard of living differs from scale or plane of living, which is merely the list of things the individual or group consumes at a given time or place. But the term is frequently used in the latter meaning.

Standard Metropolitan Statistical Area—Generally, a leading urban center together with all adjoining territory closely linked with the central city. Each standard metropolitan area must include at least one city with 50,000 or more inhabitants, or two cities having contiguous boundaries and constituting, for general economic and social purposes, a single community with a combined population of at least 50,000, the smaller of which must have a population of at least 15,000. In addition to the county, or counties, containing such a central city, or cities, contiguous counties are included if they are essentially metropolitan in character and sufficiently integrated economically with the central city. The name of the standard metropolitan area is that of the largest city. The addition of up to two city names may be made if the additional city, or cities, have at least 250,000 inhabitants, or if they have a population of one-third or more of that of the largest city and a minimum population of 25,000.

Because of the special importance of the metropolitan complexes around New York and Chicago, several contiguous SMSA's and additional counties that do not appear to meet the formal integration criteria but do have strong interrelationships of other kinds have been combined into "Standard Consolidated Areas."

The criteria for delineating SMSA's were revised in 1958. In prior years, similar areas were called "Standard Metropolitan Areas."

Supernumerary Income—Refers to that share of consumer income which is not needed for the essentials and is available for optional spending. This statistical series, developed by THE CONFERENCE BOARD, consists of all income in excess of $20,000 a year flowing to each family unit. The supernumerary income series represents a general measure of rising consumer affluence. See also Discretionary Purchasing Power.

Transfer Payments—As used in the national accounts, the sum of monetary income receipts of individuals from government and business (other than government interest) for which no services are rendered currently, government payments and corporate gifts to nonprofit institutions and individuals' bad debts to business.

Unrelated Individual—As defined by the Bureau of the Census, refers to a person 14 years or over (other than an inmate of an institution) who is not living with any relatives.

Urban Population—According to the definition adopted for use in the 1970 Census, "urban population" comprises all persons living in (a) places of 2,500 inhabitants or more, incorporated as cities, villages, boroughs (except Alaska), and towns (except towns in New England, New York and Wisconsin), but excluding those persons living in rural portions of "extended cities"—land areas usually near the city's boundary with relatively low population density; (b) unincorporated places of 2,500 inhabitants or more; and (c) other territory included in urbanized areas.

The 1970 criteria are essentially the same as those used in 1960 with two exceptions. The "extended city" concept is new for 1970. Secondly, in 1960, towns in the New England States, townships in New Jersey and Pennsylvania, and counties elsewhere which were classified as urban according to specific criteria were included in the contiguous urbanized areas. In 1970, only those portions of towns and townships in these States that met the rules followed in defining urbanized areas elsewhere in the U.S. are included.

The major difference between the 1950 and the 1960 definitions was the designation in 1960 of urban towns in New England and of urban townships in New Jersey and Pennsylvania. The effect on population classification arising from this change was actually small because, in 1950, most of the population living in such places was classified as urban by virtue of residence in an urbanized area or in an unincorporated urban place.

According to the definition used in 1940 and earlier years, the "urban population" comprised all persons living in incorporated places of 2,500 inhabitants or more and in areas (usually minor civil divisions) classified as "urban" under somewhat different special rules relating to population size and density.

In all definitions, the population not classified as urban constitutes the rural population.

Vital Statistics—Data compiled from local records on the number of births, marriages, divorces and deaths of all persons in the population.

Wage Earner—The traditional definition of a wage earner has been based upon method of wage payment. Usually, an employee whose income is computed on an hourly or daily basis, a piecework basis or other comparable basis. See Production and Related Workers.

CENSUS AND SURVEY SOURCES

Below is a brief description of the principal recurring censuses and surveys conducted by the Federal Government for the collection of data of particular interest to marketers.

Census of Population

The Constitution provides for a census of population every 10 years, primarily to establish a basis for apportionment of Members of the House of Representatives among the States. The first census was conducted in 1790 and the most recent in 1970. Each person is counted as an inhabitant of his usual place of residence. The 1950 and 1960 census were not adjusted for underenumeration, estimated at about 5.7 million persons in 1960.

In addition to general information gathered in the complete count of the population, more detailed characteristics were obtained from representative samples of the last three decennial censuses: 5 percent in 1940, 20 percent in 1950, 25 percent in 1960. A similar sampling has been made in the 1970 census. Statistics from the censuses of population, either from the sample data or from the complete count, vary somewhat from similar figures in the Current Population Surveys for the same years. These surveys are described below.

Current Population Survey

This is a monthly nationwide survey of a scientifically selected sample representing the noninstitutional civilian population. The sample is located in over 461 areas comprising more than 923 counties and independent cities with coverage in every State and the District of Columbia. About 55,000 housing units and other quarters are designed for the sample at any time.

Monthly data on the labor force, employment and unemployment are collected in these surveys. In addition, a wide range of material is gathered annually concerning the social and economic characteristics of the population and labor force.

Characteristics of the total population have been adjusted from the survey data to include the institutional population and members of the Armed Forces living off post or with their families on post. The consumer income series (providing characteristics of households, families and persons by income class) excludes inmates of institutions. Labor force characteristics refer only to the civilian noninstitutional population.

Household Survey of Purchases and Ownership

Reports based on this autumn survey provide information on ownership and purchases of cars and selected household durables. Related expenditure data are also published periodically. The sample size and scope are considerably smaller than those of the Current Population Survey.

Economic Census

Censuses of economic activity in the retail, wholesale and service trades have been taken at intervals since 1929. Beginning in 1948 these censuses have been conducted approximately every five years. The latest available figures are from the 1972 census.

These censuses contain statistics on the number of outlets, number of employees and volume of sales according to detailed kinds of business, geographical area and other variables.

Survey of Consumer Expenditures

The Bureau of Labor Statistics periodically conducts a survey of consumer expenditures as a basis for revision of its consumer price index. The most recent completed survey supplies information for 1960 and 1961. A new survey covering the years 1972 and 1973 has been tabulated and data are now being released. All portions of the 1972-1973 survey are scheduled to be published by early 1977. Data from this expenditure survey were gathered from interviews with about 20,000 families and single consumers. Published data show expenditure patterns according to various family characteristics.

LIST OF GRAPHS

LIST OF GRAPHS

Employment

Income

Expenditures

Production and Distribution

Prices

INDEX

INDEX

284

G

H

293